www.wadsworth.com

wadsworth.com is the World Wide Web site for Wadsworth Publishing Company and is your direct source to dozens of online resources.

At *wadsworth.com* you can find out about supplements, demonstration software, and student resources. You can also send e-mail to many of our authors and preview new publications and exciting new technologies.

wadsworth.com
Changing the way the world learns®

Music in Childhood

FROM PRESCHOOL THROUGH THE ELEMENTARY GRADES

SECOND EDITION

Patricia Shehan Campbell
Carol Scott-Kassner

Motivation and Management (Chapter 3) and
Technology for Music Instruction (Chapter 14)
by Kirk Kassner

SCHIRMER

THOMSON LEARNING

AUSTRALIA ✦ CANADA ✦ MEXICO ✦ SINGAPORE ✦ SPAIN

UNITED KINGDOM ✦ UNITED STATES

SCHIRMER

THOMSON LEARNING

To some of the great teachers of music we have known:
Betty Atterbury, Lucile Doersch, Claire McCoy, Dumisani Maraire,
Dordena Rogel, Jean Sinor, and Jonas Svedas

Music Publisher: Clark Baxter
Senior Development Editor: Sharon Adams Poore
Assistant Editor: Julie Iannacchino
Editorial Assistant: Jonathan Katz
Executive Marketing Manager: Diane McOscar
Project Manager, Editorial Production: Jerilyn Emori
Print/Media Buyer: Tandra Jorgensen
Permissions Editor: Stephanie Keough-Hedges
Production Service: Greg Hubit Bookworks

Text Designer: Kaelin Chappell
Copy Editor: Colleen McGuinnes
Illustrator: Lotus Art
Autographer: Mansfield Music-Graphics
Cover Designer: Margarite Reynolds
Cover Image: Comstock Images
Cover Printer: Phoenix Color Corp.
Compositor: TBH Typecast, Inc.
Printer: Quebecor World Book Services / Dubuque

Printed in the United States of America
  2 3 4 5 6 7 05 04 03 02

For permission to use material from this text, contact us by:
  Web: http://www.thomsonrights.com
  Fax: 1-800-730-2215
  Phone: 1-800-730-2214

Library of Congress Cataloging-in-Publication Data

Campbell, Patricia Shehan.
    Music in childhood : from preschool through the elementary grades : with CD / Patricia Shehan Campbell, Carol Scott-Kassner; motivation and management (chapter 3) and technology for music instruction (chapter 14) by Kirk Kassner.—2nd ed.
    p. cm.
Includes bibliographical references and index.
ISBN 0-534-58554-X
1. Music—Instruction and study—Juvenile. 2. School music—Instruction and study. I. Scott-Kassner, Carol. II. Title.
MT1.C226 2002
372.87—dc21   2001048347

Wadsworth Group/Thomson Learning
10 Davis Drive
Belmont, CA 94002-3098
USA

For more information about our products, contact us:
Thomson Learning Academic Resource Center
1-800-423-0563
http://www.wadsworth.com

International Headquarters
Thomson Learning
International Division
290 Harbor Drive, 2nd Floor
Stamford, CT 06902-7477
USA

UK/Europe/Middle East/South Africa
Thomson Learning
Berkshire House
168–173 High Holborn
London WC1V 7AA
United Kingdom

Asia
Thomson Learning
60 Albert Street, #15-01
Albert Complex
Singapore 189969

Canada
Nelson Thomson Learning
1120 Birchmount Road
Toronto, Ontario M1K 5G4
Canada

Contents

Preface to the Second Edition

Of all the beautiful things in this world, few surpass the images of music in childhood. Our own earliest memories are rich with music: soft lullabies on a parent's lap; patty-cake rhymes in the nursery; parade music played by brass bands that marched in time; seasonal songs at the dinner table, at the piano, or around the campfire; chants for jumping rope and clapping hands; and the music played with friends on homemade instruments. Music played a prominent role in our childhood then, as it still does for children today.

Music emerges magically from children, as they search for and find ways to represent their world. Intuitively and naturally, young children respond to music as they communicate through it. Music is part of their process of enculturation. They develop as members of their family, their neighborhood community, and their religious and ethnic groups through music. Parents are the first music teachers, transmitting to children the songs they remember and filling their children's ears with the music they love. Children learn a musical system—its tuning, timbres, predominant pitch and rhythmic patterns, textures, and formal structures—as surely as they learn other aspects of their family and then their community cultures. They are socialized into these groups through music and are deeply rooted in this first musical system early in childhood.

As children begin their formal schooling, in preschool or in kindergarten, they are ready to begin their formal musical education as well. With their intuitive learning in tow, children can develop musical literacy and the conceptual understanding of music as one among many disciplines featured within a school curriculum. The musical competence to sing in tune and step in time, to listen perceptively, to perform from notation, and to create a personal music that is as musically logical as it is expressive are all skills taught in a music curriculum. Unlike intuitive musical responses, however, these competencies do not appear magically. They are the outcomes of a musical education, with an expert musician-teacher as guide. If children are to become competent and even masterful musicians, a formal musical education is necessary.

Music teachers continue the musical development that began with children's early enculturation. They are the principal players in the spiraling development of children's listening, performance, literacy, and creative expressive skills. Music teachers are the catalysts that stimulate children's musical intelligence and the guides to the pathways through which children can channel their ideas. Music teachers tap the beauty that is within children, awaiting a way out.

The benefits of a musical education are many. Musically trained children are able to add layer upon layer of musical knowledge to their earliest experiences. This early training can inspire children to continue musical activities into their adult years: singing a Bach chorale after supper; reading recorder music with friends on a Sunday afternoon; becoming wholly engaged while listening to the sounds of a Beethoven sonata or a jazz session; folk dancing in time and in a musical way to the tunes of a string band; creating spontaneous harmonies vocally or on an instrument; and writing music for personal expression or to share with others. These are the sophisticated behaviors of musically educated people who were brought beyond the playful musical experiences of their childhood by teachers who taught them repertoire and notational literacy and who developed in them the skills for performing, responding to, and creating music. When people mature musically, and when they maintain musical interactions that remain meaningful to them in their adult lives, the benefits of a musical education are apparent. The beauty of music in childhood becomes more than mere memory: It is the seed that takes root and is nourished through training.

A commitment to raising more musical children requires information. We trust that the information we have provided within these pages can be translated from words to actions both by teachers who are musicians and by musicians who are teachers. With an accumulated sixty-four years of teaching music to children, teachers, and teachers-to-be between us, we offer ideas garnered from our experiences that have been evaluated, revised, and tested again, in many settings, with many students. The commitment we have to a substantive and meaningful musical education for all children is both the impetus and the desired outcome of the volume.

The following chapters delineate music and instructional approaches suited to the perceptual-cognitive, physical, and affective development of children in early and middle childhood. The various ways in which children manifest their musicality form the basis of a number of chapters: "Rhythm and the Child," "Pitch and the Child," "The Singing Child," "The Listening Child," "The Moving Child," "The Playing Child," and "The Creating Child." We have noted the natural and incipient musical behaviors associated with child development, and they become the backdrop to recommendations for teacher-directed musical experiences and educational sequences.

We have attempted to present music as a developmental process in the intellectual and affective lives of children, one that is accelerated, enriched, and deepened through the guidance of the expert musician-teacher. We offer a sampling of musical experiences that can be presented by teachers to children in graduated fashion and in

increasingly complex matrices that continue to challenge preschool and school-age children through the sixth grade. We will discuss how to

✦ structure a classroom for maximum learning

✦ preserve children's natural motivation for experiencing and knowing music

✦ plan lessons and long-term goals

✦ measure, grade, and report musical competencies of children to them, their parents, and administrators

We present models, samples, and graphs to illustrate techniques and systematic methods for teaching musical concepts and for developing musical skills in children. Scenarios, Review questions, Critical Thinking questions, and Projects are found at the conclusion of each chapter, for purposes of reviewing, extending, and putting into practice the information given. References appear at the end of each chapter.

In addition to practical information, we provide the conceptual frameworks that initiate and stimulate thinking on issues of music, teaching, and children. We have not intended this as a collection of recipe-like lessons, although examples of partial and complete lessons can be found scattered throughout the book. Instead, we present a broad array of concept-associated musical experiences in each chapter as the best way for teachers to develop lessons for children. We believe that the most successful lessons spring from the selection of a concept, embedded in a song or musical piece, which is then reinforced and expanded through a variety of instructional strategies. The full flowering of a lesson is best left to the perceptive and imaginative teacher, who can match the musical concept, repertoire, and teaching and learning strategies to the classroom context with a thorough knowledge of what children need to know.

Chapter 4 addresses method—the classic techniques and systems of Dalcroze, Kodály, and Orff; the recently emerging pedagogies; and the personal methods that evolve through experience. We believe that teachers will combine techniques from various philosophies to develop a personal pedagogy that suits them, their students, and the instructional content.

Chapters on music technology, world music and multicultural music education, and the special learner address contemporary issues that affect the teaching and learning of music. We believe that music technology should be integrated throughout the curriculum. In Chapter 14, we have provided suggestions for using technology, lists of software currently available, and ideas for funding. Regarding world music and its place in a multicultural curriculum, we have attempted to thread its themes throughout the book, while concentrating on curricular trends and issues in Chapter 15. Likewise, while we believe that each child is individual and special in his or her approach to the musical experience, and have maintained this position as central to the volume, Chapter 16 presents perspectives relevant to children who are variously challenged in learning music and who require a teacher's sensitivity to meet special needs.

Along with the developmental approach and contemporary issues we have emphasized, we hope that the reader senses the joy, the musical stimulation, and the intellectual challenge that come from teaching music to children. We have known these sensations often, and we are restored and invigorated by them. *Music in Childhood* provides a channel for teachers to develop musically and pedagogically in ways relevant to children's growth from musical intuition to musical mastery. The ultimate result of its reading—and application—may be a more musical world, through the bonding of children, music, and teachers.

Acknowledgments

We wish to thank our mentors and colleagues who have stimulated our thinking and encouraged our growth as musicians and teachers, our students who have helped to shape our ideas even as they work with them and who bring fresh perspectives to the realm of music for children, and the children themselves who have given much more than they know to the sharpening of our understanding of human musical development and its nurturance through instruction. Thanks to Rita Klinger and Patti Casey for their tuneful suggestions (and many late-night talks on music, children, and schooling in general); Dalcroze teachers Anne Farber, Herb Henke, Annabelle Joseph, Virginia Mead, Lisa Parker, Marta Sanchez, and Julia Schnebly-Black, whose ideas have "begotten" some of our ideas; Barbara Lundquist for her continuing influence on our thinking of music alongside culture; James Carlsen for his expertise in musical thinking and growth; and Shirley McRae, Jean Sinor, and Sandra Stauffer for their insightful comments along the way. Thanks to Jerry Gay for his photographs as well as to Jo Daly and the teachers at the B. F. Day School in Seattle, and to Ann Palmason and teachers at the Bush School of Seattle—and their children—for helping us to fill our book with images of joyous music making. We are enormously grateful to Kirk Kassner for writing Chapters 3 ("Motivation and Management") and 14 ("Technology for Music Instruction"). His varied experiences as a classroom music teacher offer a world of suggestions on motivating children to learn (and managing a classroom setting that is conducive to learning), and his wealth of knowledge of technology spans the continuum from the highly theoretical issues relevant to instruction to the details of technological systems and the most feasible and user-friendly classroom applications. His contributions to our book, including his editing and his ever-present good humor, have been invaluable. Thanks also to Charlie Campbell for his patience with the late-night madness of our networking sessions to put into print what we truly believe.

About the Authors

Patricia Shehan Campbell is Donald E. Peterson Professor of Music at the University of Washington. She is a certified teacher of the

Dalcroze eurhythmics and has lectured and published widely on music, children, and pedagogy. She is author of *Lessons from the World* and *Songs in Their Heads* and coauthor of numerous books on world music education, including *Multicultural Perspectives in Music Education* and *Roots and Branches*.

Carol Scott-Kassner is a writer and consultant in music education and former professor of music education. An expert in the musical growth of young children, she has written and spoken extensively on that topic. She is coauthor of three textbook series by Silver Burdett Ginn and has contributed chapters in both editions of the *Handbook of Research in Music Teaching and Learning*.

1

The Multiple Meanings of Music for Children

"I like music. I can't explain it: Sometimes it makes me happy, sometimes sad, but all the times it's there like a friend, and I need it."

—FIRST-GRADE CHILD

"I want my child to know what I never was privileged to learn, and that includes learning how to sing, dance, and draw artistically."

—PARENT OF SECOND-GRADE CHILD

"I've found enjoyable ways to achieve the curricular goals of literacy and numeracy through music, from chanting rhymes and singing songs to counting rhythms and moving in geometric patterns across the floor."

—THIRD-GRADE TEACHER

"I enjoyed the winter concert, and am especially impressed with how, as they sang and played, music seemed to bring a coalescence to a crowd of what I know to be some pretty ornery and unsettled kids."

—PARENT OF FOURTH-GRADE CHILD

"You should see what's happened to kids' interests since we added music to our classes on American history and culture. Overnight success!"

—FIFTH-GRADE TEACHER

"I think I might be making as important an impact in the musical world teaching kids to sing and play and read music, maybe as much as I might have as a world-class concert pianist. Who knows what musical minds I may tap?"

—ELEMENTARY SCHOOL MUSIC TEACHER

"Schools are reconsidering earlier educational plans that underscored the basics: We now see that guiding children's holistic development, to include experiences in the expressive arts of language, music, and the visual arts, is basic to their more complete and evolving intellectual, emotional, and physical well-being."

—ELEMENTARY SCHOOL PRINCIPAL

"I don't know everything about music yet, but I guess it just grabs me the right way."

—SIXTH-GRADE CHILD

Music is important to children. Some wish to listen to it alone through headphones, while others are inclined to sing, hum, whistle, or chant it. Some want to play it on a musical instrument—solo or with friends. Others enjoy dancing to it, and thus music gives rise to physical responses. Some wish to create "brand new music" and poems, plays, and dances to go with it. Whether listening, singing, playing, moving, or creating music, musical experiences are prominent in the lives of children. They, themselves, as well as their spokespersons—parents, guardians, and teachers—attest to this fact (Campbell, 1998).

Music's Many Functions

Music is one of life's essential ingredients. For children, it is often the substance of their playful exploration of and experimentation in the world around them, the core of their socialization and expressive communication with one another, and the refuge where they find peace, joy, and fulfillment away from the worries of their young lives. For the adults they will become, music is an avenue for expressing what cannot be verbally expressed; a source of profound enjoyment; a lighthearted amusement; a critical component of customs, traditions, and rituals; and a release valve for energy and emotions through physical response via movement and dance.

Music's powerful role offers compelling reasons for its inclusion in the schools. The numerous ways in which children engage in music underscore its appeal for them, as well as highlight the many dimensions of their beings that can be met by the musical experiences they have. Given that music is embraced by people everywhere for its unique qualities, to deny it a solid place in curricular studies would be a terrible mistake. Music is too powerful to be excluded from children's lives, whether in school or out.

The uses of music by children (and adults) of all ages and cultures are evidence of its staying power. Music has maintained its prominence among people over time and distance. Anthropologist Alan P. Merriam (1964) presented what has become a classic outline of music's many functions across cultures. These functions are relevant to children's own musical involvement—within their culture, their world—for a number of reasons.

1. *Emotional expression:* the releasing of emotions and the expression of feelings. Children may release sadness in their singing or joy in their dancing.

2. *Aesthetic enjoyment:* the use of music for deep emotional and intellectual enjoyment, for experiencing artistic and nonverbal expressions of life's beauty. The music that children listen to or perform touches them in profound ways that are not easily expressed through the words they know.

3. *Entertainment:* the use of music as diversion and amusement. Children enjoy the musical diversions presented by the media, from the current pop genres to the background music for videos, films, and television shows. Media music is effortless "easy listening" for them and greatly entertaining.

4. *Communication:* the conveying of feelings and emotions that are understood by people within a particular culture. Children receive and can be led to the musical expression of ideas and feelings in styles that are meaningful to them within their family, community, and societal cultures.

5. *Symbolic representation:* the expression of symbols exists in the texts of songs and in the cultural meaning of the musical sounds. Overlapping the communication function, children find the sounds of certain musical modes and meters more meaningful than others, through their conditioning within the musical cultures of their families, communities, and society at large.

6. *Physical response:* the use of music for dancing and other physical activity. Children are greatly affected in physical ways by the music they hear or perform and may be drawn to dance, hop, skip, or sway to the sounds. They may also be soothed to sleep by the qualities of sedative music.

7. *Enforcement of conformity to social norms:* the use of music to provide instructions or warnings. Children, especially young children, are often taught the rules of social etiquette by adults (say "please" and "thank you," wash your hands before meals) through chanted rhymes and songs.

8. *Validation of social institutions and religious rituals:* the use of music in religious services and state occasions. Children frequently build music into the rituals of their play, including chants and songs to accompany games or to select team members ("eeny meeny miney mo"). They also validate their civic and religious affiliations through the patriotic, sacred, and seasonal songs they sing.

9. *Contribution to the continuity and stability of culture:* music as an expression of cultural values. Few other cultural elements are such complete vehicles for the transmission of history, literature, and social mores as is music, offering children an understanding of the long life and stability of their culture.

10. *Contribution to the integration of society:* the use of music to bring people together. Children are socialized through music and recognize their membership within a group through music that is shared among its members. For example, singing games increase children's integration within a group, just as a school song offers children a common bond with other children.

Music is a human phenomenon, with its uses by children as widespread as they are for adults. Music is much more than an addendum in the lives of children. It is part and parcel of their development as individuals and as members of social groups of family, neighbors, and friends. While it exists "for its own sake" (as in the aesthetic principle of "art for art's sake"), music also functions as a vehicle for teaching children ways of living their lives according to the fundamental values of a culture. Countless communities of people hold music in high esteem for its functional life-guiding and life-giving properties. If music is thus understood to be at the core of human thought and behavior in so many communities, then it logically follows that it must be placed at the core of learning provided for children in the schools. Musical training can supply components critical to children's holistic development, including their intellectual, emotional, physical, and spiritual selves.

Music at the Curricular Core

Because children are drawn quite naturally to singing, moving, and other playful musical experiences, some educators have difficulty viewing music as a discipline as worthy of study as other academic subjects in the humanities, the sciences, and the social sciences. Is music truly basic to a rock-solid education or more a marginal nicety, a pleasurable pastime for the privileged classes, a channel for the talented few, to be sampled through passive watching and listening by the undertalented multitudes?

In recent years, considerable attention has been given to identifying subjects as part of an "elite core" of "basic knowledge" to be mastered by all children. Music and the arts have been marginalized by many in American schools and society, and they are viewed as less central for development than linguistic and mathematical knowledge and skills. As defined by Ernest L. Boyer (1983), however, the "basics" would seem to encompass a musical education: "Broadly defined, [a basic curriculum] is a study of those consequential ideas, experiences, and traditions common to all of us by virtue of our membership in the human family at a particular moment in history" (p. 95). Music is basic because it is a critical component of American and international societies as well as a repository of historical traditions and contemporary ideas.

Furthermore, music is a compehensive subject for study. Music is a means of knowing through perceptive listening, performance, and the creative processes of composition and improvisation, the "self" and the "other"—the world and its component parts. Samuel Hope, director of the National Association of Schools of Music, observed that "the intellectual functions of art, science, history, and philosophy come together with the knowledge, skills, subject matters and purposes of dance, music, theatre and the visual arts" (2000, p. 83). The major modes of human thought and action are experienced through inquiry in these disciplines, including music.

Music deserves a rightful place at the core of a preschool through elementary school curriculum. All children have equal rights to knowledge of their cultural heritage, including music; the development of their aural, artistic, expressive, and musical sensibilities; and familiarity with music beyond the commercially available and currently popular. *What Every Young American Should Know and Be Able to Do in the Arts: National Standards for Arts Education* (MENC, 1994) stipulates that children should know and be

Andrew playing drum

Patricia Shehan Campbell

able through training to communicate through the arts, develop and present basic analyses of works of art, and have an informed acquaintance with exemplary works of art from a variety of cultures and historical periods. In considering what a curriculum should contain, Elliot W. Eisner warned that denying children access to music as an avenue of expression is equivalent to depriving them of "the meanings that the making of music makes possible" (1982, p. 55). Estelle Jorgensen called for an awareness of music as a means of socializing children into the sensibilities of the culture, of enculturating them into the social mores and values of a group of people (1997). Schools that seek to enrich children's lives through knowledge and skill development cannot afford to relegate music to the curricular periphery but should instead place music alongside language arts, mathematics, and other basic subjects.

Music is its own discipline, while it also informs children of their world in interdisciplinary ways. Teachers need to understand the many dimensions of the musical experience for children and the significance of instruction to accomplish goals that run broad and deep, from the culturally general to the musically specific. The making of music is a discipline, in the training and rehearsal vital to the development of singing and instrumental performance skills and in the growth of critical and creative musical thinking skills. Children are stimulated intellectually, physically, and even spiritually in their recognition of music for its own sake as well as its integration with their knowledge of the humanities, the sciences, and the social studies.

Children's Musical Capacities

What does it mean to be musical? Some might say that a child who plays an instrumental piece accurately and with attention to the nuances of dynamics and tempo is more musical than one who moves easily to the rhythm of a musical beat. Or that the child with the sweet and melodious voice is more musically talented than the one who can quickly identify timbres, textures, or modes and meters in the music he or she hears. Or that the child who can create music is the most musical of all. Is there a hierarchy of qualities that make some children musical or more musical than others? Should musical training be reserved for musically talented children who will reap the greatest benefits?

All children are musical. Anthropologist John Blacking (1973) observed the musical nature of children of the Venda people of South Africa and then developed his position on the musical capacities of all children. Cognitive psychologist Howard Gardner (1983) suggested in his theory of multiple intelligences that, while children may demonstrate greater strength in one of the seven intelligences, all children possess musical abilities that can be nurtured through instruction. Christopher Small, a sociologist concerned with the manner in which humans participate in the musical process, coined the term "musicking" to embrace children and adults in the acts of singing, playing, and moving to music, noting that all are capable of more than some societies allow (1998).

In various forms and degrees, children possess the capacity to become more musical than they may currently demonstrate. Children quite naturally listen, sing, dance, play, and express themselves musically, with little or no previous training. When learning experiences are tailored to develop their musical abilities, then the complete musicians inside them begin to emerge. Certainly, because differences exist in children's individual interests and aptitudes, some variance is evident among children regarding the extent to which a particular musical intelligence, or specific musical talent, can be developed. Some may prefer to sing rather than to play, and some may be driven toward creating original musical expressions.

Children are capable of careful and attentive listening, so they are able to perceive and understand the musical language they will create or recreate. Some children will need greater help in focusing their listening and may require the removal of aural and visual distracters so that they might tune in to the components of a song or musical work. Through directed listening, children will learn a vocabulary of recurring melodic and rhythmic phrases that represent a given musical style or culture and that may reappear in music they perform or in their original improvisations and compositions. Because most children possess the physical capability to hear sounds, they can then be led to listening intelligently to the manner in which these sounds are organized as music.

Nearly all children possess the ability to sing accurately in tune, although vocal qualities may vary slightly from lighter to darker, whispery-soft to fuller in tone, and with minor differences in range. Good singers develop through frequent listening and then by replicating the sound of the singing model. Even the more powerful and resonant young singers are likely to have developed their abilities through practice, singing regularly because they enjoy it. Adults who sing regularly, in tune, for and with children, make ideal models for emulation. The capacity to sing sweetly in tune is well within the reach of children, awaiting discovery and development.

Children can respond to music through movement in controlled and expressive ways. The following of the musical pulse is just one of the initial milestones in movement development; this skill is directly related to attentive listening. Movement can demonstrate the extent to which children are focused on rhythmic durations and patterns, the rising and falling contours of melodies, or the different phrases in a musical composition. While children may need to be taught gestures, steps, and sequences, nothing can replace their careful listening so that the movement—or the dance—will be musically rendered.

Musical performance on an instrument is viewed by some as a more sophisticated musical activity than other modes of musical skills, and thus it may be deemed to suit only those who show great musical talent. However, all children who are good listeners, and who have the interest and discipline to take the daily time for building both the physical and the musical skills, will make good players. Children may begin with musical toys in their earliest years, progress to nonpitched percussion instruments, and then to xylophones, recorders, and keyboards. String, wind, and brass instruments of the orchestral and band variety are likely to be introduced to children in the intermediate grades. Given strong musical experiences in their early years, all children are thus capable of further musical growth through instrumental study.

Children are refreshingly creative when given the chance. With guidance, they can project both logic and expressiveness in their musical inventions, improvisations, and compositions. Their musical expressions are influenced by the music they know, and the choices they make as musical creators are greatly expanded through their listening experiences. Given opportunities to create, some children may require frameworks. Pitch, rhythm, and even the length of the work are some of the "game rules" they may need to guide their musical inventions. Children may also look to adults for inspiration, as well as to stories, poems, photographs, or illustrations. However, children primarily come to realize their musical creativity through an understanding of musical structure and how the components of music have been manipulated by other composers or performers before them. This understanding is attained best through instruction.

Clearly, if all children are inherently musical, then musical training should not be reserved for the hypothetical talented few. The myth that few children are musically endowed is a dangerous one that threatens the right of all to a musical education, and it may even endanger a musical culture. The work of Charles Keil and Steven Feld (1994) cries out for a recognition of the human attraction to involvement in music as an integrative mind-body experience and as a means for communicating in ways that only the human species can. Children are born with the sensory means for dancing and drumming, for singing and deep-listening potential, and they need only to be nurtured to develop their sensibilities to their maximal capacity.

Music's Historical Role in the Curriculum

Since the earliest conceptions of schools and schooling in the Western world, music has been considered a basic subject. The ancient Greek philosophers, and later the Romans, claimed music and the arts to be key to children's moral development. Through the centuries, Europeans regarded the study of music as part science, in its theoretical analysis, and part art, in its performance practice. Musical training was considered one of the high marks of refinement in the Middle Ages, from the twelfth through the fifteenth centuries. A musical education was central to those seeking to fulfill humanistic goals or striving to become "Renaissance men" (and women). Journal accounts document the significance of vocal and instrumental instruction for children not only of the nobility, but also of the rising middle class. By the time of the Enlightenment in the eighteenth century, the artistic-expressive needs of children were as likely to be addressed through schooling as their intellectual-logical needs were. Music instruction was more than window-dressing in European schools; it was viewed as basic to the education of all children.

Formalized musical training in the United States began with the establishment of singing schools in the late seventeenth and eighteenth centuries. People in towns and rural or frontier settlements were visited for a week or two at a time by singing masters who offered instruction in singing and note-reading. At the close of the day's labors, adults and children would gather to be instructed on the use of tunebooks, which featured notational exercises and hymns. Communities were well served by singing schools, and the congregational singing at church services greatly improved as a result.

Music was included in the curricular programs of private academies in colonial America, and music of the Baroque (ca. 1600–1750) and then of the Viennese Classical (ca. 1750–1820) periods was spread through the efforts of European-trained masters. While European arts and culture were a class privilege for the Southern gentry, New England progressively looked toward providing all children with cultural knowledge through education in common schools (Keene, 1982). Growing support for public education, along with the expansion of cultural societies dedicated to choral (and less frequently, instrumental) music, set the scene for the introduction of music into the curriculum of the elementary school by Lowell Mason in Boston in 1838.

The Boston schools, persuaded by Mason to test the inclusion of music in the curriculum, stipulated that children be given vocal training and music reading lessons twice weekly. Soon, children presented public concerts that demonstrated their considerable musical progress, much to the delight (and surprise) of school officials, parents, and community members. Mason's method of instruction emphasized pragmatic learning-by-doing techniques, beginning with focused listening and rote repetition of vocal music that advanced children toward music literacy. Swiss educator Heinrich Pestalozzi (1746–1827) was undeniably influential in Mason's approach, particularly as evidenced by the application of the principles of anschauung (literally, "sense intuition"), or learning through the senses. The earliest methods used in public school music instruction thus were based on the logic of "sound before sight" and "practice before theory"; listening and singing experiences led to an understanding of notation and theory.

The emergence of music as a curricular subject in the elementary schools unfolded gradually through the nineteenth and twentieth centuries. Vocal music was praised for its contribution to children's moral culture and for its functional means of cultivating the speaking voice, of developing correct expression and diction, and of providing concentration at the start and close of the day. Music listening and note-reading developed in tandem, as children were directed by the music masters to attend to the intervals between pitches, to associate solfège syllables with the melodies they sang, and to sight-read songs and exercises.

Not until schools had access to recordings and radio, however, did a more global form of music listening begin to emerge. Music appreciation classes for children were developed as early as the 1920s. The infusion of rhythmic movement and dance into children's music classes began to flourish in the opening decades of the twentieth century, when movement was recognized as offering an avenue for musical expression as well as for physical, social, and cultural growth. The eurhythmics of Emile Jaques-Dalcroze (1865–1950) first intrigued and then guided teachers toward the development of children's greater musical sensitivity through whole-body movement. John Dewey's (1859–1952) advocacy for music, movement, and the arts in a child-centered curriculum helped to stabilize music as a part of school instruction, even through the troubled economic and political times of the Great Depression of the 1930s and World War II.

Music for children was sparked by numerous innovations in the second half of the twentieth century. From Hungary came the philosophy and practices of Zoltan Kodály (1882–1967) and his associates, with their emphasis on music literacy through rigorous ear-training and vocal exercises. The early experiments in music for children by German composer Carl Orff (1895–1982), first with dancer Dorothee Giinther and then with colleague Gunild Keetman, evolved into practices that merge music with children's play and with dance and the dramatic arts. Over several decades, both Kodály's and Orff's approaches have been embraced by music educators and given American perspectives.

Various professional gatherings of teachers at conferences and in projects have had a further impact on music instruction for children. In the 1960s, the Yale Seminar, the Manhattanville Music Curriculum Project, and the Tanglewood Symposium made recommendations for (1) a broader and more representative music repertoire for listening and performance, including music of all Western historical periods, world cultures, popular, avant-garde, and American styles; (2) greater opportunities for musical expression and creativity, through composition and improvisation experiences; and (3) more extensive use of technology and the media to aid instruction. The challenges have continued into the twenty-first century, as teachers confront ways to balance experiences in European art music with the musical interests and learning styles of an increasingly diverse population of children and as they consider computers, laser discs, and interactive videos as user-friendly enhancements—not threats—to children's musical education.

Music takes its rightful place in the school curriculum today, resting on the long history of its acceptance in children's education. Through the ages, music instruction has provided children with skills for their musical expressions and knowledge of their cultural heritage(s). Despite societal changes, the need for a musical education continues. Children still learn to sing beautifully through instruction and produce sounds that please them and their listeners. They become independent musicians as they learn to read musical notation and as they become more analytical about musical sounds and structure. Through a musical education, children may learn the many facets of the uniquely aural art that allows them an opening through which to channel their many personal expressions.

Music for Children in a Changing Society

How quickly the world has changed and is changing still. Could grandparents have envisioned a world of palm-sized videocameras, MTV, and MP3s when they were young? Could parents have imagined the rise of rock music from its cult-like appeal to teenagers (only) to its pervasive presence on AM and FM radio stations, in films and on television, and even, occasionally, embedded in the music of serious composers? Could we ourselves have guessed when we were children that a global village would emerge and that the world's peoples and their cultural expressions would arrive to the shores and doors of America's society and its schools? The changes are riveting, their pace rapid and relentless, and their impact on American musical culture profound.

Children of the twenty-first century face challenges very different from those just a generation ago. They grow up within family units of various sorts, including single-parent families, working-parent families, and extended families of aunts, uncles, and cousins. They know about substance abuse and sexual abuse, some from firsthand experience. They are bombarded with media images offering examples of deviant behavior and hear dialogue on television and radio that was once considered inappropriate for previous generations. They worry about the environment, about people living in poverty both at home and abroad, about wars, and about the spread of diseases that threaten lives with no certain remedies in sight. Today's world can overwhelm children with challenges.

Enter music into this world of changes and challenges. Music is, for children, a port in the storm, a resting spot, a retreat from the madding crowd and their hectic lives. It is their safety valve, an appropriate release of energy at those times when no other channel seems possible. As music is transformed by technology and by the blending of cultural traditions from near and far, children are offered a wide array of expressions from which to choose for listening and performing. Their out-of-school musical experiences are greatly enriched by in-school instruction, so that the meaning of multiple musical expressions is deepened for them.

A Musical Future

With an understanding of the functions and meanings of music, along with a sensitivity to children's musical capacities and modes of musical experiences, teachers can develop their own personal method for stimulating the musical development of their students. Children will be guaranteed a musical future when the design of a curriculum takes into account the comprehensive goals of a musical education and the sequence for its attainment. Children have their first musical experiences in the home, under the tutelage of their mothers and fathers, but teachers are entrusted with the responsibility for building upon these experiences. The transmission of musical culture is in their hands.

Music transmission cannot be haphazard if it is to be especially meaningful. Throughout their schooling, children need musical nurturing by trained music specialists, so that the experiences they know are musical as well as thoughtfully presented. The music teacher possesses the knowledge and skills honed through many years of solo and ensemble performance experience and the study of music history, theory, and cultures. The music teacher also brings a sense of sequence, and a delivery style that appeals to children, based on an understanding of child development and pedagogical methods. Through a long and specialized training, the music teacher can ensure that quality music instruction is provided.

The musical future of children rests on careful selection of music and instructional techniques to maximize the sometimes minimal curricular time explicitly assigned to music. It rests on the imaginative ways in which creative teachers infuse music into the school days, weaving music into lessons in the language arts, social studies, mathematics, and the sciences. It rests on the belief that the tremendous cultural diversity and technological advances will enhance, embellish, enlighten, and expand the musical experiences of children.

Most important, the musical future of children rests on the teacher's confidence that he or she is first and foremost a musician, one with a lifetime of music to share. Live music making led by the teacher's own performance, along with opportunities for guided listening to performances and recordings of other professional musicians, makes music meaningful to children. While there are many effective instructional techniques, probably no certain method exists for teaching music to children, anymore than there is just one way to climb a mountain or to fall in love. The comprehensive and most effective method through which children become musically educated is to be found within the teacher's own training and interests. The possession of musical knowledge and skills, coupled with a love and understanding of children, will pave the way for a combination of techniques from various philosophical approaches into a personal pedagogy that suits the teacher, the children, and the music.

REVIEW

1. List the ten functions and uses of music. Are some more prominent in your life, and in the lives of children, than others?

2. How do children demonstrate their musical capacities?

3. How has music been placed historically within the curriculum?

4. What recommendations for changes in the music curriculum emerged from various events of the 1960s? Have those recommendations been heeded?

CRITICAL THINKING

1. Nature or nurture? Discuss your stance on children's musical abilities as natural or learned, biological or entrained. Find support for either stance.

2. In the age of DVDs and technologically wired classrooms, is the Pestalozzian concept of anschauung relevant? Explain.

PROJECTS

1. Conduct a series of interviews to determine the meaning of music to people, both currently and from their memories. Ask open-ended questions not only of children, but also of friends, family members, colleagues, and teachers. Analyze the responses according to the Merriam chart of musical uses and functions. Compare the current musical involvement of adults with their childhood memories of musical experiences.

2. Prepare a three-minute speech to be given to the board of education elucidating the benefits of music instruction for children. Present it to the class, and be prepared to respond to questions regarding your position.

3. Stage a scenario: a music teacher's consultation with a concerned parent who wonders whether her child is musical or musically talented.

4. How can in-school instruction in music expand on the musical interests and experiences that children have outside the classroom? Suggest three outside musical experiences that merit deeper exploration through the guidance of a music teacher.

REFERENCES

Blacking, J. (1973). *How musical is man?* Seattle: University of Washington.

Boyer, E. L. (1983). *High school: A report on secondary education in America.* New York: Harper & Row.

Campbell, P. S. (1998). *Songs in their heads: Music and its meaning in children's lives.* New York: Oxford University Press.

Eisner, E. W. (1982). *Cognition and curriculum: A basis for deciding what to teach.* New York: Longman.

Gardner, H. (1983). *Frames of mind: A theory of multiple intelligences.* New York: Basic Books.

Hope, S. (2000). Why study music? In Clifford K. Madsen, ed., *Vision 2020.* Reston, VA: Music Educators National Conference.

Jorgensen, E. (1997). *In search of music education.* Urbana, IL: University of Illinois Press.

Keene, J. A. (1982). A history of music education in the United States. Hanover, NH: University of New Hampshire.

Keil, C., and S. Feld (1994). *Music grooves.* Chicago: University of Chicago Press.

Merriam, A. P. (1964). *The anthropology of music.* Evanston, IL: Northwestern University.

MENC (1994). *What every young American should know and be able to do in the arts: National standards for arts education.* Reston, VA: Music Educators National Conference.

Small, C. (1998). *Musicking.* Hanover, NH: Wesleyan University Press.

2

From Theory to Practice in Teaching Music to Children

Theories of learning, teaching, and instruction are embedded in nearly every musical experience. Jeremy and Bryan playfully explore the music-making possibilities of spoons, cups, pots, and pans; Bruner (1966) and Vygotsky (1978) have developed theories to explain this behavior. Annmarie works best alone at a listening station, while Rosa grows musically when in a socially interactive group; theories on field dependence and independence explain some of the differences. Inga follows the teacher's modeling of a musical phrase and imitates it a bit better with each successive trial; both Skinner (1953) and Bandura (1977) offer theoretical explanations. Rob acquires and retains music aurally, Tony through symbols, graphs, and notes on staffs, and Charissa through associated movements and gestures; these learning modalities are theorized, analyzed, and classified in the literature on learning styles. When Donny does not attend to a listening lesson, Ausubel (1968) suggests "advance organizers" (or building a foundation of familiar ideas for the new learning situation), Gagné (1977) recommends ways of gaining attention, and Skinner offers behavioral techniques for bringing him to task.

Theories about how children learn and how teachers can help maximize this learning are at the heart of every practical musical experience that teachers provide for children. Instead of being dull, dry, and remotely related to the real-life challenges of teaching music to children, theories can illuminate for the teacher how children gain musical knowledge, skills, and values. Theories of instruction are based on effective techniques used by teachers and on scientific observation of and experimentation in how

TABLE 2.1 *Summary of Selected Theories Informing Music*

THEORIST	THEORY	PRINCIPAL FEATURES
Stage and Phase Theories		
Jean Piaget	Stage-dependent theory	Children progress through four stages of intellectual development: sensorimotor, preoperational, concrete operations, and formal operations
Jerome Bruner	Modes of representation	Learners progress through three ways of representing meaning or understanding, related to, but not dependent on, maturation: enactive, iconic, and symbolic
Lauren Sosniak	Developmental stages of the pianist or performer	Student musicians progress through three phases: tinkering, technical, and masterful music making
Gregory Bateson; Catherine Ellis	Learning I, II, III	Learners progress through three phases: enculturation, acquisition of skills or competence, and personal and aesthetic expression
Musical Play and Socialization Theories		
G. Stanley Hall	Musical play	Children train for adulthood through games; musical play leads to musical understanding
Lev Vygotsky	Socialization	Children are socialized through adult intervention and guidance; socialization leads to acquisition of cultural knowledge
Constructivist Theory		
Donald Jonassen	Constructivism	Children develop their understanding through the meaning they make from their experiences
Reinforcement and Social Learning Theories		
B. F. Skinner; Robert Thorndike	Reinforcement	Learning can be shaped through the process of positive or negative reinforcement; appropriate behaviors are shaped through successive approximation techniques
Albert Bandura	Social learning	Children observe and emulate their adult models

children learn. By understanding theory as the fruit of multiple lifetimes spent explaining how children acquire, retain, and then rework musical knowledge into their personal expressions, teachers can become more efficient at guiding this musical development. Theory is wedded to practice, in that it emanates from practical teaching and learning experiences as it also informs these practices.

Teachers need theory as a thoughtful guide to what they do. Music instruction without theories is like a car without a driver, a bird with no wings, or a computer with no program. It is helter-skelter and scattered, without offering an explanation of how children learn the music that teachers present. Teachers who think about what they do, and are informed by theory, are deeply committed to leading children to their maximal musical development.

TABLE 2.1 (*Continued*)

THEORIST	THEORY	PRINCIPAL FEATURES
Learning Style Theories		
Richard Restak	Cerebral dominance	Learners are dominated by left-hemispheric (linear) or right-hemispheric (holistic) processing
Howard Gardner	Multiple intelligences	Learners possess one or more types of intelligence or ways of being intelligent
Walter Barbe; Raymond Swassing	Learning modalities	Learners process information through a preferred sensory channel: visual, auditory, kinesthetic
Rita Dunn and Kenneth Dunn	Learning style model	A variety of factors influence learning: environmental, emotional, social, and physical
Harold Witkin	Field dependence and field independence	Learners may be content-bound, experiencing concepts as embedded within their environment; or content-independent, experiencing concepts as discrete entities removed from their background
Isabel Myers; Peter B. Briggs	Myers-BriggsType indicator	Learners may demonstrate one or several of sixteen Myers-Briggs personality types that influence the way they approach the learning task: extroversion/introversion, sensing/intuitive, thinking/feeling, judging/perceiving
Instructional Theories		
David Ausubel	Meaningful reception	Students acquire information most effectively when teachers package lessons well and prepare students through "advance organizers"
Jerome Bruner	Discovery learning; spiral curriculum	Students learn through exploration and problem solving; subject matter can be taught to children through age-appropriate experiences and can be embellished through repeated exposure
Robert Gagné	Events of instruction	Learners progress through eight instructional events, from awareness and attention through concept formation and transfer
Edwin Gordon	Music Learning Theory	Students progress through an eight-stage process that begins with aural and oral experiences with music and ends with theoretical understanding; audiation is the goal

A theory of music instruction can describe factors related to the teacher, the children, their family, social and cultural influences, and the classroom environment. A theory of music instruction is comprised of three components: (1) instruction, a set of events provided by the teacher; (2) learning processes of the child learner, including attention, perception, memory, rehearsal, and recognition and recall; and (3) learning outcomes in the forms of a child's demonstration of verbal information, intellectual skills, motor skills, cognitive strategies, and attitudes. Thus, theory directs the teacher in providing sequential experiences for understanding a rhythmic pattern or for gaining techniques necessary for playing a musical instrument. It describes the child's need for initial attention to the learning task and the progression through which the child learns and remembers it, and it suggests the means by which the child demonstrates such learning.

Theory links the teacher to the child learner, as it relates teaching events to learning processes and demonstrated learning outcomes.

Teachers—and parents—concerned with enhancing the musical development of children will be well served by the brief introduction to theories of instruction and learning that follows. Selected research and recommendations by theorists in psychology, sociology, anthropology, and education are noted, as well as the ways in which they can inform the practice of music instruction. Table 2.1 sketches selected theories that are relevant to teaching music to children.

Stage and Phase Theories

A number of theories refer to stages, phases, or levels through which children or adult learners proceed in gaining knowledge. Some of these multi-leveled theories stem from developmental psychology and are called "stage dependent," referring to the intellectual stages that children pass through as they mature. Others are not governed by maturation but nonetheless feature earlier stages of learning that provide the foundation for later, more complex learning. Whatever the emphasis, multileveled theories establish that children do not learn all at once but bit by bit and in increasingly complex ways over time.

The stage-dependent theory of Swiss biologist Jean Piaget (1952), now a half-century old, still provides an important model of cognitive development in its combination of the child's biological growth with an increasingly mature intellectual grasp of concepts. Through longitudinal observations of children from birth through late adolescence, Piaget evolved a theory that has greatly influenced views on child development. He observed that children progress through four stages of thinking: (1) sensorimotor (ages zero to two), learning through direct sensory experience; (2) preoperational (ages two to seven), learning through the manipulation of objects—noting the consequences and internalizing them for the future, thus transforming stimuli to symbols; (3) concrete operations (ages seven to eleven), viewing objects in concrete, tangible, and systematic ways but not abstractly; and (4) formal operations (ages eleven through adulthood), learning abstractly using logic and deductive reasoning.

The stages suggest that younger children in particular be given many opportunities to listen, sing, play, and move to music. The introduction of staff notation should occur only after preliminary experiences. Piagetian theory implies that music instruction follows a sound-before-symbol approach. Other notable applications of Piaget's principles to music learning indicate that age eight is a watershed year in a child's cognitive development. At this time, children are capable of identifying timbres, discriminating among random melodies, and perceiving structure in simple melodies, although they are less successful in perceiving the sound of more than one

Jerry Gay

simultaneous musical line (or harmony). As they progress into the stage of concrete operations, children also begin to conserve, or to realize the invariance of one musical element when another is altered. In other words, they begin to recognize a melody when it has been sung in a minor instead of a major modality or in triple instead of duple time. By the time they complete fifth grade, many children are capable of thinking in the abstract about music and are able to manipulate musical structures through improvisation and composition experiences.

In his modes of representation, Jerome Bruner (1966) suggests a type of stage progression that is somewhat dependent upon maturation but can be applied to all ages and intellectual stages. He proposed three teaching and learning strategies: enactive, learning through a set of actions; iconic, learning through images and graphs; and symbolic, learning by going beyond what is immediately perceptible in the environment. For example, learning to read notation can be broken into three stages corresponding to Bruner's model. Instruction may begin with arm and body movement to represent melodic contours (enactive), followed by line graphs that trace these contours (iconic), and ending with the reading and writing of notation itself on the staff (symbolic). These modes of representation are useful in providing increasingly sophisticated instructional sequences for any concept.

In a longitudinal study of concert pianists, Lauren Sosniak (1985) developed a theory also involving three phases of learning. During the initial phase, the young musician tinkers at the piano in playful exploration and is encouraged and supported by her or his parents to do so. The teacher is positive, gentle, and thus motivating for the learner. The second phase emphasizes a more systematic and technical approach to instruction. The development of playing technique brings a need for greater repetition and more careful listening to and emulating of the model, the teacher. The playfulness of the first phase is replaced by a more concentrated and serious attention to detail. In the third phase, mastery emerges in the young pianist's performance of targeted pieces. Gone is the positive and playful instructional approach as the teacher becomes more critical of the smaller flaws in an attempt to develop a near-perfect performance. The instructional mission changes, as do the student's goals, over the three phases. While the theory is hardly one of cognitive development in the Piagetian sense, progressive maturation nonetheless occurs over the time of five or ten years (or more) of lessons. A parallel can be drawn for children's study of any instrument or voice.

Anthropologist Gregory Bateson (1978) defined three broad dimensions of learning similar to Sosniak's three-phase model. These types were related to music learning by Catherine Ellis (1986). Learning I occurs without effort, as music within the environment is absorbed by the learner. Such informal encounters with music are part of the enculturation process by which children come to know the components of their society. In Learning II, thinking is combined with experience when the child learner strives to become a competent performer through lessons or classroom instruction. In this phase, the child becomes more seriously interested in music and engages in practice that develops coordination, strength, agility, and speed on a given instrument or voice. The final phase, which Ellis contends is attained only rarely, takes the performer past the technical skills to music as a personal expression of joy and even religious faith.

Children who study instruments may make their way through the phases proposed by Sosniak and by Bateson and Ellis (see Figure 2.1). Certainly, children everywhere have an initial enculturation experience. Musically, this may be their development as perceivers and performers of simple songs and instrumental pieces in their musical "mother tongue." The second phase in both theories indicates a commitment to practice to develop tech-

FIGURE 2.1

Three Phases of Musical Learning

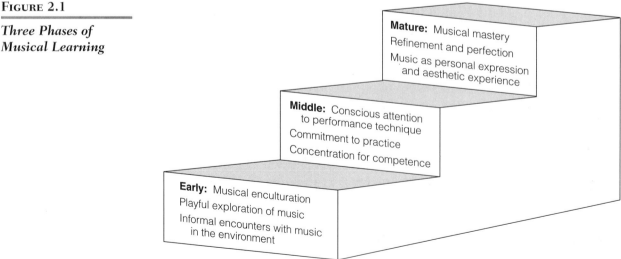

nique and build a performance repertoire. The ultimate phase is reached when performance skills are refined and the goal of music as an aesthetic expression can be attained. Few children realize this goal, although many are well on their way. The greatest focus of music instruction for children through the sixth grade is on the second phase, the skill-building stage.

Theories of Musical Play and Socialization

When children play with other children and socialize with adults, they are learning as well. Contrary to the word's connotation, play can thus be serious business for children. Socialization, a type of play in which children engage in social interactions with adult guides, can be a weighty endeavor for children with serious implications for their cognitive development. Musical play and socialization through music (and for the sake of music learning) can be bona fide means for children to gain information about the world around them.

Various schools of child psychology have supported play as a natural process and a part of child development. G. Stanley Hall and Sigmund Freud were in agreement that young children are in training for adulthood through the games they play. Musical play should be nurtured in the nursery school and continued through the primary grades, according to the pedagogies of Zoltan Kodály, Émile Jaques-Dalcroze, and Carl Orff. Singing games, newly invented songs by children, musical improvisations, and compositions that are practiced, preserved, and performed repeatedly are examples of musical play at its best.

Musical play deserves a prominent place in the education of children—at least through the primary grades—with improvisation occurring throughout the elementary grades. The key to successful music learning may be at least partly linked to the songs children know, invent, and transmit to each other while at play and to the music they create on instruments during free-play time. Certainly, a teacher's goals and well-planned lessons are necessary in the educational process, as is an open mind to the music that children know and spontaneously create. Children's musical play can be the means by which a conceptual understanding of music is more fully developed in the classroom. The teacher's role as guide, not solely as leader, can foster learning and the development of favorable attitudes toward music that will long endure.

The Russian social psychologist Lev Vygotsky (1978) established that the adult, primarily the parent and teacher, is the primary influence on a child's socialization process. The adult not only transmits music to a child, but also participates in the child's discovery and manipulation of the music to be acquired. During musical play, the teacher or parent delivers to the child cultural signs—such as verbal comments, facial expressions, or indicatory gestures—that direct the child's attention to specific elements of an experience and that activate appropriate learning behaviors. According to

Vygotsky, these signs provide the means for drawing children into knowing their culture (in this case, musical culture) while also shaping and coloring their perceptions and eventual understanding of the cultural object (the music). As the teacher interacts musically with children, for example, while singing, the children come to know that song and to progress toward singing it independently. They grow in ownership of the song and become more familiar as well with elements of that musical tradition. Their musical interactions with the adult while singing, moving, listening, and playing musical instruments are vital to their musical independence and to their coming into the musical culture itself.

A Constructivist Theory of Meaning Making

Every child has real-world experiences, and ideas become meaningful as a result of the events that happen in particular ways to each individual. Consistent with a belief in the child as an active player in the shaping of knowledge, the constructivist theory of learning explains knowledge as a result of the process by which the child creates meaning from his or her experiences. Like a carpenter or a builder of houses, learning proceeds in active instead of passive ways as the child builds up knowledge piece by experiential piece until a meaningful whole forms—and then some, for every experience to follow has also the potential of broadening as well as deepening his or her understanding. The child is the key player in this constructivist process, building a conceptualization of self, other, and outer world through each progressive experience, encounter, and interaction that comes along.

Donald Jonasson's constructivism is associated with mental constructs or principles—the germinal units that comprise knowledge—and how they are developed (Duffy and Jonasson, 1991). The reconstruction of principles by new learners of a subject is of key interest, and the shaping of experiences into new information and new interpretations is integral to the learning process. Within the instructional process, the accent shifts from the teacher to the child, from the view of teacher-as-absolute and the font of all knowledge to the child as active seeker of ideas from multiple sources. Those teachers who profess a constructivist approach to instruction become facilitators, instead of dictatorial leaders, of children. Their responsibilities are to set up an environment that is conducive to learning and to allow for the setting to support the engagement of children in experiences that lead to the acquisition of principles, skills, and understandings.

Within the realm of music in a child's life, constructivism brings with it certain images; for example, a child playing at the keyboard, trying this and then that key while creating her own tune, and figuring out a motif or gesture that is followed by its repetition and development. In such a case, the teacher is there to provide the instrument, the space (both time and measure of physical distance from the child's need for experimentation), and the occasional prompts, feedback, and encouraging and motivating remarks. Another image of the constructivist approach is the gathering of children who are working collaboratively on a project—a collective composition in which all are contributing members to the final product, a listening analysis in which children together discuss (according to pre-set guidelines) the presence and meaning of certain sonic events, a sectional rehearsal in which children take responsibility for learning (by way of teaching, reviewing, and revising component parts) of an assigned piece. In all cases, the teacher's work was in the advance planning and design of circumstances for children to explore, experiment with, accomplish general goals, and acquire understanding.

The quality of construction depends upon the range of information available to the child-constructor, and while all constructions must be considered meaningful, some are incomplete or simplistic. Learning is not a complete free-for-all in which anything goes, all outcomes are equal, and no one is in error of misinterpreting. Instead, mental constructs have been held as accurate and appropriate with societies and cultures for millenia,

---

LESSON 2.1 *Constructivist-Styled Learning*

1. *Children explore and create compositions individually on keyboards.*
   Teacher has set parameters in advance (such as 8 measures, $\frac{4}{4}$, in C, "start on C and end on C," use of ♩♪♪♩♩ rhythm at least twice); is standing by to assist and prompt; and will request that children record their piece, devise a means of notating it, and write a brief evaluation of it.

2. *Children listen and find pulse, meter, melodic and rhythmic patterns, "expressive dimensions," and general impressions, in repeated listenings to a recorded Trinidadian soca song.*
   Teacher has selected recording that illustrates musical components, accepts all children's discussion points by listing them on the board, suggests some possibilities when children struggle with descriptive words, plays the recording again so that children might review their thoughts and impressions, and prompts for ideas about song words and their musical setting.

3. *Children learn to sing "Viva la musica" in canon.*
   Teacher leads children in singing the song in unison, provides for children to conduct the group with their choices of tempo and dynamic level, allows for children's evaluation of their singing, sets children into practice teams of three—each with rotating conductors—and then brings them back together to sing in canon.

4. *Children create percussion piece on season theme.*
   Teacher has set up five groupings of two xylophones, two metallophones, a drum, and a woodblock, in the center and corners of the room; plays several examples of composed "seasonal music" pieces on recordings; notes parameters of "fifteen minutes to create 'seasonal music' (winter, spring, summer, autumn)" in ABA form; circulates to answer questions of children; and organizes the groups for class performances, discussion, evaluation.

and they form the basis of fundamental human understanding. This then becomes the challenge of constructivism to teachers: determining how to balance personal, flexible, or even free processes of knowledge acquisition by children with the initial set-up of the learning environment and guideposts along the way by teachers, so that the result is the acquisition of shared knowledge that can also be individually interpreted. Those professed constructivist teachers swear by the theory, and their children revel in what appears to be a less restrictive means of learning and more personally meaningful than that espoused by other theories (see Lesson 2.1).

Social Learning and Reinforcement Theories

Two theories from the fields of sociology and psychology, both highly relevant to teaching and learning, are linked by their examination of environmental agents that promote and influence learning. Neither is technically an instructional theory, although each targets behaviors that frequently appear in classrooms. Social learning theory explains the significance of environmental models for learning, while reinforcement theory describes the manner in which persons in the environment shape and increase learning behaviors.

Albert Bandura's (1977) social learning theory is a provocative view of the power of persons within an environment to serve as models of behavior that are later replicated by the observer. Children choose to watch and listen to their parents and teachers, whose behaviors they later emulate. Their observations of these models are mentally organized, memorized, and recalled when similar situations for thinking and acting arise in their lives.

Teacher-as-model singing with children

Jerry Gay

The process of environmental influences and social learning are played out as the student recalls the visual or aural codes of earlier observations and practices the behaviors first demonstrated by the models. Social learning theory is prominent in musical settings, because modeling is critical to the student's watching, listening, and then performing the music in the manner and style of the teacher. Children learn to sing and play instruments, as well as how to listen, by doing as their models do.

Table 2.2 shows how social learning theory can be adapted to a learning sequence that integrates the act of listening in the development of performance skills, in this case, singing. A song is learned in three stages. First, it is introduced by the teacher; second, an intermediate stage is reached several run-throughs or even weeks later; and third, a final stage of refinement is achieved some time after that. The teacher as model is central to the development of listening and performance skills. The children imitate the model and evaluate their attempts to recreate it, showing increasing ability to match the model's performance, even as they offer personal expression in their rendering of the song. Questions by the teacher direct children to careful listening to develop their ability to sing accurately and expressively. This sequence could be also contained within a single lesson; thus, it becomes a lesson plan for teaching a song.

The reinforcement theory of the behavioral school of psychology has been embraced by teachers and parents, having long provided suggestions for effective means of shaping children's behaviors toward those considered acceptable and appropriate. B. F. Skinner's (1953) classic theory of operant conditioning is at the heart of behavioral change, including learning.

TABLE 2.2 *Applications of Social Learning Theory to Music Instruction*

Early	The model (teacher) sings/children listen
	Can you sing the final tone?
	What is the meter?
	How many phrases are there?
	Are there any repeated patterns?
Middle	The model sings/children listen; children sing
	What pitches are to be accented?
	Have you lowered/raised the pitch?
	Are you sustaining for the complete duration?
	Can you achieve the rhythmic swing or flow?
Late	Children sing; the model sings/children listen; children sing
	How closely can you approximate the model?
	How might you vary the model's rendering?
	Where are the peak expressive points?
	What are the overlaps and distinctions between you and the model?

Operant conditioning is a three-part instructional "kernel," or process, comprised of a stimulus that is presented to the learner, a response that is elicited by the learner as a consequence of the stimulus, followed by the presentation of another stimulus that reinforces the response. Stimuli operating in the environment, including the verbal and nonverbal approval of a teacher, have an impact on children's learning behaviors. Skinner's reinforcement theory holds that when a child's behavior—singing in tune or playing rhythms accurately—is positively reinforced by the teacher's smile, nod, or positive comment, that behavior will be maintained or increased. Punishers can decrease inappropriate behavior through the teacher's frown, finger snap, or shake of the head.

The Skinnerian technique of successive approximation, or the shaping of behavior by reinforcing each progressive step toward an ideal, is one of the most common used by teachers. Shaping requires teachers to break songs, pieces, or musical passages into small parts; to offer approving remarks for musical behaviors that are similar to, or that approximate, the desired performance behaviors ("Yes, now you've got the right rhythm!"); and to use punishers to state what needs to change in moving learners toward the ideal ("No, you need to sing it a half-step higher"). The teacher reinforces less perfect musical behaviors in the hopes of directing children to more perfect ones. The teacher's reinforcing comments are eventually diminished, as children begin to evaluate their own musical behaviors as approximating the model or ideal sound. Reinforcement theory is recognized by behaviorists as a premiere influence on learning, with the teacher acting as environmental agent, dispenser of feedback, and model of appropriate behavior.

Reinforcement theory is also the basis of the system of classroom management called behavior modification, in which children are given external reinforcement for appropriate social or academic behaviors. In its classic form, children receive rewards contingent on or following good behavior; these rewards have included M&M candies, tokens to be applied to prizes, free time, and field trips. This system is well known for keeping children on task, or focused on goals of cooperative and nondisruptive behavior and on the completion of projects and assignments.

The work of Clifford K. Madsen and his associates (Madsen and Madsen, 1981; Madsen and Yarbrough, 1985) on the application of reinforcement theory to musical settings has inspired a host of research studies and teaching practices. They have developed four observational research principles: pinpointing a trouble behavior; observing and recording the frequency of the behavior; applying a teaching strategy to reduce the behavior; and evaluating the effect of the strategy by observing the frequency of the behavior. In countless studies, inappropriate behaviors are reduced while appropriate behaviors emerge. The key appears to be viewing the trouble behaviors one at a time and applying teaching strategies that work.

Another use of reinforcement theory as applied to music is the study of its power as a reinforcer for appropriate and nondisruptive social behaviors. This perspective underscores the function of music as a therapeutic agent.

Learning Style Theories

Several learning style theories have been developed from research on the functioning of the human brain and on the complexities of the human personality. While these are not instructional theories per se, they underscore the individual differences among children's learning styles for which an array of instructional strategies may be necessary.

Research has shed considerable light on the different but complementary tasks of the brain's right and left hemispheres. When the corpus callosum, or bundle of nerves connecting the two hemispheres, is severed, the left hemisphere responds better to verbal, sequential, and linear processing, while the right hemisphere is inclined toward nonverbal, spatial-visual, and simultaneous processing. This has led cognitive psychologists to develop a theory of cerebral dominance, which suggests that some individuals are "left-brain convergent" thinkers while others are "right-brain divergent" thinkers (Restak, 1979). More recent research suggests that, depending on the task and on the level of learning already attained, people use both sides of the brain with facility and that communication between both hemispheres is rapid and complex. Some educators have taken steps past the conceptual theory to the design of instructional strategies that reach both "brains."

Stemming partly from cerebral dominance research and from his observations of brain-damaged individuals who demonstrated specific types of intelligence even though they showed an intellectual deficiency, Howard Gardner (1983) proposed a theory of multiple intelligences. He suggested that there may be seven intelligences, one or several of which are dominant in the learner's processing of the world. Gardner was concerned that the definition of intelligence was too limited and that a person may be intelligent in more than one domain or especially strong in one area while only moderately so in another. The seven intelligences of Gardner's theory are linguistic, logical-mathematical, spatial, interpersonal, intrapersonal, musical, and bodily-kinesthetic. His recent work has probed the nature of a teacher's illumination for students of the nature of truth, beauty, and morality through carefully crafted lessons on a theory of evolution, the Holocaust, and the music of Mozart (1999). While seemingly from his earlier theory, the many dimensions of intelligence emerge in his description of the teacher's craft.

Clearly, Gardner's theory stands on its own, but if each intelligence is more centered in one hemisphere or the other, then his theory can be related to research in cerebral dominance. Left-hemisphere processes are emphasized in linguistic and logical-mathematical intelligences, while spatial intelligence reflects right-hemisphere excellence. Interpersonal and intrapersonal intelligences emanate from right-hemisphere functions. Musical intelligence is balanced by processes of both hemispheres, for it allows sequential (left-brain) processing through its perception of durational and pitch patterns and phrases, and simultaneous (right-brain) processing

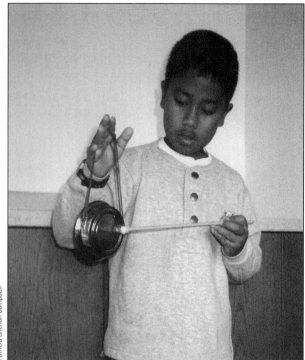

Listening, looking, doing: the multiple modalities at play

Patricia Shehan Campbell

through its perception of various polyphonic textures, including harmony. The bodily-kinesthetic intelligence is the only emphasis that appears to stem more from the motor and sensory parts of the cortex than from either hemisphere in particular. Each intelligence is like a learning style that calls for specific instructional strategies.

Along with its reference to cerebral dominance theory, Gardner's theory of multiple intelligence suggests that there is more than one intellect and that nonverbal forms of learning merit greater attention than is currently given to them by educators. If it can be accepted that the two hemispheres have specialized yet complementary functions, then it would seem critical to pay greater attention to teaching to the somewhat neglected right hemisphere. The exercise of children's subjective, affective, and divergent qualities can be greatly served through lessons in music and the arts. While music can be analyzed linearly by the left hemisphere, it can also be nonverbally experienced and creatively expressed by the right hemisphere. The nature of music instruction allows children occasions for activating the best of both brains.

A theory of learning modalities proposed by Walter Barbe and Raymond S. Swassing (1979) submits that a learner processes information most efficiently through one of three sensory channels: visual; auditory; or tactile/kinesthetic. The visual learner absorbs information by seeing, reading, and observing demonstrations by others. The auditory learner benefits from verbal instructions and from oral examples presented by the teacher, another student, or recordings. The kinesthetic learner develops knowledge and skills by touching, moving, and physically acting on his or her environment. Learning modalities are thought to be relatively stable over time, but

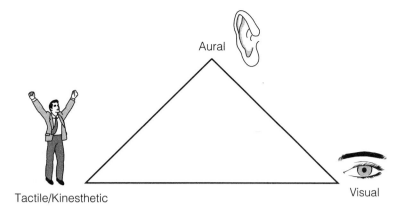

FIGURE 2.2

Learning Modalities:
Independent Yet Able
to Be Integrated

evidence also shows that very young children tend to be kinesthetically oriented, primary-grade children more inclined toward auditory learning, with adolescents shifting toward the visual modality. Figure 2.2 illustrates the modalities; their configuration within a single closed shape suggests the three modalities should all be included in lessons.

Learning modalities can be applied to music instructional approaches. While music classroom environments must be rich in stimulation for all the senses, knowing the modality strengths of individual students would be helpful. Visual learners acquire music by seeing, reading notation, and watching others make music; auditory learners from verbal instructions and musical examples; and kinesthetic learners by feeling, participating, and becoming involved with music in a physical way. The best teaching involves the stimulation of all modalities. This is particularly easy to do in music, which is multimodal by nature. Lesson 2.2 offers a sample lesson that utilizes the three modalities in developing an understanding of pitch and duration within the traditional song "Charlie over the Ocean."

Environmental, emotional, sociological, physical, and psychological issues affecting learning are addressed by Rita Dunn and Kenneth Dunn's (1984) learning style model. The environmental set of factors is perhaps the most unique aspect of the model, because it includes sound, light, temperature, and classroom design—all of which can be adjusted by the teacher. Some children are negatively affected by loud and noisy environments, while others require some ambient sound to think. Some children's quality of thinking is diminished by learning spaces that are too bright or too dull (dim). If children are too hot or too cold, they may not attain their learning potential. A fourth environmental factor involves the design of a room, which may appear too crowded, overstimulating, and distracting for some, but not stimulating.

Field dependence or field independence is postulated by numerous psychologists including Harold Witkin (1977). Field dependence is defined as the content-bound, experiencing concepts as embedded within their environment, whereas field independence is content independent, experiencing concepts as discrete entities removed from their background. The field dependent learner learns best from other people in a social setting and

Charlie over the Ocean

Char - lie o - ver the o - cean. Char - lie o - ver the sea.

Char - lie caught a black - bird he can't catch me.

Grade Level One-two

Focus d–r–m, m–r–d, d–s
$\frac{6}{8}$ rhythm: ♩♪; ♫♫; ♩.

Objectives Children will be able to:

1. Sing and chant pitch and rhythm patterns noted above, in isolation and in the context of the song "Charlie over the Ocean" (a).

2. Map the pitch and rhythm patterns as they are sounded in the song, in the air, on paper, and on the blackboard (v, k).

3. Identify pitch and rhythm patterns as they are sounded vocally or on instruments (a).

4. Walk the pulse while patting rhythm patterns (k).

5. Show pitch levels of patterns through gestures while singing (k, v).

6. Notate the song on music staff (v).

Sequence

1. Children pat the pulse, while teacher chants $\frac{6}{8}$ rhythms in various patterns:

   ♩♪ (ta-ti); ♫♫ (ti-ti-ti); ♩. (ta-i) (a).

2. Teacher chants $\frac{6}{8}$ rhythms of song in one- and two-measure phrases. Children pat the pulse while listening and then chanting in imitation (a).

3. Children pat the pulse, while teacher sings pitch patterns:

   d–r–m, m–r–d, d–s (a).

4. Teacher sings song in one- and two-measure phrases, using tonic solfa (solfège) patterns. Children pat the pulse while listening and singing in imitation (a).

5. Teacher sings song with words: in full, and then in two-measure phrases, to be imitated by children (a).

Note: a = aural; v = visual; k = kinesthetic.

6. Children sing the song, mapping in the air, on paper, and on the blackboard the pitch levels of the melody and their durations (v, k). ☏ 🏃

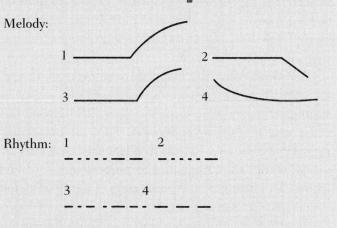

Melody:

1 _____   2 _____

3 _____   4

Rhythm: 1   2

— – · – – · – –   – · – – –

3   4

– · – – · – · – – · – –

7. When the song is learned, teacher isolates several rhythm patterns to clap or play on drum. Children chant back using rhythm syllables (see No. 1). Example:

T (claps): ♩ ♪ ♫♫

C (chant): ta ti ti ti ti

T (claps): ♪♩. ♩. ♩.

C (chant): ti ta-i ta-i ta-i

8. Teacher isolates several pitch patterns to sing on "loo" or to play on the recorder. Children sing back using tonic solfa or words. Example:

T (sings or plays): ♩ ♪ ♫♫ ♩.

C (sings with solfa): d   d d d d   s₁

C (sings words)   Char-lie o-ver the sea

9. Teacher plays the pulse on drum. Children walk the pulse. On cue, they pat the rhythms of the song (on their tummies, shoulders, and head) while walking (k). 🏃

10. While singing the song, children use hand levels to show pitch. Then they use Curwen-Kodály hand signs associated with individual pitches (k, v). 🏃 👁

11. Measure by measure, children chant the rhythm as teacher notates it above the staff (v, a). ☏ 👂

12. Measure by measure, children sing the pitches (with solfa or words) as teacher notates it on the staff (v, a). ☏ 👂

13. Teacher adjusts pitches for appropriate rhythms (v). ☏

through class discussions and teacher-directed activities. The field independent learner prefers learning alone and in an autonomous manner and is most comfortable setting his or her own goals and working at his or her own pace. In a musical setting, field dependent learners may thrive on singing games, group improvisation, and ensemble performance. Field independent learners may more easily gain knowledge through computer-assisted programs of instruction, solo practice, and individual composition. The astute observer, teacher, or parent soon distinguishes among these learners and makes allowances for them.

A related theory by Isabel Myers, Peter B. Briggs, M. H. McCaulley, and R. Most (1985) postulates that four types of personality factors inform learning: (1) extroversion/introversion, (2) sensing/intuitive, (3) thinking/feeling, and (4) judging/perceiving. They are measured through the Myers-Briggs Type indicator. Extroverted learners are more socially directed to the external world, thinking aloud to process ideas, while introverted learners require silent internal processing time to figure out what they have observed or experienced. Sensing learners rely heavily on their sensory channels to give them information, while intuitive types invent and reason new information from previous experiences. Thinking learners make decisions based on objective rational analysis, and feeling learners rely on subjective personal values as the basis of decisions. Finally, judging learners make decisions easily and promptly, while perceivers are tentative, choosing to delay decisions while gathering further information. These varied personalities challenge the teacher to carefully gauge the personalities of their students and to creatively develop ways to enhance their learning.

Theories of Instruction

Over the past several decades, instructional psychologists have developed many theories about the effects of interactions between teachers and learners. Only a small selection of the more significant theories to music instruction for children is described here.

David Ausubel (1968) maintained that a person's existing cognitive structure is the foremost factor governing whether new material is potentially meaningful as well as how readily it can be acquired and retained. In his theory of meaningful reception, the role of the learner is to receive ideas and information, with the teacher being the lecturer or explainer. Critical to the learner's meaningful reception of new information is the provision of "advance organizers" by the teacher, the structuring of a foundation of familiar ideas on which new information can be laid. The teacher who outlines the material to be covered and goals to be met is also organizing for children in advance the learning that will occur. Children must listen intently and seek actively to reorganize their existing knowledge in view of the teacher's ideas, so that they can then formulate new ways of looking at the world.

Jerome Bruner (1966) is the major proponent of the "discovery method." The discovery method is a type of learning that involves problem solving, requiring the learner to manipulate materials and to cope with incongruities from which information is derived. Discovery learning encourages taking risks, guessing, and exploring student-initiated hypotheses. Exploratory experiences and occasional nonconformity are indicators of creative thinking, which is the ultimate goal of all learning. Improvisation and composition experiences are the most obvious examples of musical exploration and experimentation, but any musical experience that challenges children to think while listening, performing, or creating can exemplify discovery learning. Musical concepts can be most effectively taught via the discovery method. By allowing children to experience a concept (such as pulse, meter, a three-pitch melody, or binary form) without initially labeling it, they can explore and be guided toward an understanding of that concept and then learn its official name.

Brunerian ideas have been influential in the development of curriculum and instruction in music, most notably on the Manhattanville Music Curriculum Project, or MMCP (Thomas, 1970). In addition to directing musical experiences for children to include musical exploration, improvisation, and composition, Bruner's concept of a spiral curriculum that allows children to learn music through age-appropriate experiences was also put to its test through MMCP. The spiral curriculum recommended that "any subject could be taught to any child at any age," so long as it is set in lessons suitable for the intellectual level of the child. Thus, the components of music—for example, melody and rhythm—can be taught to preschool and secondary school students, just as the music of Mozart and Messiaen, and from Bali and Bulgaria, can be experienced earlier and later in a child's school career.

Robert Gagné's descriptive studies of cognitive processes in the 1960s led to his development (with his colleagues) of eight "events of instruction" or "conditions of learning" (1977). The events or conditions include a progression of sensory information from perception to concept formation. These events embrace the needs for preparing children for new information, offering occasions for their responses to and practice of new information, and supporting the transfer of information gained to the greater acquisition of knowledge. The teacher's role in engaging children's interest is an important first step for knowledge acquisition; that role becomes increasingly prominent later when he or she introduces the more complex process of problem solving. More than most theories, Gagné's events of instruction are clear-cut steps that can be readily applied to music. See Box 2.1 for an application of Gagné's eight events to music for children. These steps may apply to a complete lesson or to single activities within a lesson.

Edwin E. Gordon's (1994) Music Learning Theory appears to be at least partially influenced by some of Gagné's early theoretical work. Gordon's earlier work (1971) was nearly a direct application of Gagné's events to music. Like the events of instruction, Gordon's theory is hierarchical in nature, progressing through eight levels that begin with aural or oral reception and transmission and lead to generalization, improvisation, and finally

Box 2.1 *Gagné's Events of Instruction: Applications to Music for Children*

1. Gaining and maintaining attention
   - Ask a probing question to pique curiosity
   - Present a startling statement
   - Tell a short story
   - Sing a favorite familiar song with children
   - Clap a rhythm children can imitate
   - Play a recording that encourages children's movement responses
   - Engage children in immediate participation

2. Preparing learners for instruction
   - Repeat #1, but with relevance to the new music to be learned
   - Share with children the goals and expectations of the lesson or activity
   - Present fragments and phrases of the new music to be learned as teasers for children's imitation

3. Presenting the material
   - Present the lesson's music in live or recorded form
   - Present small sections or chunks of the new music that can be linked together to form the whole

4. Prompting and guiding learning
   - llustrate problem melodic and rhythmic phrases through mnemonics
   - Call attention to repeated patterns and unusual musical features
   - Allow time to rehearse individually, in small or large groups

5. Providing conditions for response
   - Offer occasions for active participation and performance by all
   - Switch from playing to singing a piece; from singing to moving to its rhythm or pulse

6. Providing feedback for response
   - Remind children of learning goals and expectation of the lesson or activity
   - Offer specific comments when possible
   - Allow children opportunities to change and to perfect their performance

7. Promoting and measuring retention
   - Critique children's performance
   - Allow children to evaluate their performance
   - Provide opportunities for children to develop the musical ideas of the piece through improvisation

8. Enhancing transfer of learning to new tasks or information
   - Transfer concepts and skills to performance of unfamiliar piece
   - Transfer concepts and skills to listening of unfamiliar piece

music theory—the whys and hows of musical pitch and rhythm functions. Gordon compares learning music with mastering a spoken language, as a progression from first simply perceiving and responding to sounds to the advanced levels of problem solving and conceptual understanding. Gordon also addresses the sequential nature of acquiring basic discrimination and music literacy skills, and the use and transfer of these skills to bring about more sophisticated possibilities for music learning possibilities.

Gordon's Music Learning Theory is a comprehensive model of skill development, founded on the principle of audiation, or inner hearing: the ability to "hear" notation and to notate what one hears. In a Pestalozzian manner, and related to the pedagogical approaches of Lowell Mason and, much later, Europeans Émile Jaques-Dalcroze, Zoltan Kodály, and Carl Orff, Gordon's recommendations for music instruction begin with the musical sound and vocalized patterns, proceeding gradually to the notational symbols of pitch and rhythm. His music learning sequence is a prescribed succession of music skills (or performance behaviors), music content, and tonal and rhythm patterns, and it is intended to develop musical audiation and understanding. See Chapter 4 for further explanation of the method that Gordon developed from his theory.

Relating Theory to Practice

Five components of guidelines based on the theories of teaching and learning provide for the effective delivery of instruction by teachers to children in preschool and the elementary grades: the classroom environment, the child-centered curriculum, the teacher as transmitter, instructional strategies, and motivation and management.

The Classroom Environment

What Should the Music Classroom Look Like?

Theories of child development, musical play, and learning styles inform the physical setting of the music classroom. Most important, furniture in the music room must be minimal so that a great variety of musical play and performance experiences can occur. A piano is always useful, preferably one with wheels for easy maneuvering. Various types of xylophones and percussion instruments can be laid on tables for easy access by children. Larger drums and bass xylophones can be laid across the floor or kept in storage until needed. Computers for independent and small-group projects can be set up in one corner of the room, to which a Music Instrument Digital Interface (MIDI) station can be attached. Even in a medium-sized room, a small keyboard lab of four to six pianos can be placed at one end.

For seated activities, floor space is still preferable to desks. Children can pick up three-foot carpet squares (usually available as remnants from a carpet store) when they enter the classroom. Choral risers can make for useful seating or standing arrangements, especially for the upper grades. These should be located against a wall so that open space remains in the center for movement activities.

Various audiovisual resources are vital for teaching and can be kept on wheel carts for greater portability. A high-quality sound system with the capacity to play compact discs (CDs), cassette tapes, and records is basic to any successful music instruction. Overhead transparency projectors and video cassette recorder (VCR) equipment are also critical. A table with chairs, on which cassette tape players with headphones can be set, can make for an ideal independent listening and ear-training lab. A teacher's desk, files, and storage cabinets complete the list of necessary furniture.

What Should the Music Classroom Feel Like?

Teachers need to be aware of factors that create an environment conducive to music listening, performing, and creating. The music room should be well ventilated, with plenty of windows for fresh air and light. It should be low on ambient sound and moderate in temperature, ventilation, and light. Cafeterias, with the noise of cookware clanging together, are not ideal for use as music rooms. Gyms are built for sports and games, but they are not appropriate for developing musical sensitivity, performance techniques, and aural skills because of their poor acoustics.

What Other Resources Can Enhance a Music Classroom's Potential for Effective Instruction?

Visual appeal can motivate children to want to come to music and to learn. A chalkboard, preferably with staff lines, is the sine qua non of the music room, especially by the time notation is introduced. Felt and bulletin boards can be places for attractive posters and color photographs of performers, composers, dancers, instruments, maps, and timely announcements. Notational symbols make pleasant borders, and colorful lists of terms can be pinned to these boards. Instruments should be labeled in bold letters so that their names are known. Sheets of butcher paper (available from art supply or butcher's shops) are useful for writing and posting song words and key concepts of a lesson.

What Print, Audio, and Video Materials Should a Teacher Have Available for Music Instruction?

A personal collection of recordings, videotapes, books, and basal series textbooks can stimulate the design of successful lessons. An annotated listing of the contents of such a collection can trigger the memory and serve as a guide for lesson plans. Basal series textbooks often feature attractive recordings and sometimes other sources such as videotapes, posters, and computer-assisted instruction programs. Sources for beginning to build a personal library are listed at the end of each chapter. Collections of slides, color transparencies, and photographs complete a teacher's personal storehouse of instructional materials.

Whatever is not available within the music classroom may be found in a school's learning resource center, in the library, or even in the faculty lounge. When fundamental materials, such as a sound system and musical instruments, are not available, small educational grants or gifts can be obtained to provide for them.

A Child-Centered Curriculum

A child-centered curriculum offers instruction that is relevant to the child's experiences and abilities, needs, and interests. This curriculum is more playful, more integrated, and more likely to be led by the responses of children than by the whims of the teacher. What are the realities of a child-centered curriculum in music? Several key issues merit consideration in the design of a music program.

Know the Children

What musical skills and knowledge do children possess? What music interests and moves them? What are their learning styles? What subject strengths do they possess? Where are they developmentally? What are their cultural and familial backgrounds? What, if any, are the musical and educational expectations of their parents? Do they have musical goals and dreams they hope to attain? Generalizing about children leads to surefire foiled experiences that fail to reach them. By talking to teachers and parents, reviewing school files, and asking questions of the children themselves, teachers can offer far more relevant musical experiences and training.

Begin Where the Children Are

While many specific questions may be asked for which answers should be sought, universal concepts must be considered when designing music instruction for children. These include (1) providing lessons that lead children from the familiar to the unfamiliar—that is, teaching ♪♫ after they know ♫♫, and teaching ⁷₈ after they understand two- and three-beat meters; (2) giving children many occasions for active instead of passive experiences (most children achieve their greatest learning when they have actively participated through manipulation of a concept or through performance); and (3) offering children lessons with variety (various approaches to a concept, various musical examples, various musical pieces and styles).

Allow Time for Musical Play and Exploration

For young children, musical sound is a discovery of how loud and how soft, how choppy and how smooth, how long and how short, how fast and how slow, how high and how low a set of pots and pans, the teeth of a comb, or two pencils can sound. Given a drum, sandblocks, or a xylophone, how many different sounds can a young child play? For older children, the music curriculum can be linked to solving musical problems creatively through experimentation: Choose the pitches for a rhythmic pattern and create a new song; or write a poem and perform it rhythmically and with dynamic expression. Time must be allotted as well for experimentation and personal expression through music.

Integrate Music into the Other Parts of a Child's Life

Songs blend with stories, music listening mixes with movement, and a study of musical instruments is also a lesson in the science of acoustics. Like the whole language approach in other subject areas, music is not to be treated as a separate entity but can be coupled with the learning of concepts in social studies, language arts, mathematics, and the sciences. A musical experience can be enhanced by experiences in the visual arts, stories, poetry, theater, and movement and dance.

The Teacher as Transmitter

Teachers are transmitters of culture. How they package and present information to children is critical to whether the transmission process is completed; that is, whether the information is received and assimilated by children. Theories of instruction, reinforcement, socialization, and social learning underscore the powerful impact that a teacher can have on children's learning and development. Of the many qualities that good music teachers possess, several are more prominent.

Know the Subject Matter

The effective music teacher knows well the music, concept, or technique to be taught. Knowing the music requires preparation; without it, the lesson will fail. A Russian folk song cannot be taught before the teacher has practiced the song's words, melody, and rhythm. A xylophone arrangement cannot be masterfully taught if the teacher has not worked out the parts: by reading and rereading, chanting, patting, singing, or even playing them. The teacher should be able to sing, play, or move to the music selected for lessons with ease and refinement. As the teacher transmits the music, his or her enjoyment and love for it is also passed on to the children. Music concepts must be clearly understood in terms of their critical perceptual qualities so activities can be chosen to highlight those qualities.

Model the Musical Behaviors

The effective music teacher serves as the live model for the music to be learned. Performance skills are learned by children who imitate or are otherwise influenced by the behavior and comments of their teacher. Verbal explanations are far less effective than demonstration. How can children be told in words alone how to sing staccato, to sustain a sound, or (initially) to play a bourdon (bass drone) or xylophone? As the adage goes, a teacher's "actions speak louder than words." Many children will know no other musicians who can sing well and perform proficiently on musical instruments. For them, the teacher who performs is critical to their musical well-being. While absolute mimicry by children is not the goal of a teacher's musical demonstrations, model musicianship can be observed, absorbed, and reinterpreted by children in their own performance.

Present with Energy and Enthusiasm

The effective music teacher is enthusiastic about music and children, and he or she presents lessons that are charged with energy. Enthusiasm is conveyed in many ways: a broad spectrum of vocal inflections and facial expressions, steady eye contact, varied gestures and demonstrative movements of the body, and descriptive vocabulary. The teaching pace needs to at least occasionally match that of television programs to which children are accustomed, with quick changes of experiences and approaches to a musical

Children's choir in the setting of the music classroom

concept. High energy and vitality most successfully convey ideas. While enthusiasm comes naturally for some teachers, others can learn by reviewing teaching behaviors via videotaped recordings and then making a conscientious effort to increase their eye contact or to vary their facial expressions. No doubt, a teacher's enthusiasm is also related to job satisfaction as well as his or her interest in the music selected for the lesson.

Instructional Strategies

What are some of the recent instructional strategies that promote learning and develop strong and lasting interactions between teacher and children? No clearer way to understanding instructional theories exists than to apply them to your teaching. Some strategies are governed by children's age, stage, or phase of development, while others relate to their individual learning styles and personalities.

Starting the Class

The manner in which a class begins can entice and motivate children to learn or can turn their attentions away from the subject for the remainder of the period. Gaining children's attention may proceed in many ways. Play live or recorded music as children enter. Ask a question ("How might a composer portray the sound of a train?," leading to playing Honneger's Pacific 231). Tell a story ("Beauty and the Beast," leading to Ravel's piece of the same title). Make a bold and startling statement ("People in Mozambique do not sit still at concerts," leading to a lesson incorporating song, story, dance, and xylophone performance). Clap a rhythm to be imitated by children. Give a silent gesture that, over time, means to come to attention, a signal that something important is about to happen. As a musician-teacher, sing a song or play a piece. Perform a familiar song with the class. Show a photograph or illustration, in silence or with a leading question. Depending on the lesson, any number of these strategies will direct children's attention toward class.

Ending the Class

The music and the learning will linger longer when the class ends in a memorable or stimulating fashion. There are many possibilities. Sing or play a familiar song. Play or snap, clap, pat, and stamp a rhythmic piece or passage. Ask a question to be answered in the next music class ("What could we do to make this song more interesting texturally?"). Tease by previewing the next class ("And if you want to know how to play an Afro-Cuban rhythm on the conga drum, you'll have to come back next _____!"). Rapidly review the main points of the lesson. Play live or recorded music as children exit.

Supplying Feedback: The TST

The interactive instructional kernel of the teaching and learning process is a three-step process that involves the (T)eacher's presentation of information, the (S)tudents' response to that information, and the (T)eacher's specific feedback to the response. Based on operant conditioning, the TST is the Skinnerian stimulus-response-stimulus sequence that makes for effective instruction. There are multiple TST kernels in a lesson, because the teacher's feedback in the third step progresses to the next TST. An example of three TSTs in a row is this interchange at the beginning of a recorder lesson:

T: Let's learn the playing position of the recorder. Hold the recorder in your left hand.

S: (Children hold their recorders in their left hands)

T: Good. Now relax. It should feel easy, almost natural.

T: Now, let's blow air out gently, as if into a straw.

S: (Children blow air)

T: Not too hard. Gently. Pretend you're blowing small bubbles.

T: Let's try this out on the recorder. Ready, blow.

S: (Children blow air into recorder)

T: Not bad. You're on your way.

Clearly, the lack of any steps in these three TSTs means that the instruction is not complete. There must be information from the teacher, followed by a response from the children, and concluding with the teacher's evaluation of their response. From one TST to the next, the teacher is interacting with students in information given and gained.

Stimulating Aural Learning

Understanding and skill building in music require careful listening. Music literacy is advanced through aural learning, which includes the use of modeling, imitative devices, and strategies for strengthening the memory. The instructional approaches of Kodály, Dalcroze, and Orff suggest that melodic and rhythmic ideas, phrasing and form, expressive elements, and performance techniques initially can be taught aurally. The aural acquisition of music may even facilitate music literacy; it is a necessary phase toward that development. Recorded music for aural learning can be supplemented by live performances given by the teacher, older and more experienced students, visiting artists, and amateur musicians from the community. Musical patterns, fragments, phrases, and pieces can help to build in children a functional musical vocabulary for their later listening and performance. Learning by listening is a logical procedure, bringing children directly into the sound of the music.

Providing for Repetition and Rehearsal

The acquisition of performance and listening skills takes time and effort, and children can show considerable progress through repeated attempts to achieve them. Learning to sing four phrases of a traditional song such as "Charlie over the Ocean" is a complex endeavor for very young children. The words, rhythm, melodic patterns, and tonality may take many listenings and even more occasions for singing it, before the components begin to fall in place. Listening to Stravinsky's "Greeting Prelude" or to Bach's "Little Fugue in G Minor" is challenging to older children, when the object is to listen analytically for the formal organization of melodic and rhythmic ideas. Preference for, or at least tolerance of, a musical piece may require a bare minimum of ten listenings, and probably more. Fleeting experiences do not guarantee learning; repetition can.

Informed Teaching

All practices are guided by theory; music teaching and learning are no exception. Several disciplines offer theories for framing music instruction for children—developmental and stage and phase theories, musical play and socialization theories, social learning and reinforcement theories, learning style theories, and the blossoming field of instructional psychology.

Teachers engaged in the design of curriculum and instruction in music for children would do well to compare the ideas of others with their own practical perspectives. A theory can be an academic endeavor, evolved by those who once taught and later thought. It can also be a personal effort, a marriage of ideas by insightful teachers who think as they do. By knowing the literature on instructional theory and connecting it to their own practice, teachers can have a significant impact on the music instruction that children receive.

REVIEW

1. Why do teachers need theory for teaching music to children?

2. How are stage-dependent and phase theories related?

3. What theories support the following statements: (1) Good teachers are models for children to emulate. (2) Children should be allowed to learn through their own experimentation. (3) The interaction of teachers with children leads to learning. (4) Children may respond to one form of presentation more favorably than another.

4. What implications do brain and personality theories hold for instruction?

5. Are the theories of Ausubel and Bruner mutually exclusive? Why or why not?

6. Which theories govern children's motivation to learn as well as the teacher's management of their behaviors?

CRITICAL THINKING

1. Which theories can help to guide the design of a child-centered curriculum? How might such a cur-

riculum manifest itself in the behaviors of teachers and children?

2. How is it that musical play can be a child's work—a means for their development intellectually, physically, socially, and emotionally. Give examples of musical play and its effects on children's development.

PROJECTS

1. In small groups, choose a theory, articulate its principal features, and prepare for demonstration a lesson segment that illustrates the theory in action. As an alternative activity, prepare a lesson to teach and then discuss what theories are illustrated within it.

2. Observe a music class for children, and draw relationships between the instructional procedures and theories.

3. Observe the individual responses of children in music classes, and discuss learning style theories as they relate to these responses.

4. Design and teach a lesson based on Gagné's eight events of instruction.

5. Enumerate a set of behavioral rules that you will use as guidelines to ensure an effective learning environment for children.

REFERENCES

Ausubel, D. P. (1968). *Educational psychology.* New York: Holt, Rinehart & Winston.

Bandura, A. (1977). *Social learning theory.* Englewood Cliffs, NJ: Prentice-Hall.

Barbe, W. B., and R. S. Swassing (1979). *Teaching through modality strengths: Concepts and practices.* Columbus, OH: Laner Bloser.

Bateson, G. (1978). *Steps to an ecology of mind.* New York: Ballantine Books.

Bruner, J. (1966). *Toward a theory of instruction.* Cambridge, MA: Harvard University.

Duffy, T. M., and D. H. Jonasson (1991). *Constructivism and the technology of instruction.* Hillsdale, NJ: Lawrence Erlbaum.

Dunn, R., and K. Dunn (1984). Learning style: State of the science. *Theory into Practice,* 23(1), 10–19.

Ellis, C. J. (1986). *Aboriginal music, education for living: Cross-cultural experiences.* St. Lucia, Queensland: University of Queensland.

Gagné, R. M. (1977). *The conditions of learning.* New York: Holt, Rinehart & Winston.

Gardner, H. (1983). *Frames of mind: A theory of multiple intelligences.* New York: Basic Books.

——— (1999) *The disciplined mind.* New York: Penguin Books.

Gordon, E. E. (1971). *The psychology of music teaching.* Englewood Cliffs, NJ: Prentice-Hall.

——— (1994). *Learning sequences in music: Skill, content, and patterns.* Chicago: GIA Publications.

Madsen, C. H., Jr., and C. K. Madsen (1981). *Teaching/discipline* (3rd ed.). Boston: Allyn and Bacon.

Madsen, C. K., and C. Yarbrough (1985). *Competency-based music education.* Englewood Cliffs, NJ: Prentice-Hall.

Myers, I., P. Briggs, M. H. McCaulley, and R. Most (1985). *Manual: A guide to the development and use of the Myers-Briggs Type indicator.* Palo Alto, CA: Consulting Psychologists Press.

Piaget, J. (1952). *The psychology of intelligence.* (M. Percy and D. E. Berlyne, trans.) London, England: Routledge & Kegan Paul.

Restak, R. M. (1979). *The brain: The last frontier.* Garden City, NY: Doubleday.

Skinner, B. F. (1953). *Science and human behavior.* New York: Macmillan.

Sosniak, L. (1985). Three phases of learning. In B. S. Bloom, ed., *Developing talent in young people.* New York: Ballantine Books.

Thomas, R. (1970). *Manhattanville Music Curriculum Project.* Bardonia, NY: Media Materials.

Vygotsky, L. S. (1978). *Mind in society: The development of higher psychological process.* Cambridge, MA: Harvard University.

Witkin, H. (1977). Field dependent and field independent cognitive styles and their educational implications. *Review of Educational Research,* 47, 1–64.

3

Motivation
and Management

Kim began her intern teaching after several years of college preparation. She was excited about getting to teach, and she projected high enthusiasm that the students recognized and enjoyed. Most of Kim's lessons went well, but sometimes glitches arose that left her wondering how she could have managed the situation better. In one lesson, a student was knocked down and hurt in a stampede to get instruments. (Kim quickly realized she needed to organize a system for sending a few students at a time to get instruments.) In another class, three students chose to talk with each other most of the period rather than attend to the lesson. In yet another class, two students traded insults and got into a fistfight.

Kim was frustrated that her lessons had not gone perfectly, and she wanted her cooperating teacher, Mr. Chen, to tell her what to do. But Mr. Chen wisely explained that each teacher needs to develop a leadership presence and an array of interventions that are uniquely successful for herself, her particular philosophy, and the situation. He reminded Kim that the ultimate goal of any motivational or management technique is to help students learn responsibility for motivating and managing themselves. Kim experimented with several ideas and found some that worked most of the time, but nothing that worked all the time. Mr. Chen reassured Kim to be gentle with herself, relax, and not expect to be perfect. "Everyone has setbacks—even long-time teachers," he said. He even shared a poem he kept on his wall: "Ring the bells that still can ring. Forget your perfect offering. There's a crack in everything: That's how the light gets in" (Cohen, 1994). As the term progressed, Kim realized that understanding human nature and building a repertoire of skills for motivating and managing students takes a long time.

The ability to motivate and manage students is one of the most necessary skills of good teachers. Every interview for teaching positions, every job description, and every annual evaluation form include references to motivation and management. Clearly school districts, principals, parents, and students expect teachers to manage and motivate. Society as a whole expects teachers to guide students to learn and abide by the values underlying the society and the cognitive and social skills necessary for lifelong productive contributions to society.

There are many competing philosophies and approaches regarding this subject, and they can leave teachers confused and wondering what to do. Ideas run the gamut from teacher-controlled manipulation and rules enforcement to child-centered, "as-we-go-along" meaning-construction. The many discipline consultants and plans on the market tout the merits of their particular approaches, but no gimmicks or plans work for every teacher with every student at every grade level in every school in every community at every time of the year. Each teacher needs to become aware of many techniques, then develop his or her own unique philosophy and set of interventions. Motivation and management are challenging for any teacher, but more so for music teachers, because they see so many children coming from so many different class structures each day, and they have limited time options for dealing with problems.

Motivation

What Is Motivation and Where Does It Come From?

Motivation is any factor that increases the vigor of an individual's activity. Some tasks, such as doing a hobby, are enjoyable in themselves and are said to be intrinsically motivating. Other tasks are not enjoyable and people need motivation that is not pertinent to the task itself. Intrinsic motivation is a property of the task itself. Because tasks do not have the same intrinsic motivating value for all people, teachers need to be ready with some other types of motivation. Another source of motivation focuses not on the task, but on the person. Some people are motivated internally; that is, their own inner goals or values override the nonmotivating nature of an unpleasant task or add to the intrinsic motivation of an enjoyable task. Internal motivation comes from within the person. When a person is internally motivated, whether the task itself is motivating makes little difference, provided the task is perceived as helping to reach the overall goal. By contrast, external motivation is some kind of reward or feedback from others, such as grades, pressure, money, points, tokens, and so on. Table 3.1 illustrates the differences between internal, external and intrinsic motivation.

Teachers need to think carefully about the intrinsic motivational qualities of the tasks they pose to students. Tasks that most students consider

TABLE 3.1 *Four Factors of Motivation*

	PERSON IS MOTIVATED	PERSON IS NOT MOTIVATED
TASK IS MOTIVATING	Best of all worlds. Person believes the task will help achieve one of his or her goals (internal motivation) and the task is fun (intrinsic motivation). Few, if any, external rewards will be necessary.	Person does not see the relevance of the task (no internal motivation) but does the task anyway because it is fun (intrinsic motivation).
TASK IS NOT MOTIVATING	Person understands the task is necessary to reach a higher goal (internal motivation) and does the task, even though it is boring (no intrinsic motivation).	Worst-case scenario. Person does not see the relevance of the task, and the task is unpleasant. External rewards will probably be necessary to get the task completed.

enjoyable will be more motivating than dull drills and repetitive exercises. Teachers also need to present lessons in such a way that students understand the relevance of the tasks to their continued musical growth. Students are most highly motivated when they love what they are doing and know that doing it is helping them become better people. Humans are naturally curious, so the act of learning is itself usually motivational.

Some psychologists believe that motivation comes from drive reduction. This theory recognizes that human beings have drives that need satisfaction: oxygen, water, food, shelter, sensory stimulation, acceptance,

Motivation comes naturally from intrinsic and internal sources

FIGURE 3.1

*Maslow's Hierarchy
of Human Needs*

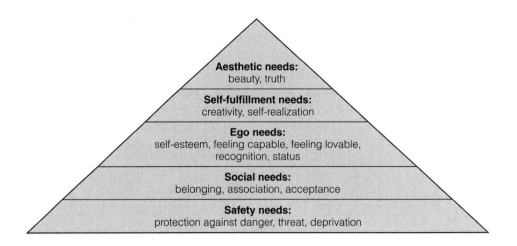

belonging—the list could go on and on. Each drive motivates behaviors in predictable and unpredictable ways. One sign of a good teacher is the ability to capitalize on students' internal drives and put them to good use. For example, a student may be continually seeking attention in class through inappropriate behaviors (off-task, hitting other children, tattling, and so on). If the behavior is caused by a need for attention, a good teacher finds an alternative, acceptable way of satisfying the need such as greeting the student when he enters the room, engaging him in a short conversation about something he is interested in, asking him to babysit a stuffed animal during class, or noticing even small appropriate productive behaviors. Maslow (1971) classifies human needs into a tiered hierarchy (see Figure 3.1).

A satisfied need is no longer motivating, but if a lower need is unmet, the person will generally stop working at the higher level and take care of the lower need. There is less consistency of importance in the higher categories. For example, a person may forgo social needs to concentrate on creative or aesthetic needs. Sometimes our efforts as teachers to motivate students in music is undercut by more basic needs (hunger, family problems, social problems, inadequate sleep), and we will probably not be effective in motivating for music until these more basic needs are met.

The illustration in Figure 3.2 is based on Maslow's hierarchy and is particularly helpful in motivating students to use rehearsals to strive for the highest fun (which is akin to making beautiful music) rather than settling for lower fun (which is equivalent to talking with friends—or making noise). As in Maslow's hierarchy, achieving the highest levels of fun is difficult when members of the group need to satisfy their lower needs.

Advocates of behaviorism believe that motivation and behavior are shaped by positive and negative reinforcement (rewards and punishments). Positive reinforcement is anything that a person seeks, and negative reinforcement is anything one wants to avoid. Sometimes people erroneously use the terms *punishment* and *negative reinforcement* interchangeably. Punishment usually is associated with imposing retribution for misdeeds, with little or no expectation for improvement. Negative reinforcement carries no moralistic connotations but is simply any action that results in lessening the probability of a behavior reoccurring. The aim of punishment is to hurt; the

FIGURE 3.2

Many Kinds of Fun— from Noise to Music

Many Kinds of Fun
—from Noise to Music
===

Super Fun
achieving high expectations
making something beautiful

}}}} Big Fun {{{{
participating in enjoyable
activities with friends

++++ Medium Fun ++++
talking or interacting with friends

//// Little Fun \\\\
being a couch potato, being bored, putting others down

—— No Fun ——
being put down, getting beat up, being with jerks

All people control the kinds of fun they will have by the ways they choose to behave and the words they choose to say.

aim of negative reinforcement is to stop inappropriate behavior. Harsh punishment is seldom effective, but skillfully administered negative reinforcement at just the right level can be highly effective in producing dramatic, permanent cessation of unwanted behaviors. Negative reinforcement, however, must be immediately followed by reinforcing desired behaviors. Good cannot be reinforced merely by negatively reinforcing the opposite. Negative reinforcement may have unpredictable results and is never a complete program in itself. (See Skinner, 1953, for more information on behaviorism and reinforcement.)

On the one hand, competition can sometimes be a source of motivation, but it can backfire. Students who enjoy challenge and risk may be motivated by competition, but students who are anxious and have low levels of expectancy may not enjoy competition. Some teachers advocate abolishing competition altogether. Kohn (1996) considers competition the number one community destroyer. He believes that any activity that rewards students for doing better than others (spelling bees, awards assemblies, segregating special needs children or gifted students) reduces students' senses of interdependence with, responsibility for, and caring about each other. Building on Kohn's work, Bennett and Bartholomew (1997) suggest alternatives to competition, rewards, and praise. Teachers whose personal theories agree with these ideas would eschew competition in favor of other forms of motivation.

Some teachers, on the other hand, find competition a useful motivator, reflective of and as preparation for life in society. In U.S. society, children are frequently exposed to competition in sporting events, card games, board games, politics, advertising, and other business promotions. Johnson and Johnson (1987) advocate using intergroup competition through team tournaments. Many children find competition in teams exciting and fun, even those who prefer not to compete individually. Competition between groups is therefore less risky than between individuals, especially when groups are well balanced between different types of students. Competition through cooperative groups can promote acceptance of diversity, sharing of effort, sharing of responsibility, orderliness, and productivity. Competition between groups in a friendly atmosphere can foster cooperation within groups, communication, a sense of belonging, and self-esteem. Low self-esteem students, who may have little chance of winning individually, enjoy feeling successful when they belong to a group that wins. Group competition must not be allowed, however, to produce hostility to people outside one's group.

Guidelines for Motivating Students

McDaniel (1985) believes that students will be well motivated if teachers follow ten commandments:

1. Build an interesting curriculum
2. Set clear goals
3. Communicate high expectations
4. Employ positive reinforcement
5. Invite success
6. Teach cooperation
7. Demonstrate enthusiasm
8. Personalize instruction
9. Induce readiness to learn
10. Encourage student responses

Some people try to motivate others through threats, intimidation, coercion, shame, rejection, belittling, sarcasm, and other power ploys. These tactics may appear to produce submission for a short time, but ultimately they lower self-esteem, foster resentment, destroy person-to-person bonds, kill initiative, and fail to build a basis for cooperation and positive self-discipline. Unfortunately, some people were raised by parents or had teachers who used these behaviors to control them. When people who are thus abused grow up, they may repeat the abuses on their own children or students. These tactics are common in totalitarian regimes of third-world countries but are decidedly undemocratic and out of place in America. Teachers need to know their own motivations, and they must employ only humane, respectful, concerned ways of motivating students. There is no latitude for choice on this issue: America's judicial system has consistently upheld students' rights.

Some Sample Motivational Ideas and Techniques

Most elementary students enjoy a small amount of friendly group competition, especially if it involves some kind of token prize. Some suitable inexpensive prizes they enjoy receiving include having music-related imprints made from rubber stamps (on paper, on the back of their hands, on their book bags, as temporary tattoos on their arm muscles, and so on), eating their lunches with the teacher in the music room, having their names printed in the school newspaper as winners in music class, being first in line to leave music class, getting first choice of instruments to play in subsequent lessons, having their names entered on a Hall of Fame poster in the music room, or getting special mention at a music program. Some music teachers find good results with giving classes a star on a chart as they leave the music room, if everyone has been cooperative and productive. When a certain number of stars are earned, students get a special music day of choosing their favorite songs to sing, playing instruments, playing music learning games, playing computer music programs, and so on. There are

Carol Scott-Kassner

Children receiving a token award after class

endless possibilities for self-esteem building rewards that are musical. Almost all children (and adults, for that matter) want to appear successful, smart, skilled, and with-it (Kassner 1996). Be careful, however, not to base motivation on tokens. Token rewards should only be insignificant manifestations of the greater inner motivation that comes from increased self-esteem (Stephens and Cooper, 1987).

Another technique to motivate appropriate student behaviors is designating a "Special Person." In each music class, a special person is elected every two weeks. The Special Person sits in a special chair, takes care of the music room mascot (stuffed animal), has first choice of instruments, assists the teacher in many tasks, and receives many other privileges. The Special Person is selected in the following procedure. (1) Captains of each Cooperative Learning group nominate and send to the front of the room a group member they believe to have shown the character trait of the week (rotating list of kind, helpful, caring, and sharing). (2) Nominees turn around and hide their eyes, then the other students vote on the person they think is best at the character trait by raising their hands when the teacher points to each contestant. (Students are reminded never to tell the nominees who voted for them or how many votes they received, so no one's feelings might get hurt.) (3) Nominees open their eyes and turn around and the teacher gives the mascot to the winner and also fills out a certificate of award for the Special Person to take home.

The Special Person designation is a highly coveted award, because students' peers elect them, not the teacher. During the election process, the teacher has several opportunities to reinforce ideas about why the characteristics of kind, helpful, caring, and sharing are important to each individual and to the smooth functioning of the entire class. After the system is established and the character traits are well ingrained, the teacher can have students evaluate inappropriate behaviors in terms of the four traits. For example, if a student intentionally sticks his foot out to trip another student, the teacher can poll the class's opinion: "Which of our Special Person characteristics does this behavior demonstrate? Kindness? Helping? Caring? Sharing?" The class usually answers "no" to each one, and the teacher concludes, "If it isn't kind, helpful, caring, or sharing, it keeps us from working well together and you should not do it." The music teacher is in a unique position to affect the entire climate of the school, and it is amazing to hear students on the playground rebuke an affront with "That wasn't very kind, helpful, caring, or sharing! You won't get to be Special Person if you keep that up."

Older students are often motivated by catching them at their best and receiving edible rewards in addition to public recognition. Whenever students answer questions correctly, perform a passage of music well, help another student, and so on, the teacher writes their names on the board. The second time students are caught doing good, the teacher writes checkmarks next to their names. The student with the most checkmarks at the end of class gets a "pizza lottery" ticket to sign and put in a drawing basket. At the end of each term, lottery tickets are drawn and the winners attend a "pizza

Carol Scott-Kassner

Special person with crown

lunch with the teacher." (Pizzas can be delivered to schools for reasonable prices or teachers could bake frozen pizzas themselves.) This is popular with students, especially if their names are written in the school bulletin or read during morning announcements that they have won and need to be excused to attend. It is also great recruiting public relations for the music program and a tremendous motivational tool to foster positive and productive behaviors (Kassner 1996).

Foundations of Managing Student Behaviors

Understanding the Role of Personal Traits and the Educational Environment

Dynamic teachers lessen the possibilities for inappropriate student behaviors with generally positive personalities that show plenty of enthusiasm, energy, self-assurance, good senses of humor, sensitivity, self-control, and sincerity. Chances for good behavior are even more assured when teachers are well organized, knowledgeable, affirming, observant, fair, flexible, punctual, and generally effective in helping students learn. Students tend to focus on good learning behaviors when the teacher challenges them with intriguing musical tasks suitable for their level of development, monitors and adjusts instruction, and varies the pace so that students do not get bored, lost, frustrated, or defeated. When students behave inappropriately, Bennett and Bartholomew (1997) suggest that teachers first consider aspects of their own behavior: "the energy level you are demonstrating[,] . . . the clarity of behavior expectations for the activity[,] . . . the level of fascination that the activity holds for the students[, and] . . . the potential for success that students see in the activity" (p. 210). These are the most important foundations for student behavior management. In a perfect world, teachers would not need anything more.

Unfortunately, some students are naturally mischievous, have quirky senses of humor, or just do not like following rules. Many students' brains do not function properly, resulting in problems with learning, attention, self-management, and social awareness. More sadly, some students do not live in loving, stimulating, peaceful, and supportive homes. Nor do all of them live in safe, quiet, respectable neighborhoods where they can be assured of walking home without assault or getting a full night's sleep. Some students arrive in our classrooms carrying unhealthy models of behavior, deep anger, hate, resentment, and hostility. Teachers need a wide variety of techniques for dealing with the different kinds and levels of class disruptions that these problems spawn. Three of the most difficult tasks new teachers face are:

1. Discerning the causes of behavior problems

2. Developing a large repertoire of management techniques

3. Knowing when and how to use the most effective technique for each problem

Richard Kindsvatter and Mary Ann Levine (1987) discuss twelve myths of discipline that are sometimes recommended to new teachers but are not best practice for classroom management. Among the myths they urge teachers to eradicate are: (1) the best teachers are those whose students do not dare misbehave; (3) good control depends on finding the right gimmick; (6) punishment is educational; (9) students do not know how to behave; (11) teachers should not look at students' records so as not to get prejudicial information; and (12) being consistent should take precedent over all other considerations. Many good reasons exist for not doing what these myths suggest.

Establishing Expectations and Procedures

Most school districts or individual schools have adopted student rights and responsibilities handbooks that all students and parents are asked to read and sign. Teachers need to be familiar with those handbooks and make sure their classroom regulations are consistent with the district's or school's master plan. Within individual classrooms, teachers need to set clear expectations and procedures, discuss them, and model them. These are the beginnings of successful student behavior management. (The terms *expectations* and *procedures* sound more collaborative, less top-down than the term *rules*, which is often used instead.) Teachers can list the expectations on a posted chart or include them in an information packet that parents and students read and sign. During the first class or two, the teacher might model several procedures and do a T-chart activity on some of the expectations. For example, if one of the expectations is that everyone be respectful of each other, the teacher draws a T-chart on large butcher paper or chart board and writes "Respect" on top of the T, then "Sounds Like" on the left side and "Looks Like" on the right side. Students contribute examples of what respect sounds and looks like and the teacher writes them down. (The teacher may need to have several ideas ready to get the discussion rolling, for example, respect sounds like "waiting for your turn to talk.") Post the chart on a wall and bring it down now and then to review and add examples to it—especially if students exhibit disrespectful behavior.

Clear expectations can also be communicated through posters. For example, students respond well to a Peanuts© panel in which Peppermint Patty says in the first frame, "Yes Mamm, I'm back from the principal's office." Second frame: "He said I should try harder at paying attention." Third frame: "How's this?" (Peppermint Patty is sitting at her desk, head straining forward, and eyes staring straight at the teacher.) The teacher reads the panel to the students, then states the expectation that every student will keep his or her head and eyes facing the teacher when the teacher is instructing. Posters with many positive messages can be purchased at learning stores, through catalogues, and through the Internet.

Stories are also great ways to convey expectations that students do not forget. Some teachers start each year telling the story of the man who wanted wisdom (see Box 3.1). After telling the story, the teacher can bring the moral home to the classroom: "Whenever I'm standing right here in my teaching station and giving instruction, I expect you to give me the attention of your eyes, ears, and brains." If some students forget to keep their eyes on the teacher, the teacher could ask someone to review the three attentions verbally or ask the wandering students to write down the three attentions. The teacher could also teach students an Asian sign of respect (palms together, fingers pointing up, and a short bow). The teacher can then inform

Box 3.1 *Attention, Attention, Attention*

A man went to a wise old guru and asked what he needed to do to become wise. The guru wrote *Attention* on a piece of paper and gave it to the man. The man was puzzled and said, "Surely there is more to wisdom than 'Attention.'" The guru smiled and said, "Yes, there is more." He took the paper back and again wrote *Attention*. The man was getting a little upset and said, "Oh great guru, I'm sure there is more to wisdom than 'Attention, Attention.'" The guru laughed and said, "Ah yes, there is indeed one more thing!" and he again wrote *Attention* on the paper. The man sputtered angrily, "I don't get it. I ask what to do to become wise and all you say is 'Attention, Attention, Attention.' What is attention, anyway?" The guru said, "Ah, you have asked exactly the right question! Now I will tell you the whole truth and you will be wise! Attention . . . is . . . Attention!" With that the guru resumed the lotus position and would say no more. The man walked toward home mumbling and complaining, until he suddenly realized what the guru meant: If you want to be wise you must pay keen attention *with* something—attention with your eyes, attention with your ears, and attention with your brain. From that day on he paid careful attention to everything and became very wise.

students that with this gesture he or she is asking for the three attentions and would like to see students give the sign back to him or her to acknowledge that they will give three attentions.

Another approach to established expectations and procedures is called Judicious Discipline. This system, developed by Gathercoal (1993), is discussed in detail by Nimmo (1997). Instead of being based on teacher power and dispensing of justice, Judicious Discipline is based on principles established in the Bill of Rights of the U.S. Constitution with the central belief that individuals have the right to maximum personal freedom as long as they do not diminish the rights of others. Expectations are developed to ensure maximum responsible freedom for the maximum number of people and fall into four large categories:

1. Safeguarding property from loss or damage
2. Promoting legitimate educational purpose
3. Protecting health and maintaining safety
4. Avoiding serious disruption of the educational process

Student behavior is discussed as it relates to time, place, and manner. When a student behaves inappropriately, the teacher's first response is to gain more information by asking questions instead of taking immediate action based on what the teacher thinks is going on. For example, "Is this the right time and place to be doing this? Is what you are doing being done in an appropriate manner?"

There are several sample questions teachers can ask students to help them understand inappropriate behavior and take responsibility for improving it:

1. Can you tell me which of our classroom expectations that action violates?
2. What were you trying to accomplish with that? Did you achieve your goal?
3. Why do you think we have a class rule about doing that?
4. What could I do to persuade you to stop that?
5. How could you do that differently next time?
6. On a scale of one to ten, how helpful to the group would you rate that action?
7. Would you recommend that everyone do that, and, if so, how would it affect our music making?
8. Would it help to clarify your values, if you wrote a description, analysis, and evaluation of this behavior?
9. That seems so unlike you—has something happened to upset you?
10. Have we reached the point where the only choice left is a parent conference/referral to principal/finding another class for you/(and so on)?

"Questioning in this way asks for more information and deeper thinking without casting blame and shame, or undermining students' self-esteem. It clearly informs students that a behavior is inappropriate and conveys faith in the students' ability to rethink the situation and come up with a better plan for the future. The focus is on education, not blame. Questions can convey possibilities for future action without the weight and force of threats, and do not have to be backed-down from or apologized for, as a statement might have to be, if new information proves a teacher's initial assessment incorrect" (Kassner, 1998).

Judicious Discipline develops a healthy educational community by sharing power between teacher and students. "When power is shared, students tend to feel more valued and respected. Moreover, they tend to be more interested in the endeavor at hand, more goal-oriented, more inspired, more integrally involved, more fulfilled, and more complete" (Nimmo, 1997, p. 32).

Learning and Remembering Students' Names

After setting expectations and procedures, the teacher needs to take the next most important step for good student behavior: learn students' names. Being able to call on each student by name helps the teacher establish a personal rapport that conveys the message, "You're unique and important." A teacher who knows each student's name is more likely to personalize instruction and less likely teach lessons to "the class." Learning names can be a daunting task, especially if the teacher is new to the building and there are hundreds of children. Many classroom teachers have younger students wear name tags for the first few days until they can associate the students' names with their faces. When students come to music classes wearing their name tags, it is much easier for the music teacher. Some music teachers make name tags for students to wear just in music class. The tags can be grouped together and put into envelopes for quick storage and distribution. This is effective, but it takes time and materials to make and keep organized.

Another aid to learning students' names is to take pictures of small groups of students and write names under faces. Pictures can be studied between classes or arranged on a poster for easy reference during music class. Students also love to see their pictures posted on the wall. This technique works better in schools with stable populations and less well in schools with high turnover.

Organizing the Classroom and Record Keeping

A less cumbersome way of learning students' names is combined with a classroom organization scheme: assigning students to particular chairs or locations and writing their names on a seating chart. This works well if the music teacher uses chairs or benches consistently arranged in the same pattern. Some teachers also make this work without seating furniture, by assigning students to specific places in the room marked by some easily identified method: carpet squares, poster signs on the wall, lines drawn on the floor with permanent marker, or banners hung from the ceiling (made from cloth or paper and differently colored or decorated). The use of tape of any kind to mark lines on the floor is not recommended, as it quickly comes loose or is picked off by students (either absentmindedly or on purpose to make tape balls to throw at others). Seating charts work well to help teachers learn student names as long as students are in their assigned spots. Until the teacher has had a chance to learn everyone's name, it is best to do lessons in which students stay in their spots or leave only for short intervals (to get instruments, for example). Seating charts also make it easier to take roll, keep track of student absences, and organize comments to help report academic and effort grades at end of term. Many teachers write lesson plan codes and codes for assessments of student skills right on the seating chart. A seating chart for each class can be placed in a loose-leaf three-ring binder and organized in a way that the teacher can retrieve most easily. For example, they can be arranged by day of the week if the teacher sees each class only once per week, or arranged by grade level, or in alphabetic order by classroom teachers' names. This system keeps everything in one place and reduces the need for a separate grade book and lesson plan book. Full lesson plans can be written on computer, printed out, and kept in or behind the seating chart book.

Figure 3.3 illustrates an effective organization of a music room. Chairs are arranged in a parabola with the open end facing the whiteboard. This gives every student a clear view of instructional material. Spaces are left between groups of chairs to delineate the groups and provide passage for walking between groups. Students are far enough away from others when sitting on chairs to discourage kicking chairs, unwanted touching, and so on.

FIGURE 3.3

Sample Seating Chart Reflecting the Room Arrangement

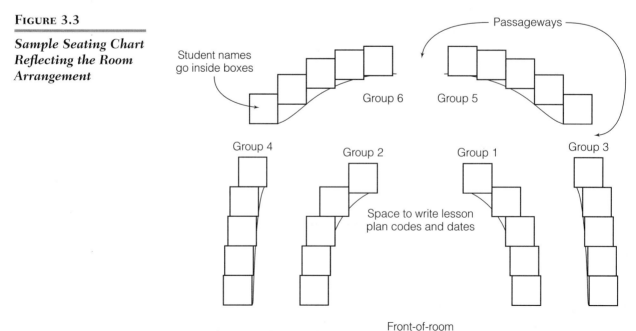

There is enough space in the center of the room for students to play instruments or to gather on the floor to observe music-related books and charts. There is enough space around the outside of the chairs to perform circle movements to music and enough space between chairs to perform snake or train movements winding between chair groups.

Organizing Classes into Cooperative Learning Groups

Cooperative Learning (CL) is a system developed by David W. Johnson, Roger T. Johnson, E. J. Holubec, and P. Roy (1984) to improve student learning of subject matter and help students become more interdependent, better self-managers, and more effective problem solvers.

Music making requires many qualities that are inherent in Cooperative Learning: positive interdependence, individual accountability, emphasis on task, direct teaching of social skills (as they relate to music making), frequent teacher observation and intervention, and group processing of musical effectiveness.

Forming Cooperative Learning groups can be easy or difficult depending on the makeup of classes, their experience with CL, and the number of individuals who bring with them difficulties relating to others or low interpersonal intelligence. Four or five students in a group is best. Fewer creates a group too small to consider divergent points of view, and more can prevent group cohesion and cause some students to retreat to wallflower status. Ideally, students of different abilities will be equally distributed in each group. Give each person in the group a specific function: The captain provides overall leadership and speaks for the group, assistant captain substitutes for the captain when absent, others can be encouragers, timekeepers, paper handlers, and so on. Inform students that groups will be changed every six to seven weeks, so that everyone will have the opportunity to function in each role.

There are many ways to divide the class into groups. Some teachers prefer to form groups through chance by having students draw colored pieces of paper out of a hat or count off by sixes (or however many groups are desired). The technique for group formation that most students prefer is to be allowed to choose their own groups. Although problems placing unpopular children may arise, these problems can usually be solved by thoughtful teacher interventions. Furthermore, these groups cohere better than randomly chosen groups.

Require those who want to be captain to find two others willing to be in their group. This eliminates the problematic waste of time when would-be captains cannot attract enough others to form a group. It also identifies and empowers the natural leaders, who help the teacher keep the others directed toward meaningful musical goals. After each embryonic group of three is established, captains choose the remaining unattached students, one at a time, until all students belong to a group.

When allowing students to form their own groups, the teacher may have to intervene at several points in the process. If past problems have

Carol Scott-Kassner

shown that some students do not do well when sitting next to each other, the teacher lists their names on the board and announces that they cannot be in the same group. If one or more students are not chosen at the end of the selection process and no captain comes forward to invite, the teacher can assign students either to the groups he or she thinks best or by using a chance system (drawing straws, lottery, coin-flip). The teacher could also take this time to talk with students about why some students are not being chosen. This must be done with care and compassion to help students learn to modify behavior without lowering their self-esteem. Skillful teachers can take this problem and turn it into a valuable learning experience in interpersonal skills (Kassner, in press).

Once groups are established, teachers can reward groups for individual team members' work. For example, when a team member answers a question or performs a musical task, the member's team is rewarded with one or more points. All the National Standards for music can be taught through CL groups. (For more details about organizing through cooperative groups, see Kassner, in press).

Strategies for Confronting Inappropriate Behavior

A variety of motivational methods is the best way to manage normal student behaviors. "I" statements usually work better than "you" statements, and noticing good behavior usually gets better results than attacking poor behavior. For example, when a group of students is talking instead of paying attention, the teacher can remark, "Thank you, [another group]. I can teach easily, because you are quiet and attentive!" Occasionally student behavior requires the teacher to use intervention techniques that are more direct, focused, and powerful.

Logical Consequences

Rudolph Dreikurs (1968) advocates managing inappropriate behaviors with natural and logical consequences. A natural consequence is something that would happen without a teacher intervention, because it is following a law of nature. For example, if a child leans back in his chair far enough, the law of gravity will eventually pull him over, resulting possibly in being hurt or embarrassed. We often cannot wait for natural consequences to occur nor want them to occur, so teachers devise logical consequences: something imposed between the behavior and the natural consequence that extinguishes the behavior before the natural consequence occurs. For example, when observing a child leaning back in his chair after being warned already, the teacher can have him sit on the floor for five minutes to help him remember to "drive" his chair more safely in school. Good logical consequences have five characteristics:

1. Are closely related to the behavior

2. Use little teacher time or energy

3. Do not disrupt the learning process

4. Are not punishment, but show respect and concern for the student

5. Employ humor when possible

Logical consequences are good ways to manage behavior by changing the rules of the game so that the student no longer gets reinforcement from the behavior.

Dreikurs also explains four levels of behavior that help teachers deal with inappropriate student behaviors. Children sometimes use Attention-Getting Mechanisms (AGMs) to bolster their self-worth; that is, they exhibit any behavior (often inappropriate) that gets the teacher's attention. If the teacher suspects the child is using an AGM, he or she can help the child find more appropriate ways of satisfying needs for attention (by helping the teacher or other students, doing better work, and so on). Sometimes children go past the AGM to Power Struggle—behaviors that challenge the teacher's authority or attempts to take over the classroom. The teacher must not get into power struggles. If he or she wins, the child may be humiliated and go into stage three (Revenge) or stage four (Assumed Disability). Even if the child does not win a power struggle, he or she does win self-esteem and the esteem of other students for standing up to the powerful teacher or at least having the power to derail the lesson and frustrate the teacher. When a teacher suspects a student is behaving in Power-Struggle mode, he or she can immediately cut off the exchange and discuss the situation privately with the student during recess or after school. In the private conference, the teacher can ask questions about what is bothering the student and what he or she can do to help. The teacher may also need to use the conference to clarify roles and expectations and possibly draft a student-learning contract that spells out student expectations and consequences for failing to meet them. In rare incidences and usually after prolonged severe mistreatment, some students turn their rage outward to Revenge (behaviors that get even with people who they believe have wronged them) or inward to Disability (refusal to even try any task). Teachers need additional help to deal with students in Revenge and Disability modes and should talk to the school counselor, principal, or parents. A behavior contract may be necessary that clearly defines Revenge and Power-Struggle behaviors and lists step-by-step warnings and consequences. The student can be given the choice to sign and abide by the contract as a condition of returning to and staying in class.

Transactional Analysis

Thomas A. Harris (1969) explained a wonderful way of understanding and managing student behavior in the popular book *I'm OK—You're OK*. Teachers can educate their older students in the basics of Transactional Analysis and ask them to use it to understand their own and others' behavior. Harris explained that all humans have three mind-states they can interact from: the Parent, Child, and Adult. The Parent is comprised of those memories and feelings from childhood that informed the child to do or not to do something because the big, powerful authority said so in an authoritative, judgmental voice. The Child is that impulsive part of human personality that wants to have fun right now and ignore the consequences. The Adult is the reasoning, thoughtful mediator. Harris envisions a social interchange as arrows going forth and back between two circle clusters or snowmen (see Figure 3.4). The best transactions are conducted between both people's Adults. For example, the teacher may say, "It seems to be getting too noisy in here. Billy, we need to use our inside voices." Billy may respond in his Adult with, "Sorry! I guess that song got me too excited."

If the teacher sends out a message from his or her Parent, it may sound like, "Billy I've told you over and over that you are making too much noise. You should be quiet right now, or else!" Parent voices often have the word *should* in them and the tone of voice that could accompany shaking the index finger at someone. Unfortunately, the Parent in one person tends to hook the Child in the other, and Billy may respond in his Child, "Everybody's talking. Why do you always pick on me?" Sometimes students respond in their Parent, "I'm not talking loud. You're talking louder than me. You be quiet!" In either case, the stage is set for an escalation, causing wasted class time and interpersonal tensions. Students can make statements in their Parent that hook the teacher's Child as in this scenario: Student: "This song is dumb. I don't know why we should sing it." Teacher: "Because I'm the teacher and I get to decide what we sing." Once Transactional Analysis has been explained, the teacher can respond by asking, "Was that statement in the voice of your Parent or Child?' How would it sound in the Adult?" Or the teacher could simply respond in his or her Adult: "What one person may think is dumb, others may find very interesting. Tell me, what is it about this song that you don't like—the lyrics, the harmony?" When the teacher understands Transactional Analysis, he or she can respond to any challenging statement at the Adult level and with hope the stu-

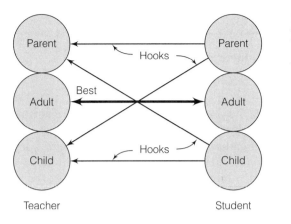

FIGURE 3.4

Transactional Analysis Diagram

dent will soon respond likewise. Only the most determined students will stay in their Parent or Child long, if the teacher skillfully stays in his or her Adult. A student who habitually operates from his or her Parent or Child can be asked to write a list of examples of statements or actions he or she has made in the inappropriate mode. The teacher and student review the list and talk together to determine if the student understands the three modes, then decide which statements and actions the student will work on first to substitute Adult mode responses for the inappropriate ones. A paper with the chosen behavior as heading and with three columns (labeled Parent, Adult, Child) and several rows (one for each future class date) is posted on a wall (without the student name). The teacher simply tallies the types of behavior the student exhibits during class. No comment is made in class and none of the other students may even be aware what is taking place. The teacher and student meet briefly after class to review progress. When the student has learned to substitute Adult mode for the named inappropriate behavior, a new behavior can be selected from the list. This procedure can continue until the student is operating in his or her Adult most of the time.

Behavior Expectation Forms and Learning Contracts

If a child repeatedly disrupts class, destroys property, or endangers his or her or others' health and safety, the teacher could send the student to a time-out chair to read, sign, and date a behavior expectation form while the rest of the class goes on with the lesson (see Box 3.2). The teacher then files the form and forgets about it unless the student behaves inappropriately again, when the exercise is repeated. Getting two different copies signed on different days establishes evidence of a pattern. On the second or third infraction, the student can be required to write out the expectations in his or her own handwriting, on the grounds that writing is a more kinesthetic way of learning than reading, which does not seem to have worked so far. The teacher might conjecture out loud, "If writing it out once doesn't work, maybe the student needs to write it five times or ten times to learn the message." Most students will assert that they do not need to write it multiple times and that they have learned the expectations and have decided it is in their best interest to follow them.

Box 3.2 *Behavior Expectation Form*

Behavior Expectations

This classroom is a place for learning. All students have a right to learn and the teacher has a right to teach. If some students behave inappropriately, other students cannot learn and the teacher cannot teach. Students are expected to respect others' rights and behave in a manner that (1) safeguards property from loss or damage, (2) protects everyone's health and safety, and (3) avoids serious disruption of the educational process.

There are many ways to disrupt a class: talking, telling other students what to do, arguing, making other sounds, making faces, threatening others, acting silly, moving to attract attention, touching others or their chairs, taking other people's property, to name just a few.

To have a peaceful, happy, and productive classroom all students must be responsible for following the behavior expectations and for paying attention.

I have read and I understand the expectations above. I want to remain in the class and I promise to behave as expected.

Student signature _____

Date _____

Behavior contracts are more individualized and specific versions of the general behavior expectations form, and they are negotiated with a misbehaving student, not imposed on him or her. Contracts often are preprinted forms with several clauses followed by blank spaces for the student to write specifics, including (1) a description of the inappropriate behavior, (2) a substitute behavior that is appropriate, (3) a plan for changing the behavior, (4) a reward for changing or a punishment for not changing, (5) a method of monitoring and evaluating progress, (6) the length of time the contract will be in effect, and (7) the student's and teacher's signature. Usually, the contract works well to extinguish the behavior problem, but if it does not, the teacher and student can discuss why the contract did not work and make a new, adjusted contract. If a student refuses to negotiate a contract, the teacher can include the refusal in a discussion with those at the next higher level (counselor, parents, vice principal, and so on). Refusal to cooperate is usually grounds for more severe consequences administered by those above the teacher. More details about behavior contracts are available in Rossman (1989).

Some problem behaviors may be so ingrained that even behavior contracts are not strong enough to effect the changes needed. More often than not, problem behaviors overlay and cover up fears of inadequacy. We need to guard against any illusions that we are trained psychologists, but music teachers can help educate students about interpersonal issues by having them write an essay about events taking place in our classrooms. Teachers could give students a paper printed with some or all of the following specifications to be included in the essay:

1. Describe the behavior that resulted in your needing to write this essay (in a complete, detailed description of the event with exact quotes when possible).

2. Write out and complete this statement: "The name of the only person in the world who can control my behavior is _____."

3. Write a detailed description of the event or events that led to this behavior. (What triggered this behavior?)

4. Describe how your behavior affected the class. (Was the learning of other students disrupted? Were other students upset? Did anyone get hurt?)

5. Describe your feelings about your behavior. (Are you feeling proud? Sorry? Angry? Sad? Happy?)

6. Describe how you think other students feel about your behavior.

7. What steps can you take to undo or lessen any bad feelings. (Apologize, promise not to repeat, give something?)

8. If you could turn back the clock and replay the events, what would you do differently?

9. If you behaved as you describe in #8, would you feel better about yourself?

10. If you behaved as you describe in #8, do you think others would feel more happy to be around you?

Completing these thought-prompts help some students do a reality check—examine and evaluate their beliefs and feelings. The teacher reads and keeps all essays for future reference. If the responses seem truthful and sincere, the teacher can congratulate the student on growth in emotional intelligence. If the responses seem untruthful, defensive, evasive, blaming others, and so on, the teacher can talk to the student about perceptions, beliefs, honesty, and such and make notes on the essay. If the student behavior improves, no follow-up is necessary. But if the same inappropriate behavior continues, one or two more essays could be required. If this does not help, the teacher could call for a conference with the parents and student to discuss the responses in the essays or append the essays (and any other documentation, such as dated behavior expectation forms) to a report to the counselor, vice principal, principal, or whoever handles inappropriate behavior at the next level. This approach provides documentation, mostly at the student's expense of time, of the interventions the teacher has used to resolve the problem and any progress or lack of progress. Such documentation helps those at the next level of power deal more quickly and effectively with the problem.

The Intervention Thermometer

Teachers may find it difficult to remember so many choices of dealing with student motivation and management and to know the proper time to use

FIGURE 3.5

*The Intervention
Thermometer*

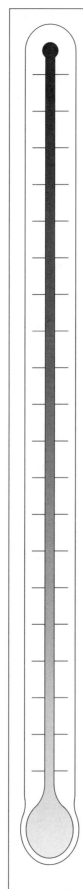

Red–Hot & Referring. Course of last resort. Referral to principal for disciplinary action, include documentation of previous interventions tried and their results.

(*Warning:* If you get to this temperature too often, the principal will start wondering about your ability to perform the job, and your evaluations may suffer. Once or twice a year in an average community is plenty at this level.)

Sizzling & Serious. Involve people with more perspectives, training, or power than the teacher. Request conference with parents, counselor, building screening committee. If appropriate, have counselor urge medical tests.

Hot & Handling It. Student suffers minor consequences for his or her behavior. Natural consequences, logical consequences, behavior contract, special essay assignments to improve interpersonal understandings, time out to think of more productive behavior options, time out to read and sign behavior expectation form, time out to copy behavior expectation form.

Tepid & Talkative. Get complete information about the problem. Discuss problems with student outside class, insist on sticking to the point, being honest, and taking personal responsibility for his or her actions. Ask probing questions that force students to think at higher levels and accept responsibility. Check with other teachers and cumulative file to see if problem is particular to your class or broad-based and long-lasting. Discuss problem with counselor or principal to get their recommendations and insights.

Warm & Wondering. Question for greater understanding and give student limited choices. Is the room too hot/cold/ dark/ bright? Are you uncomfortable? Is this task too difficult/easy for you? What can we do to make it just right? Do you understand our behavior expectations? Is there any part of our behavior expectations that you are not sure about? What is it you really want? I do not think that way is working for you. Is this the appropriate time and place to do that? Is this the appropriate manner of doing that? Can you think of another way? If you had a chance to do that over again, what would you do? Would you prefer to apologize or . . . (some consequence)? You seem to be needing a lot of attention today. Could you suggest a way we could provide the attention you need, yet still go on with the lesson?

Cool & Calm. Catch kids in the act of doing good. Ask students to review classroom expectations. Encourage students with constructive information about their behavior. Give token prizes and public recognition. Teacher moves into close proximity to student with inappropriate behavior and continues with lesson uninterrupted (teacher notices student).

each. If we envision some of the many options a teacher has to change student behavior as degrees on a thermometer, we could group interventions into six distinct temperature zones (see Figure 3.5). It is best to stay in the lowest level whenever possible. Good teachers try to stay cool at least 95 percent of the time. Knowing which levels to use and when to use them comes only with experience. Generally it is best to start at the bottom and work up, unless a student has shown a pattern of poor behavior in the past that responded to a higher level or unless the misbehavior is egregious.

Scenario

Paul taught himself to play guitar in seventh grade and, though painfully shy, performed in a few garage bands through high school for pocket money. Making music was a pleasant pastime for him, so when he heard about the shortage of teachers, he thought he might give school teaching a try. Paul had earned a college degree in liberal arts, so he was able to get an emergency teaching certificate without further college classes in music or education. He was quickly hired to teach band, violin, and general music in a small rural elementary school desperate to fill the position.

Paul's first class was a fourth-grade general music class. Remembering how cool he thought guitars were when he was young, he planned to start the year off with an impressive lesson about the guitar. As the students entered, Paul was writing guitar chords on the whiteboard and hollered over his shoulder, "I'll be with you in a minute. I'm almost done." He finally got the class started about eight minutes later by picking up his guitar, turning around to face the students, and saying, "This is a guitar. I can do some really cool stuff on it." Paul then sat down and played some chords then pointed to the board at various places and said, "Here's how you write the C chord in root position. Here's how you write the B^7 chord. You have to be careful not to play the big E string on this chord." After about ten minutes of pointing to the tablatures and showing how to play and write several chords, he said, "Now I'll put the chords in a song." He then began playing "House of the Rising Sun"—all twenty-six verses.

The children's bottoms were getting a little fatigued and cold sitting on the cement floor while he lectured and played. Billy started squirming and accidently bumped into the class bully, Mack. Mack screamed, "Get away from me, you jerk!" and pushed Billy, who fell backward, bumping his head into Stephanie's face. When Stephanie's sobs reached earsplitting level, Paul stopped playing his guitar and looked out at the students.

"This class should learn some manners. You! The kid who knocked into that girl. Get to the principal's office. The rest of you sit still and listen to this song again."

Paul started to play "House of the Rising Sun" again, but the bell rang just as he fingered the first A-minor chord. The students jumped up and ran, pushing each other, to the door. Stephanie continued to sob while looking at the bloody tooth in her hand.

Questions

1. Get into groups of three or four and reflect on Paul's lesson in terms of his motivational style, lesson appropriateness, and his student management techniques. Discuss what did and did not work in terms of principles discussed in this chapter. Share your observations and suggestions with the class as a whole. (There are at least fifteen major problems with this lesson. How many did your group find?)

2. Imagine teaching your first lesson as a school music teacher. Specify the type of class (general music, band, chorus, orchestra) and the grade level you imagine it to be. Write a detailed lesson plan for your first class that reflects better pedagogy than Paul's lesson.

   Hint. Much or all of the lesson should involve principles of motivation and class management. (As the twig is bent, so grows the tree.)

REVIEW

1. Discuss the three types of motivation (intrinsic, internal, external).

2. Discuss why negative reinforcement should never be used alone.

3. "Competition is motivational." Argue the pros and cons of this statement.

CRITICAL THINKING

1. Choose four personal traits of effective teachers (enthusiasm, energy, self-assurance, good senses of humor, sensitivity, self-control, sincerity, well organized, knowledgeable, affirming, observant, fair, flexible) that you feel are most characteristic of yourself and briefly describe an instance that you demonstrated each trait.

2. You are a new music teacher preparing for the first day of classes. What are the three most important expectations or procedures that you want to establish and how do you plan to convey these to the students?

3. You are a teacher. Describe the type of class you are teaching and the system that you have employed to be able to call on your students by name.

4. Good logical consequences have five characteristics. List all five then choose the one you think is most important and explain why. Compare your answer with other prospective teachers.

5. A student shouts, "We should not be singing this song!" In terms of Transactional Analysis, what voice is he or she in? Write two effective ways the teacher could respond in the teacher's Adult voice?

6. A large sixth-grade girl has disrupted your music classes for several days in a row by making faces at smaller girls and, when catching their eyes, shouting insults and threats at them, such as, "Stop looking at me, you little creep!" Describe your plan of action to deal with this problem. Discuss and compare it with other students' plans.

7. A fifth-grade boy seems to have some strong negative power to control most of the other students in your music class. It is barely perceptible, but you notice he seems to give silent gestures that warn others not to raise their hands to answer questions or otherwise participate in your lesson. Describe your plan of action to deal with this problem. Discuss and compare it with other students' plans.

PROJECTS

1. Customize the wording of the behavior expectation form in this chapter to reflect your own values, personality, and style.

2. Layout in a word-processing program and print a behavior contract form based on the suggestions in this chapter.

3. Layout in a word-processing program and print an intervention thermometer that you could post in your classroom to remind you of the options you plan to use to respond to inappropriate behaviors.

4. Layout in a word-processing program and print a sample list of essay thought-starters.

5. Interview a practicing music teacher to find out how he or she would respond to Critical Thinking items 1, 2, and 3 or pose the ideas on an Internet bulletin board or chat room for music teachers. Explain how and why the answers you receive compare or contrast with your own answers.

REFERENCES

Bennett, P., and D. Bartholomew (1997). *Song-Works I.* Belmont, CA: Wadsworth Publishing Company.

Cohen, L. (1994). Anthem. In D. Schiller, ed., *The Little Zen companion.* New York: Workman Publishing.

Dreikurs, R. (1968). *Psychology in the classroom.* New York: Harper & Row.

Gathercoal, F. (1993). *Judicious discipline* (3rd ed.). San Francisco: Caddo Gap Press.

Harris, T. A. (1969). *I'm ok—you're ok.* New York: Harper & Row.

Johnson, D. W., and R. T. Johnson (1987). *Learning together and alone* (2nd ed.). Englewood Cliffs, NJ: Prentice-Hall.

Johnson, D. W., R. T. Johnson, E. J. Holubec, and P. Roy (1984). *Circles of learning.* Washington, DC: Association for Supervision and Curriculum Development.

Kassner, K. (1996). Management systems for music teachers. *Music Educators Journal, 82*(5), 34–41.

———. (1998). Would better questions enhance music learning? *Music Educators Journal, 84*(4), 29–36.

———. (in press). Cooperative learning revisited: Music learning and more. *Music Educators Journal.*

Kindsvatter, R., and M. A. Levine (1987). "The myths of discipline." Reprinted in Linder, F., J. H. McMillan, eds. (1987). *Annual editions: Educational psychology 87/88.* Guilford, CT: Dushkin Publishing Group, pp. 170–174.

Kohn, A. (1996). *Beyond discipline: From compliance to community.* Alexandria VA: Association for Supervision and Curriculum Development.

Maslow, A. H. (1971). *The farther reaches of human nature.* New York: Viking Press.

McDaniel, T. R. (1985). "The ten commandments of motivation." Reprinted in Linder, F., J. H. McMillan, eds. (1987). *Annual editions: Educational psychology 87/88.* Guilford, CT: Dushkin Publishing Group, pp. 159–163

Nimmo, D. (1997). Judicious discipline in the music classroom. *Music Educators Journal, 83*(4), 27–32.

Rossman, R. L. (1989). *Tips: Discipline in the music classroom.* Reston, VA: Music Educators National Conference.

Skinner, B. F. (1953). *Science and human behavior.* New York: Macmillan Publishers.

Stephens, T. M., and J. O. Cooper (1987). "The token economy: An affirmative perspective." Reprinted in Linder, F., and J. H. McMillan, eds. (1987). *Annual editions: Educational psychology 87/88.* Guilford, CT: Dushkin Publishing Group, pp. 92–94.

FOR FURTHER READING

Bartholomew, D. (1993). Effective strategies for praising students. *Music Educators Journal, 80*(3), 40–43.

Bennett, P. (1988). The perils and profits of praise. *Music Educators Journal, 75*(1), 22–24.

Bowman, R., Jr. (1987). "Effective classroom management: A primer for practicing professionals." Reprinted in Linder, F., and J. H. McMillan, eds. (1987). *Annual editions: Educational psychology 87/88.* Guilford, CT: Dushkin Publishing Group, pp. 175–178.

Buck, G. H. (1992). Classroom management and the disruptive child. *Music Educators Journal, 79*(3), 36–42.

Erbes, R. L. (1986). The three faces of discipline. *Music Educators Journal, 73*(1), 23–26.

Merrion, M. (1992). Classroom management for beginning music educators. *Music Educators Journal, 79*(2), 53–56.

VanDerveer, E. (1989). Stopping discipline problems before they start. *Music Educators Journal, 75*(9), 23–25.

4

Methods of Teaching Music to Children

There may be as many methods of teaching music as there are music teachers. Still, certain images conjure up some of the best-known instructional approaches. Julia's bourdon playing with felt-covered mallets on metallophones recalls the Orff-Schulwerk approach, as does the rhythmic chanting of the poem that Jimmie and George set to temple blocks and kettle drums. Donna, Jeb, and Soo Mee add hand signals to the melodies of traditional singing games they know, putting the Kodály philosophy to practice. As Juan skips to a $\frac{6}{8}$ melody, changing directions at the change of phrases, two facets of Dalcroze eurhythmics are clearly evident. Angela's free exploration of sounds on bottles, boxes, and plastic balls brings to mind the Manhattanville Music Curriculum Project (MMCP). Lisa and her classmates study a Mozart minuet in the multiple ways espoused by proponents of Comprehensive Musicianship. Denny's chanting of rhythms in imitation of his teacher's presentation underscores Gordon's initial aural and oral stage, while Fatin and Catelin learn folk dances through Weikert's sequence of saying-while-doing.

Of the numerous instructional approaches used in music classes for children, some are familiar and, couched in traditions, have stood the test of time and experience. Other approaches have been developed more recently through changes in societal values, patterns of living, and technology. Some teachers hold steadfastly to a single method, while others merge techniques from many methods to convey even a single aspect of music. In the end, every teacher finds his or her own pathway to a personal teaching method that works effectively in guiding children toward the development of musical skills and understanding. This personal teaching method depends on the teacher's training and experience, the instructional goals, the classroom setting, and the musical (and extramusical) needs and interests of the children to be taught. The manner in which musicality is defined also provides for the variety of techniques used.

Some classic and contemporary methods of music instruction, many of them familiar to experienced teachers, are described here according to their principal goals and techniques. Sample experiences are presented for three of the best-known pedagogies: Dalcroze, Kodály, and Orff. Their instructional techniques are also delineated throughout the book. A comparison of the methods and further discussion of the development of a personal method conclude the chapter.

Dalcroze

"Movement with a mission" is one description of the Dalcroze approach to music instruction. Dalcroze eurhythmics has been inaccurately described as dance. The stereotypical image of a Dalcroze lesson featuring young dancers in black leotards leaping to the rhythms of improvised piano music is not complete. The Dalcroze approach is three-pronged, including not only a unique form of rhythmic movement called eurhythmics but also ear training (solfège and solfège-rhythmique) and improvisation. The key qualities that link accomplishment in each of these elements are imagination, a keen listening sense, and an immediacy of response to the musical stimulus.

The founder of the Dalcroze approach was Émile Jaques-Dalcroze (1865–1950), a Swiss musician who served as professor of solfège, harmony, and composition at the Geneva Conservatory. His pedagogy originated early in the twentieth century as he experimented with approaches to ear training. He astutely recognized that despite the advanced stages of technical proficiency that his students demonstrated through the playing of their instruments, notable gaps were evident in their musical abilities. Simple rhythms were wrongly rendered, and flaws in pitch and intonation were frequent. Students were demonstrating mechanical, not musical, understanding.

Beginning with rhythmic gymnastics that activated the diaphragm, lungs, and articulatory functions of the mouth and tongue, the students of Professor Jaques-Dalcroze were soon singing scales in dichord (d-r, r-m, m-f, and so on) and trichord (d-r-m, r-m-f, m-f-s, and so on) arrangements, in canon with the teacher, at double and half the speed of the original statement, and alternating silent internal singing and singing aloud on cue. As his eurhythmics approach evolved, students developed the muscular rhythms and nervous sensibilities that would allow them to discriminate among even the slight gradations of duration, time, intensity, and phrasing. Jaques-Dalcroze believed that people were musical when they came to possess "an ensemble of physical and spiritual resources and capacities" com-

*A **Dalcroze technique**: Children conducting while stepping the pulse*

prising the ear, brain, and body. Eurhythmics became the core of his approach and the foundation for raising each person's musical sensitivity to its fullest potential.

For experienced performers and children alike, the Dalcroze techniques lay the foundation for a thorough musicianship. The achievement of proficient eurhythmic movement requires a repertory of complex kinesthetic reactions. Children's eurhythmic movement will include any number of possibilities in space and place as well as locomotor and nonlocomotor movement—isolated gestures using the hands, arms, head, shoulders, or a combination of body parts. Their movement is a personal and immediate response to the music played on the piano, on percussion instruments, or (more rarely) on recordings or performed vocally. Children become proficient as they follow the tempo, rhythm, and meter of music with their bodies, learning to react quickly to changes in any aspects of the music, for example changes in meter, rhythm patterns, dynamics, or phrase length.

Ear training, including solfège and solfège-rhythmique, is a second critical component in a Dalcroze education. Children are taught to understand tones and semitones and their relationships in scales, songs, and musical passages. The fixed do system is advocated by most Dalcroze teachers, in which C is the starting note of the scale regardless of the tonic. For example, when the fixed do system is used, a G Major scale begins on C and contains an F♯.

Jaques-Dalcroze reasoned that children develop absolute pitch as the sense of C is impressed on the ear, the muscles, and the mind. He believed that the interrelationship of the scales would become clear, with children able to aurally determine the order of tones and semitones that constitute each scale. Singing via the Dalcroze approach is accompanied by hand gestures that show the position of the pitch in space or by movement of the fingers on the arm as an imaginary keyboard. Children are led to hearing and responding through movement to harmonic progressions: facing center for tonic, turning right for dominant, and moving left for subdominant chords.

The third Dalcroze component, improvisation, opens children to a freedom of expression through movement, in rhythmic speech, with instru-

---

LESSON ACTIVITIES 4.1 *Sampling Dalcroze*

Eurhythmics

- ✦ To teacher's drum tap, children walk the pulse. When the teacher strikes the drum rim, children stand in place and clap the pulse. Alternate between walking and clapping.

- ✦ To teacher's improvised piano music, children walk the pulse, clapping on beat one. On cue (a high piano cluster, for example), children change clap to beat two, three, or four. Extend by suggesting that children clap on several pulses: one and three, two and three, or bending the knees on one while clapping on two, three, and four.

- ✦ Children step the pulse of the teacher's improvised piano melodies lower than middle C, and clap the pulse of piano melodies higher than middle C. When a lower and higher melody are played simultaneously, children clap and step the pulse.

- ✦ With drums in hand, or wood blocks, claves, and cowbells, children listen for the recurring ostinato phrase played by the teacher on the piano and play its rhythm—without and eventually while stepping the pulse.

- ✦ Children move expressively to the teacher's piano music, realizing the meter, rhythmic phrases, dynamic changes, phrasing, and articulation through movement.

Solfège

- ✦ While conducting a $\frac{4}{4}$ meter, teacher and children chant the solfège syllables (do, re, mi, fa, sol, la, ti, do), one per beat, forward (up) and backward (down), repeating the do at either end (similar to the solfeggio exercises of Italian conservatories).

- ✦ Teacher and children sing the ascending and descending scales on solfège syllables while conducting. On cue, the syllables are sung twice as fast or twice as slow.

- ✦ Children sing ascending and descending scales, playing the imaginary keys on their forearms. Using the fixed do system, sing the C Major, G Major, and F Major scale from C to c (differentiating pitch and playing movement) for F, F♯ and B,B♭).

- ✦ Using a wide-open hand in front of them to indicate whole tones and a half-closed hand to indicate semitones, children sing ascending and descending scales (including C Major, G Major, and F Major), supported by teacher's scale-chording. They can then feel the same wide and

---

ments, or at the keyboard. Beginning with precise imitation of the teacher's or a partner's melodies, rhythms, and movements, children eventually acquire a repertory of movement and musical ideas from which they can draw for improvisation. Both eurhythmics and solfège offer a base of musical knowledge for improvisation. See Lesson Activities 4.1 for some sample experiences using Dalcroze's components.

narrow intervals with their feet, leaping for whole tones and short-stepping for semitones, as they sing to the teacher's scale-chording.

♦ Children sing familiar songs to solfège syllables while conducting the meter, clapping and patting the meter's pulse per measure (for example, a $\frac{3}{4}$ song might be accompanied by a clap-pat-pat gesture), playing the melodic pitches on their forearms, moving wide and narrow steps to indicate intervals between the melodic pitches.

Improvisation ♦ Standing in the center of a circle, the teacher taps his or her drum for four beats (or eight beats) and requests that children respond immediately with an improvised phrase of the same length on their drums or other nonpitched percussion instruments.

♦ In a circle, the first child plays an eight-beat question phrase on his or her xylophone, ending the question on sol or pitch 5. All immediately imitate the phrase, and the second child plays an eight-beat answer-phrase, ending on do or pitch 1, which is immediately imitated by all. The third child gives the next question, and the fourth child the next answer, each of whom is immediately imitated.

♦ On keyboards, partner one plays a question in an antecedent phrase, to which partner two plays an improvised consequent phrase of equal length. Parameters can be set, such as only in $\frac{6}{8}$ meter, use of just black keys, no Cs allowed, or use of D-E-F keys.

♦ With teacher or child as conductor, class group creates a collaborative piece. Conductor comes up with a subject theme, sets the pitch restrictions, conducts tempo, meter, dynamics, and entrance and exit of instruments.

♦ After listening numerous times to the recording of a musical selection (a medieval dance tune, a Guatemalan marimba ensemble, a Dominican merengue) and discussing its component parts, and then moving to some aspect(s) of it in another listening, children gather into small groups to create something on classroom instruments in the style of the studied piece. For comparison later, play the recorded selection (and move to it), followed by movement participation in the children's pieces.

Dalcroze techniques have permeated the teaching of music to children, even though few teachers in the United States are trained in the pedagogy. This may be due to the widespread recognition of movement as an important channel of musical response for children, as well as the method's longtime presence in the United States, albeit in isolated instances, since the 1920s. The training for certification in the method is challenging because of its reliance on piano as the principal medium for providing music for eurhythmic response. The certification test calls for mastery of piano improvisation that demonstrates a variety of rhythmic qualities for movement, in various keys, rendered in musically expressive ways. For further reading on the Dalcroze techniques, see the classic work by Jaques-Dalcroze (1921/1970) and the writings of Findlay (1971) and Mead (1994) for practical applications of eurhythmics with children.

Kodály

If there is a single underlying philosophy of the Kodály approach to music instruction, it is that "music belongs to everyone." Zoltán Kodály and his Hungarian associates who first evolved the method maintained that music is the right of not only the talented few but all children, who can and should develop performance, listening, and literacy skills. With music instruction beginning in early childhood, children discover folk and art music through a sequence that begins with singing and leads to the development of musically independent individuals who can read and write with ease. Kodály proponents believe that the content and sequence of the curriculum should be derived from children's musical development and from their musical literature. While hand signs and rhythm syllables are closely associated with this approach, it is far more comprehensive than these techniques suggest, with systematic training that results in musical and musically literate children at an early age.

Zoltán Kodály (1882–1967) was a composer, ethnomusicologist, and advocate of music education for children. He and Béla Bartók collected songs in Hungary, Rumania, and in other parts of southeastern Europe. Kodály's Ph.D. dissertation was on the stanzaic structure of Hungarian folk song. He lectured on composition, harmony, counterpoint, and orchestration at the Academy of Music in Budapest from 1907 to 1940. His best-known works, including the *Háry János Suite, Dances of Marosszék, Dances of Galanta,* and *Summer Evening,* feature folk song and folk-like melodies for orchestral instruments. As a vocally oriented composer, his many choruses and eleven books of folk song arrangements demonstrated the characteristic features of his cultural heritage to Hungarians and to the world.

By the early 1920s, he was writing singing and reading exercises and composing group vocal works that revived the Hungarian choral movement. Kodály started a singing movement for young people in the 1930s that soon brought about a radical change in the manner in which children were musically educated in elementary schools. Although he never taught in a primary or secondary school, Kodály's ideas on pedagogy challenged generations of musicians and teachers to raise the music potential of their students. His educational ideas on singing, solmization, reading, and folk song material crystallized in what has become known as the Kodály method. The method was elaborated by students and colleagues, including Jeno Adam, Lajos Bardos, Katalin Forrai, Gyorgy Kerenyi, Benjamin Rajeczky, and Erzsebet Szönyi. Kodály traveled through Hungary, giving encouragement to group singing as the basis for a broad musical culture. In his later years, the Hungarian government was persuaded to give financial support to strong school music instruction.

The Kodály pedagogy in Hungary stipulated four to six weekly periods of music from kindergarten through secondary levels and a sequence of musical experiences that progressed from rhythm training through singing to instrumental lessons. American-style Kodály retains the use of pentatonic folk songs, the Tonic Sol-fa approach to sight reading with its hand signs, a rhythmic system of mnemonic syllables, and an emphasis on unaccompanied song. As part of the focus on music reading and writing, a preparatory period of ear training emphasizes rhythmic and melodic patterns that are encountered in songs and later in visual form. The development of inner hearing—the capacity to think musical sounds without hearing or necessarily voicing them—is important to Kodály training.

Relative or movable do is used for solfège exercises, where the tonic of the scale moves: C is do in C Major and D is do in D Major, and so on. Such a system is seen as an efficient means of understanding the function of individual scale degrees in various keys, by allowing the tonic of the key to provide an aural anchor for dominant, subdominant, and other tonal functions. An adaptation of the French Chevé system of rhythmic mnemonics is also a

Kodály's literacy thrust: Primary-level children reading large-chart notation

Jerry Gay

Inner Hearing

◆ Recall the melody of an art-music selection or folk song, and sing it on a neutral syllable, then with solfège syllables. Later, sing with Kodály-Curwen hand signs.

◆ After singing a familiar melody, play the rhythm of the melody by tapping it on the lap, desk or table top, or floor. Chant the melody's rhythm using the French Cheve system of "ta's" and "ti's" (see Chapter 5).

◆ Sing a familiar song. On cue, continue to sing it silently. On another cue, sing it aloud.

◆ Extract and isolate a phrase from a song that works as a melodic ostinato, and divide a group of singers into melody and ostinato parts in performing it. Sing the song while patting or clapping an extracted phrase as a rhythmic ostinato.

Literacy

◆ Following study of isolated rhythmic and melodic patterns—their sounds and notational symbols—sight-read a new song that includes these patterns.

◆ Select a rhythm pattern (♩♫♩♩, ♩♩♪) or a melodic pattern (l-s-m, s-l-t-d) and find songs and recorded selections that include it.

◆ Take dictation on familiar, and later not-so-familiar, songs and musical selections. Allow the use of invented notation, then stick notation for rhythm, and finally staff notation for melodies.

◆ Using neutral syllables, sing a measure of melody or chant or clap a measure of rhythm from a song, asking children to determine from the notation which measure is being featured. Once identified, the measure can be sung with solfège or chanted with Cheve syllables.

critical technique, particularly for younger children, in learning rhythmic values and their relationships in a pattern. The chanting of "ta ti-ti's" is well known as a technique to be used by students of every level for mastering difficult rhythms. The sequence by which rhythmic and melodic phrases and fragments are taught is also specified by the Kodály approach (see Chapters 5–7).

The most basic of Kodály's ideas, that the use of good music is vital to the life of every person, is a challenging one for American teachers. Kodály recognized art music of the European tradition and its folk or traditional origins as good. He especially favored the beautiful pentatonic melodies of the Hungarians, and he greatly admired the a cappella vocal music of the Renaissance. For American teachers, not only Western European art music, but also the many coexisting musical cultures of American society present rich resources of good music for use with children. Some popular music is equally vibrant, with beautiful melodies, exciting rhythms, and resonant timbres. Lesson Activities 4.2 presents some sample experiences in the Kodály method.

Works by Choksy (1981, 1988, 1999), Szönyi (1974–1979), and Forrai with Sinor (1988) provide information on materials and sequence espoused by Kodály. Kodály's philosophical position on music instruction, and a history of the early years of the movement, are set down in his collected writings (1974).

Orff

The influence of the Orff approach on the teaching of music to children has been explosive since its introduction to North America in the 1960s. The natural behaviors of childhood—singing, saying, dancing, playing, along with improvisation and creative movement—form the basis of the Orff-Schulwerk (literally "school work"). Frequently referred to as elemental music making, the pedagogy is closely linked to the child's world of play and fantasy, of games, chants, and songs. In its original form, elemental music was preintellectual and exploratory, with music, movement, and speech interrelated and overlapping. While the prevalence of special-model Orff xylophones of wood and metal is testimony to its popularity, the Orff approach is far richer and more varied in its musical experiences than initial exposure to the pedagogy may suggest.

The Schulwerk grew from the ideas of German composer Carl Orff (1895–1982), whose experimentation with musicians and dancers in the 1920s planted the seeds for his method's association of music with dance and theater. Together with dancer Dorothee Gunther, Carl Orff established an experimental school in Munich, the Guntherschule, for the integration of the performing arts. A Guntherschule ensemble of dancers, players, and singers, many of them preparing to be teachers, performed at educational conferences throughout Europe.

With the destruction of the Guntherschule during World War II, Orff set out with a young musician-teacher named Gunild Keetman to restore the spirit of integrated music and movement through radio broadcasts, focusing on children instead of adults. Orff believed children to be naturally musical, uninhibited in their expressive movement, and more receptive to his brand of musical training than adults. The collaborative efforts of Orff and Keetman resulted in the establishment of the Schulwerk method and the publication of five volumes of chants, songs, and instrumental pieces called *Musik für Kinder* (*Music for Children*). Canadian and then American adaptations of Orff and Keetman's work in the 1960s helped to spread their pedagogy across the world.

Principal components of the Schulwerk as conceived and practiced in Europe are the imitation and exploration of music and its components, with opportunities to improvise original pieces available as learners become more

Jerry Gay

musically skilled. As adapted in the United States, the process is extended to four stages: imitation, exploration, literacy, and improvisation. Imitation may be simultaneous, or it may be canonic—either echo-like in the form of an interrupted canon (leader claps, then the group) or overlapping in a continuous canon. Imitation may occur through song, movement, or performance on pitched or nonpitched percussion instruments. Exploration challenges children's imaginations to find new ways to apply learned information, for example, "Now that we know the rhythm ♩. ♩. ♫♩. can you play it (faster or slower, louder or softer, on a different instrument, on two alternating pitches)?" Literacy, or competence in reading and writing music, is a development of children's earlier musical experiences and progresses toward the skillful use of both graphic and conventional staff notation. The Schulwerk advocates extensive musical experience before literacy can become a truly musical, instead of mechanical, tool and a means for children to preserve the music they create. Rhythmic notation for quarter notes and eighth notes may be introduced in kindergarten and first grade, with melodic notation beginning with limited pitches (sol-mi and mi-re-do) in the first grade, proceeding to the pentatonic scale by second and third grade, and extending to the reading and writing of the diatonic scale by the fifth grade.

Improvisation is the ultimate stage of the Orff process, allowing musical invention that emanates from earlier learning. It is conceivable for improvisation to occur in preliterate stages as well, but the abilities to read and write music provide children with greater knowledge of musical structures for the original works they create. In this sense, improvisation is the culminating experience that demonstrates extensive musical knowledge and creative expression. The earlier stage of growth (exploration) involves changing one component within a familiar rhythm, chant, song, movement, or instrumental piece, while improvisation is the combination of skills and understanding into new and original forms. In this way, improvisation becomes the ultimate aim of Comprehensive Musicianship for children through the American-style Orff approach. Because of the extent of improvisational qualities in many of the world's musical cultures, the Orff process provides a natural opening into an understanding of these cultures. In particular, the improvised drumming traditions of Ghana, xylophone music of Zimbabwe, and percussion music of China can be learned by children in a manner of expressive creativity outlined by the Orff-Schulwerk.

The Orff process is complemented by the use of such musical features as folk and folk-like songs in the pentatonic mode; ostinato patterns that are spoken, sung, played, and moved; tonic drones or pedal tones; and static and moving bourdon accompaniments on xylophones and various other percussion instruments. These are the more prominent facets of the Schulwerk; the modes of music making in the four-step process are its pedagogy. Lesson Activities 4.3 offers some suggestions for incorporating Orff approach into classes.

Among the most thorough accounts of the Orff-Schulwerk are the volumes by Frazee (1987), Steen (1992), and Warner (1991), while Keetman (1970) presents earlier perspectives on the Schulwerk. The classic Schulwerk contained within Orff and Keetman's *Musik für Kinder* (1950–1954) and the English-language version by Hall (1956) are particularly valuable to those wishing to pursue the historical foundations of the approach.

Other Approaches

Comprehensive Musicianship

The interdisciplinary study of music is the thrust of the approach called Comprehensive Musicianship, which advocates the integration of performance, theory, history and literature, and composition in the music

Imitation
- ✦ Imitate eight-beat body-percussion rhythms by having one child offer a rhythm followed by the group.
- ✦ Imitate a partner's eight-beat body percussion piece. Turn the piece into a movement piece, again with one partner following the movement immediately after its performance by the other partner.
- ✦ Imitate the rhythms of body-percussion gestures on unpitched instruments. For example, finger snaps can be played on triangle, claps on wood blocks, and stamps on drums.

Exploration
- ✦ Experiment with different ways of rendering a familiar folk song, altering just one musical element at a time (for example, dynamics, tempo, mode, meter, accompaniment).
- ✦ Sing a familiar major-key melody in minor.
- ✦ Play on percussion instruments a variety of accompaniments (with combinations that produce varied textures).

Literacy
- ✦ Compose an eight-beat piece that can be graphically notated. Write it as closely as possible to its intended sound on staff notation. Pass the piece to a friend or a new group to perform.
- ✦ Realize the shapes and contours of contemporary art work in music, assigning a conductor to clarify which component should inspire the musical expression. (Allow scientific graphs to be read as musical direction.)
- ✦ Play a simple song's melody. Develop variations of the melody and accompaniment. Notate these.

Improvisation
- ✦ Select a simple rhythm, and see what permutations a group of singers and players can create. Do the same with a melody.
- ✦ Choose a poem. Chant it rhythmically, and then add a nonpitched percussion accompaniment. Turn it into a three-pitch song with pitched accompaniment and movement to express its form.
- ✦ Select a story, and figure ways of musically enhancing the story through the provision of a soundscape, musical responses to the story, other musical insertions, interludes, introduction, and closing music.

curriculum—all in a single lesson. The Ford Foundation funded the Contemporary Music Project (CMP) in 1963 to reshape school music programs to give greater emphasis to creative composition and contemporary music, to bring composers into contact with children, and to reduce the compartmentalization of the music profession into separate subdisciplines.

The CMP sponsored a Seminar on Comprehensive Musicianship at Northwestern University in 1965. This seminar changed the direction of CMP from one of contemporary music in the schools to that of the broad-based teaching of all musical styles through the development of performance, listening and analysis, and compositional and improvisational competences. A series of regional institutes brought these ideas on curriculum revision to collegiate, secondary, and elementary teachers.

While Comprehensive Musicianship was intended to influence all levels of music instruction, it appears to have naturally found a home in music classes for children. One of its major thrusts is the common elements approach to music, such that music of any style can be studied through its sound properties of frequency (pitch), duration (rhythm), intensity (loudness), and timbre. These elements make for convenient organizers of listening lessons, suggesting questions on high and low pitches, short and long rhythmic values, loud and soft volumes, and the quality of instrumental, vocal, and other sounds. They are related to the six elements made popular by the basal music textbook series: melody, rhythm, texture, form, dynamics, and timbre.

Children who are taught with the goals of Comprehensive Musicianship in mind are actively involved in listening to and performing representative music of many cultures and time periods. Few lessons are devoted completely to singing or playing of instruments without some opportunity to experience the real thing on recordings, as performed by trained musicians. Children are led to understand music by listening analytically to a piece, performing it when possible (or sampling fragments of it, such as a recurring rhythmic pattern or melody), and by taking what they know and transferring it creatively to new compositions and improvisations they invent. Fuller explanations of Comprehensive Musicianship can be found in Thomson (1974) and by Choksy, Abramson, Gillespie, and Woods (2000).

Gordon

American music educator Edwin E. Gordon (b. 1928) began to develop a sequence for music instruction in the 1970s, culminating in the formulation of his Music Learning Theory. He coined the term *audiation* to refer to the goal of music instruction: inner hearing (or hearing music in the mind when it is not physically present). Similar to the classic European pedagogies, Gordon supports the sound-before-symbol approach to music instruction. As in the development of language, children listen to tonal and rhythm patterns, imitate them, and then read and write them. Audiation occurs when children have had ample listening experiences, so that they can see a notated rhythm or melody and make musical sense of it, hearing it even if it is not sounded aloud.

Gordon's theory of music learning suggests a hierarchy of musical skill building that begins with aural perception and discriminative listening, progresses through the development of music reading and writing, improvisation, and on to a theoretical understanding of music. The eight-step hierarchy of his learning sequence is:

Discrimination learning

1. Aural and oral
2. Verbal association
3. Partial synthesis
4. Symbolic association
5. Composite synthesis

Inference learning

6. Generalization
7. Creativity and improvisation
8. Theoretical understanding

Discrimination learning begins with listening and imitation of small patterns of sound, often on a neutral syllable. These tonal and rhythm patterns are then given verbal associations by way of solfège syllables and a set of mnemonic rhythm syllables (for example, ♩♫ = du du-de or ♩♬ = du du-ta-de-ta). Partial synthesis is the testing of children to determine how well they are able to aurally recognize and discriminate tonal and rhythm patterns that have been taught. Their success in this stage prepares them for symbolic association, the introduction of the written symbols for the solfège and rhythmic mnemonic syllables students have listened to, imitated, and aurally identified. There is no discussion, for example, of quarter notes and eighth notes at this level, but instead the shift of what they hear to how it is symbolized—and vice versa—is considered. A composite synthesis is achieved when isolated notational patterns can be grouped in a series (in a song's notation) and read with ease. Likewise, children should be able to notate an aurally dictated melody or rhythm that uses familiar patterns that have been previously sounded and symbolized.

Inference learning is a higher-order learning, largely of unfamiliar stimuli. It begins with generalization, a test of whether children can transfer familiar tonal and rhythm patterns to new pieces, to be read or written. Improvisation and composition encourages the use of learned patterns in new and personally creative ways, with opportunities for children to notate what they have invented. The final stage, theoretical understanding, allows for the acquisition of knowledge about why music is what it is, as well as what meter and key signatures mean, how lines and spaces of a staff are lettered, what relationships a series of pitches may have, and what the mathematical values of rhythms are. Theory is last in the sequence, following all opportunities to know music aurally, orally, and symbolically.

Gordon's sequence is further revealed in the textbook series he coauthored with David Woods, *Jump Right In!: The Music Curriculum* (1990). Exercises and songs that reinforce tonal and rhythm patterns are included for children from kindergarten through middle school. The theoretical framework for the series is found in Gordon (1994).

Manhattanville Music Curriculum Project

During the review and redesign of music instruction programs in the 1960s, the Manhattanville Music Curriculum Project emerged as one of the most progressive and influential programs. Funded by the U.S. Office of Education and named for Manhattanville College where it originated, it was as intensive as it was extensive. The project resulted in a comprehensive curriculum for grades three to twelve that derived from children's instead of

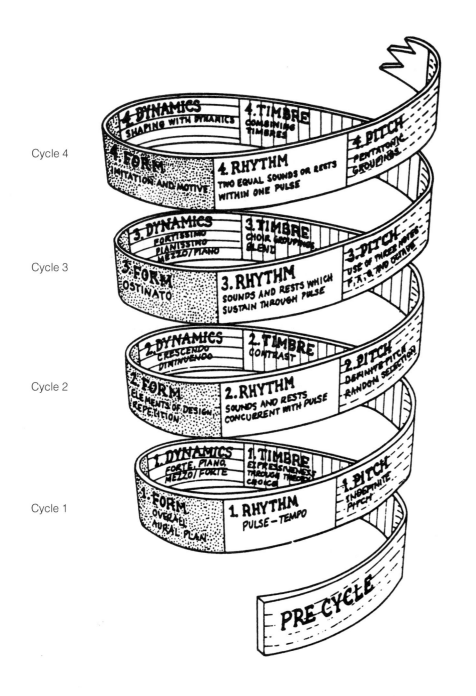

FIGURE 4.1

Manhattanville Music Curriculum Project Curriculum Concept Spiral

Source: Thomas (1970).

the teacher's perspective, providing a sequence of basic musical concepts to be learned through exploratory yet teacher-guided experiences. MMCP connected learning from one grade level to the next via a spiral of progressively more sophisticated aspects of the musical elements, in a variety of musical styles.

MMCP is strongly anchored in the tradition of perceiving by exploring and of understanding by creating, improvising, and composing. Children are encouraged to experience music by sampling their own sound world, by making sounds with their bodies: snapping, clapping, patting, stamping, whistling, tapping, shuffling, moaning, and various vocalizations. They are stimulated to produce found sounds through objects they gather and new instruments they can build. They develop concepts of pitch (melody and texture), rhythm, form, dynamics, and timbre by creating their own musical expressions, and eventually notating them. These concepts become increasingly more sophisticated as children mature (see Figure 4.1).

As advocated by director Ronald B. Thomas (1970), MMCP includes seven types of experiences: MMCP strategies (composing, performing, evaluating, conducting, listening), student recitals, listening to recordings, research and oral reports, guest recitals, skill development, and group singing. Children's musical expressions are stimulated through new ideas in the music selections they hear. Composed pieces are approached holistically, so that children not only listen to them, but also conduct them, perform them, invent variations, and then create entirely new compositions inspired by them. MMCP supports the development of aural, dexterous (performing and conducting), and translative (notational) skills—with emphasis on graphic forms invented by children.

MMCP has fostered an attitude that some of the most meaningful music learning occurs when the environment is informal and relaxed, and when the teacher's approach is flexible enough to accommodate children's unique learning styles. Effective music instruction incorporates alternative sound sources for making music, the room and space for movement and for gathering in groups of performers and composers, and enough time to work through musical problems.

Music in Education

In the 1980s, technology-assisted music instruction entered the realm of the music classroom. The Yamaha Corporation developed a new interest in children's conceptual learning of music through the computer and computerized keyboard programs. Its Music in Education (MIE) approach suggests that children supplied with keyboards can build aural, performance, and rotational skills in an integrative way.

The MIE goals are to develop intelligent listeners who can describe and discuss the music they hear, make, and create. The curriculum includes print materials, software, and hardware, integrated with one another and divided into 145 learning modules that focus on specific elemental areas and musical concepts—from beat and meter to tonality and atonality, and from ostinato accompaniments to chord progressions in major and minor keys. The curriculum offers a repertoire that includes folk songs ("New River Train"), patriotic songs ("America"), pop songs, songs from popular musicals ("My Favorite Things"), and classical selections ("Eine Kleine Nachtmusik"). Children progress at their own pace through exercises in melodic and rhythmic dictation, composition, and keyboard performance. Ensemble and independent performances, and class and independent study, are possible through MIE.

The computer is critical to the MIE program, allowing children access to instruction, rehearsal and review, and evaluation of their skill and knowledge attainment. It is central in providing children with performance experience on keyboards that utilize MIDI (Music Instrument Digital Interface) technology. Children thus learn concepts, performance skills, and repertoire through the synthesized MIDI sounds they make and create. Pilot programs have proven MIE to be a highly successful curriculum for attaining music literacy. The continuing evolution of MIE is traced in two manuals entitled *Program Components* and *Scope and Sequence* (Music in Education, 1989a, 1989b).

Education through Music

As the sound of its title indicates, Education through Music (ETM) is a holistic approach to music instruction. American music educator Mary Helen Richards was fascinated with ways in which the Kodály pedagogy could be adapted to the needs of children and teachers in the United States. Following extensive correspondence with Zoltán Kodály and observations in Hungarian schools, she began her adaptation of the Kodály principles to English-language songs and American curricular emphases. In the 1960s, Richards published her songs and instructional sequence in *Threshold to Music*, a series of books and charts that were a prelude to ETM. She used Kodály's suggestions in finding folk songs from the North American continent to introduce to children, and she became fascinated with the relationship between the ways songs and language were acquired through pattern recognition.

The first- and second-level goals of ETM are to bring children comfort and self-esteem, as well as cooperation with others, within the context of group music making. These are followed and supported by the goals of aural skill acquisition and an understanding of the melodic and rhythmic patterns of the musical language. The ETM approach makes use of folk songs and singing games of the United States and British Isles. Many of the songs are selected because of their involvement of children in both singing and kinesthetic experiences (actions, circle games, line and partner dances, and so forth). Movement is viewed as a necessary technique for leading children in their discovery of melodic and rhythmic patterns, and repeated words and word-phrases. The pattern recognition touted by ETM prepares children for sight-reading. With literacy accomplished, the relationship of ETM to the Hungarian approach is undeniable—and is certainly acknowledged by its founder. Bennett (1987) offers a more complete description of the ETM approach, as do Bennett and Bartholomew (1998).

Weikert

The growth of interest in movement as a component of music instruction in the 1980s led to the acceptance of the work of Phyllis Weikert. In her work in physical education and recreational folk dance, Weikert observed that people struggle with basic movement because they cannot maintain a steady beat. She devised a sequence for teaching folk and choreographed dance that takes into account the relationship between language and movement and that underscores the development of beat competence through movement and dance. That four-step process has been found to be effective by music teachers who incorporate structured movement in their music classes, particularly folk dance, and who view the development of the feeling for steady beat as a primary instructional objective. Weikert's process is as follows:

Step 1.   Say "Step-hop, step-hop, side-close"

Step 2.   Say and do "Step-hop, step-hop, side-close"

Step 3.   Whisper and do "Step-hop, step-hop, side-close"

Step 4.   Do (think and do) "Step-hop, step-hop, side-close"

Weikert's sequence is straightforward and can be used by classroom teachers and physical education instructors with limited musical training. Its chief contribution in music education is as a technique for teaching steady beat, not as a comprehensive method. It may best be used in remedial ways or as a supplement to more musical pedagogies such as Dalcroze eurhythmics or Orff-Schulwerk. Weikert (1982) has published several volumes of folk dance instructions that are accompanied by recordings of arranged dance music.

A Comparison of Methods and Techniques

Table 4.1 (pp. 90–91) offers a comparison of the various pedagogical approaches, focusing on several categories: goals, recommended musical material, principal experiences, aural skills and ear-training techniques, approaches to literacy and notation, and instructional structure. Because of the necessary brevity of the chart, prominent factors are highlighted instead of all aspects of the pedagogy.

Carder (1991), Choksy, Abramson, Gillespie, and Woods (2000), and Shehan (1986) discuss and compare several of these pedagogies.

A Personal Method

Despite the myriad of techniques intended to advance the musical development of children, each teacher in the end chooses to incorporate those pedagogical aspects that are harmonious with his or her personal goals and definitions of music education. Often, those goals are based upon the teacher's own musical strengths and personal preferences in music and instruction. Singers may be inclined to sing more than to move or to play, pianists may be more prone to utilize a keyboard laboratory or to accompany songs and movement on the piano, and kinesthetically oriented teachers may center their music instruction on assorted movement experiences. There is no one correct way to teach musical understanding, skills, and values, nor is there only one of ten standard ways to approach these goals.

"We teach as we have been taught" is an adage relevant to the philosophy that guides instruction and to the techniques selected and blended into each teacher's personal pedagogy. Undergraduate programs leading to degrees and teaching certification in music provide teachers with extensive preparation in applied music, aural and keyboard skills, ensemble performance, conducting, theory, and history and culture, with occasional courses in improvisation and composition. This training, when coupled with methods courses that emphasize musical materials and techniques proven to be effective in teaching children, holds the potential for producing independent and successful musician educators.

Instruction is further shaped through additional training in music. A postgraduate course in conducting may direct a teacher's attention toward potential movement and expressive gestures that children may learn to use as they listen and perform a song. A clinic taken in improvisation may inspire lessons in creative musical thinking and doing. A string of workshops in technology-oriented instruction or in the music of world cultures will provide a teacher not only with new musical materials, but also with innovative instructional techniques. A graduate course in ear training, theory, or analysis will hone a teacher's listening skills, while also providing approaches for training children's ears. The development of musicianship is an ongoing process. To use colloquial expressions, when we don't (continue to) train, we don't gain, and when we don't use it (the musical skills we may have earlier developed), we lose it.

Training in the classic and contemporary methods of music instruction for children can greatly enhance the development of a personal teaching method. Summer courses in Kodály, Dalcroze, and Orff are provided at universities throughout North America and abroad, with certification available following extensive coursework and demonstration of selected proficiencies in music, teaching, and planning. Also, summer courses are available on the approaches espoused by Gordon, Weikert, Education through Music, and Music in Education. Training in these methods leads to the adaptation of aspects of their philosophies, goals, and techniques, for these all are logical pathways that have been tested with children. In the end, however, the

TABLE 4.1 *A Comparison of Methods for Teaching Music to Children*

METHOD	FOUNDER	GOAL	MUSICAL MATERIAL
Dalcroze, or Dalcroze eurhythmics	Émile Jaques-Dalcroze, theorist and composer	Natural rhythmic movement of the body to improve aural skills	Improvised music on the piano
Kodály; the Hungarian method	Zoltán Kodály, composer and ethnomusicologist	Musical literacy and inner hearing	Traditional folk music and art music (in Hungary, Hungarian music first)
Orff-Schulwerk	Carl Orff, composer	Musical experience, expression through music	Folk songs and children's melodies
Comprehensive Musicianship	Norman Dello Joio, composer (Contemporary Music Project); Robert Werner, music educator; and others	Descriptive, performing, and creative competence	Composed music, including contemporary, and traditional and world music
Gordon; Music Learning Theory	Edwin E. Gordon, music educator	Audiation (hearing music in the mind)	Tonal and rhythm patterns; folk and composed songs in *Jump Right In!*
Manhattanville Music Curriculum Project (MMCP)	Ronald Thomas, music educator, and others	Improvement of musicianship through experimentation and exploration	Contemporary and other composed music; children's sound pieces
Music in Education (MIE)	Yamaha Corporation	Keyboard, aural, and notational skills	Keyboard arrangements of folk, patriotic, popular, and classical works
Education through Music (ETM)	Mary Helen Richards, music educator	Musical literacy and inner hearing	Traditional folk music of the United States and British Isles
Weikert	Phyllis Weikert, physical education specialist	Development of feeling for steady beat	Recorded arrangements of folk-dance music

teacher's interests, strengths, and classroom needs emerge again to bring about the blend of a newly acquired layer of skills with those that the teacher has used for some time.

A personal method of music instruction does not preclude the opportunity to find affinities with certain established methods. More than likely, the teacher who strives for greater musicianship will seek out the set of techniques that appeal to his or her personal interests. But does the provi-

PRINCIPAL EXPERIENCES	AURAL SKILLS	NOTATION	INSTRUCTIONAL SEQUENCE
Eurhythmics, solfège, improvisation	Fixed do, dichords, trichords, solfège combined with conducting and movement	Phrases are mapped; single- and double-line staves lead to full staff	Germinal, building from rhythmic phrase to a complete piece
Singing (a cappella), directed listening, folk songs, singing games, folk dance	Movable do and rhythmic mnemonics	Song patterns are heard, then sung or chanted, then notated	Sequential development of melodic and rhythmic vocabulary
Speech chants, movement, singing, instrumental performance, improvisation	Imitation and exploration of rhythmic and melodic patterns	*In its original form:* No prescribed system, preliterate experiences. *In its American adaptation:* Experience precedes notation symbols	From imitation to exploration (to notational literacy) to improvisation
Relating theory and history to performance and composition; common elements	Listening and performing large works and discrete patterns	Representational icons leading to conventional notation	Sequence stemming from working curriculum
Listening, reading, writing discrete tonal and rhythm patterns	Aural and oral rote learning to movable do and rhythmic mnemonics	Easy, moderate, and difficult patterns to hear, read, and write	Eight-step process in two phases: discrimination and inference learning
Exploring, creating, performing	Listening to environmental sounds and composed pieces	Emphasis on invented icons and graphs	Stemming from children's needs and interests; seven guides
Keyboard experiences	Melodic and rhythmic dictation exercises at the keyboard	Staff notation and terminology through keyboard performance	Designated through 145 instructional modules
Singing, directed listening, games and dances	Movable do and rhythmic mnemonics	Song patterns are heard, sung, and chanted, then notated	Sequential development of melodic and rhythmic vocabulary
Folk dancing	Not addressed	Not addressed	Four-step sequence for folk-dance instruction; books with recordings

sion of movement experiences classify her as a follower of Dalcroze? Does an emphasis on folk song and the great art music make him a Kodály teacher? Does the rhythmic chanting of poetry brand them followers of Orff? Or is there variation among the practices of teachers who have been influenced by the pedagogical emphases of Dalcroze, Kodály, or Orff? How are culturally based pedagogies blended with standard instructional methods when teaching a Zulu song or a Brazilian Samba? All teachers make choices in the techniques and musical materials they select for use with children, and most might conceivably be judged as showing an inclination toward one or another known method. Still, the personalization of these techniques and methods following training is the true test of the teacher's independent musicianship and ability to lead children in their own musical development.

REVIEW

1. Which pedagogies stress the use of movement as an instructional technique? To what extent does movement advance musical understanding in these pedagogies?

2. What is the relationship of inner hearing to audiation? Which methods espouse these goals?

3. Which approaches are American-made? In what ways? Are the European methods suitable for adaptation in American settings? How?

CRITICAL THINKING

1. What are the relationships among the three classic European methods (Dalcroze, Kodály, Orff) regarding the development of aural skills, musical literacy, and creative musical expression?

2. What aspects of these notated pedagogies for children can be continued into the realm of music instruction for adolescents? Adults? In choral settings? Instrumental settings?

3. Experiment with the samples of the Dalcroze, Kodály, and Orff pedagogies. Design and implement original examples of the principles.

PROJECTS

1. Identify and observe the teaching of those trained in the techniques of a specific pedagogy. Discuss with them their philosophy and goals, and note their use of specific techniques and media.

2. Select a musical concept: $\frac{3}{4}$ meter, m-r-d, ♩♫♩♩, binary form. Design three (or more) ways of teaching the concept, using the distinctive techniques and materials of three (or more) methods.

3. Interview teachers regarding their personal goals of music experience and instruction for children, their preferred techniques, and professional activity and advanced training and certification. Later, note any overlap of goals and techniques.

4. In a letter to the principal, describe your personal method of instruction. Include a statement of goals and experiences you have and musical materials and techniques you use.

REFERENCES

Bennett, P. (1987). The evolution of education through music. *Music Educators Journal*, 74, 1.

Bennett, P., and D. Bartholomew (1998). *SongWorks I* and *SongWorks II*. Belmont, CA: Thomson Publishing Company.

Carder, P., ed. (1991). *The eclectic curriculum in American music education.* Reston, VA: Music Educators National Conference.

Choksy, L. (1981). *The Kodály context.* Englewood Cliffs, NJ: Prentice-Hall.

———. (1988). *The Kodály method.* Englewood Cliffs, NJ: Prentice-Hall.

———. (1999). *The Kodály Method* (2nd ed.). Upper Saddle River, NJ: Prentice-Hall.

Choksy, L., R. M. Abramson, A. E. Gillespie, and D. Woods (2000). *Teaching music in the twenty-first century.* Upper Saddle River, NJ: Prentice-Hall.

Findlay, E. (1971). *Rhythm and movement: Applications of Dalcroze eurhythmics.* Evanston, IL: Summy-Birchard.

Forrai, K., with J. Sinor (1988). *Music in preschool.* Budapest, Hungary: Corvina Press.

Frazee, J. (1987). *Discovering Orff: A curriculum for music teachers.* New York: Schott.

———. (1999). *Discovering Keetman.* New York: Schott.

Gordon, E. E. (1994). *Learning sequences in music: Skill, content, and patterns.* Chicago: G.I.A. Publications.

Gordon, E. E., and D. Woods (1990). *Jump right in!: The music curriculum.* Chicago: G.I.A. Publications.

Hall, D. (1956). *Music for children.* Mainz, Germany: B. Schott's Söhne.

Jaques-Dalcroze, Émile (1921/1970). *Rhythm, music, and education.* (H. F. Rubenstein, trans.) London, England: The Dalcroze Society.

Keetman, G. (1970). *Elementaria: First acquaintance with Orff-Schulwerk.* London: Schott.

Kodály, Zoltán (1974). *The selected writings of Zoltán Kodály.* (F. Bonis, ed.; L. Halapy and F. Macnicol, trans.) London, England: Boosey and Hawkes.

Mead, V. (1994). *Dalcroze eurhythmics in today's music classrooms.* New York: Schott.

Music in Education. (1989). *Program components.* Buena Park, CA: Yamaha Corporation.

———. (1989). *Scope and sequence.* Buena Park, CA: Yamaha Corporation.

Orff, C., and G. Keetman (1950–1954). *Musik für Kinder.* Mainz, Germany: B. Schott's Söhne.

Shehan, P. K. (1986). Major approaches to music education. *Music Educators Journal, 72*(6), 26–31.

Steen, A. (1992). *Exploring Orff.* New York: Schott.

Szönyi, E. (1974–1979). *Musical reading and writing* (3 vols.). New York: Boosey and Hawkes.

Thomas, R. B. (1970). *Manhattanville Music Curriculum Program: Final report.* ERIC document ED 045 865. Washington, DC: U.S. Office of Education, Bureau of Research.

Thomson, W. (1974). *Comprehensive musicianship through classroom music.* Belmont, CA: Addison-Wesley.

Warner, B. (1991). *Orff-Schulwerk: Applications for the classroom.* Englewood Cliffs, NJ: Prentice-Hall.

Weikert, P. S. (1982). *Teaching movement and dance* (2 vols.). Ypsilanti, MI: High Scope.

ORGANIZATIONS

The Dalcroze Society of America. Julia Schnebly-Black, president. School of Music DN-10, University of Washington, Seattle, WA 98195.

Education through Music. Richards Institute of Music Education and Research. 149 Corte Madera, Portola Valley, CA 94028.

Institut Jaques-Dalcroze. M. Dominique Porte, directeur. 44 Rue de la Terrassiere, Geneva, Switzerland 1206.

Organization of American Kodály Educators. Richard Merrill, executive director. 823 Old Westtown Road, West Chester, PA, 19382.

International Kodály Society. P.O. Box 8, H-1502, Budapest, Hungary.

American Orff-Schulwerk Association. P.O. Box 391089, Cleveland, OH 44139.

Music Learning Theory. Edwin E. Gordon. G. I. A. Publications, Inc. 7404 S. Mason Ave., Chicago, IL 60638.

Music in Education. Yamaha International. 6600 Orangethorpe Ave., Buena Park, CA 90622-6600.

5

Rhythm and the Child

Rhythm is everywhere in the lives of children. When children speak, their words tumble and flow in regular streams of sounds, in starts and stops, with emphasis or not. When they move, they step regularly; they run, hop, jump, and skip in rhythms of their own. The rhythms they experience extend beyond speech and movement: Maria hears the rhythm of her mother's heartbeat, soft and steady, and is soothed by it. Aaron can feel the throbbing of his own pulse as he holds his wrist, feeling it gradually decrease in speed as he settles down after hopping around the playground. When Lamont recites a favorite poem, he gives accent and rhythm to the rhyming words, shaping them into units of loudness and softness, and faster and slower sounds. Jacqueline pours her own rhythm into the teddy bear, dancing him in time to the tune she hums. When the grind of a homework assignment presses him, Robby raps as he rhythmically reads aloud his weekly list of spelling words. With surprising frequency, rhythm emerges in the things that children do.

Children at play or at work show their natural attraction to and fascination with rhythm. The word comes from the Greek verb *rhein*, meaning "to flow." Children flow eagerly through rhythmic experiences that engage them in listening, speaking, or moving. They develop greater rhythmic facility naturally and easily while singing and when rhythm is embedded in language and movement. The counting of beats can be experienced later as a higher level of musical knowing, but children's first experience with rhythms is through their daily speech and movement.

Children learn to understand concepts of rhythm in music through their teachers and musically sensitive parents. In school music classes as well as through private instrumental instruction, children learn by participating in the activity of a sequenced curriculum. Children chant, sing, listen, play, read, and write their way to a thorough knowledge of pulse (or beat), subdivisions and extensions of the pulse (for example ♫ and ♩), other durations and patterns of rhythm (and their related rests), accents, meter, syncopation, and polyrhythms. Children's natural affinity for rhythm is more fully realized through training, taking them from the experiences of listening and responding to rhythms to reading and writing the notes that symbolize them; that is, music literacy.

Rhythm and Child Development

The mother's heartbeat, initially experienced in the prenatal environment, may be the earliest rhythmic experience of all. In early infancy, children then add the rhythmicity of sounds in their environment—the rocking movements and rhythmic cooings made by their parents, the pulse of music emanating from televisions and stereos, and the often regular loud-soft and fast-slow gradations of speech in conversations that surround them. Well within their first year, children respond rhythmically to music as they sway, rock, and bounce. Toddlers may show their perception of rhythm through the rhythmic dance-like movements they perform, first with others and then by themselves. Young children experience rhythm by feeling, hearing, and moving to it. Table 5.1 summarizes aspects of children's developmental stages of rhythmic perception and understanding.

The spontaneous songs children sing become increasingly rhythmic with age. Beginning with musical babbling at one year to eighteen months, when their singing is often a string of pitches with occasional and often irregular pauses for breaths to occur, children at two years may already be framing their melodies around steady beats within and between phrases. By three years of age, children's songs may take on rhythmic structures that include strong metric tendencies and recurring patterns. With increasing exposure to standard nursery rhymes, chants, and songs, as well as to folk and popular songs, preschool children are often integrating rather sophisticated rhythmic patterns into their spontaneous songs. Their attempts to reproduce songs presented to them also become more accurate in both rhythmic and melodic elements as they approach school age.

Moorhead and Pond (1978) observed that preschool children's spontaneous sounds are first regular in pulse but unaccented. Keeping a steady pulse appears to be developmental. While few three-year-old children can tap, clap, or pat in time to a set regular pulse, most six-year-olds accomplish this task with great accuracy. Beat competence is widely evident by first grade, and yet some children still require training, or at least reinforcement of the skill, to maintain a steady beat. The accurate replication of short rhythmic patterns by young children reveals a similar developmental progression from toddler through kindergarten age. Not only does rhythmic perception develop early, but also the abilities to perform (or produce) pulse

TABLE 5.1 *Children's Rhythmic Development*

AGE	DEVELOPMENTAL SKILL
Less than one	Demonstrates rhythmic swaying, rocking, bouncing
One to two	Demonstrates babbling in irregular rhythmic patterns
	Performs dance-like rhythmic movements
Two	Sings spontaneous songs framed around regular rhythmic pulses and patterns
Three	Sings spontaneous songs with some feeling for meter and with regularly recurring rhythmic patterns
	Imitates short rhythmic patterns
Four to five (Kindergarten)	Taps in time to a regular set pulse
	Begins to develop rhythmic clapping and patting
	Replicates short rhythmic patterns on instruments
Six to seven (Grades one and two)	Distinguishes fast and slow, long and short
	Can perform songs faster and slower
	Can PRW quarter-, eighth-, and half-note rhythms
Eight to nine (Grade three)	Can PRW dotted-quarter and eighth notes (♩. ♪), and syncopated quarter- and eighth-note rhythms (♪♩ ♪)
	Can recognize and conduct music in $\frac{2}{4}$, $\frac{4}{4}$, $\frac{6}{8}$, and $\frac{3}{4}$ meter
Nine to ten (Grade four)	Can PRW sixteenth-note patterns (♬♬ ♫♬ ♬♫)
	Can recognize and conduct music in cut time and compound meters ($\frac{9}{8}$, $\frac{12}{8}$)
Ten to twelve (Grades five and six)	Can PRW dotted eighth- and sixteenth-note patterns (♫. ♪♫.)
	Can recognize and conduct music in asymmetric meters ($\frac{5}{8}$, $\frac{7}{8}$)

Note: PRW = perform, read, and write.

and to reproduce patterns emerge even before most children begin formal schooling.

With increasing musical exposure, children in the elementary grades evolve a sophisticated understanding of how music is organized rhythmically. Primary-grade children demonstrate their readiness for learning about tempo, durations, and metric groupings through their rhythmic chants and through the rhythmic recitation of numbers, letters, words, and word-phrases. They learn to use the regular rhythmic pulses and patterns of spoken language, and how to use expressively the accents, flow, and shadings of language in ways that parallel musical expression.

In first grade, children typically can discern fast from slow and long from short. This prepares them for experiences in performing songs faster and slower, and for recognizing the sounds of quarter notes and their eighth-note subdivisions. By second grade, they usually are capable of reading and writing various rhythmic patterns based first on quarter and eighth notes, and then with the addition of half notes. Third-grade children (who have had sufficient practice with earlier durations) are ready for directed listening and the performance of music with dotted quarter notes and syncopated patterns that mix quarter and eighth notes (♪♩♪) and can develop the skills to read and write patterns with these durations. During this period, children become capable of discerning the metric grouping of pulses in simple duple ($\frac{2}{4}$ and $\frac{4}{4}$), compound duple ($\frac{6}{8}$), and triple ($\frac{3}{4}$) time, showing their knowledge through conducting patterns and various other movements.

With a solid foundation of rhythmic understanding, and the development of skills for performing, reading, and writing, children in the intermediate grades can progress easily into experiences with rhythms of greater complexity. Sixteenth notes, along with patterns combining sixteenth and eighth notes (♫♪ and ♫♪), can be introduced to fourth-grade children, dotted eighth- and sixteenth-note patterns (♪♫ and ♫♪.) to fifth-grade children, and triplets to children in the sixth grade. With an understanding of music in $\frac{2}{4}$, $\frac{4}{4}$, $\frac{6}{8}$, and $\frac{3}{4}$ under way, children can then explore other compound meters ($\frac{9}{8}, \frac{12}{8}$), cut time or alla breve ($\frac{2}{2}$) as symbolized by ¢ as opposed to common time ($\frac{4}{4}$), and irregular or asymmetric meters ($\frac{5}{8}$ and $\frac{7}{8}$, for example). Many of the more sophisticated rhythmic concepts targeted for learning at the intermediate level are nonetheless inherent in popular music and children's listening preferences, and thus were experienced at younger ages.

The logic of a rhythm learning sequence must be set by teachers with a comprehensive knowledge of music and children's developmental levels. A large part of children's rhythmic perception develops without training, but the capacity to perform it, code it through notation, and decode it by reading the notation is dependent on instruction and a long experience in hearing these rhythms. A refined ability to discern the rhythmic nuances of music also is greatly enhanced through the directed listening that teachers provide. The rhythmic development and training of children is explored in a classic text by Hood and Schultz (1949) and more recently by others noted in this chapter.

Rhythm in Speech

The rhythm of spoken language is the natural gateway to musical rhythm. Words and word-phrases provide children with every component of rhythm—from the basic pulse to the multilayered complexity of polyrhythm.

Words become musical when:

1. They are spoken over the foundation of a set pulse.

2. Their sounds are transformed into chants of longer and shorter musical durations.

3. Some words in a group are emphasized over others.

From the discovery of language in early childhood through the sophisticated wordplay of preadolescence, children develop musical understanding in their rhythmic chants.

Children can be made aware of musical rhythm through experiences that engage language as a tool for learning duration, accent, and temporal units. Because speech is oral, children learn its rhythmic patterns through enculturation, for example, by listening to their parents, older siblings, relatives, neighbors, and friends, as well as to speakers on the television, radio, and film. The media present universal patterns of the rhythmic flow and stress of language, a homogenized pronunciation of words and phrases. Children are not likely to intentionally distort or perform inaccurately the spoken language they have learned orally and thus are readied for learning concepts of musical rhythm by the very nature of their extensive listening to language and speaking of it.

The Orff approach adheres to the development of rhythmic understanding through chant. Words of one, two, and three syllables form the building blocks of music, because they provide the substance for the recitation of longer and shorter durations equivalent to quarter, eighth, half, whole, and sixteenth notes, as well as triplets. Typically, children's names, or names of colors, fruits, or animals, provide occasions for chanting to a steady pulse. From single words, children can explore word-phrases, sentences, and paragraphs that equate to half-phrases of two measures, full phrases of four measures, and musical forms such as binary, ternary, and rondo. Greetings and farewells, colloquialisms, proverbs, rhymes, famous quotations, and poems are rich with potential for musical rhythm. As children recite these bits of speech and language, they come into contact with rhythmic values and nuances.

The pedagogy of Orff-Schulwerk provides experiences not only for rhythmic chanting, but also for the abstraction and accompaniment of speech rhythms by clapping, tapping, snapping, and stamping. While Carl Orff did not specify the transfer of rhythmic speech to the reading and writing of rhythmic notation, American proponents of the approach have successfully developed music literacy by following the extensive rhythmic experience with wordplay that they provide for their children. See Lessons 5.1 through 5.7 for examples of rhythm embedded in spoken phrases that can be incorporated within a lesson on pulse, durations, and durational patterns.

Because language is so fundamental to children's daily lives, they comfortably and easily express rhythmically its phonemes (sounds, including syllables) and phrases. While rhythmic chant is a musical realization of language, the challenge is to eventually perform the rhythms of the words while silencing the words themselves, to achieve a more complete musical understanding of the rhythmic components. After chanting, patting, clapping, tapping, stamping, and stepping the rhythm, can children fade away the words and maintain the integrity of the rhythm itself? After internalizing the rhythmic phrase, can they graph it—through dots, dashes, lines, and

LESSON 5.1 *Rhythmic Duration through Name Chants*

Patting the pulse, chanting the words:

LESSON 5.2 *Rhythmic Chants: Colors*

Patting the pulse, clapping the off-beats, chanting the words:

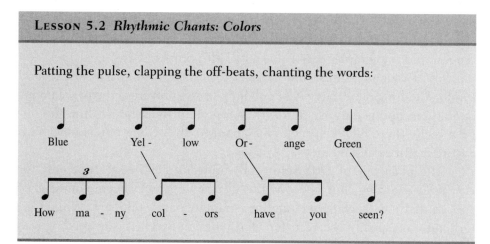

LESSON 5.3 *Rhythmic Chants: Animals*

Patting the pulse, clapping the off-beats, chanting the words:

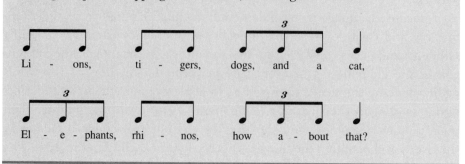

LESSON 5.4 *Rhythmic Chants: Fruits*

Chanting with body rhythms:

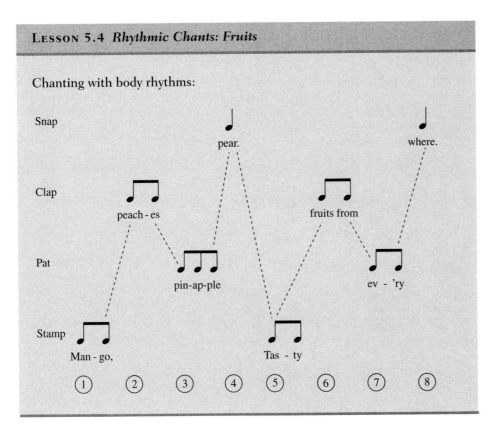

LESSON 5.5 *A Half-Phrase of Rhythm*

Patting the pulse, chanting the words:

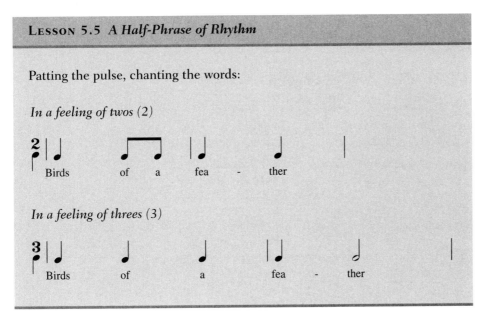

shapes? Can they notate it? Can they hear the rhythm of the word-phrase in a new musical context—a song or recorded piece? Can they recognize the rhythm and read it when it occurs in notated music? These are sophisticated skills in the development of rhythmic understanding. It all begins with an awareness of the rhythm of speech. The work of Frazee (1987),

LESSON 5.6 A Full-Phrase of Rhythm

Patting the pulse, chanting the words:

In a feeling of twos (2)

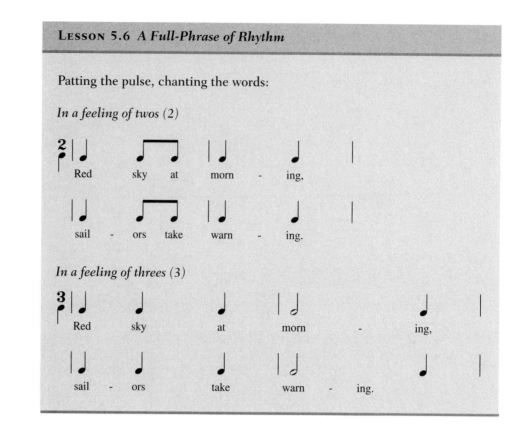

In a feeling of threes (3)

LESSON 5.7 A Musical Form: Rondo

Chanting the words, choosing the body rhythms:

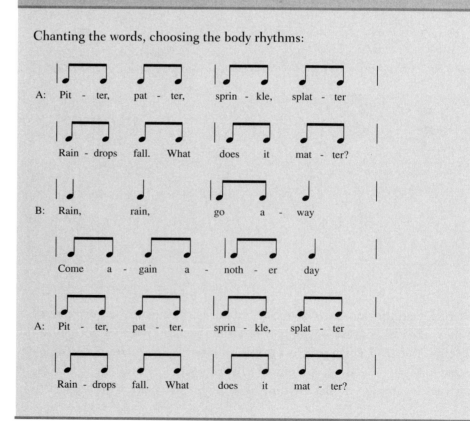

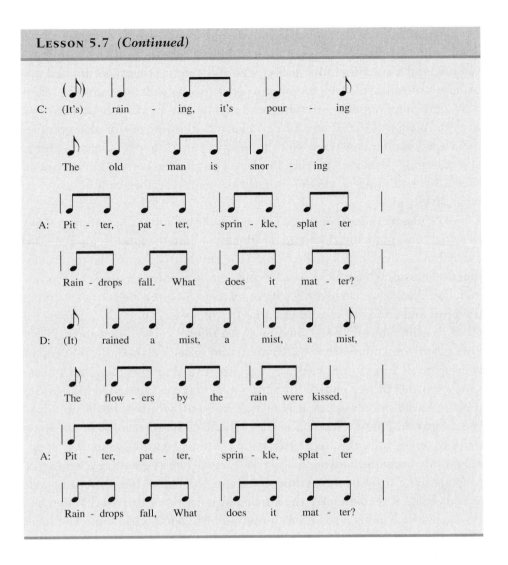

C: (It's) rain - ing, it's pour - ing

The old man is snor - ing

A: Pit - ter, pat - ter, sprin - kle, splat - ter

Rain - drops fall. What does it mat - ter?

D: (It) rained a mist, a mist, a mist,

The flow - ers by the rain were kissed.

A: Pit - ter, pat - ter, sprin - kle, splat - ter

Rain - drops fall, What does it mat - ter?

Keetman (1974), Orff and Keetman (1956), Steen (1992), and Warner (1991) provide many examples of Orff practices of rhythmic speech, as do works by Goodkin (1998, 1999).

Rhythm in Movement

Children of all ages enjoy physical activity. Together with speech, movement is a natural means by which children can develop an understanding of rhythm. Their movement to an underlying pulse, to subdivisions of the beat, and to rhythmic patterns almost guarantees their understanding of these musical elements. Once their ears receive and bodies respond to rhythm, children internalize the sound and feeling, leading to conceptualization. They come to know quarter notes, because they have walked them, and a pattern such as ♩♪ because they have skipped it. No mathematical analysis or counting-out procedure is necessary. No notation is meaningful to children until they have sensed through movement its rhythmic essence.

When children are provided with occasions for moving rhythmically to music, they develop conceptual understanding relative to their natural developmental stage. Rhythmic movement may require their coordinated use of larger muscles in such locomotor activities as walking, running, skipping, galloping, hopping, jumping, or swaying, and in kinesthetic activities such as swinging the arms and conducting. Movement can also complement speech chants when children engage in patting, clapping, snapping, and stamping. Whether moving in place or across space, children grow in their understanding of rhythm when they can kinesthetically respond to what they hear.

The classic music pedagogies underscore the importance of movement as a tool for enhancing rhythmic development. The techniques of Dalcroze eurhythmics are based on the belief that rhythm is the fundamental element of music, whose source is the natural locomotor rhythms of the human body. Dalcroze eurhythmics includes exercises in conducting, stepping the beat, and changing movement qualities of speed, direction, and weight, all in an effort to reflect the rhythm of the music through movement. Carl Orff's elemental approach is based on the premise that rhythmic movement is inseparable from music itself, as it is also critical to the child's natural responses to his or her world. Rhythmic movement is not as central to the broader-based Schulwerk as it is to Dalcroze eurhythmics, but it nonetheless is an important avenue through which children can learn to sense rhythms more fully through basic body rhythms (patting, clapping, snapping, and stamping) and locomotor activities. The sequential teaching of proponents of the Kodály method maintains the use of folk dances as well as songs, and it recommends the curricular infusion of dances that demonstrate rhythmic concepts such as pulse, pattern, and metric unit. The logic of teaching rhythm through movement is undeniable and is woven throughout these and other pedagogies. See Chapter 8 for sample experiences in rhythmic movement for children.

The Pulse

Of the fundamental elements of rhythm, none is more basic in the Western world (and perhaps universally) than the pulse, or beat. Its presence is heard or felt in almost all music. It regulates music, because it is a recurring and steady stress underlying a variety of other rhythms, melodies, and textures. Regardless of whatever else is sounding within the music, "the beat (usually) goes on."

Children may demonstrate a sensitivity to the pulse as toddlers, rocking steadily to recorded music. Other children are still coming to terms with a feeling of pulse in the intermediate grades. While sensitivity varies, most children can maintain a steady clapping pulse by the age of eight. For a comprehensive rhythmic development to occur, children must first be able

to follow the pulse present in the music. Lesson 5.8 can be expanded to a complete lesson, offering experiences that serve to establish a sensitivity to musical pulse.

Meter

In most music, the steady and regular pulse, or beat, is defined by accent, or emphasis that is given to some but not all pulses. The recurring pattern of stronger and weaker pulses is called meter. More than independent pulses, an understanding of meter enables the listener to perceive the flow of musical ideas.

Time signatures at the beginning of a notated piece are indications of meter, or the number of pulses in a musical unit or measure. Bar lines separate one measure from another. In general, the top number shows the number of pulses, while the bottom number signifies the value of the note that receives one pulse. For example, in $\frac{2}{4}$ meter, there are two pulses per

1. Play a recording of a Sousa march or a rock song. Ask children to clap the pulse. Model the clapping of the beat in correct time. Pat the beat on the shoulder of those who are having difficulty or place your hands on theirs to direct their clapping.

2. Ask children to show the pulse by patting their knees. On the cue word *change,* children show the pulse elsewhere (clapping hands, patting shoulders or head, snapping fingers).

3. Write the one-syllable names of children in the group horizontally across the board. Ask children to pat a steady pulse on their knees and then to chant:

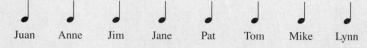

Juan   Anne   Jim   Jane   Pat   Tom   Mike   Lynn

4. Ask children to pat the pulse on their knees as they sing familiar songs such as "Knick-Knack Paddy Whack," "Frère Jacques," or " Old Joe Clark."

5. Play a steady pulse on a drum or a melody with a steady pulse on piano or xylophone. Ask children to sit facing a partner and to roll balls or pass bean bags to each other on every pulse.

6. Ask children to form small groups and to create a chant of one-syllable and two-syllable words to a single category: colors, animals, insects, flowers, and cars. Ask them to determine a way of sounding a steady beat as they prepare their chant pieces for performance.

measure, and the pulse is notated as a quarter note ($\quarternote$). In a compound meter such as $\frac{6}{8}$ or $\frac{7}{8}$, there are six or seven pulses per measure, and the pulse is notated as an eighth note ($\eighthnote$). An exception to this rule is when the tempo quickens: The six eighth notes in $\frac{6}{8}$ are heard and felt in two groups of three instead of as six separate pulses ($\eighthnote\eighthnote\eighthnote$ $\eighthnote\eighthnote\eighthnote$). For children, the feeling of a quick $\frac{6}{8}$ in a song such as "Oh Dear, What Can the Matter Be?" or "The Farmer in the Dell" is easily felt; it is only the explanation that appears complex.

Children come to understand meter through attentive listening and through kinesthetic responses that follow the musical flow of stronger and weaker sounds. As early as age three or four, children listen and respond to music in two or four beats (or duple meter), three beats (or triple meter), and a quick-paced compound meter. Some children respond naturally by rocking, swinging, swaying, chanting rhymes, and singing, but most require a model to lead them to sensing the appropriate loud-and-soft metrical pulses. Children in the intermediate grades who are skilled in identifying these basic meters can be challenged to combine 2 + 3 pulses or 3 + 2 + 2 pulses in asymmetric meters such as $\frac{5}{4}$, $\frac{5}{8}$, $\frac{7}{4}$, or $\frac{7}{8}$, or to alternate meters such as $\frac{4}{4}$ and $\frac{3}{4}$ in mixed meter.

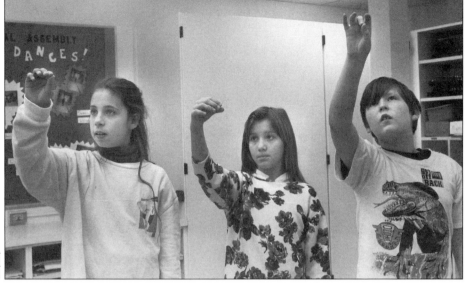

Jerry Gay

Various approaches lead children to an understanding of meter, some requiring movement. Speech rhythms accompanied by rhythmic ostinatos involving body movements such as patting, clapping, snapping, and stamping reinforce the concept of meter. Conducting is another primary means of sensing the strong and weak pulses: The strong pulse of each measure is shown by a vertical downbeat, while all other pulses are indicated somewhat horizontally. Children are frequently adept at learning conducting patterns for some of the commonly found meters. The experiences in Lesson 5.9 are useful in developing a sense of meter; they are techniques and strategies to be used in lessons of various levels. Taken collectively, they are the substance of a lesson on meter.

Durations and Their Patterns

As the fundamental pulse, or beat, and then the accented and unaccented pulses of meter are understood, children gradually become aware that chants, songs, and recorded musical works contain other rhythmic elements as well. While keeping the pulse, children may be rhythmically chanting two words or three syllables. They may be singing songs that appear to have faster rhythms; for example, with more rhythmic durations and pitches than they are conducting. In fact, the rhythms are more accurately viewed as shorter rather than faster (and also longer rather than slower) than the pulse. As they listen to a recording, children may be finding more rhythmic diversity than the meter beats they have been asked to identify. Rhythm is fundamental to music in its underlying pulse, but it also decorates and energizes music through its many durations that are longer and shorter, and faster and slower, than the pulse.

1. Play a selection of recordings in various meters. Ask children to pat their knees on the strong beat and to hold on the weak beats. Play the recordings again, asking children to continue to pat their knees on the strong beat and to find another movement (clap, snap, or pat floor) for each of the weak beats.

2. Lead children in chanting the following phrases while patting the strong beats and clapping the weak beats (p = pat, c = clap).

Durational values may be viewed as subdivisions or extensions, for example, elongations, of the basic pulse. If the pulse is symbolized by ♩, then its subdivision is ♫ or two eighth notes. Twice the length of the quarter-note pulse is ♩, and four times the pulse is o. While these durational values can be analyzed mathematically, this is not the manner by which rhythm is perceived by children—or adults. Instead, music is commonly perceived as

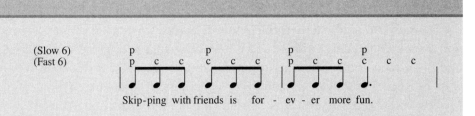

(Slow 6)
(Fast 6)

Skip-ping with friends is for - ev - er more fun.

3. Draw basic conducting patterns on the board. Lead children in drawing the conducting patterns in the air. Chant aloud the words *strong* for the first downbeat and *weak* for all other pulses. As children learn the conducting patterns, sing or hum familiar songs in the appropriate meter.

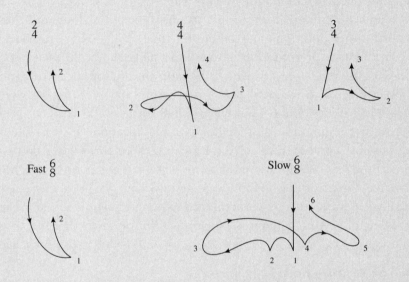

4. Ask children to play improvised melodies on the piano or xylophone. Other children can listen, step the pulse, and identify the meter by conducting.

5. Sing a familiar song such as "Row Your Boat" or "Yankee Doodle" in a different meter while patting and clapping or conducting.

6. In small groups, create a recurring movement pattern that can be repeatedly performed to a predetermined song or recording.

patterns of durations and pitches, not as single isolated sounds. These patterns often occur more than once in a song or musical composition, offering coherence, tying musical ideas together, and giving the work a sense of a unified whole. Thus, children learn rhythmic durations with relative ease when sounds are linked together in patterns instead of when single sounds are treated mathematically.

When rhythmic patterns are associated with the chants and songs children have performed, their learning is accelerated. Once children have had opportunities to perform rhythmic patterns within the music, these patterns and even individual durations can be extracted, chanted, played on pitched and nonpitched percussion instruments, and used as a basis for improvisation. Further rhythmic development can occur as children are challenged to identify these patterns in new songs, to create chants and songs that incorporate them, and ultimately to read and write them.

Proponents of the Kodály method offer a sequence for the teaching of rhythmic patterns that derive logically from traditional songs that children sing. The sequence begins with quarter- and eighth-note patterns and is followed by the introduction of the half note, sixteenth notes, syncopated patterns, and patterns of compound meters such as $\frac{6}{8}$, $\frac{9}{8}$, $\frac{5}{8}$, or $\frac{7}{8}$. The first patterns of quarter and eighth notes are usually four pulses long, but those patterns with other durations may be briefer than that. Box 5.1 provides a logical order for the presentation of rhythmic patterns to children, along with familiar children's songs in which the patterns are found. Information on Kodály-inspired sequences for teaching rhythm may be found in works by Szönyi (1974–1979) and Choksy (1981, 1988).

Many other permutations of single rhythmic durations are possible; in fact, the possible combinations of durations are nearly infinite. Likewise, most songs probably contain more than one pattern that can be highlighted and extracted for chanting, clapping, stepping, and playing experiences. The pedagogical mission is to lead children to a more complete and lasting understanding of rhythm when it is experienced in the songs that they sing.

Box 5.1 *A Sequence of Rhythmic Patterns*

Box 5.1 *(Continued)*

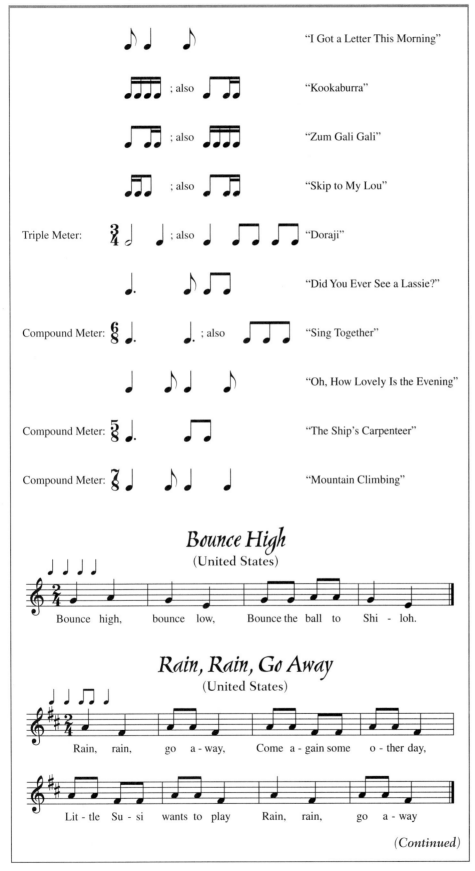

Box 5.1 *(Continued)*

Box 5.1 *(Continued)*

(Continued)

Box 5.1 *(Continued)*

Box 5.1 (*Continued*)

Did You Ever See a Lassie?
(United States)

Sing Together
(United States)

Oh, How Lovely Is the Evening
(England)

(*Continued*)

Box 5.1 *(Continued)*

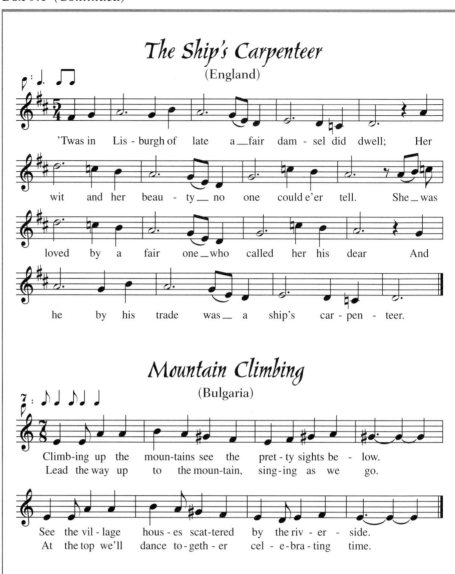

Mnemonics

Because music is an aural phenomenon, it is logical to assume that rhythm can be learned by listening—at least at first. In many cultures, rhythms are transmitted by master musicians and teachers to their students without the assistance of notation, graphs, or other visual aids (Campbell, 1991). While literacy is an important goal of school music instruction, it cannot be fully developed without children first internalizing the sound of the rhythm. As in many oral cultures, rhythm is thus effectively taught to children through rhythm syllables called mnemonics (pronounced, "neh-*mon*-iks"). These mnemonics have no semantic meaning and are associated with specific rhythmic durations.

Several mnemonics systems have proven successful in introducing rhythms to children, have developed their inner hearing of these rhythms, and have lead to their reading and writing of rhythms. These systems include the word-chant system similar to the speech rhythms of Orff-Schulwerk and to Kodály and Gordon syllables. There are also notable historical systems, counting systems, culture-specific systems, and systems that combine duration and drum syllable strokes. Those systems most commonly and effectively used in teaching rhythm to children in American schools will now be described.

In that speech rhythms are fundamental to the Orff-Schulwerk, the fixed word-chant system may have been derived from that approach. In the word-chant system, each rhythmic duration is assigned a specific word, often at the discretion of the teacher. These words may be chosen from one category or another. For example, if "fruit" is the selected category, then a quarter note may be chanted as "pear" whenever it occurs in a pattern, eighth notes as "ap-ple," sixteenth notes as "boy-sen-ber-ry," and so on. Any word combination is possible in a longer phrase, and because these words designate specific durations, they serve as mnemonics for internalizing the rhythms and patterns.

One well-known tool of the Kodály method is its rhythm duration syllables. The syllables are related to the French Chevé system of mnemonics that dates to the early nineteenth century and was practiced in conservatories throughout Europe before the Hungarians popularized them in their musical education of children. The crisp dental "t" sound begins most syllables, and the more sustained syllables are sounded as "ah" for each pulse. Like the Orff-inspired word-chant, the Kodály syllables can be combined in as many ways as there are rhythmic patterns and phrases. The chanting of these syllables is known to lead successfully to the reading and writing of notation.

Edwin E. Gordon has proposed another mnemonics system, based on the rhythm syllables first suggested by McHose and Tibbs in the 1940s. Similar to the word-chant and Kodály systems, syllables are learned orally so that audiation, or inner hearing, can be developed before the introduction of notation. Similar to the Kodály syllables, there is a crispness to the "d's" and "t's" that initiate them. In the Gordon system, "du" is used whenever the melodic rhythm pattern coincides with the underlying macro beat feeling. For example, in $\frac{4}{4}$ where four macro beats are felt in a measure, a series of eight eighth notes would be "du-de-du-de-du-de-du-de," and if only two macro beats were felt in the measure, the syllables would be "du-ta-de-ta-de-ta-de-ta." While Kodály syllables are always associated with the same written note value regardless of the rhythmic feeling or meter, Gordon's syllables are associated with the sound of the rhythm patterns as they relate to the feeling of the underlying macro and micro beats that constitute the meter.

Box 5.2 offers a comparison of the word-chant, Kodály, and Gordon syllable systems, featuring rhythmic durations and patterns that can be offered intact or adapted to suit the musical needs of children. In all three systems, rests are taught as beats of silence. They may be chanted in

Box 5.2 *Rhythm Mnemonics*

Duration	Word-Chant	Kodály	Gordon
♩	pear	ta	du
♫	ap - ple	ti - ti	4/4 du - de
♪	date	ti	du, de, or ta
(sixteenths)	boy - sen - ber - ry	ti - ri - ti - ri	2/4 du - ta - de - ta
(triplet 3)	pine - ap - ple	tri - o - la	2/4 du - da - di
♩.	peach	ta - i	du –
(dotted eighth-sixteenth)	co - co - nut	tim - ri - ta	4/4 du - ta du
♩ (half note)	plum	ta - ah	du du –

Phrase

4/4 ♩ ♩ ♫ ♩
pear   pear   ap-ple   pear
ta   ta   ti - ti ta
du   du   du-de   du
1   2   3   +   4

2/4 (sixteenths) (triplet 3) 2/4 ♩
boy - sen-ber-ry   pine-ap - ple   plum
ti - ri - ti - ri tri-o - la   ta - ah
du - ta - de-ta   du - da - di   du
1   e and a   2   and a   3 - 4

4/4 (dotted eighth-sixteenth) ♩ ♫ ♩
co   –   co - nut   ap - ple pear
tim –   ri - ta   ti - ti   ta
du   –   ta   du   du - de   du
1   –   a   2   3   +   4

4/4 ♩.   ♪ (dotted eighth-sixteenth) ♩
peach   date co - co -nut
ta - i   ti   tim - ri - ta
du   –   de   du - ta du
1   +   2   + 3 - a   4

hushed tones or their durational words and syllables merely thought and felt instead of voiced.

The use of a mnemonics system is an important part of children's music learning, and it is most effective when used consistently and without overlap into other systems. Rhythm syllables allow children to build an extensive vocabulary of rhythmic patterns and to discriminate between individual durations, their patterns, and the characteristic meters in which they are set. Children who have internalized rhythms through chant are thus prepared to read and write the notation that symbolizes their sounds.

Notation

All avenues of musical experience lead eventually to notational literacy, so that children may attain a comprehensive musicianship. While a sensitivity to music's rhythm—its pulse, meter, and durations—is developed through chants, songs, and movement, a child's musical education is more encompassing when he or she becomes musically literate. Music literacy is the ability (1) to see symbols and to think or reproduce the sound, and (2) to hear the sound and to think or write the symbols. Just as the reading of words can be systematically learned by children following their experience in the spoken language, music notation can be learned when its teaching is systematically addressed.

The adage of "sounds before symbols" serves as a slogan for the teaching of rhythmic notation to children. A rhythmic pattern sounded by the teacher played on piano, xylophone, or hand drum often is understood by children through movement. When children coordinate their bodies to step, clap, or realize this pattern through a combination of body rhythms, they are then prepared for the Dalcrozian "dash-a-note" challenge. Children can draw horizontal dashes from left to right on a chalkboard to represent what they hear and feel: the longer the sound, the longer the dash. The dashes are eventually converted into notes, with vertical stems and noteheads drawn. Dash-a-note maps can be drawn in the air or on paper, but the rhythmic patterns require ample large-muscle movement experience before they can be accurately drawn. Before and after the advent of literacy, this technique can solidify the relationship of rhythmic sound to symbol.

One of the tools of the Kodály practice involves the initial use of note stems for rhythm reading. All stem notes (except half notes) are notated without the body of the note (for example, | = ♩ and ⊓ = ♫). This releases children from the time-consuming act of coloring in the noteheads, so that dictation can then envelop a greater number of rhythms per class period. Rhythmic patterns are heard and quickly depicted by writing only the stems. Variations of this technique include the use by younger children of Popsicle sticks, rhythm sticks, and dowels for representing patterns.

The whiteboard as an aid for teaching rhythm

Jerry Gay

If children can learn to read and write letters, words, and sentences, they can also decipher, interpret, and write rhythmic notation. Through the kindergarten year, rhythmic learning should be experiential, while children are discovering the sounds of their environment and playing with them. By first grade, children are ready to match rhythms to circles or discs, squares, diamonds, hearts, stick-people, or vertical lines. These images represent the rhythms of familiar songs children have previously sung. As children hear the various combinations of quarter notes and eighth notes, they can follow the images that represent the pulse and its subdivision, pointing to the sounds that are ordered from left to right on the blackboard, feltboard, or

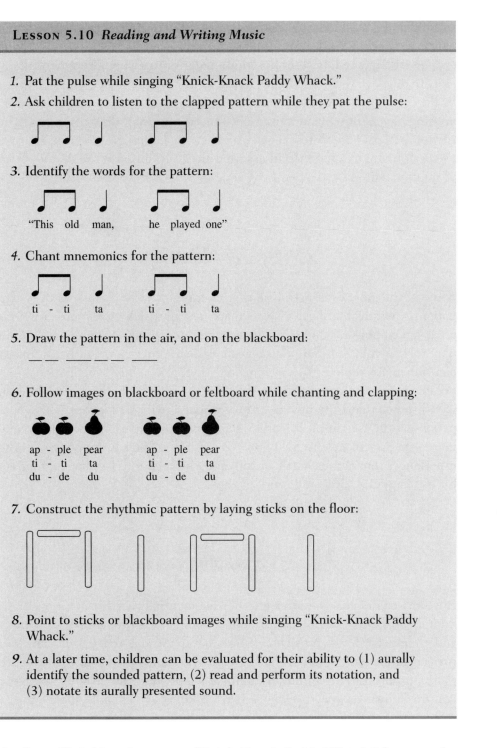

1. Pat the pulse while singing "Knick-Knack Paddy Whack."

2. Ask children to listen to the clapped pattern while they pat the pulse:

3. Identify the words for the pattern:

"This old man,   he played one"

4. Chant mnemonics for the pattern:

ti - ti ta   ti - ti ta

5. Draw the pattern in the air, and on the blackboard:

6. Follow images on blackboard or feltboard while chanting and clapping:

ap - ple pear   ap - ple pear
ti - ti   ta   ti - ti   ta
du - de   du   du - de   du

7. Construct the rhythmic pattern by laying sticks on the floor:

8. Point to sticks or blackboard images while singing "Knick-Knack Paddy Whack."

9. At a later time, children can be evaluated for their ability to (1) aurally identify the sounded pattern, (2) read and perform its notation, and (3) notate its aurally presented sound.

the floor. If children have sung "Knick-Knack Paddy Whack," for example, and have chanted the syllables for some of its patterns, then they are ready to read the images that represent the rhythm and to write them out using selected shapes or sticks. Such a lesson appears in Lesson 5.10 and is suitable for children in grades one and two.

The process for learning to read and write other patterns continues similarly as the children mature, using rhythms that are increasingly complex. When they have developed their ability to print legibly (no later than second grade), children are also ready to take rhythmic dictation with paper and pencil. They no longer require the iconic visual images. Sticks and shapes are replaced by stem notation, and eventually children gain the facility to quickly attach noteheads to the stems. With practice, this can occur by the fourth grade. Central to the process of reading and writing, however, are singing, chanting, and movement experiences that must come first. The rhythm patterns presented above provide a logical progression for not only the performance experience in assorted rhythms, but also the development of rotational literacy.

Syncopations

Some of the most exciting music that children can know consists of syncopation—rhythms that have displaced accents, in which unaccented rhythms are given emphasis while normally accented pulses are deemphasized. Popular, rock 'n' roll, Sub-Saharan African, African American, and Latin American music are replete with syncopated rhythms. While syncopation in its notated form is seldom introduced before the intermediate grades, children have listened to off-the-beat rhythms for many years. The concept of syncopation can be taught at an earlier stage through experience, analysis, and more experience. Lesson 5.11 (pp. 124–125) provides a sampling of these experiences that can be partly or fully incorporated into lessons appropriate for use in grades three and four.

Polyrhythms

Rhythms can occur one after another (sequentially) or they can occur simultaneously. In the polyphonic music from the European Renaissance, and in much of the music of Sub-Saharan Africa, the Caribbean, and African-influenced music of both North and South America, two or more rhythmic layers that sound simultaneously provide the striking rhythmic feature known as polyrhythm. When children are capable of keeping a steady pulse and of chanting, clapping, and playing rhythmic patterns that last eight or more pulses, then they have achieved the musicianship required to perform one rhythm as other rhythms are sounding. By the third grade, most children possess the rhythmic stability necessary for performing polyrhythmic pieces. It will take the teacher's careful sequencing of lessons, however, for children to perform them cleanly, steadily, and independently yet cooperatively, as is the nature of polyrhythm. Lessons 5.12 through 5.14 suggest three sets of experiences that easily comprise three single lessons to develop an understanding of the intricacies of polyrhythm.

*Children playing
polyrhythms on
African and Latin
instruments*

From Natural Rhythms to Rhythmic Training

Children demonstrate their natural rhythms in nearly all that they do, but primarily through speech and movement. The challenge for teachers is to channel these natural rhythms into an understanding of one of music's most elemental parts. The challenge becomes greater when teachers recognize the need to season instruction with the playfulness with which children have perceived and explored rhythm from their earliest years. Some of the most powerful musical experiences children can know may be the discovery of how their own physical energy can be ordered, regularized, and combined with others in rhythmic chant, song, and movement. Rhythm may be the magical dynamism that attracts and maintains the interest of children in music, both in school and out.

Teachers and parents can explore with children the rhythmic components of language and the manner in which rhythmic movement can add to their enjoyment of singing a song or listening to music. Children's conceptual understanding of rhythm—its pulse, meter, and durations—can be developed further through experiences that associate listening with speech and movement, leading to inner hearing. There is a logical sequence in the introduction of rhythm patterns from pulses and their subdivisions to

1. Clap or pat even pulses, accenting the first of every two.

2. On the cue word *change*, syncopate by accenting the second of every two pulses.

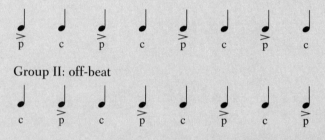

3. In two on-beat and off-beat groups, accent the first or second of every two pulses by patting the accent and clapping the unaccented pulse.

   Group I: on-beat

   Group II: off-beat

4. Practice chanting rhythm syllables and applying body rhythms for syncopated patterns.

date	pear		date	date	pear		date
ti	ta		ti	ti	ta		ti
du	de		de	du	de		de

5. Seek out the syncopated patterns in these songs, chanting and clapping them while tapping the steady pulse or conducting the meter.

Bucket of Water
(Jamaica)

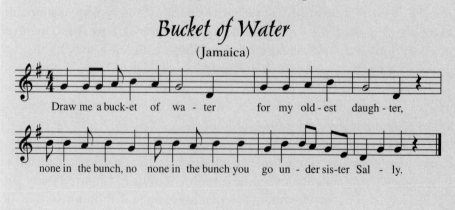

Draw me a buck-et of wa - ter   for my old - est daugh - ter,

none in the bunch, no   none in the bunch you   go un - der sis-ter Sal - ly.

Sansa Kroma
(Ghana)

San - sa kro - ma Ne nay woo ah chay chay ko - ko - ma.

San - sa kro - ma Ne nay woo ah chay chay ko - ko - ma.

Kye Kye
(Ghana)

Kye kye ku - le Kye kye ku - le Kye kye ko - fee - sah
(Chay chay koo - lay)

Kye kye ko-fee - sah ko-fee - sah lang - a ka-ka shi-lang - a

Ka - ka shi-lang - a ka-ka - shi-lang - a kum a-den - de
(day)

kum a - den - de kum a - den - de Hey!
(day) (day)

1. Learn to perform the eight-count polyrhythm.

   (a) Chant the two rhythmic patterns separately.

   (b) Clap and chant the patterns separately.

   (c) Clap and (silently) chant the patterns separately.

   (d) Divide into two groups; clap the patterns separately.

   (e) In two groups, clap the patterns together (four or more times).

   (f) For greater rhythmic clarity, choose different body sounds on which each group plays its rhythm: hand-clap, lap-pat, foot-stamp, finger-snap, vocalizations.

(1)   1 — 3 4 — 6 7 —

(2)   1 2 — — 5 6 — 8

---

2. Follow the same sequence as above, but increase the groups in clapping this four part polyrhythm. Tranfer to different body rhythms and instruments.

   (a) (clap, woodblock)

   1 — 3 4 — 6 7 — 9 10 — 12

   (b) (snap, rattle)

   1 2 3 4 5 6 7 8 9 10 — —

   (c) (pat, iron bell, tone bell)

   1 — — — 5 6 — 8 9 — 11 12

   (d) (stamp, drum)

   1 2 3 — 5 6 — 8 — 10 — 12

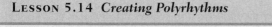

3. Challenge children to perform a personal polyrhythm in their bodies.

(a) Clap and chant the following rhythm:

♩	𝄽	♩	𝄽	♩	♩	♩	𝄽
1	—	3	—	5	6	7	—

(b) Step and chant the following rhythm:

𝄽	♩	𝄽	♩	𝄽	𝄽	𝄽	♩
—	2	—	4	—	—	—	8

(c) Combine the stepping and clapping patterns.

(d) Create new eight-beat patterns that interlock with (a) and (b), to be snapped and patted.

sixteenth notes and to syncopations, and from rhythms in duple meter to those in triple and compound meters. There is a logical learning order as well in the progression from sound to symbol, as teachers guide children through listen-and-response experiences in rhythm, to chanting their mnemonic syllables, to reading the rhythms that are notated, and to notating the rhythms that are heard. This is the musical foundation that can be formed in the elementary grades and from which more sophisticated musical understanding can proceed.

REVIEW

1. Differentiate between speech and rhythmic speech. In what ways does language offer a means by which rhythmic understanding can be developed?

2. In what order should these rhythmic concepts be presented to children and at what ages or grade levels: accents, duration and durational patterns, syncopation, pulse, meter, polyrhythms?

3. Why is $\frac{6}{8}$ called a compound meter? How does the definition apply to $\frac{5}{8}$ or $\frac{7}{8}$?

4. Discuss the function of mnemonics, and compare the grammar of the more frequently found systems. What other systems are in use?

CRITICAL THINKING

1. How does the achievement of music literacy contribute to the comprehensiveness of children's musical sensitivity and understanding?

2. To what extent might rhythm be the featured activity in learning a song to sing? For example, discuss multiple ways of underscoring rhythmic components in "Zum Gali Gali" and how these strategies enhance song learning.

PROJECTS

1. Listen to recordings of musical works of various styles. Compile a list of ten works that can be used in teaching concepts of rhythm to children. For each work, determine its meter and prominent rhythmic patterns.

2. Choose five colloquialisms, proverbs, or famous quotations. Recite them aloud, listening for accents and durations. Notate their rhythms in duple and triple meter.

3. Select a rhythmic pattern, and prepare a ten-minute lesson that incorporates rhythmic speech chant and body rhythms.

4. Analyze the rhythmic contents of ten traditional children's songs. Arrange them in order of complexity, noting the repeated rhythmic patterns that might be highlighted in a lesson for children. Recommend the grade level at which the song's rhythms would be suitable for learning.

REFERENCES

Campbell, P. S. (1991). *Lessons from the world.* New York: Schirmer Books.

Choksy, L. (1981). *The Kodály context.* Englewood Cliffs, NJ: Prentice-Hall.

———. (1988). *The Kodály method* (2nd ed.). Englewood Cliffs, NJ: Prentice-Hall.

Frazee, J. (1987). *Discovering Orff: A curriculum for music teachers.* New York: Schott.

Goodkin, Doug (1998). *A Rhyme in time.* Miami: Warner Bros. Publications.

———. (1999). *Name games.* Miami: Warner Bros. Publications.

Hood, M. V., and E. J. Schultz (1949). *Learning music through rhythm.* Boston: Ginn.

Keetman, G. (1974). *Elementaria: First acquaintance with Orff-Schulwerk.* (M. Murray, trans.) London: Schott.

Moog, H. (1976). *The musical experience of the preschool child.* (C. Clarke, trans.) London: Schott.

Moorhead, G. E., and D. Pond (1978). *Music of young children.* Santa Barbara, CA: Pillsbury Foundation.

Orff, C., and G. Keetman (1956). *Orff-Schulwerk: Music for children* (5 vols.). English adaptation by Doreen Hall and Arnold Walter. Mainz, Germany: B. Schott's Söhne.

Szönyi, E. (1974–1979). *Musical reading and writing* (3 vols.). New York: Boosey and Hawkes.

Steen, A. (1992). *Exploring Orff.* New York: Schott.

Warner, B. (1991). *Orff-Schulwerk: Adaptations for the classroom.* Englewood Cliffs, NJ: Prentice-Hall.

6

Pitch and the Child

Jeffrey listens dreamily to the rise and fall of his parents' voices as he plays with his toys. Later, he is rocked to sleep by the soothing sounds of a lullaby. Mindy hums a self-made song to her doll as she dresses it. Tyler and Jared look forward to times on family vacations when they all sing together in the car. Katie laughs with the surprise of recognition as her music teacher introduces a song based on the melodies of some of her favorite television jingles. Melody, the linear use of pitch and rhythm, comes to children in many places and forms, sometimes through listening and sometimes through performing. These experiences create a foundation for building conscious understanding of melodic concepts.

Eventually, children also become aware of harmony, the simultaneous sounding of pitches. Ian's dad plays a guitar as they sing together. Esther hears people sing in harmony in her church and she eagerly joins in. Rashad's class is learning to play the Autoharp to accompany some of their songs. Arianne sings second soprano in her fifth-grade choir. As children experience different harmonies, feeling the tension and release that results from the various uses of consonance and dissonance, they build the concrete basis for understanding harmony's theoretical structures.

The word *melody* comes from the Greek words *melos* meaning "song" and *aeidein* meaning "to sing." In the Greek sense, melody is inextricably bound with the idea of song. For children, song is undoubtedly the most immediate experience they have of melody. The ability of children to master the production of melodies and, eventually, to sing in harmony will be addressed in Chapter 7.

The focus here is on ways teachers and parents can enhance children's perception and understanding of different aspects of melody and harmony. Numerous techniques for developing sensitivity to pitch and pitch patterns will be provided. These activities are important in helping children to

1. Think about music
2. Discuss what they notice happening in musical events—eventually using musical terms
3. Use these ideas creatively

These techniques will help children focus on pitch, as a part of an entire lesson. Teachers can incorporate them in lessons as a part of ongoing work on pitch development.

Growth in Understanding of Linear Pitch Structures

Many challenges face children as they grow in their ability to perceive and understand the pitch-related aspects of melody.

- ✦ At the most basic level is the task of discrimination—Are two pitches, patterns, or melodies the same or different?
- ✦ At the next level is recognition of shape or contour—What is the overall curve of a melody?
- ✦ These abilities, along with the ability of children to form aural images of songs, result in recognition—Is the melody familiar?

Next comes a focus on more discrete aspects of melody.

- ✦ Pitch register—Are pitches relatively high or low?
- ✦ Pitch direction—Is the melody moving upward or downward?
- ✦ Pitch motion—Are the pitches moving by steps, leaps, or repeats?
- ✦ Interval size—Are the leaps large, medium, or small?

Later children become aware of

- ✦ Tonality—What is the focal point of the melody?
- ✦ Melodic phrase—What constitutes a complete idea melodically?
- ✦ Scale—What is the underlying pattern of tones for the melody?

And they become aware of additional concepts such as major modes, minor modes, and melodic sequence.

At a remarkably early age, children develop a sense of their own culture's ways of constructing melodies, probably in the same way they develop a sense of the syntax of their native language. Such sensitivities emerge

Children associating sounds of pitches with notation

gradually and are retained through adulthood, regardless of training in music. A knowledge of when these perceptual sensitivities emerge can help the parent or teacher plan developmentally appropriate activities.

The teacher or parent can help children move from percept (the ability to notice these various qualities of melody) to concept (the ability to identify these qualities in a variety of settings and permutations). However, they need to be conscious of the readiness of children for a particular level of thinking. For example, a child may perceive that some pitches are high and some are low but may not be able to group the highest and the lowest ones in separate categories. In addition, the child may or may not be ready to explain his or her thinking in familiar terms such as high and low or upward and downward.

Table 6.1 presents an appropriate sequence for teacher activity during children's melodic development. As the table shows, rapid growth in pitch perception occurs in the early childhood years, birth through age eight. Percepts and concepts stabilize and refine after that. The development of individual children can vary. Some musically experienced children may have clear, foundational pitch concepts at the age of four. Most children seem to develop these concepts around the ages of six to eight, in the primary grades.

Discrimination and Contour Awareness

Although infants are capable of noticing the difference between two pitches or two melodic contours, the task for older children is to begin to describe what they notice. At first, they may say "same" or "different" in response to

TABLE 6.1 *Children's Melodic Development and Teachers' Guidance*

AGE	PERCEPT AND CONCEPT	TEACHER ACTIONS
Less than six months	Responds to differences in pitch. Can match vocally sustained pitches and begins to imitate sounds.	Sing with words or neutral syllables such as "loo." Sustain pitches in middle register. Imitate sounds. Generate new ideas.
Six to eighteen months	Differentiates between pitch contours. Sensitive to phrase endings and intervals.	Continue vocal play. Sing nursery songs and other simple songs from child's culture. Play recorded music.
Eighteen months to four years	Able to recognize familiar phrases and songs based on contour and rhythm. Increased ability to replicate familiar material. More attention to absolute value of pitches than to relative value. Sensitivity to phrase, shown through movement.	Sing many songs with children. Engage in vocal play, extending the range upward and downward. Add words to vocal play upward and downward and high and low to match pitch patterns. Experiment with keyboards and computer programs that reinforce contour and pattern discrimination skills. Show contour and phrase with bodies.
Four to eight years (kindergarten to grade three)	Beginning to conceptualize aspects of pitch and melody such as high and low, upward and downward. Able to demonstrate this knowledge first (age four to five) through showing and later (age five to six) through telling. Sensitivity to intervals and to tonality emerges. Continued development of phrase as unit.	Provide many opportunities through singing, movement, use of bells, and use of computer programs to demonstrate pitch concepts and contours. Have children vocally supply endings to familiar songs. Help them add musical vocabulary to describe melodic events. Respond to phrase endings.
Eight to twelve years (grades three to six)	Can identify discrete aspects of pitch motion such as steps, leaps, and repeated tones. Perceives patterns moving downward most easily—later moving upward. Recognition of melodic sequence. Can build concepts of scale and mode around age ten to eleven.	Continue to build experience with melodies through singing, shaping through movement, and playing instruments. Add reading of contours and patterns using precise notation.

patterns or "I know that song!" or "I don't know it" in response to questions regarding the familiarity of various songs. Preschool-aged children usually show their recognition of familiar songs simply by joining in and singing along. Around the age of three, children may recognize that the contours of familiar songs are the same, for example, "The Alphabet Song," "Baa, Baa Black Sheep," and "Twinkle, Twinkle Little Star." And, as children between ages four and seven develop relational concepts such as high and low, they can begin to describe the movement of contours and the relationship among different pitches (see Music Example 6.1).

The activities in Box 6.1 are designed to increase children's sensitivity to pitch differences and melodic contour through active experimentation and discovery. Although these are being presented in separate categories of singing, playing, moving, listening, and creating, most children will benefit from multiple approaches. These percepts are basic to the formation of other pitch understandings and need to be developed regardless of the age of the child.

Kodály and his proponents adapted John Curwen's (and Sarah Glover's) nineteenth-century British hand sign system. The technique illustrates the power of a combined perceptual approach for pitch development. In this system, each pitch of the diatonic scale is associated with a

MUSIC EXAMPLE 6.1

Finding Repeated Patterns in Songs

Old John the Rabbit
(African American Singing Game)

Reproduced with permission from *World of Music*, Grade 1 (Parsippany, NJ: Silver Burdett Ginn, 1992).

Box 6.1 *Age-Appropriate Activities in Pitch Discrimination and Contour*

MODE	AGES FOUR TO EIGHT	AGES NINE TO TWELVE
Singing	Learn more songs to use as images of shapes and patterns. Echo different shapes with voice or kazoo. Find repeated patterns in songs —"Old John the Rabbit" (Music Example 6.1).	Sing many songs Signal when all voices match pitch. Sing familiar songs or patterns on "loo" and identify them from their contours.
Moving	Shape contour with hands or bodies as children listen or sing—add flashlight for variety. Learn Kodály-Curwen hand signs; practice and identify patterns from hand signs.	Take aural dictation of different melodic shapes by listening, then moving using either levels or Kodály-Curwen hand signs; discover those patterns in songs.
Playing	Have children generate contour at keyboard that teacher imitates— label *same*; then teacher plays contrast—label *different*. Play single pitch, see if child can match it on another instrument; expand to two, three, and four pitches.	Echo—play individual pitches or melodic contours by ear on keyed percussion instruments or soprano recorders or both.
Listening	Play two pitches or contours, children show palms down if same and palms sideways if different.	Listen to melodies on recordings. Shape with body or hand signs or trace on paper.
Reading	Present children with various visuals of melodic curves. Have them sing or play. Have several children hold a long rope with both hands and shape a melody by raising or lowering hands. Use computer software programs that connect sight and sound: *Music Ace I*; *Making Music I*; *Thinkin' Things I* and *II*.	Give children tracing paper to place over melodies in books. Have them connect the notes in a dot-to-dot fashion. Discuss contours. Place melodies of familiar songs on bulletin board or overhead—see how quickly children can name the tune from the contour. Use software programs that connect sight and sound: *Music Ace I* and *II*; *Making Music II*; *Musica Practica*. (See music printing programs in Chapter 14.)
Creating	Improvise a short piece on keyed percussion, taking melodic contours and displacing them. Compose using software *Making Music I*.	Compose a piece using contrasting contours jagged or smooth. Compose a piece using a skyline of a city or mountain for a contour.

hand sign (see Figure 6.1). Children use simultaneously the visual, auditory, and kinesthetic modalities as they respond to individual pitches, pitch motion, interval relations, and melodic contours. This system encourages children to use the hand signs when they sing out loud or to themselves and to model aural perception of various melodic and harmonic events in music.

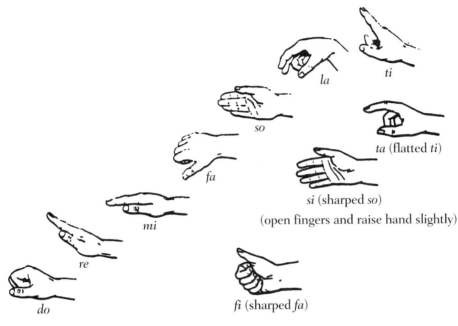

Reproduced with permission from Choksy (1981).

Figure 6.1

Kodály-Curwen Hand Signs

Children creating string melody

Pitch Relations and Melodic Motion

Around the age of four, most children begin to demonstrate the ability to categorize specific aspects of pitch as being relatively the same. For example, they might group three relatively high pitches together and two relatively low pitches together. Or, they might recognize that two melodic contours are the same even though they use different pitches to shape them. Often it is easier for them to demonstrate their understandings through pointing, grouping, or playing than through telling.

The words *high* and *low* or *up* and *down*, when applied to pitch, are confusing to young children. Because pitches are not high or low acoustically and because most keyboards are presented to children on a horizontal plane, children are understandably confused by the vocabulary used to discuss pitch. In addition, the words *up* and *down* are often used to talk about volume as well as pitch; for example, "Turn down the TV, it's too loud!" Finally, pitch notation is an arbitrary system that is often confusing for learners, because it places pitches in a two-dimensional visual plane that does not match the acoustic sense perceivers have of pitch.

Teachers and parents wishing to help children apply terminology correctly should use words such as *upward* or *downward* and moving *higher* or *lower* to describe pitch motion. Other strategies, using step bells, slide whistles, movement, and vertically oriented xylophones, may also help. Ultimately, because music is more than pitches in isolation, it is desirable to present children with patterns taken from melodies of familiar songs and instrumental works to build their sense of pitch relations.

Box 6.2 gives strategies and age-appropriate activities designed to help children form concepts about discrete aspects of pitch relations such as high and low; upward and downward; stepwise, leaping, or repeating mo-

Children with step bells and vertical glockenspiel

tion; and small, medium, or large intervals. Singing, moving, and playing instruments provide the most concrete means of experiencing pitch relations. Listening and reading involve greater intellectual abstraction, and creating allows children to synthesize the new understandings they have developed.

Box 6.2 *Age-Appropriate Activities in Pitch Register, Motion, and Interval Size*

MODE	AGES FOUR TO EIGHT	AGES NINE TO TWELVE
Singing	Have children imitate high and low sounds—sing songs with exaggerated differences of high and low. Sing scale songs and describe upward and downward motion. Develop a sense of interval size and melodic motion through use of Curwen hand signs.	Sing upward-moving passages of a familiar song out loud and downward-moving passages internally. Use words *upward* and *downward* and *high* and *low* to describe passages in songs. Sing songs with various kinds of motion. Discuss effect of size of leaps, steps, repeated tones.
Moving	Make high or low motions in response to individual pitches or pitches embedded in songs. Move gradually upward and downward to glissandi and scale songs.	Walk forward if melody moves upward, backward if melody moves downward, and step in place when it repeats. Refine by stepping if melody steps and leaping if melody leaps.
Playing	Place "lower <—> higher" on body of keyed instruments. Have children play high, medium, and low sounds in response to cues. Suspend a small xylophone vertically on pegboard, high pitches on top; connect with staff notation. Use step bells to reinforce sense of upward and downward movement. Play various kinds of patterns—stepping, leaping, repeating—to accompany songs.	Experiment with tuning bottles in a stepwise tuning. Color cold water and use to accompany various patterns in songs or to play ear tunes. Notate using colors. As children are preparing to play various ostinati, bourdon, and other accompaniment patterns, discuss the movement of the patterns and the relative size of the intervals.
Listening	Show upward motion by pointing upward; downward by pointing downward; and repeated tones with palm flat, facing floor. Circle iconic patterns on response sheets that represent different kinds of melodic motion: a) ↗ b) ↘ c) ↗↘ d) ↘↗	Learn to identify melodic patterns within recorded works; read and play or sing them first, then identify them. Select patterns on response sheet as numbers are called while listening to: a) b)

(Continued)

Box 6.2 (*Continued*)

MODE	AGES FOUR TO EIGHT	AGES NINE TO TWELVE
Reading	Make a score out of dots at various levels in different patterns; have children play on keyboard: Show pitch motion and intervals on a hand staff (palm facing chest) or by placing buttons on a paper staff.	Work with software programs to practice the various concepts (see Chapter 14). Notate or highlight various repeated note, stepping, and leaping patterns. Play on keyed percussion instrument. Begin to associate staff locations and pitch names.
Creating	Create a high and low contrast piece; record it and add movement to it. Experiment with how to create glissandi on various instruments. Create a piece for glissandi using various tone colors.	Have children notate a melody as if on a walk, incorporating steps, leaps, and repeats. (Notation could resemble a map.) Perform pieces on pitched instruments.

Advanced Pitch Concepts

Around the age of six or seven, children begin to develop a clear sense of tonality, or that a piece of music is centered within a logical system and moves within that system to a final point of resolution or rest. They bring to this an already developing sense of melodic phrase (music is expressed in a series of ideas that have a sense of completeness).

These percepts can be developed into concepts during the primary grades. Then, in combination with concepts of melodic motion, they can be refined into more specific concepts regarding pitch organization during the intermediate years. These concepts include:

1. Scale—the underlying set of tones for a melody. It is from the Latin word *scala*, which means ladder or stairs. Scales use specific intervals as they rise and fall. The size of those intervals varies with the type of scale and the tuning systems used in the culture in which it occurs.

2. Major and Minor Modes—the two most commonly used modes in the Western tradition. They are distinguished by a difference in the treatment of the third and sixth tones of the scale. Each is used for different musical effects.

The major scale consists of stepwise intervals in the pattern of:

The minor scale pattern is:

3. **Melodic Sequence**—a short melodic pattern repeated at different pitch levels. It is used as a forming device for building melodies.

The activities in Box 6.3 suggest concrete ways of involving children with these ideas. Because many of these activities are dependent on understanding of and experience with foundation concepts, the preponderance of the activities are geared toward the older elementary child. Many of the activities listed here for children aged four to eight could be adapted for older children if necessary.

Box 6.3 *Age-Appropriate Activities in Tonality, Phrase, Scale, and Sequence*

MODE	AGES FOUR TO EIGHT	AGES NINE TO TWELVE
Singing	Ask children to supply the final note of both familiar and unfamiliar songs; label that as the home tone; note the strength of the home tone in scale songs. Have groups of children sing alternating phrases in a song; identify as phrases.	Learn to shape phrases expressively, discuss various effects. Using familiar songs, notice differences between strong and weak phrase endings. Sing a given song in a major key and then a minor key; discuss differences. Sing songs in other scales: pentatonic, whole tone, chromatic. Discover sequences in melodic patterns; assign singing of each to different groups.
Moving	Move around the room to a melody, coming to rest at the final point. Use arms, scarves, or streamers to shape phrases in air. Move in style to song, changing direction at end of phrases.	Choreograph various phrases in recorded music; if phrase repeats, repeat movements. Learn Kodály-Curwen hand signs for scales; note relationship of minor half step to other tones; discover whole- and half-step differences in major and minor scales. Move major and minor scales through room taking full step on whole step and smaller step on half step; sing or play scales while moving. Move sequential patterns with body in space; alternate with a partner.

(Continued)

Box 6.3 (*Continued*)

MODE	AGES FOUR TO EIGHT	AGES NINE TO TWELVE
Playing	In songs with equal phrase length, play finger cymbals to highlight end of each phrase. Give each child a set of diatonic octave bells; have them play the tonal center in tonic-oriented songs. Have children play the final phrase of songs on keyed instruments; relate sense of close to tonal center.	Highlight phrases by playing contrasting rhythm instruments on beat or melodic rhythm. Learn to play major and minor scale patterns on piano, chromatic bells, or synthesizer. Begin with C Major and A natural minor; transpose patterns to other starting points; improvise within those scales. Play handbell or tone bell to highlight beginning of each occurrence of a melodic sequence.
Listening	Trace phrases on paper while listening to recorded works, compare lengths.	Using randomly ordered pitches from the C Major scale, give one tone bell and mallet to each of eight children. Line them up and have them play. Encourage other children to place them in correct order to form a human scale; play scale song. Use human scale to add black keys, and discover whole and half-step relationships for both major and minor scales.
Reading	Find beginning and ending pitches in songs that end on do; develop understanding that most songs move toward tonal center at ending though they may not begin there. Discover repeating and contrasting phrases in songs by looking at notation; listen to confirm perception.	Take melodic dictation for phrases using Kodály techniques. Help children associate different tonal centers with different scales and different keys. Give pairs of children a familiar melody and some staff paper; extract the various pitches from the melody and notate them; discover whether the melody uses all of the pitches of the scale on which it was based. Highlight melodic sequences on score.
Creating	Once children become aware of tonal center, challenge them to end vocal or instrumental improvisations on do. Improvise in call-and-response form across an eight-beat phrase.	Improvise using various scales structured on Orff instruments. Using a chromatic instrument, invent a scale and compose a four-measure melody using it. Compose a piece using melodic sequences as a structural device; try inverting them for variety.

Growth in Understanding
of Vertical Pitch Structures

Musically perceptive listeners are not only aware of what is occurring melodically in music. They also are aware that sounds occur simultaneously and that those vertical arrangements of sound result in something called harmony. This harmony can be created by a combination of independent melodic lines (polyphonic texture) or a stacking of pitches (homophonic texture). The progression of harmonies through a piece of music and the choice of harmonic colors create various feelings of tension and release in the listener.

Once again, this awareness builds gradually and is influenced by the cultural and stylistic norms for what constitutes agreeable and disagreeable combinations of sounds and sequences of those combinations. Table 6.2 describes the course of that growth based on current research (see Colwell, 1992; Peery, Peery, and Draper, 1987; Hargreaves, 1986; and Serafine, 1988).

Box 6.4 suggests a range of ideas for the development of percepts and concepts related to harmony and texture. As in Box 6.2, the majority of the activities are aimed at older children. Many of the activities for younger children can be adapted and used with older children as necessary.

TABLE 6.2 *Children's Harmonic Development and Teachers' Guidance*

AGE	PERCEPT AND CONCEPT	TEACHER ACTIONS
Five to seven (kindergarten to grade one)	Developing sensitivity to relation between melody and harmony—harmonic fit. Small number of children beginning to notice separate vertical events. May perceptually combine two pitches into one.	Help children distinguish between accompanied and nonaccompanied music. Ask children to indicate when chords need to change as accompaniment to a melody.
Eight to ten (grades two to four)	Stronger ability to notice numbers of vertical events. Beginning to sense closed or strong and open or weak cadences	Build triads and add to songs. Sing songs with combined lines such as ostinatos and rounds. Add Autoharp accompaniments to songs.
Eleven to twelve (grades five to six)	Able to correctly identify number of simultaneous events. Clear sense of strong and weak cadence. Can harmonize accurately by ear.	Keep refining perception of simultaneous sounds through listening. Have them use simultaneous sounds and cadences creatively. Give students melodies to harmonze with basic chords.

Numerous resources offer additional strategies to develop pitch awareness. Ideas on how to reinforce children's perceptions and build them into concepts can be found in Edelstein et al. (1980), Findlay (1971), Mead (1994), Steen (1992), and Aaron (1976), as well as many contemporary music series texts. Materials to implement multicultural strategies can be found in Anderson and Campbell (1996) and Jessup (1992). Strategies that extend to creative application of pitch concepts can be found in Thomas (1970), Schafer (1976), and Paynter and Aston (1971).

Helping Children to Think Musically

Research in pitch perception clearly shows that people develop sensitivities to pitch and pitch structures as a natural part of responding cognitively to the music that surrounds them. The challenge for the teacher is to build on these percepts and expand them into conscious concepts that can be applied through a lifetime of musical experiences.

As teachers strive to make musical learning meaningful, they need to be selective, choosing activities that will stimulate musical growth. However, any activity, done in isolation, runs the risk of simply filling time in interesting or not-so-interesting ways. A well-developed series of strategies

Box 6.4 *Age-Appropriate Activities in Harmony and Texture*

MODE	AGES FOUR TO EIGHT	AGES NINE TO TWELVE
Singing	Sing songs with and without Autoharp or guitar accompaniment; discuss differences.	Sing two- and three-chord songs, indicating chord changes with I, IV, or V fingers or root of chord with hand sign.
	Age seven and beyond: sing vocal ostinati to accompany songs; keep track of lines.	Sing songs that alternate strong and weak cadences; discuss differences.
		Sing rounds in two, three, and four parts; tape and listen to differences in texture.
		Add vocal chording on I, IV, and V chords to accompany songs.
Moving	With a two-chord song, move through general space, changing direction when chords change.	Make up different movements, alone or with a partner, to show I, IV, and V chords; move in response to music.
		Choreograph the melody of a round with simple movements; perform the song and movements in a round; note layers.
		Learn to lead two-part singing with Kodály-Curwen hand signs.

Box 6.4 (*Continued*)

MODE	AGES FOUR TO EIGHT	AGES NINE TO TWELVE
Playing	Have children accompany songs with Autoharp, bell chords, or automatic chords on a synthesizer; begin with one-chord songs and move to two-chord songs in which they identify changes by ear. Accompany melodies with ostinati, bourdons, or descants; discuss texture and harmony.	Accompany songs using chords on Autoharps, bells, or keyboards by ear and then by sight. Play two-, three-, and four-part rounds on recorders or pitched percussion; discuss textures created. Build triads on every pitch of the diatonic scale; identify them as major or minor. Learn the chord progression for a favorite pop tune or twelve-bar blues, play to accompany songs. Learn to perform various African rhythm complexes with rhythmic percussion instruments such as from Ghana or on xylophones such as the Mandinka would play; discuss textures created by layers.
Listening	Age six or seven on: listen as teacher sings a song with a harmonic accompaniment; raise hands to indicate when chords need to change.	While listening, mark beats to a song with pens, changing colors when the chords change or hold up different color cards as chords change (that is, red = tonic, blue = dominant, yellow = subdominant). In a small group, develop a listening map to show the overlapping lines of a polyphonic work; check the map against the music.
Reading	Age seven and up: learn to track chord changes in music while playing an accompaniment.	Follow the relationship of lines in a two-line polyphonic piece on listening map, and later with music. Learn to build root-position triads using buttons on a paper staff.
Creating	Improvise an accompaniment to a pentatonic melody on an Orff-keyed percussion instrument	Improvise an accompaniment using broken chords. Using the pentatonic scale, compose a piece for three different melodies that are layered to create various textures. Compose a piece for chords, experimenting with different progressions and rhythms; use different instruments for variety; start with root position triads, later add sevenths, ninths, or elevenths.

involves a variety of modes: singing, moving, playing, listening, reading, and creating. Discussion and reflection will also be a regular part of the process of learning. Strategies carefully selected, ordered, and implemented across time, at levels appropriate to a child's development, have a much greater likelihood of expanding the ability of children to think about music.

REVIEW

1. What is the difference between a percept and a concept? How are the two related?

2. At what point are children developmentally ready to explore ideas related to tonality? What are some ways to reinforce that perception?

3. At what point can children accurately perceive the number of simultaneous sounds in a piece of music? What kinds of tasks might you create to test that ability?

CRITICAL THINKING

1. If children automatically gain perceptions of pitch and pitch structures as a result of growing up in a musically rich environment, why should parents and teachers devote time to expanding those perceptions? List three reasons.

2. Why is it important to have a developmental perspective, beginning from the early childhood years, regarding what children are capable of perceiving? What meaning might that have for an elementary general music specialist?

PROJECTS

1. Create music manipulatives such as a dowel staff or magnet board that you can use with children to reinforce various musical concepts.

2. Using the model of moving from concrete activities of singing, moving, and playing instruments to more abstract experiences of listening, reading, and creating, plan a series of activities to teach and extend the concept of upward and downward pitch motion to second-grade children. Work in a team to plan the activities. Use music series texts as basic resources. Feel free to go beyond those sources as needed.

3. Select a perceptual task that children should be able to perform at the age indicated in this chapter. Work with another person to devise a way to test whether children have that percept or concept. Implement this test with at least five children to determine where they are developmentally. Bring your results back to class and present your discoveries.

4. Select an activity or a series of activities from this chapter designed to expand understanding of pitch and implement them with children. Modify them as necessary to fit the unique needs of the children involved.

5. Review some of the musical activities suggested in Anderson and Campbell (1994). Select two that could be used to develop pitch related concepts. List what those concepts are.

6. In one of the books on musical creativity listed in the references, find a strategy related to pitch development and implement it with children.

REFERENCES

Aaron, T., ed. (1976). *Musicbook O.* St. Louis: Magnamusic-Baton.

Anderson, W. M., and P. S. Campbell, eds. (1996). *Multicultural perspectives in music education* (2nd ed.). Reston, VA: Music Educators National Conference.

Choksy, L. (1981). *The Kodály context.* Englewood Cliffs, NJ: Prentice-Hall.

Colwell, R., ed. (1992). Section D: Perception and cognition. In *Handbook of research on music teaching and learning.* New York: Schirmer Books.

Edelstein, S., L. Choksy, P. Lehman, N. Sigurdsson, and D. Woods (1980). *Creating curriculum in music.* Menlo Park, CA: Addison-Wesley.

Findlay, E. (1971). *Rhythm and movement.* Evanston, IL: Summy-Birchard.

Hargreaves, D. J. (1986). *The developmental psychology of music.* Cambridge, England: Cambridge University.

Jessup, L. (1992). *World music: A source book for teaching.* Danbury, CT: World Music Press.

Mead, V. H. (1994) *Dalcroze eurhythmics in today's classroom.* NY: Schott.

Paynter, J., and P. Aston (1971). *Sound and silence.* Cambridge, England: Cambridge University.

Peery, J. C., I. W. Peery, and T. W. Draper, eds. (1987). *Music and child development.* New York: Springer-Verlag.

Schafer, R. M. (1976). *Creative music education.* New York: Schirmer Books.

Serafine, M. L. (1988). *Music as cognition.* New York: Columbia University.

Steen, A. (1992). *Exploring Orff: A teacher's guide.* NY: Schott.

Thomas, R. (1970). *Manhattanville Music Curriculum Project (MMCP) synthesis.* Bardonia, NY: Media Materials.

7

The Singing Child

For the child, to sing is to turn interests, experiences, and feelings into a personal musical expression. Kimberly sings about flowers, David about trains, and Tony about lions, bears, dogs, and dragons. Michelle chants with Rosalita and Candy the songs of their hand-clapping games. Robert and Charoen trade songs they learned at church and in the temple, making up new words and tunes as they sing them. Lonnie sings before sleep, while Tuyen invents new tunes in the morning. Diana sings to the wind's drone, her head leaning out of the window of her father's car. Wayne mixes singing with lip-syncing all the latest tunes on MTV. Heather eagerly awaits her weekly choir rehearsals, while Marla sings her solos like the singing star she dreams of being.

The sounds of singing children can bring joy to those who listen, for these sounds emanate from their childlike thoughts and experiences. The quality of children's voices reflects a combined innocence, playfulness, and energy that befits them. Children sing alone and together, with and without the accompaniment of instruments or the electronic media of tapes, television, and radio. They sing spontaneously and often without knowing it—at meals, while walking to school, and in the middle of an independent school project. As they imitate and personalize the songs they have heard, children bring joy to themselves as well as to those who listen.

In today's high-tech societies, some may say that the singing child is an anachronism—a symbol of days gone by. Some may believe that "children would rather be entertained than to entertain" themselves and others by singing, that "boys beyond grade two do not sing," and that "folk song singing has been replaced by rock song shouting." This gloom-and-doom perspective can discourage teachers and parents who recall their own active childhoods as singers and who wish to incorporate songs within the learning experiences of children.

Are children singing less (and less well) in the contemporary world of high-tech media? While the media may appear to pacify children as they entertain them, children begin to sing at or before the stage at which they acquire speech—at a time before they may even be attracted to the media. It follows that children will continue singing when given opportunities to do so. Away from their tapes and television, they sing a great deal. Teachers and parents can provide occasions for singing—before classes and assemblies, at the start and close of the school day, after dinner, before bedtime, or while camping, walking, or riding in the car or on the bus. These are the times for singing favorite songs as well as for learning new ones. As for the media, rather than reducing children's singing, radio, recordings, and television may be stimulating their songfulness as well as adding to their repertoire (Campbell, 1998).

What Every Young American Should Know and Be Able to Do in the Arts: National Standards for Arts Education describes singing as primary content in a sequential program of study (MENC, 1994). From kindergarten through the elementary grades, children can develop the skills to sing independently and together, on pitch and in rhythm, with appropriate timbre, diction, and posture. With the appropriate instruction, children in the elementary grades learn to sing expressively with regard to the appropriate use of dynamics, phrasing, and interpretation. Further, children should be singing a varied repertoire of songs representing genres and styles from diverse cultures, and they should progress from singing melodies with simple ostinatos to rounds and canons. These goals are attainable by children when led by trained music teachers in programs with instruction that is thorough and consistent.

Singing is a phenomenon for all ages, times, and cultures, but it begins and is nurtured in childhood. Children's vocal development can be greatly enhanced through training. The teacher who understands the physiology and capabilities of the young voice will select an appropriate repertoire and instructional techniques for children from preschool through the elementary grades. Contrary to the myth that singing lessons should begin in or after adolescence, vocal technique can be taught from the earliest ages by knowledgeable teachers.

The Developing Child Voice

As early as infancy, as children begin to discover their vocal capabilities, they are making musical sounds. Playfully, they explore sounds with the vowels and consonants that they have heard before, extending their duration, repeating them rhythmically, and in rising and falling pitch passages. Like the babbling that precedes speech, musical babbling is the vocalization that precedes the performance of melodies (Moog, 1976). As they toddle toward two years, children progress in their vocalizations, producing increasingly longer melodic phrases spontaneously. While young children may seldom use words in their spontaneous songs, they string nonsense syllables together in small intervals of seconds and thirds. By the age of three, children begin to develop the periodic accents of regular rhythmic patterns in their spontaneous songs, and slightly larger intervals may occur. Besides their own invented songs, children reproduce the short songs of nursery rhymes and childhood chants at this age, including the simple movements associated with them. An outline of children's vocal development can be found in Table 7.1. See also Music Example 7.1.

Children four and five years of age begin to discover the difference between their singing and speaking voices. Their singing may shift from a light, airy sound to a playground yell for lively songs. While their spontaneous singing may span nearly two octaves, the range at which they can sing accurately in tune may extend only five pitches, from d to a. As children learn new songs, they progress through five stages, reproducing the words, the rhythm of the words, a general but inaccurate sense of the melody's contour, a more accurate sense of individual pitches within the melody, and the tonality of the song across all its phrases. They learn songs through imitation of a model and require the teacher's step-by-step guidance toward more accurate reproduction.

As children learn to sing a repertoire of songs, they also acquire rhythmic and melodic fragments that spill into their own musical play and invented songs. In many Western cultures, children through the elementary grades may incorporate in their invented songs the descending minor third often accompanied by a fourth.

"Rain, Rain Go Away" and "Little Sally Walker" are examples of Western traditional children's songs that feature this common melodic pattern. However, it may be premature to suggest that, despite its frequent presence, the minor third is the first or most frequent interval to emerge in children's vocalizations, especially before systematic study of children in other world cultures has been undertaken. As children in the West gain exposure to popular music, the songs they strive to sing and create anew may contain the syncopated rhythms and the melodic patterns characteristic of the popular sound. Similarly, children's extended experience with any other musical style is likely to influence their accumulated repertoire and to flavor their musical expressions.

Children in the primary grades are more apt to sing in tune than younger children. Their singing range widens from C to b for six-year-olds to about an octave by second grade, from C to d′, and from about B♭ to e♭′ by third grade. Their tessitura, or the average range in which most pitches of a song lie, is somewhat smaller. So although children are capable of a larger vocal range, songs that linger on the lowest to highest pitches should be

TABLE 7.1 *Children's Vocal Development*

AGE	DEVELOPMENTAL ACTIVITY
Less than one	Vocalizes (babbles) vowels and consonants
One to two	Babbles in irregular rhythmic patterns
	Imitates the contour of songs' melodic phrases, but not discrete pitches
Two	Babbles in extended melodic phrases
	Babbles in small intervals of seconds, thirds
	Imitates occasional discrete pitches of songs
Three	Invents spontaneous songs with discrete pitches and recurring rhythmic and melodic patterns
	Reproduces nursery rhymes and childhood chants
Four to five (kindergarten)	Discovers differences between speaking and singing voices
	Shifts song qualities from light and airy to the playground yell for lively songs
	Sings spontaneous songs spanning two octaves
	Sings in tune within range of five pitches, d to a
Six to seven (grade one)	Sings in tune in range of C to b, with smaller tessitura
	Can begin to develop head voice, with guidance
	Begins to have expressive control of voice
Seven to eight (grade two)	Sings in tune in range of octave, about C to c' or d to d', with smaller tessitura
Eight to nine (grade three)	Sings in tune in range of B♭ to e♭', with smaller tessitura
	Can perform fundamental harmony songs such as melody over vocal ostinato or sustained pitch
Nine to ten (grade four)	Sings in tune in range of A to e', with smaller tessitura
	Sings with increasing resonance (grades four, five, and six)
	May experience first vocal change (boys, beginning age ten)
	Can perform canons, rounds, descants, countermelodies
	Can sing with appropriate phrasing, with guidance
Ten to eleven (grade five)	Sings in tune in range of A♭ to f', with C to c' octave tessitura
	Is increasingly selective of song repertoire
	Prefers songs in middle range
	Prefers songs without sentimental or babyish texts
	Can perform two-part songs
Eleven to twelve (grade six)	Sings in tune in range of G to g', with C to c' octave tessitura
	Can perform three-part songs

Note: c = middle c; c' = one octave higher; C = one octave lower than middle c.

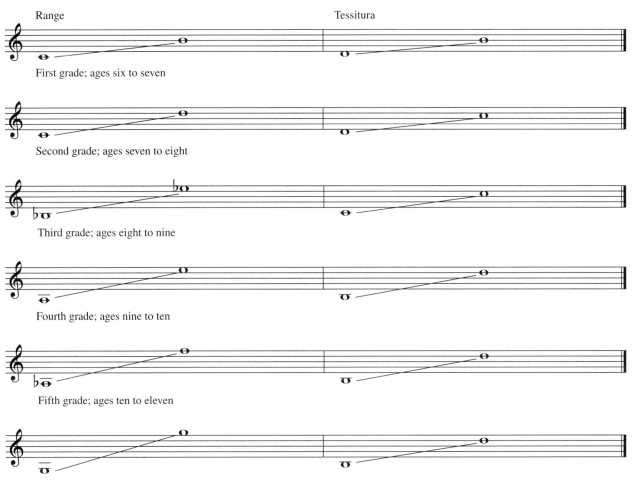

Range and Tessitura for Children's Voices, Ages Six to Twelve

avoided. Children may continue to sing as they do at play, in their lower chest range, unless their head voice is developed—particularly through pitch-matching exercises. The use of a pure neutral syllable such as "loo" will assist children in concentrating on appropriate vocal production through their ranges.

At eight years (or by second grade), children are likely to be able to maintain the same tonality throughout a song. As their musical memory increases, they are able to learn longer and more complex songs. By the age of nine, children may succeed at performing fundamental harmony songs—those with a recurring vocal ostinato, or sustained sounds overlapped by moving melodies. Their need for socialization with friends may nurture their interest in singing with others, while at the same time their perceptual development offers them a greater awareness of blending their voices with the ensemble of singers.

In the intermediate grades, when children are showing signs of rapid physical development, their voices are also affected by the maturation process. Their singing quality is fuller and more resonant in the fourth, fifth, and sixth grades than in the primary grades, although some children may feel more self-conscious about singing (especially solos) and thus may sound softer and lighter than their full-volumed capacity. The range of children's voices before the first changes that accompany adolescence typically spans from A to e' for fourth graders, from A♭ to f' for fifth graders, and from G to g' for sixth graders. The tessitura for children ten through twelve years may be limited to about one octave. Some boys will experience a first vocal change by age ten or eleven, although others will sing well into early adolescence with a robust yet pure quality unmatched by children at any other age.

Children begin to manifest the signs of physiological and psychological changes typical of adolescence by the close of their elementary years. Unless they are accustomed to singing, they may lose interest and resist any occasion to sing. While in some societies singing is an act of great pride that brings on admiration by members of the opposite sex, in American schools it is not unusual to find girls who are embarrassed to sing in front of boys and boys who view singing as a feminine or at least a less virile activity. To many children on the brink of adolescence singing is no longer cool. Maintaining children's interest in singing requires a careful selection of songs with texts that are meaningful to them (and not too sentimental or babyish), with melodic ranges well within the safety of their tessitura.

The changing male voice is a symptom of the hormonal changes that begin to occur at the onset of puberty. When boys show a sudden growth spurt and a physical awkwardness, they may also demonstrate a heavier quality as they speak and sing. Their voices may occasionally crack as they reach beyond their middle range. While experts vary somewhat in their approaches to boys' changing voices, most recommend singing within the middle and most comfortable section of their range and avoiding register extremes.

As children come to understand the vocal mechanism, they are better able to use their voices productively. Children in the intermediate grades also are capable of performing with appropriate phrasing, diction, and intonation—all important facets of choral singing. Because they can perceive more than one simultaneously occurring musical line at a time, and because their voices are stronger and more independent than earlier, they can sing in harmony the rounds, partner songs, and part-songs that comprise the repertoire of children's choirs. As they mature, children are able to sing expressively and to evaluate their own musical and vocal performance in terms of accuracy and appropriate tone, blend, and style.

Physical Training for the Child Voice

Beyond the natural development that occurs from preschool through the elementary grades, children's voices can be greatly enhanced through training. This is not to say that private singing lessons are advisable for children; lessons may best be reserved for the later years of adolescence and adulthood when vocal development is complete. The astute teacher, however, who knows and provides occasions for exercising children's voices through songs, vocal games, and drills, will quicken the pace of development and extend the capacity for musical expression. Daily or even twice-weekly "group sings" will undoubtedly create more musical singers at an earlier age.

Perfect singing posture, or PSP, is prerequisite to gaining good breath control, producing a beautiful tone, and phrasing a set of tones expressively (see Box 7.1). Although they are physically active and seldom sedentary, children require regular coordination, conditioning, and postural-development exercises. Imagery and exercise (instead of verbal explanations) can lead to the correct stance (or sitting position) for singing.

One of the most complete means for attaining appropriate alignment of the body parts for PSP is the image and imitation of a marionette puppet. Children begin this exercise by standing tall and imagining that there are two strings attached to them—from the ceiling to the bottom of their back and to the top of their head. An invisible puppeteer loosens the string, and the children drop from their waist, with heads and arms hanging down past their knees, to the floor. In that position, they gently bounce. When the puppeteer begins to pull at the strings, the marionette children slowly rise and realign themselves: chest, shoulders, neck, head, and arms fall relaxedly into place.

PSP can be achieved in a sitting, as well as standing, position. The alignment of the middle- and upper-body transfers from standing to sitting positions. Children on chairs should sit on the front half of the seats with

Perfect singing posture (PSP)

Box 7.1 *Perfect Singing Posture*

Perfect singing posture (PSP) involves bottom-to-top body parts. Here are some suggestions for how to achieve the correct position.

1. Feet should be flat on the floor, about six inches apart, with one foot slightly ahead of the other. The weight is on the balls (not the heels) of the feet. Practice in shifting the weight from heels to toes will bring about an awareness of where the weight should be.

2. Knees need to be relaxed and not locked. A light bouncing in place, one knee alternating with the other, and then both knees, can eliminate tightness and tension.

3. The spine is to be lifted up and away from the hips. It should be straight but not stiff. Leading with the arms extended, and hands clasped backward, a spinal stretch can extend down to the toes, outward from the chest to the front, right, and left sides, and then high above the head. A return back to center will move the spine gently into place.

4. The chest should be slightly raised. Movement of the arms in a circular breast-stroke gesture from the middle of the chest to above the head and down to the side can loosen yet also coordinate the musculature of the chest, rib cage, lungs, and sternum.

5. Shoulders are held back slightly and down. Shoulder rolls are helpful: Rotation of the shoulders forward, down, and up will decrease tension; the reverse movement (backward, down, and up again) can also be helpful.

6. The head is held high, as it rises up out of the spine and neck and rests level and well aligned. Head rolls achieve this position, by dropping the head to the chest, rolling it to one side and then the other.

7. Arms and hands should hang easily down at the sides. This can be achieved at the end of the spinal stretch or breast-stroke gesture, although attention may need to be called to the position of the arms and hands.

their feet flat on the floor. For those whose feet do not touch the floor, they should sit further back on the seats while hooking their feet on the front rung of the chair. Children who sit on the floor can be coaxed to cross their legs, raise themselves out of their hips, and lean slightly forward. No one position should be maintained for too long a time; standing and sitting positions can be taken alternately throughout a singing session.

Breathing for singing is similar to breathing for high-endurance sports such as swimming and long-distance running. Children are intrigued when they discover the physicality of good singing and the parallel of singing to athletic endeavors. With perfect singing posture, their bodies are readied for the deep breathing that must initiate and sustain the vocal sound. The image of filling the feet, the knees, the stomach, and the diaphragm (and the lungs) with air shows how complete and all-encompassing the breathing must be. Children can come to understand that as they fill themselves with the air of a very deep breath, their lower rib cage expands along with their lungs. Like a balloon or a bagpipe, they have the air within them that can be

Jerry Gay

moved up the windpipe and across the vocal cords causing vibration to occur and sound to be produced.

Breathing exercises should precede singing activity. Children can take in air as they would sip soda through a straw: With puckered lips, they slowly sip the air in a manner similar to drinking. Because sipping is an easy and gentle action, there should be no tension in the exercise. Taking the image of the balloon, children can compare the expansion of their own lungs to the fullness of a blown balloon. They can imitate the roundness of a balloon as they breathe in through their mouths, their arms curved in front of them, fingers touching. The more air they inhale, the wider the balloon becomes; their arms move out more widely so that their fingers can no longer touch. As air in a balloon is slowly released, they can slowly release air without producing a vocal sound, and their fingers touch again. The inhaling and exhaling process can challenge children physically, especially when the appropriate vocal sound to which the exercises lead is demonstrated.

Vocal exercises that combine the inhaling, sustaining, and releasing of air develop control essential to good singing. Lesson 7.1 provides several suggestions for warming up the voice with attention to the breathing mechanism.

Toward Accurate Singing

Children who can hear and perceive melody are well equipped for singing accurately. The ability to hear is a physical endowment, but to perceive the melody of a song well enough to sing it requires focused and attentive listening.

The Ha–Ha

Imitate the quick, deep breathing of a dog panting at the end of a long and energetic run. Place the hands just under the rib cage at the diaphragm, take a deep breath, and exhale in short "ha-ha's." Breathe again, and while exhaling, sing the "ha-ha's" on one pitch. A third variation is to sing the "ha-ha's" stepwise from do to sol and back again, and then on a triadic do-mi-sol-mi-do.

The Cool "OO"

Because the *u* vowel, as sounded in *new*, resonates well and is a relaxed sound for children to produce, it is commonly used in warm-ups and tuning voices to one another. Using a descending stepwise pattern that ends in a skip of a fifth up and down, sing an "oo" sound with the letter *I* interspersed. Care should be taken not to form the lips too tightly. A relaxed and slightly dropped jaw will allow maximal air flow without changing the vowel sound.

The "No–ah's Ark"

The pure *o* as in *cold* requires the jaw to drop more than in the *u*. It should also have little of the "vanishing oo" sound of "no"; that is, "no-oo." The *a* of *father* is sounded by dropping the jaw to a space long enough to allow the insertion of two fingers vertically. A slight smile contributes to a brighter *a*, not the "uh" sound. By singing "No-ah's Ark," children exercise two distinctive positions of the mouth and thus two separate vowel and vocal sounds. A smaller- and larger-ranged version of ascending and successive thirds is appropriate for children in the primary and intermediate grades.

The "Mmmmm" on the Vowels

Using the "m" sound to lead easily to vowel sounds, sing on one pitch the vowels *i* sounded as "ee," *e* sounded as "ay," *a, o,* and *u*. The *i* is like the sound in "green" and is produced with the lips slightly puckered so that the sound does not spread too widely. The *e* is a diphthong similar to the sound in "play," with an emphasis on "eh" that closes on "ee." In this exercise, five vowels are sounded on a single pitch. The transition from the consonant *m* to each vowel and back to the consonant again should be smooth, connected, and all on one sustained breath. The exercise can be accompanied by I, IV, I, V7, I.

The Echo

The modeling of pitches and pitch patterns by a leader is then imitated by the children. In leader-follower fashion, sing patterns and phrases from familiar songs as well as those yet to be learned. Use neutral syllables such

(Continued)

as "loo," "noo," "la," and "bee" for tuning voices and solfège syllables for building understanding of pitches and their relationships.

"Tinga Layo"

loo loo loo loo   noo noo noo noo noo noo

"Little Sally Walker"

la   la   la   la   la   la
(sol sol   mi   la   sol   mi)

"Music Alone Shall Live"

bee bee bee   bee bee bee   bee bee bee   bee

The percentage of problem singers is greater now than ever before, and some children will need care and consistent instruction to become proficient singers. In order from having less to more singing skill, presingers do not sing but chant the song text, speaking-range singers sustain tones within the speaking voice range only, limited-range singers typically sing only from d to f, initial-range singers sing within a range of d to a, and full-fledged singers can sing in a range beyond the minimal register (B–d). Individual and small-group instruction via games and activities that combine singing with socializing experiences can camouflage the disciplined exercise that needs to occur to develop children's voices (Rutkowski, 1996). Patience is key, however, because an entire academic year may be necessary for more effective singing to break through and remain consistent.

Children need the teacher's direction to attend to the pitches, phrases, and contours of a melody, as well as its rhythm, text, and formal organization. Some learn best through repeated listenings alone, others learn well when visual means (including color-coded shapes, numbers, pictures, and graphs; staff notation; and the printed song words) are applied, and still others require the use of their bodies to feel the melody. One means of focusing children's listening is the use of direct questions, such as "Does the melody move mostly upward or downward?" or "Which word sounds the highest pitch of the song?"

Children can draw the melody's movement with their fingers, hands, arms, or even torso. This graphing of the melody's rise and fall is sometimes referred to as mapping. Such mapping can be broad and involve the entire body, or it can be contained within a very small space. Mapping may consist of a line drawing that moves each phrase from left to right with a finger in the air, on chalkboards with chalk, or on large pieces of paper with crayon.

Another means of directing children's attention to individual pitches and their relationships is through the use of a hand sign system first developed by Sarah Glover and John Curwen in England in the middle of the nineteenth century. The system was later popularized by proponents of the Kodály approach, and it is often referred to as Kodály hand signs (see Figure 6.1). In this system, each pitch of the diatonic scale is associated with a hand sign. Additional signs are used to indicate chromatic pitches, or accidentals outside of the song's key signature. Children can be taught the hand signs with relative ease, as they sing the pitch names of the diatonic scale or as they learn the melodic fragments and tonal phrases of the songs they know. The hand sign system is effective as a technique for teaching melodic direction and shape, and it is enjoyed by children as a game that challenges their listening, critical thinking, moving, and singing skills.

Children are more likely to sing accurately when they can discriminate among higher or lower pitches and when they are presented with occasions for reproducing short melodic phrases. Pitch matching requires not only listening perception and short-term memory skills, but also the skills of vocal production. Through a series of echo-chants built on neutral syllables, solfège syllables, or word-phrases, children can match the pitches of short melodic phrases that are sung to them. These phrases may be embedded in familiar songs, or in songs they will eventually learn to sing, or in a familiar music repertoire. These melodic phrases may also be built into conversational or dialogue phrases, in which the same pitches used for a question may be used by children in their response.

Lesson 7.2 presents a sampling of musical fragments for pitch matching, proceeding from simple to more complex content. When such phrases

LESSON 7.2 *Pitch-matching Samples*

Assorted Phrases

(Continued)

are accompanied by appropriate gestures to indicate pitch direction and pitch relationships, children may sing them with even greater accuracy.

As children develop the abilities to discriminate pitches and to sing in tune, they should also be developing tonal memory. The teacher can guide children in strengthening their tonal memory by playing "name that tune," in which they identify the title of a familiar song that is sung by the teacher or selected leader without words on a neutral syllable. Another playful approach to strengthening the memory is to lead children in singing a song, and on a prearranged cue (such as a tap on the drum) to sing silently, only to return to singing aloud when given the cue again. Children must retain a sense of pulse, tempo, and pitch while silently performing the melody so that they can join in together again when the cue is given. Tonal memory, like rhythmic memory, requires children's utmost concentration. With it, their musicianship—and their repertoire of songs—can grow.

For every phrase or song that is sung, the pitch and tempo must be set by the teacher. Children need to know on just what pitch they are to begin their singing, or all attempts at accurate singing are foiled. Familiar songs can begin with the teacher's sounding of the tonic or home tone of the song and then the 1-3-5-3-1 (d-m-s-m-d) of the key. A piano, xylophone, guitar, or other pitched instrument may be more helpful to the teacher than to the children, who may need to hear the vocally produced pitch to match it. Even in teaching individual song phrases by rote, the teacher should make a practice of sounding the first pitch, vocally, on a neutral syllable such as "loo" or "la," and then signaling the children to sing that pitch on that syllable before repeating the phrase. The pitch and tempo for familiar and new songs can be set together by conducting the meter while singing an initial phrase on the first pitch of the song. One example for pitch and tempo setting at the same time is shown in Music Example 7.2.

MUSIC EXAMPLE 7.2

Starting a Song

As children listen to song phrases and fragments, they must also strive to learn and retain their components to sing them accurately. They learn the words, rhythm, and melody of a song through repeated listening, and then by imitating the singer who serves as model for them. Young singers require far more repetition of songs and song segments than they typically receive to grasp all the musical details. For example, an eight-measure melody such as "Hey, Betty Martin" may require six or eight repetitions before a group of seven-year-olds can retain and reproduce the song with the words, melody, rhythm, and tonality intact. The teacher can sing alone while the children listen or the children can sing while following the teacher's lead. A longer and more complex song such as "Tinga Layo" may necessitate as many (or more) repetitions for a group of ten-year-olds to learn it.

Not all children sing accurately in tune, although the great majority of children are capable of it. Children who sing daily at home or in school develop in-tune singing by the end of the second grade. For those in environments without regular opportunities to listen to music and to sing, vocal troubles may require attention. Instead of labeling the uncertain singers as monotones or nonsingers, teachers may need to devise remedial exercises within class and help sessions before school, after school, or at recess. Some children need coaxing to find their singing voice, and they may need to sing close to the pitch of their speaking voice. Others need to know that it is safe to sing aloud (and possibly solo). This will entail discussing the rules of etiquette with the group while singing alone, so that all children can be helped in becoming a part of their singing team. A series of siren-like sound effects can be modeled and then imitated, to extend the range of children who drone on one or two pitches or who sing below the appropriate pitch (see Music Example 7.3).

MUSIC EXAMPLE 7.3

Extending Voice Range

The sound of a ghost is another aural image that can assist children in hearing and feeling how their voices can reach registers not usually associated with their own speaking ranges. Likewise, children can imitate the sound of "yoo-hoo" or a train whistle.

These experiences can lead to pitch-matching exercises and to songs with simple rhythms and small melodic ranges. Unless children have physiological conditions (such as damaged vocal cords or severe hearing deficits) or the rare condition known as amusia, they can learn to sing accurately. The patient teacher's knowledgeable and inventive remedies can ensure success.

The Vocal Model

Children tend to sing a song in the manner and style in which it was presented to them. Thus, the presence of an accurate vocal model is critical to the instructional process. Whether the teacher, parent, or other adult seeks to teach a song, attention must be paid to musical style and voice quality as well as to the components of the song itself. If children are to sing in a light head tone, then the song must be sung by the model in that way. If a song is to be sung with vigor at high volume, then that model should be presented. If a song is suited for a softer and slower performance, then children must hear it that way. Children will sing a song presented in legato style in that manner, just as they are likely to sing a song in as many phrases (with as many breaths) and as many accents and dynamic nuances as they hear from the model.

The teacher or other singer who models for children should assume a singer's posture: straight and well aligned, but not stiff. Children need to see and hear what is expected of them. They need to see a singer's facial expression and gestures reflecting the mood and text of the song and hear the singer's energy and enthusiasm for the song, because the singer's performance can convince them that they should learn the song. Most important,

Male singer with children—from light falsetto to characteristic register

Jerry Gay

the singer who models for children should sing the song musically—in tune, in its correct rhythm, and according to its stylistic nuances.

If the voice quality of the model is in many cases imitated by children, then what can be said about the male singer intent on teaching children to sing? Until the fourth grade, even children who sing regularly may have difficulty matching pitches when they hear the male voice sounding an octave below their own register. Some children attempt to sing at the lower octave, while others target a set of pitches somewhere between the model's pitch and that of the higher octave. Male singers working with young children or with children inexperienced in singing make more effective models for children when they sing using a falsetto quality. This falsetto sound should not be forced or at the full volume of a countertenor. Instead, the sound should be light and somewhat softer than the full dynamic intensity of the real voice. As children are able to transfer the sound of a male voice to their own register, often by fourth grade, they can begin to reap the benefit of hearing the male voice in its characteristic register.

Although much of the singing children do can be led by the teacher without the aid of other accompaniment, the use of instruments may enhance the vocal sound. A tasteful accompaniment for recorder, xylophone ensemble, guitar, or piano can add musical interest, particularly for public performance (for the parents' club meeting or a school assembly, for example). A recorder descant played by a small group of children can provide a light contrapuntal line to the voice melody. The percussive quality of xylophone bourdons and ostinatos can provide striking contrast to smooth and well-supported singing. By strumming or plucking a guitar, the teacher can move closer to the children to hear and to help them with singing problems. The piano can provide an excellent support to singing, although it must be played with sensitivity to the vocal balance. However, because school music classrooms are often outfitted with a piano, it is tempting to overuse it in the early stages of learning a song so that children cannot listen to the teacher's (or their own) voice.

Should recordings be used in teaching children to sing? This is an irresistible proposition, and when instruments beyond those of the classroom appear on a recording, there may be greater musical intrigue and possibly greater motivation for children to sing. Some recordings have the advantage of demonstrating to children the ideal aural image of how their own young voices should sound. A recording can make a most acceptable model of a perfected sound and can be used to introduce a song, or to later reinforce it. Still, it may be largely the task of the teacher to start and stop the song, and to raise and lower the pitch, tempo, and volume of the song, according to the vocal abilities and musical needs of the children. No recording or other electronic apparatus can do this with such ease and immediacy.

Selecting and Teaching Songs

Processes for teaching songs to children range from rote to note, or combinations of the two. Teaching a song by rote is transmitting the song orally, while teaching by note clearly involves children's ability to read music. The process depends on the teacher's perspective, the lesson objectives, and the children's skill levels. Yet even before the teaching process begins, initial steps can be taken to ensure children's successful singing. The critical first step is selecting songs that are musically, textually, and developmentally appropriate. Guidelines for song selection are noted in Box 7.2, along with other preparatory issues. (See also Table 13.1 for a guide to authenticity in the selection of music.)

Song collections are plentiful, with songs of every genre—traditional, patriotic, art and classical, composed, popular, and even songs transmitted and preserved by children. The collections of Erdei and Komlos (1974), Fowke (1969, 1977), Lomax (1960), and Seeger (1948) contain songs from North America. A rich collection of rounds suitable for children has been compiled by Finckel (1993), and a set of British traditional songs is the result of research by Langstaff, Swanson, and Emlen (1999). Songs and chants for young children are found in volumes by Feierabend (1999) and Kleiner (1996). For examples of children's songs from other world cultures, see Adzinyah, Maraire, and Tucker (1986), Campbell, McCullough-Brabson, and Tucker (1994), Campbell with Frega (2001), Kwami (1998), Lavendar (1998), Nguyen and Campbell (1992), and Campbell, Williamson, and Perron (1996), all accompanied by recordings. The music textbook series published by Macmillan and Silver Burdett Ginn contain a wide variety of songs appropriate for use with children from kindergarten through the eighth grade.

One of the most popular ways for the teacher to present a song is through oral and aural means, or by rote. In the rote approach, children are

Box 7.2 *Song Selection and Preparation*

1. Select a song that is age-appropriate.

    Check the song's range.

    Check the song's tessitura.

    Check the text:

    > Is it too babyish?

    > Is it too grown-up or lovey-dovey?

    > Will the subject matter interest children?

    > Does it contain offensive language (perhaps unintended)?

    > If in a foreign language, can you pronounce it?

2. Select a song in a style that you can sing.

    Check the style: If it is outside your training and experience, can you learn to sing it in its appropriate style?

3. Review the song for its musical and textual highlights.

    Check the melody: Are there tonal phrases to sing in isolation?

    Check the rhythm: Are there rhythmic phrases to chant in isolation?

    Check the text: Are there ideas that relate to a story, poem, discussion of a historical or cultural issue?

given numerous opportunities to listen to the complete song. Fragments of the song are then presented sequentially to the children (oral) in small phrases or chunks; children listen (aural) and then echo these fragments. These chunks are sung repeatedly until accuracy is achieved, and then the chunks are combined with other chunks until the whole song is learned. The children's imitation of the model is a necessary strategy in the rote approach, which can nearly guarantee the development of a large repertoire of songs.

Another approach to teaching a song involves children in the reading of notation. A selected song may contain melodic and rhythmic patterns that were sung, chanted, and played in earlier lessons. Given the great array of songs in series textbooks and in song collections, children can be challenged to seek familiar notated patterns within the new song and to perform them. Rhythms can be chanted according to the preferred system, and melodic patterns can be sung on neutral syllables or with solfège syllables. While there may be unfamiliar patterns to be learned by rote, by trial and error, or by putting to practice the logical and analytical skills required of reading words or notes, children can connect the familiar to the new patterns in learning the song. The teacher may eventually sing the entire song to provide them with a coherent image of the song. Children can feel accomplished in having the ability to decode the notation themselves. Lesson 7.3 presents both rote and note approaches to teaching "Kookaburra."

Rote and note are two approaches, although combinations of these approaches are also possible. The immersion process is another means for

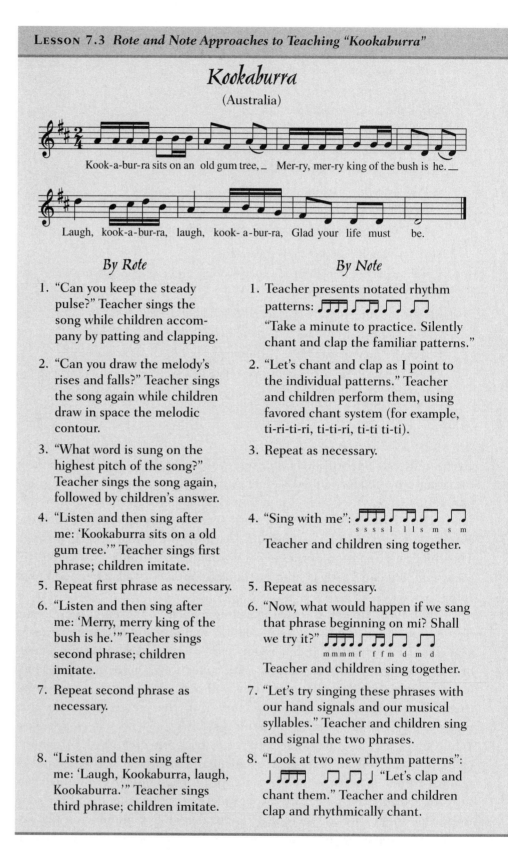

Kookaburra
(Australia)

Kook-a-bur-ra sits on an old gum tree, ___ Mer-ry, mer-ry king of the bush is he. ___

Laugh, kook-a-bur-ra, laugh, kook-a-bur-ra, Glad your life must be.

By Rote

1. "Can you keep the steady pulse?" Teacher sings the song while children accompany by patting and clapping.

2. "Can you draw the melody's rises and falls?" Teacher sings the song again while children draw in space the melodic contour.

3. "What word is sung on the highest pitch of the song?" Teacher sings the song again, followed by children's answer.

4. "Listen and then sing after me: 'Kookaburra sits on a old gum tree.'" Teacher sings first phrase; children imitate.

5. Repeat first phrase as necessary.

6. "Listen and then sing after me: 'Merry, merry king of the bush is he.'" Teacher sings second phrase; children imitate.

7. Repeat second phrase as necessary.

8. "Listen and then sing after me: 'Laugh, Kookaburra, laugh, Kookaburra.'" Teacher sings third phrase; children imitate.

By Note

1. Teacher presents notated rhythm patterns: "Take a minute to practice. Silently chant and clap the familiar patterns."

2. "Let's chant and clap as I point to the individual patterns." Teacher and children perform them, using favored chant system (for example, ti-ri-ti-ri, ti-ti-ri, ti-ti ti-ti).

3. Repeat as necessary.

4. "Sing with me": *s s s s l l l s m s m* Teacher and children sing together.

5. Repeat as necessary.

6. "Now, what would happen if we sang that phrase beginning on mi? Shall we try it?" *m m m m f f f m d m d* Teacher and children sing together.

7. "Let's try singing these phrases with our hand signals and our musical syllables." Teacher and children sing and signal the two phrases.

8. "Look at two new rhythm patterns": "Let's clap and chant them." Teacher and children clap and rhythmically chant.

learning a song, in which children hear the song sung by the teacher, parent, or another child to the extent they individually require before joining in. When a song is learned, children can then be led to related activities, including playing body percussion on ♩, ♫, and ♬♬; creating a dance to re-

By Rote	*By Note*
9. Repeat third phrase as necessary.	9. "What if we added pitches to those rhythms? Could you sing them?" Teacher presents notation for last two phrases.
10. "Listen and then sing after me: 'Glad your life must be.'" Teacher sings final phrase, children imitate.	10. "What's the highest pitch?" (Do.) Listen and follow with your hand signs: ♩ ♫♫♩ ♫♫♩ ♫ d l t d l s s l s f m d d d
11. Repeat final phrase as necessary.	11. "Now sing with me." Teacher and children sing last two phrases with syllables and hand signals.
12. "Let's sing the first two phrases, first me and then you." Teacher sings phrase one and two; children imitate.	12. Repeat as necessary.
13. Repeat as necessary.	13. Teacher presents the notated song. "Can you clap and chant the whole song?" Teacher and children clap and chant together.
14. "Let's sing the last two phrases, first me and then you." Teacher sings phrases three and four; children imitate.	14. "Can you, slowly, sing the melody with our musical syllables and hand signals? Watch me when you get lost." Teacher and children sing and signal together.
15. Repeat as necessary.	15. Repeat as necessary.
16. "Now we're ready to sing the whole song." Teacher and children sing together.	16. "Let's read the words to this song in rhythm."
17. "Can you sing the song without me? I'll get you started." Teacher sets pitch and tempo; children sing.	17. "Let's sing the song with the words."
	18. Repeat as necessary.
	19. "Can you sing the song without me? I'll get you started." Teacher sets pitch and tempo; children sing.

flect its phrases and form; accompanying the song with ostinati on classroom instruments; improvising a variation on recorder; or including it in a performance of other songs and chanted poems on similar subjects. However, any possibilities for extending their capabilities for singing expressively requires their full knowledge and skills in performing the song. With this accomplished and with the vocal production capacity in good working order, children can then be taught to sing musically.

How to Teach Singing in Parts

When children have developed the perceptual and productive skills that come with singing in tune, the next natural stage is to sing in harmony. Children in the third grade can be successful in singing songs in two-part arrangements: melodies with drones and ostinati. Fourth-grade children perform canons (or rounds), descants, partner songs, and countermelodies well in two independent groups; three-part canons can be reserved for children in fifth and sixth grades. When music instruction has been consistent and strong, bona fide two-part choral pieces can be read, rehearsed, and perfected for performance in the last years of elementary school.

In testing children's ability to sing in independent groups, songs such as "Old Texas" with active melodies sung over the sustained pitch of a second group can be selected (see Music Example 7.4). The teacher can lead the singing, sustaining as children sing in imitation. Eventually, two groups can perform this fundamental form of part-singing.

Among the first attempts at singing in parts is the use of a repeated melodic pattern, or ostinato, to accompany the melody, as in "Hey, Ho, Nobody Home" or "Ah, Poor Bird" (see Music Examples 7.5 and 7.6). Ostinato parts are created by examining the melody for its harmonic possibilities and sampling on a pitched instrument one- or two-measure segments that jell harmonically with each measure of the song. While seconds or sevenths occasionally may sound together in passing, so long as they are resolved to

MUSIC EXAMPLE 7.4

Melody over Sustained Pitch

Old Texas
(United States)

Melody over Sustained Pitch

I'm goin' to leave _____ Old _ Tex - as now

I'm goin' to leave _____ Old _ Tex - as

They've got no use for the long-horn cow.

now They've got no use for the long-horn cow.

Hey, Ho, Nobody Home
(England)

Melody with Ostinato (also, Round)

Hey, Ho! No-bo-dy home, meat nor drink nor mon-ey have I none,

still, will I be mer-ry, ve-ry mer-ry.

ostinato:

Hey, ho, Hey, ho

Ah, Poor Bird
(England)

Melody with Ostinato (also, Round)

Ah, poor bird, take your flight, Far a-bove the sor-rows of

this sad night.

ostinato:

Poor bird, poor bird

MUSIC EXAMPLE 7.5

Melody with Ostinato (Also, Round)

MUSIC EXAMPLE 7.6

Melody with Ostinato (Also, Round)

thirds, fourths, or fifths on the strong beats, the ostinato will probably be satisfying.

Canons and rounds comprise some of the most fulfilling musical experiences for children in their elementary years. Critical to that fulfillment, however, is the process by which they are taught. First, the teacher should be certain that the children are secure in singing the song's melody as a larger group, and then in smaller groups. Second, the teacher can cue the class to begin singing and then can begin softly singing the second part at the canon. The number 2 on the scores signifies the point at which the group must be when the teacher begins singing. Third, a small group of children can be selected to sing with the teacher at the canon. Finally, the class can be divided equally, so that the two groups can maintain their independent parts while performing. "Scotland's Burning," "Kaeru No Uta," "Autumn's Here," and "Viva la musica" are examples of canons that work with children's voices (see Music Example 7.7).

A descant is an independent melody that can be added above a first and usually more familiar melody. It is higher in pitch than the main melody. Conversely, a countermelody can be added below a familiar main melody. Using some of the procedures for teaching a round, children can sing the melody while the teacher softly adds a descant or countermelody; the class can gradually be divided into two groups. The songs "Skye Boat Song" and "Yo Mamana, Yo!" illustrate the use of the countermelody and descant (see Music Examples 7.8 and 7.9).

Skye Boat Song
(Scotland)

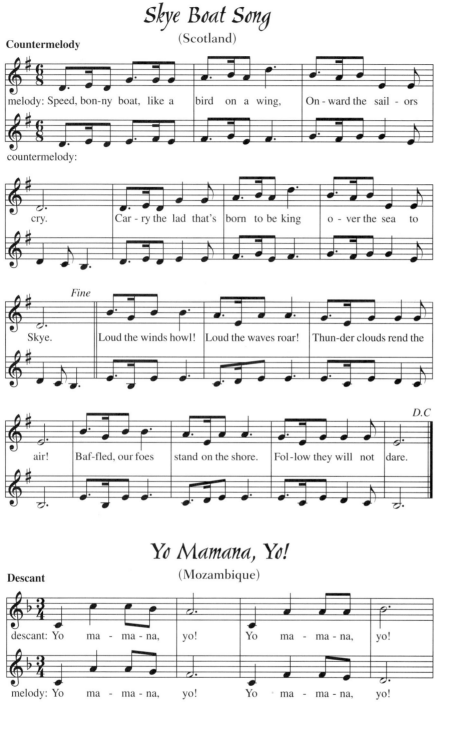

Yo Mamana, Yo!
(Mozambique)

Source: As sung by Salamao Manhica. From *Roots and Branches*. © 1994 World Music Press. Used by permission.

Some musical traditions of the world are best sung in unison if a culturally authentic sound is to be rendered. Still, harmony is an important feature of many songs from Anglo-American and African American traditions, as well as from parts of sub-Saharan Africa, the Pacific Islands, and much of the Hispanic world. Excerpts from three pieces appear in Music Example 7.10: "Savalivalah" from Samoa, "Ambozado," from Puerto Rico, and "Mbube," from South Africa.

MUSIC EXAMPLE 7.10

Songs with Harmony

Savalivalah
(Samoa)

Three-Part Song

"Sa - va - li - va-lah" means "Go for a walk." "Tau - ta - la - ta - la" means

Ooh "Go for a walk." Ooh

"Sa - va - li - va-lah" means "Go for a walk." "Tau - ta - la - ta - la" means

"Too much talk." "A - lo - fa iā te oe" means

"Too much talk." "A - lo - fa iā te oe" means

"Too much talk." "A - lo - fa iā te oe" means

"I love you." "Take it ea - sy," Fai Fai - le - mu.

"I love you." "Take it ea - sy," Fai Fai - le - mu.

"I love you." "Take it ea - sy," Fai Fai - le - mu.

Ambozado
(Puerto Rico)

Three-Part Song

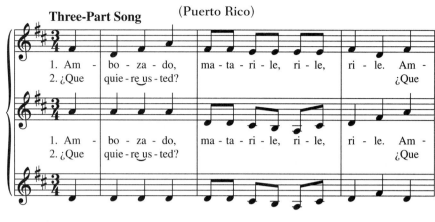

1. Am - bo - za - do, ma - ta - ri - le, ri - le, ri - le. Am -
2. ¿Que quie - re us - ted? ¿Que

bo - za - do ma - ta - ri - le re - le ron.
quie - re us - ted?

3. Yo qui-ro un pa-je.

4. Ella dice que-lo quie-re.

(El)

Mbube
(South Africa)

Four-Part Song

(1) In the jun - gle the qui - et jun - gle the li - on sleeps to - night.
(2) In the jun - gle the might - y jun - gle the li - on sleeps to - night.

M-bu-be m - bu-be m-bu-be m - bu-be m-bu-be m-bu-be m-bu-be m-bu-be

M-bu-be m - bu-be m - bu-be m - bu-be m - bu-be m - bu-be m - bu-be m - bu-be

M-bu-be m - bu-be m - bu-be m - bu-be m-bu-be m - bu-be m - bu-be m - bu-be

Two- and three-part songs for children in the intermediate grades are increasingly available from publishing companies that specialize in choral music. Children's ability to sing in tune, to sing in harmony, and to render songs with musical sensitivity makes singing a pleasure for them as well as for their listeners.

Children's Choirs

When children have been raised to enjoy singing, they may be eager for the additional musical experiences that membership in a choir provides. Children's choirs in schools, churches, and communities are a growing phenomenon. When viewed as much as an educational entity as a performance one, the choir can extend the musical goals as well as the vocal development of children. Aural skills can be refined, pitch matching can be improved, and children can become exposed to a variety of the historical and cultural repertoire. Within the framework of the school curriculum, a twice-weekly choir meeting of forty-five minutes to an hour can greatly enhance children's vocal and musical development.

School choirs often open membership to children of mixed ages beginning in the third or fourth grade, although two or three choirs can be formed according to age and experience. A public performance for parents or at a school assembly may be one of the choir's targeted goals, so that children can know the joy of performing for others. Seasonal, holiday, and graduation programs that feature children from all classes and grade levels can be capped off with a set of songs performed by the school choir. Citywide or districtwide festivals of elementary school choirs are other occasions for sharing with an audience the results of children's efforts in their rehearsals.

An audition is useful if only to emphasize the commitment of children to singing in a choir, and so that there is an understanding that each child's voice is important in its contribution to the group sound. This is not to say that the choir should be exclusive in its acceptance of only the most talented children. All children who express interest in singing in a school choir should be given a fair chance to become a member of the singing team. An audition allows the director to know the vocal quality and musicianship of each child and helps to guide the type of vocal exercises and repertoire to be used in rehearsal. Children who need remedial work also can be identified through the audition process.

Auditions can take place before or after school or at recess, but preferably not during the music class. To determine range and pitch accuracy, each child can be asked to sing a familiar song such as "America" or "Are You Sleeping?" first in a comfortable middle-range key, and then in higher and lower keys. Vocal quality and range also can be assessed by singing a descending major scale on a neutral syllable, starting first at c′ (c above middle c), then at d′, e′, and so forth. Another test of pitch accuracy is having each child sing a set of short melodic patterns that are first sung or played by the teacher. Tonal memory can be tested by lengthening the melodic patterns to be imitated from four to six to eight beats. Finally, vocal independence can be evaluated by asking the student to sing a familiar song ("Are You Sleeping?," "Row Your Boat," "Music Alone Shall Live") while the teacher sings it in canon. These tasks offer the information teachers require in selecting and arranging music for the choir, while they challenge children musically and vocally.

A choir rehearsal may progress in several stages, beginning with physical warm-ups and vocal exercises. To maintain attention, a rehearsal should contain a variety of musical selections and approaches to them. One rule of thumb is to efficiently rehearse each song, or song section, for a maximum of seven minutes before proceeding to a new piece. In the case of a part song, those who are not singing should be silently following their part, which they may be directed to sing on cue at any given moment. When children show signs of distraction or inattention, a physical exercise or rhythmic pattern can be introduced to restore focus and energy. All rehearsals, regardless of how close a performance may be, should close with a familiar song that is guaranteed to send children on their way with good sounds and feelings about themselves and their membership in the choir. For further advice on organizing a children's choir, see McRae (1991).

Assessment of Singing

Children's singing skills grow through use and the concentrated effort it takes to develop (1) musical (tonal and rhythmic) accuracy, (2) the physical capacity to support a clear and focused vocal quality, and (3) the expressive nuance that flows from understanding the intent of the composer, the poet, and the cultural tradition. The teacher's own vocal training provides not only a model for children to emulate in their process of learning to sing, but also the musical intelligence to be able to distinguish when children's vocal skills are keeping pace with their potential at given ages and stages. Children can also be drawn into understanding what is, and is not, musical, vocally balanced, and expressive singing. Just as a listening ear is vital to the growth of singing skills, listening is key in children's assessment of their own vocal development.

The following questions are useful to have at hand as children sing alone or together, and as they listen to themselves in the act of singing or as they play back a recording of their singing for later critique.

1. Was the singing in tune? Was it flat or sharp? (Could you have filled yourself with deeper breaths and greater energy to support your singing?)

2. Was the singing in time? Was it rhythmically alive? (Could you have been more aware of the music and text ahead of you, and more prepared to sing each pitch, word and syllable, and phrase?)

3. Was the singing relaxed and open, or tense and tight? (Could you have stood taller and with better alignment of your feet, spine, chest, shoulders, and head? Could you have opened yourself up to fuller breaths?)

4. Was the singing expressive of the text? (Could you have put more into making the song meaningful, to charge the listener and give him or her goose bumps in receiving the musical message?)

As children practice singing and hear good singers perform live and on recordings, they will naturally be drawn into grasping the components of singing well. They will come to recognize different vocal styles and the spectrum of expressive qualities of which the voice is capable for conveying various meanings. The teacher may wish to record children's singing progress by arranging for periodic tape-recording sessions of students on a given song or exercise. Such a procedure can happen at the end of a scholastic term, or following a study unit or a concert program, or on a bimonthly basis, when children can file one by one to a closet or out to the hall to sing a song or several phrases into a tape recorder. Such recordings can become a part of student portfolios, tracing the development of children's vocal range and tessitura, vocal strength, musical accuracy, and expressivity. Children can be given these tapes at the end of the year as documentation of their growth as young singers, to be shared with their families. Asssessment of children's singing, however, occurs naturally in the daily process of a class singing activity, when a teacher may ask children in rapid-fire succession to sing a phrase or a song segment in small groups, duos, and even individually. He or she is in effect providing assessment at every step of the instructional process.

Reasons to Sing

Children are still singing despite rumors that the media-rich world in which they live has turned them to passive listeners and lip-syncers. The voice is the one musical instrument that all possess and for which no rental fee or elaborate arrangement for private instruction is necessary. For many children, singing is the path that they will choose to experience as participants and performers the great joy of music. Teachers who enjoy singing will further kindle the interests of children, because enjoyment is irresistible; it is contagious.

Teachers and parents may be teaching more than musicianship when they sing with their children. A great many ideas can be advanced through song. The link between language, speech, chant, and song is undeniable, such that children can expand their vocabulary as well as understand ways in which words fit together as they learn new songs. Cultural values can be advanced through songs, and songs from various cultures and historical periods can present children with glimpses of different worlds and eras. Song texts cover nearly every subject under the sun, so that there are countless songs about animals, food, modes of transportation, flowers, rivers, patriotism, and family, friends, and neighbors. Singing can be combined with other musical activities, too, so that children can sing as they play instruments, move, and create new music.

Scenario

It is September, and Ms. Patterson has begun the school year with a plan for her fourth-grade children at Thompson Elementary School: to learn to sing in parts. Her students arrive, settling in at the outer rim of a large braided carpet of many colors, three girls here, a couple of girls there, and the eleven boys packed in shoulder to shoulder within about one-third of the rim. Ms. Patterson stands by the piano, just outside the circle, plays a few chords to bring children to attention, and announces the plan: "Because you have all had four years of experience in our music program, and your voices have developed such strength, we will be learning to sing harmony this year—in parts." She shares the sequence of the day's lesson with them: "We'll begin with some vocal warm-ups, and then we'll be ready to learn our first real part song, 'Old Texas.'" With a flourish of several more chords to set the key, she directs them to sing a major scale on a neutral syllable and then on solfège syllables, accompanying them chordally on each pitch they sing. Most of the girls are with her, and a few of the boys, while others are chanting and half-shouting the syllables (but in a very rhythmic manner). She proceeds to pitch-matching exercises, playing a brief melodic phrase at the piano to which they respond in imitation on a neutral syllable. "Pretty good," she says, in part to balance her remarks to a group of both in-tune singers and others who seem uncertain, uninterested, or unable to match pitches.

As promised, Ms. Patterson proceeds to introduce the children to "Old Texas." She steps into the middle of the circle and sings the melody to the children in a light voice. To connect to the children, she moves from child to child, making eye contact as she sings the song four times through. Most of the children are attentive, and two or three children are already singing along with her. Having introduced the song, she then breaks the song into two-measure phrases, singing and then cueing the children to sing after her. There is a sequence, first she (and then the children) sing the phrase with the song's words, then on neutral syllables, and lastly with solfège syllables. Phrase by phrase, most of the children are coming to grips with the song melody (five or six of the boys are singing with a cowboy twang and swaying left to right, but Ms. Patterson finds their performance otherwise acceptable—and amusing).

Ms. Patterson directs the children to sing the song in unison from start to finish, and they do so with gusto, so she announces that they will now sing in parts. "I'll sing first and then you follow, on cue, in imitation of what I just sang. Listen to me, watch, and sing when I signal you." She sings with her strong and clear voice, and as she sustains the pitch, she cues the children who stagger in after her. She acknowledges their efforts, and they try it again. About half of the class is entering on cue, while the others are losing interest. Ms. Patterson continues to walk around the circle, trying to make eye contact as she sings and then signaling the children in. She then divides the class into the girls as leaders and the boys as followers, and she directs the two groups in their performance of "Old Texas" four times through. The attempt is a shaky one, as the girls outsing the boys by twice as much strength, and the girls are singing head-tones while the boys continue to twang. "It's a start, and you're on your way to singing in harmony," Ms. Patterson concludes aloud, knowing that they will take up the song again in the next class.

Questions

1. Were Ms. Patterson's exercises appropriate in warming up the young singers? Why or why not?

2. How was Ms. Patterson effective in her teaching of the melody of the song and the elementary part-singing? What might she have added or deleted to make for a more effective lesson?

3. How might Ms. Patterson extend and develop this beginning lesson in part-singing in the next class?

REVIEW

1. Trace the development of children's voices from early childhood through the intermediate grades, with special attention to changes in range and quality.

2. What is PSP? How is it attained?

3. What is a developmental sequence for children's part-song singing?

4. What are the components of an audition for membership in a children's choir?

CRITICAL THINKING

1. Cite evidence to support the view of singing as a physical as well as mental endeavor.

2. Choose a traditional song and write a vocal ostinato for it that suits second graders and fourth graders.

PROJECTS

1. Prepare a song to teach by rote and by note. How do the approaches differ? How might aspects of each be combined over several lessons?

2. Collect ten songs that you feel all children in preschool or elementary school should know. Analyze the songs for their melodic and rhythmic content, order them from less to more complex, and determine the grade level at which you would teach these songs.

3. Visit a music store specializing in choral scores, and begin a card file of the song title, composer and arranger, publisher, range and tessitura for songs and part-songs useful in music class and in the school choir. Select a set of songs that could conceivably comprise an autumn, winter, or spring program.

REFERENCES

Adzinyah, D. M., D. Maraire, and J. C. Tucker (1986). *Let your voice be heard.* Danbury, CT: World Music Press.

Campbell, P. S. (1998). *Songs in their heads.* New York: Oxford University Press.

Campbell, P. S., with A. L. Frega (2001). *Canciones de America Latina: De su Origen a la Escuela.* Miami, FL: Warner Bros. Publications.

Campbell, P. S., E. Mccullough-Brabson, and J. C. Tucker (1994). *Roots and branches.* Danbury, CT: World Music Press.

Campbell, P. S., S. Williamson, and P. Perron (1996). *Songs from singing cultures.* Miami, FL: Warner Bros. Publications.

Erdei, P., and K. Komlos (1974). *150 American folk songs for children to sing and play.* New York: Boosey and Hawkes.

Feierabend, J. (1999). *First steps in music.* St. Louis, MO: Magna Music Baton.

Finckel, E. A. (1993). *Now we'll make the rafters ring: 100 traditional and contemporary rounds for everyone.* Pennington, NJ: A Cappella Books.

Fowke, E. (1969). *Sally go round the sun.* Garden City, NY: Doubleday.

———. (1977). *Ring around the moon.* Englewood Cliffs, NJ: Prentice-Hall.

Kleiner, L. (1996). *Kids make music, babies make music, too.* Miami: Warner Bros. Publications.

Kwami, Robert Mawuena (1998). *African songs for school and community.* New York: Schott.

Langstaff, J., P. Swanson, and G. Emlen (1999). *Celebrate the spring: Celebrations for schools and communities.* Watertown, MA: Revels.

Lavendar, C. (1998). *Songs of the rainbow children.* Milwaukee, WI: Hal Leonard.

Lomax, A. (1960). *The folk songs of North America.* Garden City, NY: Doubleday.

McRae, S. W. (1991). *Directing the children's choir.* New York: Schirmer Books.

MENC (1994). *What every young American should know and be able to do in the arts: National standards for arts education.* Reston, VA: Music Educators National Conference.

Moog, H. (1976). *The musical experience of the preschool child.* (C. Clarke, trans.) London: Schott.

Nguyen, P., and P. S. Campbell (1992). *From rice paddies and temple yards: Traditional music of Vietnam.* Danbury, CT: World Music Press.

Rutkowski, J. (1996). The effectiveness of individual/small group singing activities on kindergartners' use of singing voice and developmental music aptitude. *Journal of Research in Music Education* 44(4), Winter, 353–368.

Seeger, R. C. (1948). *American folk songs for children.* New York: Doubleday.

8

The Listening Child

Courtney concentrates happily as her mother sings a new song to her. When her mother stops, she says, "Sing it again, Mommy, sing it again!" Her mother sings it over several times and, finally, Courtney joins in, singing the song accurately. Josh walks down the street, almost dancing, as he listens through his headphones to his latest purchase, a tape of his favorite pop group. Ofewe sets a rhythm pattern on his synthesizer, focuses on its flow, then begins to improvise a melody to it. Michiko practices a phrase from her latest piano piece, shakes her head in frustration, tries it again, then smiles with satisfaction.

Each of these children is engaged in the perceptive activity that is at the heart of all that is done with music whether singing, dancing, creating, or playing. That activity is listening. Music is an aural art that stimulates ears and challenges minds, usually bringing a pleasure and satisfaction that transcends much of what is experienced in life. Most music is received through the ear, not the eye. And most music performed throughout the world is aurally transmitted and will never be written down. Development of the ear is crucial to development of musicianship.

Learning to listen perceptively is a skill that can grow as surely as the gourmet can learn to detect the ingredients in a dish from a single taste. The reward of developing that skill is the same as any person feels at being perceptively sensitive, at being able to notice the subtleties and nuances present in an experience. Of all the musical abilities teachers try to help children develop, the ability to listen with focus and insight is perhaps the most important and long lasting. Of all the ways people interact with music, the most frequently used lifelong skill is through listening.

To help children develop their aural perceptive abilities, teachers and parents need to engage children in what R. Murray Schaefer (1976) calls "ear cleaning." This is difficult to achieve in a world in which people are constantly bombarded with sounds and quiet is virtually impossible to find. To counter the effects of noise pollution, children's ears and minds must be opened to events in all aspects of music making: singing, playing instruments, moving, conducting, composing, and reading. Children need to learn to reflect on the quality of their own and others' performances.

Increased sophistication in listening can also be developed through listening to recorded music. This does not mean the kind of functional listening most people do when they use music as a background to help them celebrate, relax, clean house, or study. In most of those instances, the music is a kind of tonal bath that surrounds and washes over them but is not seriously attended to. The teacher needs to foster active listening, in which the learner focuses on musical events such as patterns that repeat and contrast, the creative use of tone colors, or the shaping of the music through dynamic change. Increased sophistication also comes through exposure to and development of a wide repertoire of music of various styles, cultures, and genres—from Bach to rock or from Indonesian gamelan music to Native American flute music.

The Development of Perceptive Listening

Key to the development of listening skills is the ability to perceive sounds and to form thoughts about those sounds. The auditory sense develops early and is remarkably keen in most children. Infants at birth can differentiate between pitches and quickly learn to identify the sound of their mother's voice. All babies go through a babbling stage in their first six months of development, in which they become increasingly sophisticated in matching vocal and mouth sounds that their parents generate. It is through this listening and corresponding vocal play that children are forming the mental constructs for language production and for the music of their culture.

Children as young as three months, perhaps younger, can vocally match sustained pitches. Children as young as six or seven months appear to have acquired a sense of musical phrase, and by eight months a sense of what constitutes a good fit melodically in their culture. By the time children are in preschool they are developing vocabulary to describe what they hear. Concepts of tone color, dynamics, tempo, and style seem to emerge early. Concepts of pitch, rhythm, and form emerge later, around the age of four or after. Children continue to grow in their perceptiveness and can show that in remarkable ways. Older children are able to recognize and apply a wide range of concepts to musical listening experiences, provided they have had a strong foundation in music education (for further detail on the development of these skills see Scott-Kassner, 1992; and Haack, 1992).

Everyone can aurally identify hundreds, if not thousands, of pieces of music that he or she has been exposed to through a lifetime, explain details about the music and the context in which particular pieces are known, and attach personal meaning to that music. Music, in many ways, is a thread connecting the different periods of one's life, marking special moments.

The Development of Attitudes toward Music

Most music teachers are eager to have their students love music. That often translates into the selection of works for performance and listening that have an immediate appeal but may not have lasting value. Many complex factors besides the music itself enter into the development of attitudes toward music. A number of these factors are outside the teacher's control. A child's gender, ethnic background, age, personality, socioeconomic status and the ensuing beliefs, feelings, and values that emerge all contribute to the formation of attitudes toward music. Teachers, families, peer groups, the media, and other adult authority figures also have an influence.

Young children from preschool through the age of eight are usually remarkably open to all kinds of music. This period of children's lives seems to be a good time to introduce them to a wide range of excellent music of many styles, genres, and cultures.

About the age of nine or ten, children begin to exhibit much more sensitivity to peer culture and the influence of the media, often rejecting, on a surface level, music that is not endorsed by that culture. Tests of preference show that children of this age prefer music that is loud rather than soft, fast rather than slow, and music that has a strong beat rather than less intrusive music. They are also drawn to humorous music. Teachers need to encourage children of this age to be receptive toward music that they do not necessarily prefer, so that they can learn about and from that music.

As most people mature, they will once again open themselves to a wider range of music than what they were attracted to during their teenage years. At the same time, music they associate with certain times or events may continue to appeal to them throughout a lifetime.

Teachers can take heart in the knowledge that, in spite of children's preferences and tastes in music, they can be helped to understand a wide range of music through active involvement in listening. Because the area of attitude development is so complex, teachers cannot guarantee that experiencing a work of music will cause a student to like that work. However, there is some evidence that human organisms:

- Are drawn to complexity
- Tend to value what is familiar and feel uncomfortable with the unfamiliar
- Can learn to focus their perception on subtle changes
- Can change their attitudes through learning in spite of enculturated tastes

These findings should encourage teachers to formulate an approach to active listening in which children

1. Regularly listen to music that is more complex and challenging than much of the music they are exposed to in their daily environments

2. Listen to pieces of music enough times so that those works become familiar and no longer seem exotic

3. Gain the conceptual tools for discussing and analyzing music and perceive and respond to musical events in increasingly refined fashion

4. Discuss their preferences (a choice between two different events) and attitudes (a more generalized network of beliefs, values, and feelings) without being told that their choices or feelings are incorrect

5. Engage in listening activities that allow them to reflect and document what they have perceived and felt

Once children express an attitude about a piece of music, whether positive or negative, they need to be encouraged to go to the next step and describe what about the music makes them feel that way. A fifth grader, Steve, said he "loved" the song "Bridge over Troubled Water" as sung by Simon and Garfunkel. All of the other students agreed. The teacher played the recording again, asking the children to connect their feelings to what was happening musically. At the end, Steve eagerly raised his hand and offered a detailed analysis of the dynamic and melodic shaping of the A section of the piece that built emotional tension, then released. This was in contrast with the B section that was all on one level dynamically and melodically. He then went on to discuss the lyrics in each of those sections and how they fit expressively with what was going on in the music. Steve had clearly connected his affective response with actual musical events.

Building Skills of Aural Perception

A program in active listening has several goals:

- Build heightened aural perception and sensitivity to music and musical events (aural skills development)
- Illustrate and reinforce or expand concepts of music

- Build an aural repertoire that represents a wide range of styles, cultures, and genres of music and places music within a context
- Link children's felt responses to their perceptions and understandings

Although these may seem to be discrete activities, they are interdependent; growth in one area affects another. For example, the greater your ability to perceive musical events, the more likely you are to form concepts about those events, and the richer your experience of listening to all kinds of music becomes. Growth in one or all of these skills should lead to greater aesthetic satisfaction through listening.

Learning to listen perceptively demands focus and attention. Teachers can use a variety of techniques to help children become aware of sounds.

1. Have children close their eyes. Drop a familiar object, such as keys or a pencil, and have children name the object.

2. Have children close their eyes. Drop a piece of chalk from a certain height and ask children to show that height with their hands above a desk. Try this with several different heights.

3. Have children hide behind a screen and play different rhythm instruments while other children name what they hear.

4. Ask a child to close his or her eyes and then identify the voice of a classmate, after hearing a sung phrase.

5. Have children shape the upward or downward sounds of a slide whistle as they listen with their eyes closed.

Each of these listening activities helps children focus on aural stimuli by eliminating visual cues. This training leads naturally to the more difficult task of listening for specific events in recorded music—a more difficult task because the music is usually more complex with more things occurring, not just one. To help children focus, teachers need to develop active listening strategies.

Active listening to recorded music means involving more than the ears and the mind. To help children focus on a particular aspect of the music, teachers may use some physical means, such as having students perform, read, or move as they listen. In many instances, only a segment of a recorded work will be played. Sometimes, an entire work or section of a work will be used.

Lesson Activities 8.1 through 8.6 suggest a variety of active listening strategies designed to focus attention on different aspects of music: tone color, rhythm, pitch, texture, dynamics, form, and style. These strategies are designed for use with a broad variety of recorded music and with live performances by children, teachers, and guests. Specific concepts appropriate to the elementary curriculum are listed on the left, and ideas to focus children's perception by using movement, performing, or reading are listed in their respective columns. Such experiences will provide a variety of opportunities for children to develop National Standard 6—listening to, analyzing, and describing music. (See also Figure 8.1, p. 192.)

Concept	Moving	Performing	Reading
Voices or instruments alone Voices or instruments in groups	Raise your hand when you hear the first trumpet; tap your head when you hear the first trombone. Clap to the pattern the bass drum plays. Pretend to play the violin whenever you hear it. Listen to a movement in a string quartet. In a group of four, assign each person to listen for a different instrument and decide how to move when each hears the sounds of his or her instrument.	Sing with the pattern of the two-toned bell. Sing with the female voice only; listen to the male. Identify the pitches of the marimba ostinato and play it on the bass xylophone while listening to the recording. Select a rhythmic percussion instrument that would fit stylistically with a given piece, and improvise a rhythm to accompany the recording.	Circle the names or pictures of the instruments you hear in this piece. List in order of entrance the instruments you hear. Make a simple score of entrances and exits and relationships of the instruments in a work featuring three contrasting timbres. Visually follow a simple score, and cue the instruments or voices as they enter. Follow a call chart like the one shown on the facing page.

Active listening strategy with listening chart

Jerry Gay

A Call Chart helps students track events by tone color, dynamics, and tempo. Students follow events as they listen to a recording with numbers spoken as events occur.

1. Introduction-full orchestra; *ff*; fast.
2. Low strings, low brass; *f*, then *mf*; slow.
3. English horn, clarinet, strings, tambourine; *mp*; slow.
4. Clarinet and piccolo solos, strings accompany; *mf*; slow.
5. Horns, woodwinds, tambourine; *f*; fast.
6. Strings, tambourine, brass; *ff*; slow.
7. Oboe, clarinet, low strings *pizzicato* (plucked); *mp*; slow.
8. Woodwinds, strings, brass, percussion; *ff*; very fast.
9. Full orchestra, brass section predominates; *f*; fast.
10. Full orchestra to end; bass drum "stinger."

Source: Call chart for "Sailor's Dance" from *The Red Poppy* by Reinhold Glière. Reproduced with permission from *World of Music*, Grade 7 (Parsippany, NJ: Silver Burdett & Ginn, 1992).

LESSON ACTIVITIES 8.2 *Active Listening to Rhythm*

Concept	Moving	Performing	Reading
Beat Rhythm Meter Tempo Syncopation	Tap the beat, off-beat, or rhythm on various parts of the body. Move around the room to the rhythmic flow of a piece; change directions at the ends of phrases. Create a movement pattern using different body levels (stomp, pat, clap, snap) to accompany patterns in a recording. Pass a ball around a circle to the beat, changing direction when the tempo changes. Work with a partner to show meter through movement; make the downbeat a strong motion. Bounce a ball on the accented beat; catch, roll, or hold on the weak beats.	Select instruments that complement a recording and add an accompaniment that highlights the beat, rhythm, and meter. Create a rhythmic ostinato to accompany the music. Identify a repeated pattern in the music; play along with it whenever it occurs.	Learn to read the rhythm of the main motivic pattern in a piece of music; find that pattern whenever it enters (aurally and visually). Read and notate the rhythm patterns in a work that features layered rhythms. Read and interpret by conducting the various meters in works in single meters and works that change meters. Read and maintain a rhythm pattern as an accompaniment to the music.

Concept	Moving	Performing	Reading
Horizontal 　Upward and 　downward 　High and 　low 　Step, leap, 　and repeat 　Melodic 　curve and 　patterns 　Phrase 　Scale 　Tonality 　Range and 　register Vertical 　Chords 　Cadences 　Clusters	Alone and with a partner, shape the general curve of the melody. Show the highest and lowest notes of the recorded work by using high and low movements. Shape phrases. Develop discrete movements to show steps, leaps, and repeats in a melody. Discover the main theme or motives in a work; create a movement to represent each motive; perform the appropriate movement when you hear each theme. Move through general space, pausing at cadence points; make contrasting motions to show half and full cadences. Change motions each time a chord changes. In a group of three, have one person move on the I chord, a second on the IV chord, and the last on the V chord.	Sing along with the melodic line of a work using words or a neutral syllable. Play the melodic line with the recording. Play or sing motives or melodic themes with the recording. Develop a melodic ostinato to play as an accompaniment to a pentatonic melody. Play chord progressions on a synthesizer along with a pop or rock piece.	Look at the melodic shape or notation of a motive, pattern, or theme. Notice each time it occurs in the music. Draw the shape of the melody as it unfolds. Read through the melody on a score ahead of time. Notice its shape: smooth or angular; its register: high or low; its range: low to high; its use of steps, leaps, and repeats. Imagine what it will sound like, then listen to test your perception. As you listen, notate the chord changes and number of beats on each chord of a blues or pop song. Circle the cadence points on a score as you listen. Listen again, and mark them as half or full.

Concept	Moving	Performing	Reading
Texture 　Monophonic 　Homophonic 　Polyphonic 　Mixed	Move in the line of a single melody; upper body in personal space, then through general space. In a group of three or four, have each person move to a	Sing or play in unison with the melody of a mono-phonic work. Sing or play with various lines or chords of other works, adding to the texture; fade the volume to listen to	Trace the line on a score of a monophonic melody as you listen. Draw or notate the line as you listen.

Concept	Moving	Performing	Reading
	different line in a polyphonic piece.	students, then increase volume.	Visually track the entrances and exits of lines in a polyphonic work.
	Show the layers of a round or canon by moving in concentric circles to the lines as they enter (each circle represents a different part).	Add a countermelody or ostinato to a recording to create a polyphonic texture.	Using different colors, draw the separate lines as you listen.
		Add chords to a recording of a melody to create a homophonic texture.	Follow the notation of a homophonic work noting the relation between the melody and the chords.
	While one group moves to a melody, have another show the pattern of the underlying chords.	Shift textures in your accompaniment to create mixed textures.	Follow a call chart that outlines the textures in a mixed texture work.
	Create different movements to show that you hear various textures.		Invent your own call chart.

Dynamics
  Loud
  and soft
  Dynamic
  accent
  Gradual
  change
  Sudden
	Show changes from loud to soft through changes in energy and flow.
	
	Show dynamic accents through angular movements.
	
	Develop group crescendo/decrescendo.
		Clap or play a rhythm instrument on selected or all dynamic accents.
		
		Play rhythm instruments to accompany gradual and sudden changes.
			Follow the dynamic markings on a score, gesturing or conducting to show changes.
			
			Draw a score of the dynamic changes while listening.

LESSON ACTIVITIES 8.5 *Active Listening to Form*

Concept	Moving	Performing	Reading

Repetition and contrast
  Phrase
  Unitary
  Binary
  Ternary
Rondo theme and variations
Through composed
Tone poem
	Make up one motion for initial idea, contrasting motions for other idea(s); perform motions solo or in groups.
	
	Change directions with each new phrase, showing repetition and contrast in phrases with specific motions.
	
	Show a rondo by using different colored scarves
		Select different instrumental or vocal timbres to accompany various phrases or sections of a work.
		
		Using only hands as a sound source, accompany a recorded rondo; change the playing technique (clap, rub, snap) with each theme.
		
		Learn to perform the theme by playing or singing, then
			Have simple shapes such as triangles, squares, and circles at your desk to show the structure of a piece as you listen (AA, AB, ABA, ABACABA).
			
			Follow the score as you listen; label each section as it occurs.
			
			Read the theme before you hear the music; note the contour and rhythm;

(*Continued*)

Concept	Moving	Performing	Reading
Program music	and movements; assign each section to different groups. Have one group pattern the theme through movement while additional groups pattern the variations, incorporating the theme. Develop creative movements or dramas to tell the story or convey the mood as a piece unfolds.	identify it in each of its incarnations. Play or sing the main themes of the characters or sections before listening such as in the listening guide for *Carmen*, below.	discuss ways it might be varied; chart the variations on a piece of paper as you listen. Follow or draw a storyboard of a piece as you listen. Follow story in book, with puppets, or illustrate storyline or mood.

A Notated Listening Guide for "Prelude" from Carmen by Georges Bizet

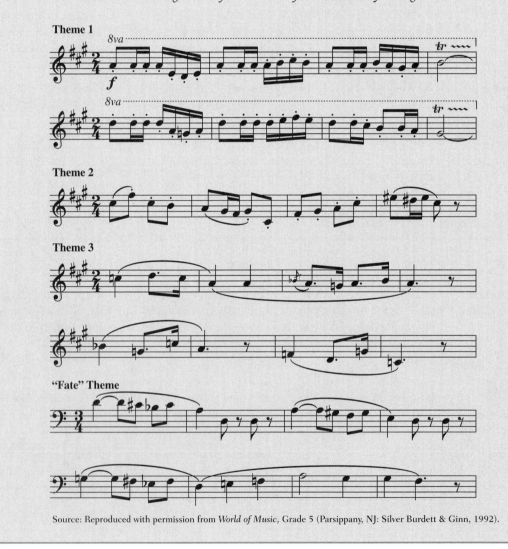

Source: Reproduced with permission from *World of Music,* Grade 5 (Parsippany, NJ: Silver Burdett & Ginn, 1992).

Concept	Moving	Performing	Reading

Style is the result of the combination of the elements of music reflecting cultural or personal choices	Change the quality of movement to reflect the style of the music (curved and flowing versus sharp, short, and angular moves).
	
	Learn specific dances or patterns of movement from various times and cultures to show styles of music.
	
	From Greece: grapevine step, arms at shoulders.
	
	From some parts of Africa: knees bent, arms bent slightly, palms down, eyes downward, movement toward ground, feet toward ground, upper body moves in and out.
		Add a clapping or percussive accompaniment that fits the style of the music on the recording. For clave in a calypso piece:
		
		Imitate through singing or playing the vocal or instrumental style used on a recording (blue notes, chest resonated voice, open sound toward front of facial mask).
			Select from a set of style cards that match the music being played.
			
			Set 1 (touch)
			  Velvet
			  Gravel
			  Steel wool
			  Lima beans
			  Bubble plastic
			  Plush rug
			  Fake fur
			
			Set 2 (art)
			  Impressionist
			  Baroque
			  Classical
			  Romantic
			  Abstract
			
			Set 3 (images)
			  Houses from different periods
			  Costumes from different periods
			
			Set 4 (cultures)
			  Native American
			  African American
			  Latin American
			  Sub-Saharan African
			  East Asian
			
			Children should be able to describe why they made a certain style choice in terms of the music.

FIGURE 8.1

Listening Map for Thenody for the Victims of Hiroshima by Krzysztof Penderecki

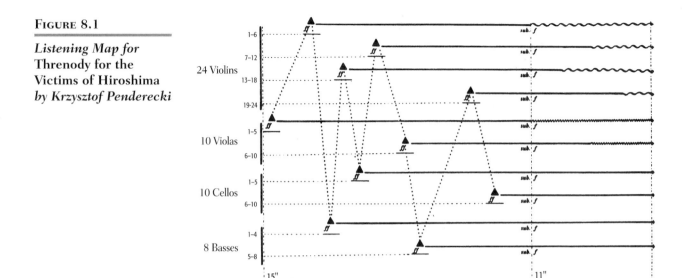

Source: Reproduced with permission from *Music and You,* Grade 6 (New York: Macmillan, 1989).

Children playing marimba to accompany recording

Student Construction of Listening Experiences

Current theories of learning suggest that using strategies in which children solve problems leads to the formation of mental constructs or schemas that are much deeper and more well formed than approaches that are completely teacher-directed. Such strategies invite students into the music by having them use one or more modalities—kinesthetic, visual, or verbal—to represent what they notice happening in the music. In these approaches, teachers structure the types of activities and select the music to be explored, but they turn the response to the music over to the students. Children work individually or in small groups and represent the music in some way such as speaking about it, drawing aspects of it, solving puzzles in which they put themes in order, moving to the music using their own ideas, or creating their own works based on it. Because this process requires multiple hearings of the music, it is advisable to select short works or sections of works lasting under two minutes. If several tape recorders are available, students can work at their own pace, determining when they need to re-listen. These activities can also be done with the group as a whole.

Mary Helen Richards (1980) has long advocated having children draw their own maps of music or musical events. The maps may be drawn most successfully after children have physically responded to the music through movement of their hands to shape dynamics or tempo change or melodic and rhythmic ideas or timbral changes. Children could try to represent only one of these elements or they could represent a combination of elements. Espeland (1987) and a group of teachers from Norway developed a number of ways that children might respond to the music. They call their program "Music in Use." Figure 8.2 suggests a variety of ways to engage children in constructing their response to a piece of recorded music.

Kerchner (1996) views this type of listening as engaging students in creative approaches that demand "cognitive acts including perception,

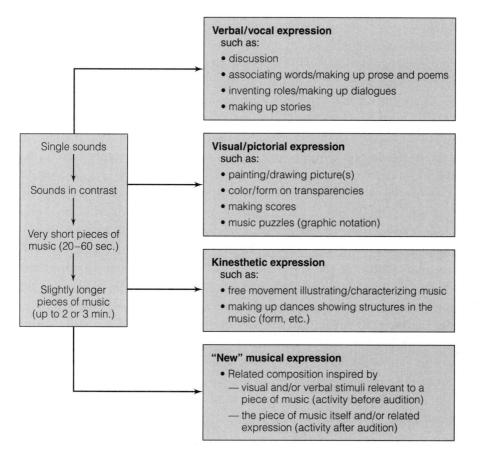

FIGURE 8.2

"Music in Use" Activities

Source: Espeland (1987, p. 288).

CHAPTER 8 / THE LISTENING CHILD

193

focus of attention, recall, and comparison. The process also includes anticipation or expectation." In mapping, students can draw maps, add to their maps through multiple hearings, and share their maps with others, asking them to respond to the drawings. Students could use limited movement of their upper bodies to physically map a portion of a piece then gradually work into whole body movement or plan a group choreography of a piece. It is worthwhile to have several groups visually map or choreograph the same piece of music and then have the students share their ideas followed by a discussion of similarities and differences and the reasons underlying their choices.

Building an Aural Repertoire

Teachers will often want to play a work of recorded music across a series of lessons or several times throughout a year. This approach helps children take works into long-term memory, so they become internalized references for a lifetime of musical learning and valuing. Repeated hearings help children become friends, not simply acquaintances, with the music that teachers, parents, and the children themselves find significant.

One approach to repertoire building is to utilize techniques outlined in the last section on student construction of listening experiences. These techniques involve students deeply through their own explorations and representation of the music and necessitate listening to the music many times. Another approach to repertoire building is to take a gestalt or holistic point of view. This allows the children to hear the entire piece, section, or movement in the initial listening. Subsequent hearings may concentrate on smaller parts for a particular focus. A final listening returns to the whole. This whole-part-whole approach to listening can take advantage of many active-listening techniques already discussed in this chapter. This is often teacher-directed.

Ideally, the repertoire should come from a wide range of music of the highest aesthetic quality, well crafted and well performed. This could include masterworks of Western art music, as well as folk, traditional, and popular music from any culture. Teachers may wish to set a goal of building deep knowledge of six works each year. Works could be organized around themes such as composer, artist, or culture of the month. At the elementary school level, children can become acquainted with individual styles within the Western art music tradition but are not yet ready for a strict historical approach to that music. At the same time, placing music in a cultural and historic context helps create deeper meaning for the students. A contextual perspective connects the work to the culture and time in which it was written to help students gain insight into ideas of cultural meaning, style, and performance practice.

Resources for listening are abundant, as close as the nearest record store or music site on the World Wide Web. Recordings and listening lessons are also incorporated in music series texts. Visuals, such as charts and music maps (for example, those in the lesson boxes), are included to assist learning. *Music Smart!* by Hotchkiss (1990) provides a rich resource of listening lessons. Other delightful recordings about the lives of composers are available from Classical Kids Productions in Toronto. Many children's books have been written to tell the stories of recorded works and composers. Such publications, along with music videos to enhance listening, can be found in such sources as the *Music in Motion* catalog or in local music stores that feature materials for teachers. The Metropolitan Opera in New York publishes *The Metropolitan Opera Boxes*. The Smithsonian Institution in Washington, D.C., publishes a wide range of educational recordings including folk and traditional music from throughout the world. Other ideas can be found in *Teaching General Music* (MENC, 1991) and MacGregor (1995) as well as music series texts.

In addition, listening lessons can be developed by teachers using any available recorded music. In the pop and jazz fields, it is often advisable to purchase "Best of" albums from artists who have demonstrated staying power in constantly changing fields.

Listening Sequence

A listening sequence (adapted from work by Sandra L. Stauffer), whether completed in one day or spread across many class periods, includes several steps.

Step 1: Prepare

Children need to be prepared to listen. The preparation will depend on the purpose of the listening. They could listen to a story such as *The Nutcracker*; they could be told the background of the culture the music is from and be asked to find the region on a map; they could view a painting or picture that helps establish a mood or sense of style; they could hear a story of the composer, composition, or the lives of the people from whom the music originated; or they could sing a melodic theme or sing and clap a pattern or motive they are to notice (this could be taught by rote or from a score). It is very important to give children something specific to listen for and a way to show that they hear it. These should be quiet responses such as raising hands, pointing, or writing so that all children can concentrate on the music. (Ideas for directing and monitoring perception appear in Lesson Activities 8.1 through 8.6.)

Step 2: Listen

Play the recording, and check students' perceptions or feelings through class discussion.

Step 3: Activate and Participate

Listen again, while actively involving students in performing or moving in some way to the music. These exercises can be repeated more than once and over time. It is a wonderful way to build a work into children's internal repertoire. For example, young children never seem to tire of moving like dwarves to *In the Hall of the Mountain King* by Grieg.

Step 4: Question and Discuss

Discussion should take place throughout this sequence, and can address the music, portions of the music, the activities the children are doing, or their emotional response to the experiences or the music.

Step 5: Listen Again

Listen to the recording quietly, simply to notice familiar moments, expand insight into the music, and reestablish the work as a whole.

Step 6: Extend the Listening

Use this listening as a stimulus to have the children:

1. Compose music in similar forms or with similar characteristics

2. Listen to other music by the same composer or culture that has similar or contrasting characteristics

3. Listen to other music by other composers or cultures that has similar or contrasting characteristics

The activities shown in Lessons 8.1 through 8.3 illustrate these principles and suggest possible ways to approach repertoire building with selected works. Music teachers who see children only once or twice a week may wish to enlist the help of classroom teachers in reinforcing listening experiences with children. [Remember that dubbing tapes or compact discs (CDs) and distributing copies to others is illegal under the copyright law. However, tapes and CDs owned by the school or district may be used in any classroom.] Lesson 8.1 is based on a familiar piece of Western classical music. Lesson 8.2 is adapted from suggestions in the book *Multicultural Perspectives in Music Education* (2nd ed.) by Anderson and Campbell (1996). The music is available on the tape that accompanies that book. This is one of many resources now available to help build listening repertoire from multicultural sources. Lesson 8.3 is an example of a listening strategy developed from recordings by contemporary artists and integrated with children's literature. Note that each series of activities strives to attain many goals related to musical elements, skills, repertoire, cultural or historical context, or other disciplines.

Grades	Second to fourth.
Repertoire and Context Goals	To internalize Beethoven's "Minuet in G" to gain a sense of musical style typical of his period and to learn something about Beethoven.
Concept Goal	To understand that ABA form can exist in an orchestral work. To put into words the musical differences between the sections.
Skills Goals	To perceive the differences in the sections. To coordinate movements to the sections.
Day 1	Show a picture of Ludwig van Beethoven. Ask the children if they have ever heard his name. (Discuss what they know about him.) Explain that he wrote many kinds of music, including music to be danced to. A popular dance of his day was called a minuet. Tell them you are going to play a particular minuet called "Minuet in G." Listen to this music and try to imagine the dancers. What kinds of motions might they be making and why? (Play recording. When it is finished, have children demonstrate some motions and discuss their choices.)
Day 2	Put "Minuet in G" on chalkboard. Have children tell you what they remember about the piece. Tell the children they are going to help invent a dance to do to the music but first they need to develop a sense of the way the music is organized. Review AB and ABA form. Ask them to listen to the music and to discover which pattern best fits its structure. Once children have discovered ABA form, show pictures of people dancing the minuet. Discuss the style of dress and hair. Discuss the elegance of the posture. Have them suggest stylized motions to do during the A section and contrasting motions during the B. Try those with the music. Note whether they change movements with the change in sections. Have them discuss how effective their choices were in terms of the music.
Day 3	Play "Minuet in G" as a mystery tune on a recording or on the piano. See how long it takes the children to name it and the composer. Put two words on the board: *even* and *uneven*. Tell them you want them to clap the rhythm of the melody of the "Minuet in G" as they listen and decide which word best fits the A section and which best fits the B. Later, help them to discover other ways the two sections contrast.
Extensions	1. Play the audio or videotape of the program *Beethoven Lives Upstairs* by Classical Kids Productions from Toronto. Have the children select other works by Beethoven they want to know.
	2. Invite a guest artist to play some Beethoven and discuss why the children are attracted to his music.
	3. Learn steps from the minuet and practice dancing them to the Beethoven selection.
	4. Compose an ABA form piece for instruments in which each section is sixteen beats long.

Using *In Praise of Oxala and Other Gods: Music from Colombia, South America,* Nonesuch Records

Grades	Fourth to sixth
Repertoire Goal	To internalize the piece "San Antonio," gaining a sense of style represented by African-derived music from Colombia.
Concept Goals	To understand that this music is created by the use of layers of various percussion instruments playing ostinati plus voices singing in call-and-response fashion. To understand the context in which the piece is used.
Skills Goals	To perceive the layers and specific rhythm patterns of the instruments. To be able to replicate by ear at least one of the patterns. To name the instruments being played. To play and sing the parts with accuracy. To add vocal harmony.
Day 1	Find Colombia on a map of South America. Discuss the fact that a large part of the country is a tropical rain forest and that much of it can be reached only by boat because the vegetation is so thick. Most of the people are very poor and make their money from growing bananas and catching fish. African slaves were brought to this region to work in the gold mines. The people who brought them left, and the blacks stayed. About 5,000 blacks live there today. Although Colombia is a Spanish-speaking country, much of the music has been influenced by the music that the African people brought with them. Tell the students that in the religious music that comes out of the Catholic church, the people often sing songs to saints. The song "San Antonio" is a song to Saint Anthony and is usually sung on Christmas Eve as a lullaby. It is sung in Spanish, but there are some African influences including the instruments used. (Review some of the traditional African instruments learned in an earlier unit.) Listen to "San Antonio," and notice the instruments used. Be ready to name them. (Discuss the use of marimba, rattles, and drums.) Listen again and notice the relation between the two voices and the instruments. Focus particularly on patterns that repeat. (Discuss the call-and-response vocal form and the instrumental ostinato.)
Day 2	Show children the notation for the call-and-response section of "San Antonio." Teach them the response pattern. Sing the call, and have them respond. Play the recording and have them join in each time they hear the response. (They may be able to sing this in harmony.) Ask for volunteers to learn the call. Take turns using different leaders. Other children may wish to add the rattle or drum part, learning it aurally.

Day 3	Echo clap the rhythms for the call and response in the marimba part for "San Antonio." Have children discover those patterns in the score of the marimba part. How are they similar to the sung line? Teach some children to play those patterns on the marimba or keyboard. Put the whole piece together.

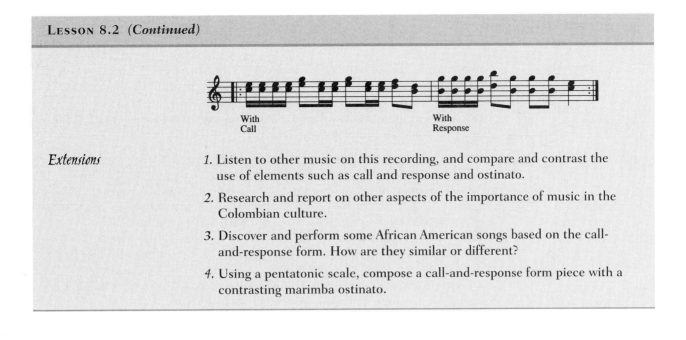

Extensions

1. Listen to other music on this recording, and compare and contrast the use of elements such as call and response and ostinato.

2. Research and report on other aspects of the importance of music in the Colombian culture.

3. Discover and perform some African American songs based on the call-and-response form. How are they similar or different?

4. Using a pentatonic scale, compose a call-and-response form piece with a contrasting marimba ostinato.

LESSON 8.3 *"Hush Little Baby"*

Using "Hush Little Baby" by Heidi Grant Murphy and Auréole and *Hush* by Yo-Yo Ma and Bobby McFerrin

Grades

Pre-K to second.

Repertoire Goals

To internalize a sense of style that comes from contrasting versions of a familiar song. To understand that one piece can occur in many different arrangements.

Concept Goals

To review the meaning and traditional style of a lullaby. To understand that improvising is a way to be musically playful.

Skills Goals

To physically and vocally respond to the flow and mood of the music. To aurally perceive ways that a familiar work has been altered. To experiment with musically altering other familiar works.

Literature Goals

To become familiar with contrasting styles of illustrating a familiar song and to connect that with similar styles in music. To write and illustrate an arrangement of that song.

Day 1

Read the picture book *Hush Little Baby* as illustrated by Aliki (1968). Discuss the sequence and the predictability of the rhymes. Learn to sing the folk song "Hush Little Baby." Sing it as you follow the pictures in the book.

Day 2

Bring in a doll or stuffed animal. Pretend to put it to sleep by rocking it. When it resists falling asleep, suggest that a lullaby might help. Have the children listen carefully to see if they can help rock pretend babies and also sing the lullaby. Begin to sing "Hush Little Baby" on the neutral syllable "loo." Watch to see when children recognize the song and enter in. Have them name the song and then sing it while they pretend to rock their babies and put them to sleep. Gently place the sleeping babies away as you play the

(Continued)

recording of "Hush Little Baby" by Heidi Grant Murphy and Auréole. Invite children to stand, find a place in space and gently move to the flow of the music. Extend their movements by having them used colored scarves or streamers to show the flow. Invite children to share what they noticed about the music and how it made them feel.

Day 3

On the board, put the words *word* and *bird*, *sing and ring*, *down* and *town*, and so on. Invite children to help to read them. Ask them what song the words are from. Sing the song using soft, soothing voices. Discuss the flow (gentle) and dynamic quality (soft) of the lullaby. Tell them you are going to play a recording of two men performing "Hush Little Baby." Ask them to listen to decide whether they think it will put the baby to sleep or not. Listen and discuss their responses as to why it would not put the baby to sleep. (It is loud and fast.) Have the children stand, face a partner, and hold hands. Play the recording again while the children rock back and forth to the flow of the music, creating an imaginary cradle.

Day 4

Introduce children to the names of the two musicians who performed "Hush Little Baby." Show them their pictures. Discuss the fact that they are both famous musicians who love to experiment or play with sounds. (Children may have seen them on *Sesame Street,* on *Mister Rogers' Neighborhood,* or in TV ads.) Listen to their arrangement of "Hush Little Baby" to discover what they did to make it different from the original. Discuss those ideas (faster, louder, different words, higher pitches, sliding, mouth sounds, clapping). Have children join in vocally with the recording, trying some of the techniques. Discuss the delightful character of this style of singing. Read the book *Hush Little Baby* illustrated by Margot Zemach (1976). Does its quality capture more of the original version of the song or the YoYo Ma–McFerrin version? Why or why not?

Teacher with young children and dolls, singing "Hush Little Baby"

Extensions

1. Have the children develop their own vocal improvisations (playing with sounds) using familiar nursery rhymes.

2. Take another lullaby and turn it from a gentle piece to an upbeat piece by improvising.

3. Share the book *Hush Little Baby* by Sylvia Long (1997). Have the children discuss what is different about this book. Encourage them to create their own version of "Hush Little Baby," illustrate it, and then bind it into their own book.

4. Listen to other selections from the album *Hush* such as "Flight of the Bumblebee" by Rimsky-Korsakov. Discuss how the various effects were created.

5. Find out more about Bobby McFerrin and Yo-Yo Ma (videotapes from PBS, other recordings). Build their names into the children's vocabulary. Compare Yo-Yo Ma's cello style on "Hush Little Baby" with a more traditional style. Discuss the differences.

Assessment of Listening

Many ways exist to understand what children are hearing and feeling as they listen. One tool that is commonly used in music series texts to test for aural perception of discrete elements is "what do you hear?" charts (see Figure 8.3). These focus narrowly on whether or not students have formed a concept or understanding of an element and whether they can identify it in a short segment of recorded music. Lesson Activities 8.1 through 8.6 include many techniques for observing what children are perceiving in the music.

The ability to identify a musical work studied during the year could be assessed through having children listen to a range of familiar pieces, name them, and share something they remember about each piece.

A much richer understanding of what students are hearing and feeling can be gained by asking them to describe the music in some way—verbally, kinesthetically, or visually. Rodriguez and Webster (1997) found clear age-related differences in the quality of verbal descriptions children offered in response to recorded music. They asked children four questions to get at their cognitive responses, knowledge of how to create music, awareness of their feeling response to music, and musical features that evoked these feelings.

The questions were:

1. What were you thinking when you listened to this music?

2. If you were going to make music like this, how would you start?

3. How does this music make you feel?

4. What in the music makes you feel that way?

FIGURE 8.3

"What Do You Hear?"

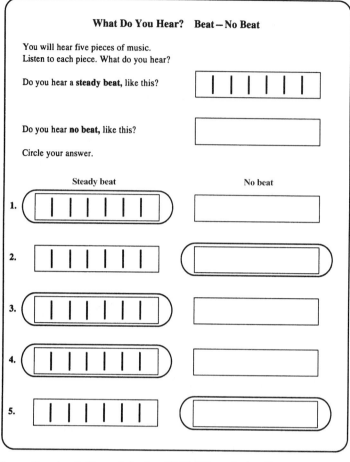

Source: Reproduced with permission from *World of Music,* Grade 1 (Parsippany, NJ: Silver Burdett & Ginn, 1992).

Generally, as children mature, they are more able to connect feelings with the music, use musical terminology, and understand the need for training, organization, and collaboration in making music. Responses to such questions could become part of a child's portfolio, either in written form or taped form. Kerchner (1999) found that children were more detailed in their descriptions of music when they drew maps or responded kinesthetically than when they tried to describe the music verbally. This research points to the value of including several ways of having children describe music and their responses to the music, and it suggests that different modes will be preferred by different children. Children's musical maps or videos of their movement solutions and reflections on those solutions could also become part of a portfolio.

Keys to Listening

Opening ears and minds to the sounds and subtleties of music and watching the discoveries children make and the excitement they feel bring great satisfaction to the teaching of music. To do this successfully, teachers need to continue listening themselves—not just to familiar works but also to unfamiliar ones, and to the comfortable and uncomfortable. Teachers need to bring attitudes of openness, curiosity, and discovery to the act of listening. They need to be willing to engage in focused listening, not just passive listening.

Teachers who actively nurture their own musical growth through listening have greater riches to offer their students. The keys to listening can be developed and, through them, worlds of pleasure unlocked. To paraphrase philosopher Harry Broudy, teachers need to develop their own connoisseurship to help their students engage in a lifetime of enlightened cherishing.

Scenario

Mrs. Delacorte has been eager to share a recording of the overture to Mozart's opera *The Magic Flute* with her fifth graders. The music is playing as the children enter the room. They move to their assigned seats with their cooperative groups. Mrs. Delacorte has trained the students to be prepared to describe something they notice about the music that is playing when they enter. When the music stops, she gives the groups a short period of time to discuss what they noticed. She has each team captain share ideas, and she lists them on the board. Mostly the children name the instruments that they heard and their responses to the lively style of the music. Some talk about the tempo and sudden dynamic changes.

Next Mrs. Delacorte invites the children to listen to the music again and imitate her hands as she moves them upward and downward to the shape of the melody. She adds dynamic emphasis as she moves. Some children have a hard time imitating the movements as the music moves by so quickly. Two or three children start to laugh, but Mrs. Delacorte ignores them and continues to map the music through movement of the arms and hands. Once the music finishes, she asks the students to describe what more they noticed. The children begin to talk about the shape of the melodies and the repetition of some of the patterns.

Mrs. Delacorte asks the team captains to distribute drawing paper and colored pens to each member of their team. The assignment is to . . .

Questions

1. What approach to active listening is Mrs. Delacorte using?

2. Discuss what might happen next in this lesson. What will the assignment be?

3. How will the children report back to the rest of the class?

4. What else might be valuable for children to understand about this music?

5. How might Mrs. Delacorte approach this music another day to expand student understanding of it?

REVIEW

1. What is the difference between active perceptive listening and passive functional listening? What are three techniques to enhance active listening?

2. At what age or stage are students likely to form strong preferences for particular kinds of music? How might that influence what recordings you use with them?

3. What are useful steps for planning listening lessons designed to build repertoire?

4. What are the benefits to having children construct their own responses to listening experiences?

5. What techniques can be used to assess listening?

6. How can teachers nurture their own ongoing growth as perceptive listeners?

CRITICAL THINKING

1. How would you justify spending class time having children listen to recorded music?

2. How might a teacher respond to older elementary children's requests to bring pop music recordings to music class?

3. Discuss with others in your class the validity of the following statement: "A teacher can make children like music that the teacher likes."

4. Which approach(es) to listening outlined in this chapter seem to hold the most potential for having children own a piece of music and why?

PROJECTS

1. Interview two kindergartners, two second graders, two fourth graders, and two sixth graders about what kind of music they like and why. Are their stages of preference similar to those outlined in this chapter? Summarize and report your findings to your class.

2. Select a piece of recorded music you find exciting. Determine why you find it exciting. Using the steps outlined for a listening sequence, plan a series of activities to share this music with children.

3. Develop a set of materials that children can use to enter more actively into the listening experience. These could include ideas from the reading column of Lesson Activities 8.1 through 8.6 or others.

4. Develop a listening map to help children track events in a recorded work.

5. Find a listening map in a music series text or create one of your own. Cut it into phrases and cre-
ate a puzzle for children to place in order as they listen to that music. Try it with children of different ages and see whether they are able to solve the puzzle.

6. Closely examine different music series texts to see how they incorporate listening to music. What literature have they chosen? How have they helped get children actively involved? How have they helped to build repertoire, if at all? Teach one of those lessons to your class or to a group of children.

7. Interview children of different ages using the questions designed by Rodriguez and Webster (1997) in response to a piece of music. Compare the responses you collected to those in their article.

REFERENCES

Aliki (1968). *Hush little baby: A folk lullaby.* New York: Simon & Schuster Books for Young Children.

Anderson, W., and P. Campbell (1996). *Multicultural perspectives in music education* (2nd ed.). Reston, VA: Music Educators National Conference.

Cain, T. (1988). *Keynote.* Cambridge, England: Cambridge University.

Espeland, Magne (1987). Music in use: Responsive music listening in the primary school. *British Journal of Music Education,* 4(3), 283–297.

Haack, P. (1992). The acquisition of music listening skills. In D. Colwell, ed., *Handbook of research on music teaching and learning,* chapter 29. New York: Schirmer Books.

Hotchkiss, G. (1990). *Music smart!* Reston, VA: Music in Motion.

Kerchner, J. L. (1996). Creative music listening. *General Music Today,* Fall, 28–30.

———. (1999). Children's verbal, visual, and kinesthetic responses: Insight into their music listening experience. *Bulletin of the Council for Research in Music Education,* 142, Fall, 84–85.

Long, S. (1997). *Hush little baby.* New York: Scholastic.

Ma, Yo-Yo, and Bobby McFerrin (1992). *Hush.* Sony Masterworks SK 48177.

MacGregor, H. (1995). *Listening to music: Elements age 5+.* London, England: A & C Black.

MENC (1991). *Teaching general music.* Reston, VA: Music Educators National Conference.

Murphy, H. G., and Auréole (1999). *Dreamscape: Lullabies from around the world.* Koch 3-7433-2HI.

Richards, M. H. (1980). *Aesthetic foundations for thinking: The ETM process.* Portola Valley, CA.: Richards Institute.

Rodriguez, C. X., and P. R. Webster (1997). Development of children's verbal interpretive responses to music listening. *Bulletin of the Council for Research in Music Education,* 134, Fall, 9–30.

Schaefer, R. M. (1976). *Creative music education.* New York: Schirmer Books.

Scott-Kassner, C. (1992). Research on music in early childhood. In D. Colwell, ed., *Handbook of research on music teaching and learning,* chapter 45. New York: Schirmer Books.

Zemach, M. (1976). *Hush, little baby.* New York: E. P. Dutton.

CATALOGS AND RESOURCES

Classical Kids Productions. 1988. *Beethoven Lives Upstairs.* The Children's Group, 561 Bloor St. W., Suite 300, Toronto, Ontario, Canada M5S I Y6.

Claudia's Caravan (a catalog of multicultural and multilingual materials). P.O. Box 1582, Alameda, CA. 94501; (510) 521-7871.

The Metropolitan Opera Box for ages eleven through eighteen. Education at the Met, 1865 Broadway, New York, NY 10023.

Music in Motion (a music education and gift catalog). P.O. Box 833814, Richardson, TX 75083-3814.

Roots and Rhythm Mail Order (a catalog of blues, folk, world music, and pop recordings and books). 6921 Stockton Ave., El Cerrito, CA 94530; (510) 525-1494.

The Whole Folkways Catalog (a catalog of historic folkways recordings). Smithsonian/Folkways, Center for Folklife Programs and Cultural Studies, 955 L'Enfant Plaza, Suite 2600, Smithsonian Institution, Washington, DC 20560; (202) 287-3262.

World Music Press/West Music (a catalog of world music resources). West Music, 1208 Fifth Street, P.O. Box 5521, Coralville, IA 52241.

9

The Moving Child

In the world of children, music and movement are nearly inseparable from one another. Clear the room, set the rules, start the music, and watch the movement begin: Rochelle pirouettes like a ballerina to the light and whirling music of the flute. Ally glides like a swan to the cello's melody. Nicolas hops, then jumps in one place to the dialogue of the clarinet and bassoon. With the entrance of the brass instruments, Sally marches with her knees high and her toes pointed. Sean, Li, and Tommy strut forward with long legs overlapping, arms stretched across each other's shoulders. Jimmie jogs with an imaginary basketball to the pulse of the percussion section. Consuela and Trina find the pulse and clap hands, forward, backward, and upside down. Anna stands at the center of it all, conducting.

Children love to move. With the sound of the music, they release their bundles of energy. Heads nod; toes tap; bodies rock; arms swing. Even without music, while children play, they often move in some semblance of a musical rhythm. Moving children skip, hop, walk, run, slide, gallop, jump, twist, and turn. Movement—of all kinds—is one of their favorite things to do.

The foundation of music for children is ultimately and intimately entwined with their physical selves. Music, the aural art, is also music, the kinesthetic art. Children develop their musical abilities through a combination of what they experience through their ears, eyes, and bodies. As children listen, sing, or play instruments—even as they read music—their aural, visual, and kinesthetic senses are activated. Movement is thus vital to their musical development and basic to all that they do.

Children mirroring
movement patterns

Jerry Gay

Music classes for children in elementary schools and in early childhood settings are animated affairs. The teacher's task is to harness, shape, and direct the spontaneous and natural movements of children toward an understanding of rhythm, melody, phrasing, texture, dynamics, and form. Under a teacher's guidance, children combine their movement with body sounds: stepping, clapping, patting, or snapping. They sing songs with associated actions or games. They practice the preparatory movements that ease them toward the playing of musical instruments. They move creatively to express what they hear and feel. They learn the structured steps of a dance. For all of these experiences, the teacher uses logic and creativity to steer children through their movement toward musical understanding.

Movement helps children to internalize musical concepts. While there is no explicit content for movement within the National Standards for music (MENC, 1994), teachers with years of successful experience assume that movement is the means for leading children to more musical singing and instrument playing, to composing and improvising in meaningful ways, and to showing evidence of listening with a clear understanding of music's structures and sonic flow. The National Standards in dance (MENC, 1994) prescribe content standards in the elements and skills of moving with artistic purpose, but the use of music in the musical education of children presumes no artistic end. Instead, it is a means for learning musical ideas and expressions. It is also used by teachers to allow children to let off steam and to change the classroom pace from a sit-down activity to a move-around exercise that rewards children for hard work well done. Movement gives opportunities for socialization and cooperation through singing games and dances. It offers children a means for understanding other cultures through folk dances. It stimulates thinking, including musical thinking. It is an important means by which children can express themselves. Movement balances the academically passive parts of the school day with the children's characteristically active nature. Movement can successfully merge children's energies, attitudes, and ideas.

Movement responses to music may be instinctive and natural, but children's instincts can be further developed and refined through instruction. When children are receptive to musical sound, the rhythm or melody will inspire them to actively participate in the music through the movement they imitate or invent. They are capable of responding to music with motion and emotion; it evokes in them both kinesthetic and aesthetic reactions. Children's natural movements can be used as avenues to music learning when lessons are designed by teachers to match movement to musical concepts.

Movement and Child Development

From infancy, children listen attentively to music and respond by moving to its rhythm. Moog (1976) noted that by the age of six months, when infants are increasingly able to coordinate the actions of their sense organs, they move their whole body in a generalized—albeit not synchronized—manner. By two years, toddling children are seen rocking from side to side, bouncing up and down, and waving their arms in conducting patterns. As children begin to listen more attentively to music at the age of three to four, the variety of their movements declines and they enter into a period of practicing and perfecting the movements they already know. Their physical coordination improves as they enter kindergarten, when four- to six-year-olds are able to move more often than not to the pulse of the music.

Children develop their capacity to use their large muscles necessary for such locomotor activities as walking, running, and hopping before they can control the small muscles they need for writing, drawing, or playing such instruments as the recorder or keyboard. By the time they are in kindergarten, children have usually developed the coordination that enables them to hop, gallop, skip, and jump rope. They enjoy physical activity and move successfully to singing games, action songs, and simple folk dances. They also seize opportunities to respond freely to recorded and live music. They enjoy creating movements to music in individually expressive ways.

Movement ability and the psychomotor skills necessary for performance improve with advancing age. Petzold's (1966) classic study found that, by third grade, most children can accurately maintain a steady beat through tapping. Developmental patterns are apparent, in that when children in the primary grades are asked to reproduce rhythms, they do so most accurately by chanting the rhythms, moderately so by clapping, and least accurately when stepping them. Children show a gradual but marked increase in accuracy through the first three grades in these types of rhythmic movement, with girls generally outperforming boys who may lag about a year behind. While children's larger muscles develop earlier than their small

TABLE 9.1 *Children's Movement Development*

AGE	DEVELOPMENTAL SKILL
Less than six months	Responds to music through generalized body movement; movement not yet synchronized to rhythm
Two years	Responds by rocking, bouncing, waving arms to rhythm Develops walking and running skills Attempts to imitate clapping and patty-cake movements
Three to four	Practices known movements by repeating them Invents and imitates new movements Begins to develop large muscle coordination for jumping, hopping Can perform simple action songs and game songs
Five to six (kindergarten)	Begins to develop rhythmic clapping and patting Begins to develop skills for galloping (one-sided skip) and jumping rope Can perform simple folk dances in circles and lines Begins to develop small muscle coordination for drawing and printing (writing)
Six to seven (grades one and two)	Begins to develop skipping skills Responds (frequently) to music through hand-clapping; achievement of beat competence Can follow the pulse and dynamics of music and respond to gradual changes through movement Can perform beat on drum, rhythm sticks; can play sustained bourdons on xylophone (but requires prepatory movement to precede performance)

muscles, the extent to which they can fine-tune coordination of the torso, the arms, and the legs to express themselves musically improves gradually through the age of ten or eleven years. This complex perceptual-motor co-ordination is vital to reading and performing music. See Table 9.1 for a summary of children's movement development.

Through the primary grades, as children develop strength, agility, and flexibility, they increase their ability to play with some control percussion instruments such as the drum, tambourine, claves, and maracas. They can play simple accompaniments on xylophones and bells, including sustained bourdons and simple ostinato patterns. Preparatory movements performed initially without the instruments will provide children with the motor patterns necessary to play them with rhythmic accuracy and fluency of movement. The motor coordination necessary for the performance of wind, brass, stringed, and keyboard instruments is usually not well developed before the age of eight or nine years. However, those children presented with opportunities to play these instruments will develop the necessary muscles

TABLE 9.1 (*Continued*)

AGE	DEVELOPMENTAL SKILL
Eight to nine (grade three)	Can maintain a steady beat while tapping, patting, clapping
	Can accurately reproduce rhythms by chanting, tapping, patting, clapping, or stepping
	Can perform ostinatos on xylophones (but requires preparatory movement to precede performance)
	Develops small muscle coordination for playing recorder, keyboard
	Can respond quickly and accurately to musical changes (in tempo, rhythmic patterns, texture) through movement; can have quick reactions
	Can perform more complex folk dances in circles, lines, squares, and partners
	Can conduct meters with rhythmic accuracy
Ten to twelve (grades four to six)	Girls begin to show early signs of physical maturation
	Develops small muscle coordination (and dual coordination of breathing and fingers) for performing wind and brass instruments
	Enjoys active physical involvement; may prefer sports to dance
	Can perform rhythmic canons by moving to music that is previously sounded (four beats earlier) while listening to other music
	Can respond to two distinctive features of music through simultaneous movement (stepping the rhythm while conducting the pulse)

to do so, should they be motivated to heed the adage that "practice makes perfect."

Action Songs and Singing Games

From the perspective of child development, movement is more than just the motor coordination necessary for the performance of a musical instrument. It is the essence of children's play and the manner through which they come to know their world. From early childhood, children move playfully as they sing songs associated with games, actions, and dances. The melodies of action songs and singing games draw from children the movements they have naturally encountered in their free play. These movements are recalled and organized by children to express the song's rhythmic and expressive qualities. Even in the upper elementary grades, carefully selected songs to appeal to the interests of older children can provide the orderly release of physical energy that the music requires.

*Movement for tight
spaces and confined
areas*

Jerry Gay

Eurhythmics

Eurhythmic activities, in which children are encouraged to "do what the music tells you to do," can be designed to be in step developmentally with children's physical capacities. Children from preschool through the sixth grade can be motivated to use their bodies to illustrate music's salient features. By stepping the pulse, conducting the meter, tapping the melody's repeated rhythmic pattern, or drawing the melodic contour or shaping the phrase length in the air, children can demonstrate without words their understanding of musical concepts. Through eurhythmics, the body becomes a personal instrument for realizing the music from the simplest to the more challenging exercises.

Creative Movement

While the development of feeling for a steady beat may be one among many musical goals, it may not always be necessary that children synchronize their movement with others or to a unifying pulse. In creative movement, children may be guided to develop their own repertoire of movements to express loud or soft, slow or fast, high or low, or choppy or smooth. They may explore a single movement, repeating it and expanding it, or take the movement modeled for them and vary it. By imitating the teacher or another student, children build their movement vocabulary for later recall and use. Music supplies the impetus for children to assemble new and familiar movements in ways that are personally expressive.

Dance

The structured movements of dance require the basic skill of keeping time with the music. Even in the primary grades, children frequently are able to perform simple folk dances in a synchronized manner, although this is partly dependent on their physical development. The synchronicity required for perfecting the structured steps and formations of circle, square, partner, and line dances should not necessarily delay the teaching of these dances. The practice of doing the dances will provide children with the exercise for developing their sense of rhythm and time.

Precepts and Principles of Movement

In designing lessons and experiences for children that unite music with movement, the teacher will want to include musical concepts and genres of movement that children potentially can develop. The teacher with musical training will recognize the musical concepts as fundamental to children's understanding of "what makes music tick." The teacher who has observed children at play will recognize that the movement genres describe the natural inclinations of children toward physical activity (see Table 9.2, p. 214). The challenge is how to match musical concepts with movement genres. How can these repertoires be merged? How does movement teach a musical concept? How does a musical concept motivate movement?

Movement and music are both concerned with time, and so the concepts of pulse, duration, accent, and tempo figure prominently in each. Of all the possible combinations of movement with music, then, the most obvious is the ways in which these rhythmic (pulse, duration, accent) and expressive (tempo) concepts might be expressed through movement. But melody, timbre, form, and texture can also be expressed physically by children through various locomotor and nonlocomotor movement styles and through variations in space, time, and energy. The action songs, singing games, eurhythmics, creative movement, and dance lessons suggested below will illustrate how.

For movement-based musical experiences to be educationally sound, the teacher also needs to consider a set of precepts and physical arrangements to ensure the success of these exercises with children. The following items are intended to guide the teacher in the planning of music-and-movement lessons for children (see also Box 9.1 and Box 9.2, p. 215).

Prelude to Movement-Based Musical Experiences

In beginning to develop a sensitivity to music through movement, children need to be aware of (1) the potential of their bodies to move in place (nonlocomotor) and across space (locomotor), (2) the relationship of their bodies to people and objects in the room, and (3) the related qualities of space, time, and energy found in both music and movement. Exploratory movement ideas suggested in Table 9.3 on page 216 act as a prelude to movement-based musical experiences and can be performed with and without musical accompaniment.

TABLE 9.2 *Musical Concepts and Their Related Movement Genres*

MUSICAL CONCEPTS	MOVEMENT GENRES

Rhythm
  Pulse (beat)
  Duration
  Accent
  Meter
  Patterns
Melody
  Pitch: high and low
  Contour
  Repeat, step, skip
Timbre
  Musical sound and not-musical
    sound
  Voices (type)
  Instruments (type)
    Alone
    In groups
Form
  Repetition
  Variation
  Contrast
Texture
  One line
  Multiple lines: simultaneous
  Multiple lines: independent
Expressive qualities
  Tempo: fast and slow
  Tempo: changing
  Dynamics: loud and soft
  Dynamics: changing
	Nonlocomotor (in place)
	  Stretch
	  Bend
	  Swing
	  Twist
	  Bounce
	  Shake
	  Push
	  Pull
	  Sway
	  Rise
	  Collapse
	Locomotor (across space)
	  Walk
	  Run
	  Jump
	  Hop
	  Gallop
	  Skip
	  Slide
	  Leap
	  Lunge
	  Strut
	Movement variations
	  Space
	    Shape (round, angular, bodily
	      designs)
	    Size (large, small)
	    Level (high, middle, low)
	    Place (in place, through space)
	    Direction (forward, backward,
	      sideways, turning)
	    Pathway (straight, curving)
	  Time
	    Pulse (beat)
	    Duration (long, short)
	    Accent (force)
	    Tempo (fast, slow)
	  Energy
	    Attack (sharp, smooth)
	    Weight (light, heavy)
	    Flow (bound, free)
	    Strength (tight, loose)

Exploratory movement experiences can be initiated or further developed by the classroom teacher or physical education instructor. Nonetheless, the music teacher may use these suggestions for movement as a means of warming up children's physical selves in preparation for musical exercises that require agility, grace, flexibility, and the coordination of thinking with doing. Children enjoy the discovery of the capacities of their bodies to move

Box 9.1 *Preparation for Music-and-Movement Experiences*

1. Observe children at play during recess. Notice their energy, speed, direction, levels, and various locomotor and nonlocomotor genres of their movements. Note the distinctions in the movement of boys and girls and among children of various age groups.

2. Consider ways in which the movement qualities of athletic activities, sports, and playground games can be brought into lessons that explore musical concepts.

3. Be prepared to model a variety of movement possibilities for children's imitation and eventual variation and personal interpretation. Also, take note of children who move with ease and flair and can serve as models of movement for their peers.

4. Encourage children to explore the variety of ways in which the various body parts can be moved, including experiments with the energy, speed, directions, and levels in space.

Box 9.2 *Arranging for Music-and-Movement Experiences*

1. Make room for movement. Move chairs and desks to the side of the room, go outdoors in the good weather, and use cafeterias, gyms (although acoustics can be a problem), lobbies, and hallways.

2. Explore the possibilities for movement in tight spaces, in chairs, and at desks. Some of the most fulfilling movement can be done sitting down and snapping, clapping, patting, stamping, and conducting.

3. While allowing children the freedom to express musical ideas through movement, set movement rules (move without touching anyone, listen before moving) that will organize what might otherwise prove chaotic to the classroom.

4. Choose live music (on piano, for example) and recorded music in a variety of styles that will motivate children to want to move in various expressive ways.

as suggested and to act on command; such exercises are inherently motivating. Children can be led toward problem solving, presented as questions or creative imagery, as they offer solutions through the most personal of entities: their bodies. For the music teacher, however, the end-product of all movement experiences is the development of children's musical understanding, skills, and values.

Action Songs and Singing Games

For young children from the toddling stages through the primary grades, action songs and singing games help develop coordination, synchronized rhythmic movement, and the singing voice. Many children's songs that are performed in schoolyards during recess are oriented toward actions and games. The movements of these songs offer a release for pent-up energy and may serve as a memory cue for learning the words of those songs. The

TABLE 9.3 *Exploratory Movement with and without Music*

GOAL	EXPLORATORY TASKS
Body awareness	Find different ways of moving your fingers, hands, arms, elbows, shoulders, feet, legs, head, and hips
Body relationship	Walk your own path without touching anyone; walk around every chair, block, or hoop placed on the floor
	Touch two fingers to the two fingers of your neighbors as you pass them
	Follow teacher across the floor in exactly the same way (but after teacher has completed movement)
Time (speed)	Move a body part: fast, faster, slow, slower, gradually faster or slower
Space (direction)	Walk forward, backward, sideways, toward the door, toward the windows
Space (levels)	Walk high, low, medium; alternately high and low
Energy (weight)	Make yourself heavy, light, strong, limp
Energy (flow)	Walk without stopping; stop suddenly or gradually
Nonlocomotor movement	Draw with your hands, elbows, head, or feet a straight line, a curved line, a zigzag, a loop; shape your body into a box, a triangle, a *T*, a *V*; move from one shape to the next within four beats or seven beats
Locomotor movement	Walk, leap, lunge, run, jump, hop, gallop, skip, strut, slide

songs provide avenues for channeling children's energies toward meaningful movement.

Action songs are those to which rhythmic gestures are added, often to coincide with the meaning of the song text (see Lesson 9.1). These songs can usually be performed with little previous training and without movement exercises preceding them. As a lullaby, "Suogan" suggests the rocking of a baby to sleep, while the texts of "Johnny Works with One Hammer" and "Teddy Bear" tell the young singers to hammer with one or more hammers and to turn around and touch the ground, respectively. Beyond the traditional action songs, children may enjoy inventing gestures for familiar songs.

Many children's traditional songs incorporate games (see Lesson 9.2). Singing games may have survived many generations because of the joy they bring to children. The games typically require children to gather in circles, lines, small groups, or with partners, and the movement they perform is often matched to the pulse or melodic rhythm of the song. Counting songs and hand-clapping songs are singing games as well, and children enjoy the excitement of songs that have a game goal in mind. "Ring around the Rosy" and "London Bridge" are well-known singing games in English-speaking countries. From Cambodia, "Leak Kanseng" involves a scarf and a chase around the circle. "Guru Ndiani" is a children's singing game from

Suogan
(Wales)

Su - o - gan, do not weep, Su - o - gan, go to sleep,

Su - o - gan, Moth-er's near, Su - o - gan, have no fear.

Song   "Suogan"

Level   Early childhood through grade one

Movement   Cradle the baby in the arms, rocking it back and forth to the musical pulse.

Johnny Works with One Hammer
(United States)

John - ny works with one ham-mer, one ham-mer, one ham-mer.

John - ny works with one ham-mer, then he works with two.

2. two hammers, then he works with three.
3. three hammers, then he works with four.
4. four hammers, then he works with five.
5. five hammers, then he goes to sleep.

Song   "Johnny Works with One Hammer"

Level   Early childhood through grade one

Movement   Verse 1, pound one fist on knee. Verse 2, pound two fists on knees. Verse 3, pound two fists and one foot. Verse 4, pound two fists and two feet. Verse 5, pound two fists, two feet, and nod head. On "then he goes to sleep," rest head on hands.

(Continued)

Teddy Bear

(United States)

Ted - dy bear, ted - dy bear, turn a - round, _____
tie your shoe, _____
go up - stairs, _____
turn out the light, _____

Ted - dy bear, ted - dy bear, touch the ground.
that will do.
say your prayers.
say good - night.

Song	"Teddy Bear"
Level	Early childhood through grade one
Movement	Act out the words of the text.

Zimbabwe. Like action songs, the children's own singing provides the necessary accompaniment to the movement and the game.

There are historical collections of action songs stemming from the late nineteenth century and a wide variety of Kodály- and Orff-based published materials. Forrai with Sinor's (1988) collection of action songs and singing games is especially noteworthy for those teaching younger children.

Dalcroze Eurhythmics

Principles developed by Swiss musician Émile Jaques-Dalcroze provide the single most complete system of rhythmic training to appear in the twentieth century. He recognized movement as the foundation of a thorough musicianship and thus developed a means of communication linking the ear, the brain, and the body. He established eurhythmics (good rhythm) as an alternative to dance and gymnastics, developing in his students a fuller musical consciousness through directed and improvised physical responses to music. While few teachers today submit to the rigorous training of the Dalcroze approach, partly because of the challenges of learning the keyboard improvisation that Dalcroze used to accompany these movement exercises, eurhythmic experiences can be integrated within music classes for children in modified ways, using drums or prerecorded music as the impetus for movement.

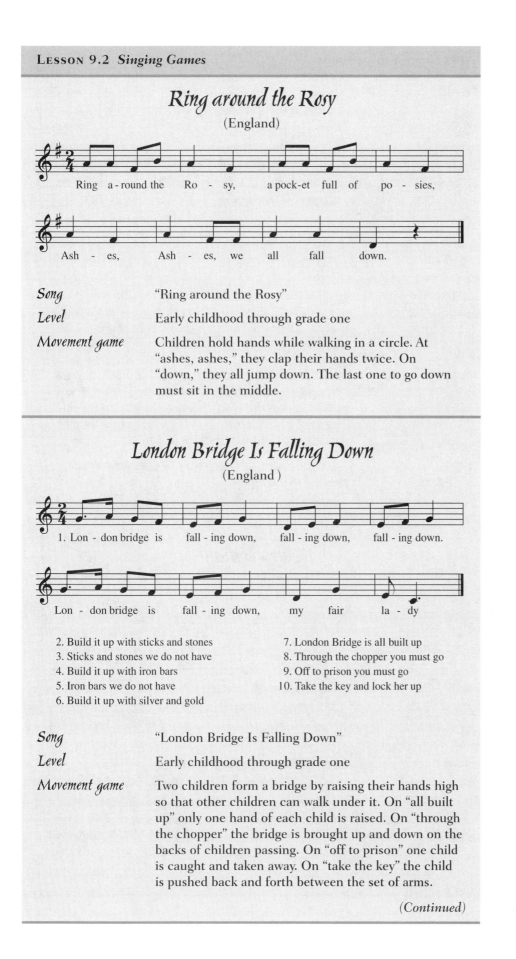

Ring around the Rosy
(England)

Ring a-round the Ro - sy, a pock-et full of po - sies,

Ash - es, Ash - es, we all fall down.

Song	"Ring around the Rosy"
Level	Early childhood through grade one
Movement game	Children hold hands while walking in a circle. At "ashes, ashes," they clap their hands twice. On "down," they all jump down. The last one to go down must sit in the middle.

London Bridge Is Falling Down
(England)

1. Lon - don bridge is fall - ing down, fall - ing down, fall - ing down.

Lon - don bridge is fall - ing down, my fair la - dy

2. Build it up with sticks and stones
3. Sticks and stones we do not have
4. Build it up with iron bars
5. Iron bars we do not have
6. Build it up with silver and gold

7. London Bridge is all built up
8. Through the chopper you must go
9. Off to prison you must go
10. Take the key and lock her up

Song	"London Bridge Is Falling Down"
Level	Early childhood through grade one
Movement game	Two children form a bridge by raising their hands high so that other children can walk under it. On "all built up" only one hand of each child is raised. On "through the chopper" the bridge is brought up and down on the backs of children passing. On "off to prison" one child is caught and taken away. On "take the key" the child is pushed back and forth between the set of arms.

(Continued)

Leak Kanseng

(Cambodia)

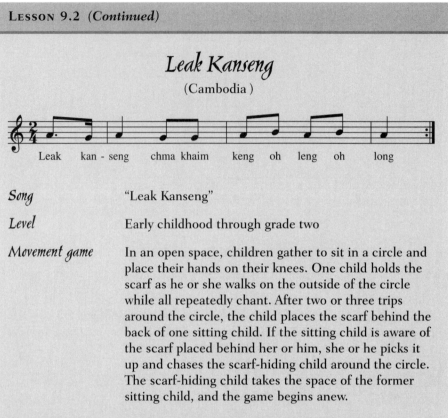

Leak kan - seng chma khaim keng oh leng oh long

Song	"Leak Kanseng"
Level	Early childhood through grade two
Movement game	In an open space, children gather to sit in a circle and place their hands on their knees. One child holds the scarf as he or she walks on the outside of the circle while all repeatedly chant. After two or three trips around the circle, the child places the scarf behind the back of one sitting child. If the sitting child is aware of the scarf placed behind her or him, she or he picks it up and chases the scarf-hiding child around the circle. The scarf-hiding child takes the space of the former sitting child, and the game begins anew.

Source: "Leak Kanseng" as sung by Sam-Ang Sam. From *Silent Temples, Songful Hearts: Traditional Music of Cambodia.* © 1991 World Music Press. Used by permission.

Guru Ndiani

(Zimbabwe)

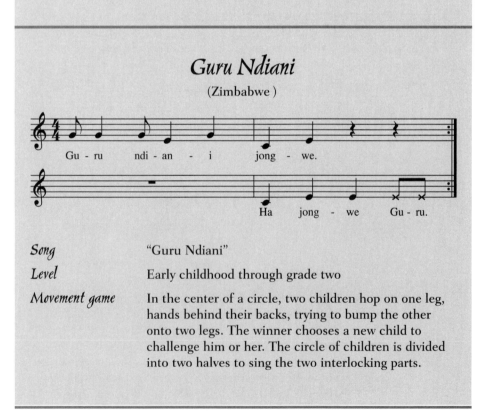

Gu - ru ndi - an - i jong - we.

Ha jong - we Gu - ru.

Song	"Guru Ndiani"
Level	Early childhood through grade two
Movement game	In the center of a circle, two children hop on one leg, hands behind their backs, trying to bump the other onto two legs. The winner chooses a new child to challenge him or her. The circle of children is divided into two halves to sing the two interlocking parts.

Children engaged in Dalcroze eurhythmics, with teacher at the piano

Jerry Gay

Eurhythmics has been misinterpreted frequently as physical conditioning exercises, creative movement, or dance; it is none of these. Still, eurhythmics requires children to be limber, quick, and controlled. It requires them to express the music they hear through a creative reorganizing of the movements they already know. It sets their bodies to dance (in a figurative sense) to the musical sounds they perceive.

Elements of music, including basic sound awareness, pulse (beat), tempo, articulation, style, dynamics, accent, meter, melody, phrases, anacrusis (upbeat), duration, proportional relationships, and timbre, can be taught through Dalcroze eurhythmics. Little is needed to bring children into contact with music through eurhythmics: a large space, a drum, a piano, a stereo, and rules for boundaries and acceptable behavior that all children understand. Lesson 9.3 presents a sampling of suggestions for eurhythmics experiences. The creative teacher will use these as springboards for further development into ten-minute experiences, full lessons, and experiences that extend for days, weeks, or months.

At times, recorded music can be used to stimulate movement, but the live and partly spontaneous music played by the teacher on piano or percussion instrument is best. Children learn at different paces. Some need to hear a musical idea many times, and with the teacher's access to an instrument, the music can be easily slowed down, repeated, or given more emphasis. Whatever the instrument, the teacher should feel comfortable with it. Basic rhythms, melodies, and harmonies can stimulate sensitive movement when they are played musically.

Short composed piano pieces also provide the impetus for teaching musical concepts through movement. In planning a lesson that emanates from a composed piece, the teacher should thoroughly analyze its rhythmic

CHAPTER 9 / THE MOVING CHILD   *221*

LESSON 9.3 *Sample Experiences in Dalcroze Eurhythmics*

MUSICAL CONCEPT	EXPERIENCE
Sound versus silence	Children move when music is heard and freeze during silences.
Pulse (tempo)	Children step to the pulse of one child (no music). As teacher calls out the name of another child, children step the tempo and quality of that child's walk.
Pulse (tempo, timbre)	Children step to the beat of the drum. When the drum stops, children stop. When teacher taps the rim of the drum, children change the direction of their walking. (Variation: Children continue walking to the same beat even when the drum has stopped, testing their internalization of its sound.)
Articulation	Children hop or jump to choppy, staccato music, and glide, slide, or sway to legato, smooth music.
Dynamics	Children improvise strong movements for loud (forte) music and quiet, subtle movements for soft (piano) music. As music crescendos, children gradually enlarge their movements, diminishing them for diminuendo parts.
Style (tempo, dynamics, articulation)	Children clap, step, or follow teacher's improvisation on piano or xylophone. They should be encouraged to use as much variety of space, time, and energy as is necessary to kinesthetically realize the music.
Tempo	The room is divided into two parts: a slow and a fast half. Without music, children move from one side to the other using the designated tempo of each half. When teacher plays music, children resolve their movement to that new tempo. Teacher demonstrates a movement that children imitate. Then, as music in various tempos is played, children perform the movement slower or faster.
Accent	Children walk, run, or skip through the forest. On accent, they jump behind a tree to hide from a bear.
Phrase	Children move in response to musical phrases. After several listenings, they use the same movements for the repeated phrases and change the movement for contrasting phrases.
Timbre	As teacher plays piano in various registers, children clap the high melodies and step the low melodies. Challenge them to coordinate the two when both treble and bass parts are sounding.

and melodic nuances, phrasing, and overall formal organization, as well as the expressive markings that indicate tempo, dynamics, and articulation. The piece may require concentrated practice in preparation for the lesson, so that the composer's musical intentions are artfully presented to the children. When the teacher has reached a level of familiarity and confidence

MUSICAL CONCEPT	EXPERIENCE
Meter	Children walk the pulse and clap on the first beat of each measure to teacher's improvised music in twos, threes, fours, fives, sixes, sevens, and so on. Choose a number, and while teacher plays music, children clap, pat, step, and rest for that number of beats. Challenge children to respond to the call of other numbers with the same sequence of movements. (For example, on four, children clap, pat, step, and rest for four beats each, and on seven, children clap, pat, step, and rest for seven beats each.)
	In partners or a circle of children, choose a way to demonstrate a meter of two, three, four, five, six, seven, and so on, by rolling, tossing, or passing a ball. (For example, in a $\frac{2}{4}$ meter, partners might bounce and catch the ball. In a $\frac{3}{4}$ meter, a circle of children might bounce, hold, and pass the ball.)
Melody	As ascending music plays, children rise like the sun. They fall slowly like the sun setting on the horizon with the sound of descending music.
	Children move forward to ascending melodies, backward to descending music, and stand in place for melodies of static and unchanging pitch.
Anacrusis	Children step the pulse and conduct the meter. On music with an upbeat, or anacrusis, they step counter-clockwise and on music with a downbeat, or crusis, they step clockwise.
Duration	Children walk the quarter notes of teacher's improvised music on drum or piano, and stop and clap when eighth notes are played.
	Children sit in a circle. As the teacher improvises music on piano or drum, children walk the quarter notes by patting their laps, run the eighth notes by clapping, pat the half notes on their head, and tap the whole notes on the floor in front of them.
Proportional relationships	Children step the pulse of the music. When a verbal or musical clue is given, they step twice as fast or twice as slow.

that will allow him or her to occasionally glance away from the instrument so as to be able to evaluate the movement responses of the children, then that piece is probably ready for teaching. Lesson 9.4 presents a sampling of technically easy, and commonly found, piano pieces along with suggestions for musical concepts that can be highlighted through eurhythmics.

Schumann: "The Wild Horseman"
(*measures one to eight*)

Musical Concepts

Pulse; tempo; style
(Gallop like a horse) ♩ ♪♩ ♪

Triplet figure of melody
(Clap the continuous trotting sound) ♫♪

Two-measure accompaniment figure
("Hop, hop – – step, hop, hop") ♪ 𝄾 𝄾 ♪ 𝄾 𝄾 | ♩ ♪ 𝄾 𝄾 |

Melody and accompaniment
(Group one trots while group two hops)
(Group one plays on woodblock, while group two plays on drum)

Beethoven: "Ecossaise in G"
(*measures one to eight*)

Musical Concepts

Steady eighth-note accompaniment pattern ♫♫
(Lightly step the steady accompaniment pattern)

Two similar four-measure phrases: A A′
(Change direction at the end of each phrase, but retain same quality if the phrase is the same)

Two-measure crescendo, two-measure decrescendo <>
(Enlarge movements for crescendo, and decrease size and space for decrescendo)

Anacrusis ♫ | | ♩
(Make a movement that leans into the first pulse, of measure one and five)

Staccato and legato ♫ ♩ ♫♫
(Glide on legato and give a slight hop to the staccato sounds)

Accent
(On measures two and six, hop and land on the accented pitch e′)

Rhythmic pattern in treble ♫ ♪♫♫ ♪♩
(Step the rhythmic pattern, with attention to articulation, accent, dynamics, and anacrusis)

Schumann: "Soldier's March"
(*measures one to sixteen*)

Musical Concepts

Pulse; tempo; style
(March like a soldier)
♫ ♩ ♪ pattern, measures one, five, nine, and thirteen
("Skip-ty, step" [binary] or "step-hop, step")

Four-measure phrases: A B A B
(Change direction at the end of each phrase, and move at distinct levels for A and B phrases)
(In partners, create movements for A and B)

The teacher who incorporates Dalcroze eurhythmics in music lessons will find that children become astute listeners for musical elements to meet the challenges of these movement games. While specialized Dalcroze training will shape the teacher's ability to improvise at the piano, a good musician who takes time out for practice will be capable of facilitating fundamental eurhythmics experiences into classes. Further information on eurhythmics can be found in the writings of Abramson (1973), Aronoff (1969), Black and Moore (1997), Findlay (1971), and Mead (1994).

Creative Movement

Creative movement is a form of dance that is personal, interpretive, and expressive. It can be used to socialize children, provide entertainment to an audience of parents, and communicate ideas and feelings more directly or deeply than words. Unlike most dance forms, creative movement lacks authoritarian structure. There is no one right way of doing things, and there are no specific steps to learn. It is inspired by verbal and musical imagery, and it is an extension of exploratory movement experiences. It primes the kinesthetic impulses for responding to a stimulus. It may spring from a musical source, but it is not as closely united to specific musical concepts as required by eurhythmics. Creative movement links children's emotional and inventive selves with the kinesthetic skills of their bodies to utilize space, time, and energy in a unique dance.

The concepts to be taught should be presented as questions and challenges that inspire individual solutions. The Socratic method should be prominently used when the teacher guides children's movement through such questions as the following: "How do squirrels scamper?" "What parts of the squirrel's body move?" "Can you swing like a puppet blowing in the wind?" "Can you swing high or low?" "Can you swing while you walk, run, or skip?" "Can you swing in an even rhythm or uneven rhythm?" Children should be encouraged to explore and discover the concept of breath, body parts, sounds, shapes, accents, levels, and pathways instead of being told or shown what to do. The teacher may lead children in preparatory movement experiences; select and present the stimulus for creative movement; direct attention to the concept through imagery that may be verbal, visual, or musical; and shape the final form of the experience through suggestion and approval. The learning, however, emanates from the child's own willingness to discover the expressive potential of his or her body.

Creative movement can be inspired by a word, a picture, a poem, a story, a song's melody, a rhythmic pattern, or a symphonic work. Teachers who strive for the development of musical understanding through creative movement may begin with any of these stimuli but are certain to reinforce a selected concept as an aid to the children's realization of an image or to incorporate music at the culmination of the exercise. To ensure learning, the teacher must be certain that the lesson is based on a preset goal; that children are informed of the goal; that they are presented with a variety of questions, problems, and stimuli; and that they are encouraged to achieve the lesson goal (if they do) through particular attention to the strengths of individual children as well as the group as a whole.

LESSON 9.5 *Experiences in Creative Movement*

GOAL	EXPERIENCE
To portray words in movement and sound	In partners or small groups, present children with words to be turned into movement and sound pieces: yawn, tramp, spin, shuffle, ooze, flutter, drip, explode, crack, spurt, swish, ripple, crunch, stir, sprinkle, plunge, slither. In a presentation to the class, these pieces may be moved silently and then presented with vocal, body, and instrumental accompaniment.
To portray musical terms in movement	Assign groups of children various musical terms, and ask that they express them through movement: legato, staccato, forte, marcato, sforzando, cantabile, piano, piacere, lento, allegro, appassionato, doloroso. (First they must learn the meanings of these terms as applied to music.) They may later invent a melody to express the term and to coincide with the movement.
To depict a musical in movement	Play a recording of Camille Saint-Saëns' "The Lion" from *Carnival of the Animals*. Direct children's attention to pitch register and direction in the lion's growl. Through repeated listenings, ask that they move like a lion (large, strong, forceful), stopping to growl at the appropriate time. Ask children to listen to a recording of Aaron Copland's *Fanfare for the Common Man*, to note the sounds and the silences, to identify the long and sustained sounds, the instruments, the melodic leaps, the changes in dynamics. Play the opening forty-five seconds of the recording repeatedly, giving children the task of finding their own individual movements to personify the piece.
To create a movement-and-music version of a visual image	Show children a copy of a painting or a photograph. In small groups (depending on the number of figures), encourage them to make the visual image come to life. They will need to discuss what the people are doing, where they are going, and how they are moving. Their tableau should begin as a still image and can proceed through a movement piece that communicates without words. Vocal, body, and instrumental music may be improvised by another group of children to accompany the tableau. Paintings such as George Caleb Bingham's *Raftsmen Playing Cards*, Frederic Remington's *Howl of the Weather*, or John Steuart Curry's *The Mississippi* may inspire movement.

Suggestions for experiences in creative movement are found in Lesson 9.5. Some will encompass complete lesson periods, others can be included as short segments within a lesson, and still others may require several periods and much practice to fulfill. The creative teacher will likely extend, vary, and develop these experiences to suit the needs of children.

GOAL	EXPERIENCE
To create a movement piece from a collection of individual movements	Gather children into groups of four to eight. Ask that each child invent a movement to be included in a movement collection; each group should have as many movements as there are children. As a group, they practice their collective movements until one flows easily to the next. As an extension, they can choose to allow each movement one, two, or four pulses, or repeat some or all of the movements. Children can develop different levels of energy and space for these movements, should they wish to express them as tired, intimidated, angry, or gentle. Musical accompaniment can be suggested, selected or created.
To express a poem through movement	A poem paints a visual image that can be realized through movement. Children can choose to follow the rhythm of the words or move more freely to the images that strike them.

The Puzzled Centipede (Anon.)

A cen' tipede' was hap' py quite,'
Until' a frog,' in fun,'
Said, "Pray,' which leg' comes af' ter which'?"
This raised' her mind' to such' a pitch,'
She lay' distract' ed in the ditch'
Consid' ering how' to run.'

The Animal Dance (P. S. Campbell)

The owl,' the skunk,'
The bull,' and the bear'
Went dan' cing one eve' ning.
They let' down their hair.'

The owl' did wad' dle.
The skunk' gave a twirl.'
The bull' hopped on two' feet.
The bear' took a whirl.'

Closing in' on a cir' cle,
They turned' to their right.'
Holding paws,' hoofs, and feath' ers,
They took' off in flight.'

(Continued)

The skunk' set the speed'
For all three' of his friends.'
Fast. Fas' ter. They cir' cled
And spun' to the end.'

Centri' ugal force,'
As they laughed' and they screamed,'
"We're the an' imal danc' ers!
We dance' in your dreams'!"

To express a story
through
movement

Action stories inspire movement. Collections such as Joanna Cole's *Best-Loved Folktales of the World* provide many examples for dramatization. One story, with potential for both movement and musical accompaniment, is "A Crocodile's Tale" from the Philippines.

A Crocodile's Tale

A little boy named Juan saved the life of a crocodile by untying a rope around his neck. But instead of thanking him, the crocodile sweeps little Juan up with his tail and wraps it around him. He wants to eat the boy. While the crocodile catches fish from the river as "appetizers," Juan cries for help. He is heard by a monkey sitting in a tree on the bank of the river. The monkey shouts to the crocodile, "What are you doing with Juan?" To which the crocodile replies, "I'm going to eat him." The clever monkey shouts "Can't hear you! What did you say? Come a little closer." The crocodile swims to the middle of the river, with his tail wrapped around Juan. "I'm going to eat him, and maybe you, too." Again the monkey shouts "Can't hear you! Come a little closer." The crocodile swims to the bank and shows his teeth to the monkey in the tree. In an instant, the monkey lunges down with a rope to tie the crocodile's snout tightly shut, and Juan frees himself from the tail and jumps to safety. The monkey and Juan celebrate by joyfully dancing the Tinikling, a traditional dance of the Philippines (see Lesson 9.7 on how to perform the Tinikling dance.)

Creative movement generates enthusiasm among children. It gives them permission to explore and express freely and playfully the ideas that are brought to mind by poems, pictures, music, and stories. It gives them freedom to experiment with their own space, time, and energy, leading them to a discovery of the language of movement. The use of music as a stimulus for movement, as part of the learning process, or as a component of the final product provides a more fulfilling and integrative experience for children. In this manner, children learn music as they also learn to speak through their bodies. For additional ideas on creative movement, see Joyce (1980).

Dance

Dance is a purposeful, choreographed, and much-rehearsed movement to music. Dance knows many forms: classical ballet; modern dance as inspired by Martha Graham or Katherine Dunham; classical court dances of Southeast Asia, theater dances of China and Japan, martial arts-inspired dances of Latin America; dances that involve entire communities in sub-Saharan Africa or Native American pow-wows; and ballroom, hip-hop, and a grand variety of folk dances. To dance well, these forms involve physical training that is dependent on technique, knowledge, and experience. Unlike other types of movement for children, dance is an art. It is structured and premeditated movement that demands concentration in learning the postures, positions, and steps and that requires practice to keep the specific movements in the memory.

For children through the elementary grades, folk dance is one of the best avenues for experiencing music, cultures, and movement all at once. The first dances attempted should be those with simple and repetitive footwork set to music with a clearly defined pulse. Line and circle dances are often easier for beginners than partner dances because they can focus on the steps instead of their relationships to their partners. Emphasizing physical education goals, Weikert (1982) suggests a progression for learning folk dances. However, the sequence shown in Lesson 9.6 is more effective when the accent is on music and music learning through movement (Shehan, 1984).

LESSON 9.6 *An Effective Sequence for Teaching Folk Dances*

Listen	As an introduction to the musical style of the dance, the teacher should guide children to listen carefully to the music. Children can attend to musical details. What instruments are playing? Which are the melody instruments? Do they hear repeated rhythmic patterns? Can they chant, clap, or write them? Is the melody wide or narrow in range? Can they sing the melody? Is the texture of the combined instruments chordal, unison, or heterophonic (simultaneous variations played by several melody instruments)? Concentrated and repeated listenings will create a more comfortable dance experience, and the music will be better understood and appreciated.

(Continued)

Respond	The teacher should direct children to listen to the recording (or to the song as it is sung or played), and respond to the underlying rhythm in the bass line, the chordal accompaniment, or the percussion instruments. By patting the accented beats on their laps, children are responding to the dance rhythm. When learning a dance to a song, instead of a recorded musical piece, the teacher can nonetheless present the steps as a clapped or patted ostinato rhythm for all to follow.
Chant and Pat	Ask children to chant descriptive words to indicate the motion of the dance. By chanting "step," "hop," "pause," "left," "right" and the like, children will more easily perform the necessary rhythmic movement of the feet. The words are spoken in the rhythm of the steps, which are danced with the hands on the lap.
Chant and Step	The transfer of movement from the hands to the feet occurs next. The repeated rhythmic chant should continue, so that the children match the steps to the descriptive words. This speech-action activity is initially more successful without the music, which may confuse some students who will be distracted by other musical aspects such as timbre and melody.
Step and Internalize	In the final stage, the music returns to accompany the movement. Children begin to internalize the rhythmic chant, thinking and doing the steps. As a result of earlier stages in the sequence, children develop an inner hearing for the rhythm and a kinesthetic ease in performing the movement.

Lesson 9.7 presents instructions for a selection of folk dances, along with their associated melodies and references to accessible recordings. Melodies played on classroom instruments by children can provide the culminating performance for programs and for children's own pleasure.

The movements of folk dance are natural and unaffected, stylized but not stilted, offering a means of socialization, enrichment of school programs, and exposure to the folkways of world cultures. As a movement-based musical experience, folk dance makes a meaningful contribution to the musical development of children. Folk dance collections by Longden (1998) and Longden and Weikert (1992), with their accompanying recordings of dance arrangements, are useful for teachers who can modify the instructional sequence to suit their musical goals.

Skip to My Lou
(United States)

Phrase 1   **2**

Fly's in the but-ter-milk, Shoo fly   shoo,   Fly's in the but-ter-milk, Shoo fly   shoo,
Chorus: Skip____ Skip____   Skip to my Lou   Skip____ Skip____   Skip to my Lou.
Where's my partner?   Skip to my Lou   Where's my partner?   Skip to my Lou.

3   **4**

Fly's in the but-ter-milk,   Shoo fly   shoo   Skip to my Lou my   dar - ling
Skip____ Skip____   Skip to my Lou   Skip to my Lou my   dar - ling.
There's my partner.   Skip to my Lou   Skip to my Lou my   dar - ling.

Song: "Skip to My Lou" (Anglo-American)

Level: Early childhood through third grade

Recording: American Folk Songs for Children (Rounder 8001/ 8002/8003)

Sequence: Circle; all join hands

                 Phrase 1—Circle-right-3-4 (4 beats)

                 Phrase 2—Circle-left-3-4 (4 beats)

                 Phrase 3—"Where's my partner?" (4 beats)

                        Break formation, search for lost partner

                 Phrase 4—"There's my partner" (4 beats)

                        Finds a new partner

                 Chorus—Partners circle with elbows hooked

Dance the Kolo
(Serbia)

Come a - long and   dance the ko - lo,   ha - ha - ha,   Dance the ko - lo,
Flute and drum and   tam-bou-rine to   Tam-bou-rine to

ha - ha - ha,   Dance the   ko - lo,   hey,   hey,   hey.
give us joy: Mus - ic   for the   ko - lo   dance.

Song: "Dance the Kolo" (Serbian, Yugoslavia)

Level: Grades two to six

(Continued)

<table>
<tr><td>*Recording:*</td><td>*Hi Neighbor!* CMS Unicef 6</td></tr>
<tr><td>*Sequence:*</td><td>Circle; all join hands with arms down</td></tr>
</table>

Four-measure repeated pattern:

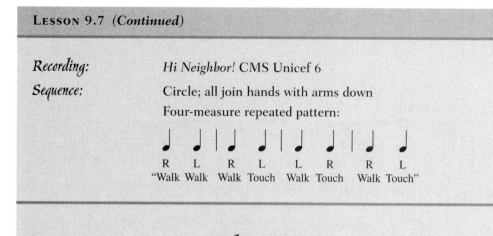

R   L   R   L   L   R   R   L
"Walk Walk Walk Touch Walk Touch Walk Touch"

Sakura
(Japan)

Song:	"Sakura" (Japan)
Level:	Grades two to six
Recording:	*Art of the Koto: The Music of Japan*
Sequence:	Independent, in lines or circle (phrase = 4 beats)

Phrase 1—Arms extended, nod right, nod left

Phrase 2—Make right arm circle, left arm circle

Phrase 3—Move right arm side-front, left arm side-front

Phrase 4—Hands pat right lap, hands pat left lap

Phrase 5—Repeat 3

Phrase 6—Repeat 1

Phrase 7—Raise right arm, fingers skyward, left hand below right elbow, then reverse with left arm

La Raspa
(Mexico)

La ras - pa yo bai - lé   al de-cho y al re-vés.   Sí

quie - res tú   bai - lar,   em - pie-za a mo - ver   los pies.

Brin-ca, brin-ca, brin-ca tam-bién,   mue-ve, mue-ve mu-cho los pies.   Que la

ras - pa ras a bai - lar   al de - re - cho y al re - vés.

Song: "La Raspa" (Mexico)

Level: Grades three to five

Recording: *Folk Dance Fun* (Kimbo 7037)

Sequence: Partners, facing each other, hands on hips

Phrases 1-8

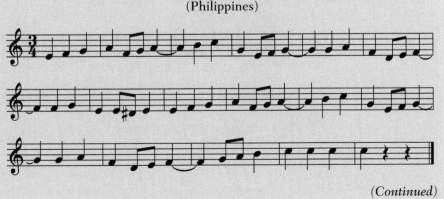

R   L   R   L   R   L   y   y
"Step Step Step Clap Clap Step Step Step Clap Clap"

Measures 9–10—Link right elbows, skip once around

Measures 11–12—Link left elbows, skip once around

Tinikling
(Philippines)

(Continued)

Song: "Tinikling" (Philippines)

Level: Grades three to six

Recording: *Folk Dance Fun* (Kimbo 7037)

Sequence: Two poles of six to ten feet on the floor

Child holding two poles at each end

Pole movement:	Count 1—Strike poles together
	Count 2—Poles apart, strike floor
	Count 3—Poles apart, strike floor
Dance movement:	Count 1—Jump out, spreading feet apart
	Count 2—Jump in, with feet together
	Count 3—Jump in, with feet together

Schottische

(Sweden)

Song: "Schottische" (Sweden)

Level: Grades four to six

Recording: *Folk Dances for All Ages* (RCA Victor 1622)

Sequence: Partners side by side, in circle facing right, inside hands linked

Phrase 1—Move apart

R	R	L	L	R	R	L	Pause
"Step	Hop	Step	Hop	Step	Hop	Step	Hop"

Phrase 2—Move together

R	R	L	L	R	R	L	Pause
"Step	Hop	Step	Hop	Step	Hop	Step	Hop"

Gerakina

(Greece)

Ger - a - ki-na's at the fair,   Ger - a - ki - na with her gol-den ban-gles on,

There's mu-sic ev -'ry - where.   Ring, pret-ty gol-den ban-gles, jin-gle, jin-gle,

jan - gle. Sing in the   air, Ger-a-ki - na danc-ing at the   fair. All the vil-lage

boys will come to the   square For the jin-gle   jan - gle dance at the   fair

Song:	"Gerakina" (Greece)
Level:	Grades four to six
Recording:	*Dances of the World's People* (Folkways FD 6501)
Sequence:	Line, all join hands
	Shoulder hold
	Two-measure repeated pattern

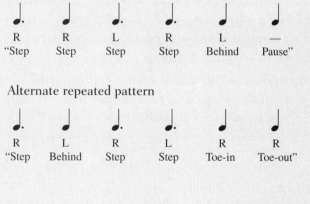

Alternate repeated pattern

Assessment of Moving

If movement is a pedagogical tool for achieving musical understanding and a means for demonstrating musical perception and cognition, it can also be an artistic end-product of instruction for children who learn to connect their ears, minds, and bodies in expressive ways. The teacher needs to consider what place movement will hold in a curricular program—whether part of the instructional process that leads, for example, to more perceptive listening or whether the product and programmatic result of a lesson are intended to complement and elaborate upon a sung song or instrumental piece. For some, the choice may one or the other, while for others it will seem natural to expect children to grow musically through movement possibilities as well as to move in an expressive manner approaching the art of dance. In any case, movement with musical intent will be more than free and unbridled motor energy; it will be an entity that can be assessed.

Assessment questions that the teacher can ask and that can comprise a guide to children in their attempts to engage in movement with a musical focus include the following:

1. In the case of action songs and singing games, are you rhythmically on time with your gestures, steps, and other means of physical movement? Or are you performing out of sync with the song, the game, and fellow players?

2. In the case of eurhythmics, are you able to capture the musical feature (pulse, meter, rhythmic pattern, melodic contour, form) in your movement? Or are you drawn to some other musical feature than the one prescribed? Why?

3. In the case of creative movement, are you able to move in a way that feels good to you, with thoughts given to the use of space, time, and energy in your own personal way? Or are you simply following someone else's ideas?

4. In the case of dance, are you following the sequence of movements required of the dance, in proper order, in rhythmically accurate time, and within the expressive style associated with the dance?

Movement can easily go awry with children, in that it can be filler (and a time-killer) within a class and a cute and clever addition to a program, but with no merit or real contribution to musical understanding. It can be so much more than that, however, and a view toward how children might be assessed in their movement development can ensure that musical goals surround and steer its use in music instruction. Along with the above questions that can be posed to them as a framework for their more thoughtful movement, children can grow in understanding both the commonalities and the differences between movement for recreation (sports and other playful endeavor) and movement as an expressive extension of the self, incited and supported by music. These questions can be considered by children in group discussion, on paper (as in short journal-like accounts), or in silent ways that nonetheless direct their careful attention to how their bodies respond to the music that propels them.

Movement for Musical Development

Teachers are sometimes hesitant to initiate movement experiences. What if the music room is too small? Explore the school building and schoolyard for alternative spaces. Modify the size and scope of some of the movement experiences. What if the children do not know their left from their right? Most action songs, singing games, eurhythmics, and creative-movement experiences do not require a knowledge of left and right. In learning folk dances, children can tie a ribbon around their left (or right) wrists. What if the children are not getting a musical concept? Focus their attention. Repeat the melody, the rhythm, the chant, and the directions. Model the movement. Sequence the activity, breaking it into smaller segments. Give them time to practice. What if they get rowdy? Set the rules at the start, remind children of the penalties for broken rules, and follow through on them. What should the rules be? That depends on the activity, the goals, the space, and the age of children. Keep the rules simple and straightforward; sometimes no-touch and stop-when-the-music-stops rules are enough. What if the children will not move? Determine whether the movement is age-appropriate. For older children, opportunities for teaching each other and working in small groups may be more readily received than too many teacher-directed lessons.

Movement is more than an occasional experience. It is an integral part of children's musical education. Children develop musical sensitivity when their natural movements are channeled toward the discovery or reinforcement of musical features and components. The musically trained teacher who recognizes children's movement capacities is critical to advancing their musical knowledge, skills, and sensitivities.

Scenario

The late-afternoon class of third-grade children is lively, even for them, on one Tuesday afternoon in February, and Mr. Robinson is convinced that they are one of his more kinesthetically prone classes that will do well to spend much of their music time in movement. His classroom, a 1970s-style portable building of aluminum exterior siding set at the far end of the parking lot, is conducive to movement, too. There are no desks or chairs, no clutter of books or instruments on the floor, and the tile floor stretches a space as large as a standard school cafeteria.

The children have taken their places in a standing circle, and although most are either laughing, or talking loudly, or twirling, or even stamping in place, Mr. Robinson moves quickly to the middle of the circle with a colorful Ghanian-style djembe drum hung from his shoulder. Without a word of instruction, he slaps his hand on the head of the drum, and the deep-sounding "thud" signals the children to turn to their right, tune their ears to the beat, and walk. Mr. Robinson's third-grade music class has begun.

For nearly two minutes, the children walk when the drum sounds and freeze when the drum rests. They match the tempo of the $\frac{6}{8}$ drum beat, from moderately fast, to medium, to slow, and to a gradually increasing speed that turns around again to become so slow as to finally stop. Mr. Robinson then sets his drum down and without words signals the children with his arms to slowly sit down. "You're tuned in," he compliments the children. "Your energy is going into all the right moves, and your ears are leading the way. Good job!" He asks the children to remember the rules for moving in music class, and they raise their hands to tick off two: "Use your ears to move" and "Move safely." Mr. Robinson has made his way to the piano just outside the circle and asks the children to follow his beat with hands on the floor. They bend over to the floor and as he plays a jig-like melody at the piano (with a left-handed drone accompaniment), the children pat their palms onto the floor. They are not together, however, and some children are patting eighth notes while others have found the dotted-quarter note to pat.

"Listen to the low sounds, and pat softly," he calls out to them, and then he drops the melody out and gives accent to the drones. The children are soon patting together. He brings the melody back, and most (but not all) of the children are able to retain the dotted-quarter pat. A cluster of high pitches signals the children to stop.

"Jimmy, Jacob, Kelly, Sean, take a stack of hand drums and pass them out." Mr. Robinson plays Schumann's "The Wild Horseman" as the drums are distributed. Children are playing various $\frac{6}{8}$ rhythms, from ♪♪♪ to ♩♪, and also ♩., most of them a little faster than the piano's tempo.

"Shhh," Mr. Robinson reminds them, and the children lighten their drum taps but then play a tad slower as well.

"Two fingers," he cautions, and the drum taps become even lighter. "Bounce lightly," he suggests, and they begin to get more of the character that Schumann had intended. This continues through several repetitions of the piece, and it seems that Mr. Robinson's goal is to allow the children to keep a steady rhythm going—any rhythm that fits within the piece.

He asks the children to stand with their hand drums, tells them that the entire classroom is their space, that they can go wherever they wish, but that they must walk the beat when they hear high-pitched music and play the beat on their drums, standing still in one place, when they hear low-pitched music. Beginning with the "The Wild Horseman" again, Mr. Robinson plays first the left hand's low pitches and then the right hand's high pitches, one section at a time. He plays again, alternating between high and low pitches, phrase by phrase. The children have the gist of the game, responding to the highs and lows by playing or walking, but they are tuned to the rhythm of the pitches they hear (as they had been in the previous activity)—not to the beat.

Mr. Robinson calls the children back to the circle and directs them to sit with their drums in their laps. He sits himself between two of the liveliest boys. "Here's a poem for you. If you can find the beat, you can tap it on your drum—with one finger only."

He chants "The Animal Dance" with a $\frac{6}{8}$ metric feeling, and three children are immediately on the beat with him. Others join in a scattershot kind of sound. He stops and starts to sway, subtly, from the right to the left, and soon the children are with him, swaying and tapping their drums. "Keep it slow, keep it steady," he cautions them in a $\frac{6}{8}$ rhythm and begins the poem again. The children are more able to keep the dotted-quarter-note beat, and they continue to sway as they do so.

"Which words are 'moving words'?" he asks, and the children call out "dancing," "waddle," "twirl," "hopped," and "turned." Mr. Robinson challenges them to a waddle, grabs his djembe drum to play a waddle rhythm, and the children are up on their haunches, falling over, colliding, laughing; about half the class in total confusion. He runs for the light switch and flicks it off until the children settle down.

"Is that moving safely? No, so watch yourselves, or you'll lose your privileges." The children are better at following the turning, hopping, and twirling rhythms that Mr. Robinson plays, and they use the floor space well to get into the flow of the drum's sounds. Mr. Robinson calls the children back to the circle, compliments them on "what was mostly a very good class," and informs them that they have begun to get a sense of $\frac{6}{8}$ meter.

Questions

1. What was the theme of Mr. Robinson's class? In what ways was it demonstrated?

2. What factors made for successful movement experiences? What adjustments might be made to the class setting and plan to ensure greater success?

3. Should any of these activities be repeated in another class session or extended? How?

REVIEW

1. Discuss the musical and social outcomes of including movement in a music lesson for children.

2. Define the movement components of space, time, and energy.

3. At what age would action songs be appropriate for use with children? Singing games?

4. List musical goals for teaching folk dance to children. How would they differ from the goals of a physical education instructor who teaches folk dancing?

CRITICAL THINKING

1. How are eurhythmics and creative movement related? How are they different?

2. Why would movement as employed by music teachers not be likely to meet the achievement expectations outlined in the National Standards in dance?

PROJECTS

1. Visit a school or park playground to observe the movement of children at play. What games do they

play that include songs and movement? What movements can older children perform for which younger children have not yet mastered the coordination? Make a list of your observations regarding children's use of space, time, and energy.

2. Begin a collection of songs, including game, dance, and action songs, that require or suggest movement. Organize the songs chronologically according to the level of kinesthetic development necessary to enable children to successfully perform them.

3. Choose a musical concept and prepare a set of movement experiences appropriate for children in kindergarten, grade three, and grade six.

4. Select a sample experience in Dalcroze eurhythmics, and prepare a ten-minute lesson to teach in class. Develop that same idea into a thirty-minute lesson.

5. Listen to recordings of music from various historical periods and cultures. Select one or more musical concepts from each, and consider ways in which movement can be applied as a vehicle for developing children's understanding of the concept(s).

6. Write a letter to your principal to explain how the movement experiences he or she observed in your music class were educationally justified. Include an explanation of which specific musical concepts were learned by children through the movement demonstration.

REFERENCES

Abramson, R. (1973). *Rhythm games*. New York: Movement Press.

Aronoff, F. W. (1969). *Music and young children*. New York: Turning Wheel Press.

Black, J. S., and S. Moore (1997). *The rhythm inside*. Portland, OR: Rudra Press.

Findlay, E. (1971). *Rhythm and movement: Application of Dalcroze eurhythmics*. Evanston, IL: Summy Birchard.

Forrai, K. (1988). *Music in preschool*. (J. Sinor, trans.) Budapest, Hungary: Corvina Press.

Joyce, M. (1980). *First steps in teaching creative dance to children* (2nd ed.). Palo Alto, CA: Mayfield.

Longden, S. H. (1998). *Living ethnic dances*. Chicago: Folkstyle Productions.

Longden, S. H., and P. S. Weikert (1992). *Cultures and styling in folk dance*. Ypsilanti, MI: High/Scope Press.

Mead, V. (1994). *Dalcroze eurhythmics in today's classroom*. New York: Schott.

MENC (1994). *What every young American should know and be able to do in the arts: National standards for arts education*. Reston, VA: Music Educators National Conference.

Moog, H. (1976). *The musical experience of the preschool child*. (C. Clarke, trans.) London: Schott.

Petzold, R. G. (1966). *Auditory perception of musical sounds by children in the first six grades*. Cooperative Research Project No. 1051. Madison, WI: University of Wisconsin.

Shehan, P. S. (1984). Teaching music through Balkan folk dance. *Music Educators Journal*, 71(3), 44–49.

Weikert, P. S. (1982). *Teaching movement and dance*. Ypsilanti, MI: High/Scope Press.

10

The Playing Child

Strike up the band, and the child is captivated by the colorful sounds of musical instruments. As the instruments thump, soar, chime, rattle, slide, shimmer, ring, bellow, and shake, the various timbres are as stimulating to children as they are spellbinding. And when children are given the chance to play, they do so with great pleasure. Janie beats the drum at a snappy and spirited speed. Julie shakes the maracas, first with her right hand, then with her left, and then both at once. LaToya concentrates on the different sounds she can make on a tambourine. Andrew and Jorge hammer out melodies together on wooden xylophones. Shannon sings a song she knows while pushing chord keys on an Autoharp. Marcus practices two guitar chords over and over, creating new rhythmic strums as he goes. Rex and Evan are at the keyboard, playing a blues progression that matches a popular song's harmonies.

Children of all ages are players of musical instruments, or they would like to be. Infants shake rattles, toddlers bang on cardboard boxes, tables, chairs, or pots and pans. Toy pianos, flutes, and guitar-like instruments make popular birthday gifts for preschoolers. In early childhood centers, the highlight of any day is music making—especially when it includes the playing of drums, jingle bells, wooden sticks, and tambourines.

As children mature, pitched instruments available at home and in their elementary school classrooms can offer them challenging and gratifying musical experiences. Some instruments, such as xylophone, recorder, and tone bells are for playing melodies; some, such as Autoharp and guitar, primarily produce harmonies or chords. Ensembles of xylophones or recorders provide both melody and harmonic accompaniment. Keyboard instruments such as piano, organ, MIDI (Music Instrument Digital Interface) synthesizers, and small tabletop or lap pianos provide musical challenges to older children.

Children continue to be fascinated by nonpitched rhythm instruments through the elementary years, particularly by drums of all sizes and shapes—kettle, bongo, conga, and hand drums. Whether they play alone, in small groups, or full ensemble, children will play to be heard and to hear themselves play.

Because of their natural attraction to the sounds of musical instruments, it is well within the realm of reason for children to achieve the skills set by the National Standards in music (MENC, 1994) for their age and grade levels. They are capable of playing at least one instrument—be it recorder, keyboard, xylophone, guitar, or one of a wide selection of percussion instruments, band and orchestral instruments, or instruments of the steel drum (pan), mariachi, gamelan, and other heritage ensembles—accurately and independently, alone and in ensemble, with appropriate playing techniques. Given the opportunity, children will perform the music of diverse genres and cultures with expression and technical accuracy. Their curiosity for instruments piqued early in their development, children are able to produce instrumental sounds by ear and to read the music that corresponds to a selected instrument. In a curricular program that allows for exploratory experiences and regular, sequential instruction, children can become proficient on nearly any instrument they choose.

Beyond the solo performance of an instrument, or its performance in a standard ensemble, instrument playing is often the icing on the cake in the performance of sung music in a class lesson. Songs such as "Hey, Betty Martin," "Tinga Layo," "I Got a Letter This Morning," "Skye Boat Song," and "Sansa Kroma" can be enhanced through accompaniments on pitched and nonpitched percussion music, by the addition of a countermelody on recorder, or chordal harmonies on keyboard or guitar. Children can learn just enough on classroom instruments to provide ostinati for songs like these, for interludes, and for introductions and codas. They can also grow to a greater level of accomplishment and provide more intricate, polyphonic textures for a vocal line. They can also create new musical expressions through the instruments they play, working individually and in partners and small groups to come up with fresh new pieces that fit the structural parameters of a particular style, genre, or teacher-prescribed activity. Along with their use in singing and creating experiences, instruments can underscore and reinforce concepts that are the focus of a listening lesson and even be used as accompaniment to any number of folk dances. From preschool explorations with instruments, children can be guided to grow their instrumental skills to a level that will serve them in many musical ways.

Developmental Sequence

Children's abilities to play musical instruments are closely related to their physical development. An example of this relationship might be seen in the playing of maracas or gourd rattles found in much African and Latin American music. Infants in their fourth and fifth months master the task of grasping toys and other objects, including their own baby rattles, and are already on their way to making music. By the time children are three years old, they have usually developed the muscle control that goes with playing and silencing the rattle at will. Primary-grade children have the coordination as well as the perceptiveness to keep the musical pulse and to play basic rhythmic patterns. Children in the intermediate grades can become adept at playing a host of rhythms on maracas, due to their physical maturation, musical perception, and cognitive understanding of the characteristics of the music they are making.

While rhythmic skills are usually the first to emerge—as early as the first year of life—the muscular coordination essential to playing musical instruments may develop much later. The early rhythmic rocking of an infant leads later to the swinging of the arms (about age three), which progresses to the alternation of one hand and then the other for playing two mallets on a drum (about age five or six). The more sophisticated eye-hand coordination skills begin to be refined from the age of seven onward, becoming more perfect through practice. For example, eye-hand coordination allows the child's visual sense to signal and set in gear his or her neurophysical system in the complex operation of striking a xylophone key. Something so seemingly simple as playing a melody on piano requires motoric machinery that involves the eyes, ears, and multiple muscles of the finger, hand, and forearm. Add to that the coordination of the breathing apparatus in the playing of wind instruments, and it is no wonder that recorders are only introduced to children in the third or fourth grade, with instruction on orchestral wind and brass instruments initiated at the close of the elementary school years, in fifth or sixth grade.

The pedagogy of Shinichi Suzuki has been widely recognized for the manner in which it develops listening skills and performance techniques at an early age. While the image of pint-sized violins comes to mind, it is the philosophy and practices of the Suzuki approach that attracts parents and their children. Suzuki called the method "Talent Education" and based it on the premise that all children are born musical. The tenet that children learn musical instruments in the same way they learn to speak is reflected through seven principles of Suzuki's method: (1) begin early, with listening at birth and lessons from about two-and-a-half years onward; (2) delay music reading until musical skills and performance techniques have developed; (3) involve parents in lessons and home practice; (4) use excellent music literature that is developmentally appropriate; (5) balance private lessons (for attention to technical skills) with group lessons (for motivation and socialization); (6) repeat, review, and reinforce the performance of previously learned music; and (7) accentuate self-development while deemphasizing competition. The Suzuki method maintains that children will develop musically through their instrument, when they are given occasion to develop the motor abilities necessary for performance on violin (or cello, piano, flute, and numerous other instruments).

But because motoric development progresses naturally and is largely unassisted by such specialized instruction as Suzuki, children will learn best when presented with experiences in playing musical instruments that match their developmental abilities. This is not to say that the exploration of assorted sounds that musical instruments can produce cannot be initiated in earlier stages; such discovery learning should be encouraged at every age. Still, children are likely to cultivate performance techniques on an instrument when they are physically ready to do so, thus the importance of matching motoric development to instruments. Table 10.1 provides a sequence for

TABLE 10.1 *Developmental Sequence for Playing Instruments*

AGE	MUSICAL-MOTORIC DEVELOPMENT	INSTRUMENTS; INSTRUMENTAL TECHNIQUES
Less than two years	Rocking, nodding, swaying Capacity to grip and grasp	Rattles (shaking) Jingle bells (shaking)
Two to three	Short periods of rhythmic regularity	Hand drum (hand tapping) Sticks (striking)
Three to four	Longer periods of rhythmic regularity Sensitivity to pulse Swaying of arms	Claves (striking) Sticks (rubbing) Woodblock (mallet striking, rubbing) Sandblocks (rubbing) Tambourine (shaking, striking) Guiro (rubbing) Maracas (shaking) Gong (mallet striking) Cowbell (mallet striking)
Five to six (kindergarten to grade one)	Maintenance of pulse Alternation of hands Basic eye-hand coordination	Finger cymbals (striking rim to rim) Bongo drums (hand striking) Timpani (mallet striking) Cymbals (striking) Triangle (mallet striking) Keyboard (one hand)
Seven to nine (grades one to three)	Eye-hand coordination	Finger cymbals (striking; attached) Slit log drum (mallet striking) Temple blocks (mallet striking) Conga drum (hand striking) Goblet drum (hand striking) Double iron agogo bells (mallet striking) Tone bells (mallet striking) Xylophone (simple drone, bourdon, ostinato; two mallets striking) Keyboard (both hands, melody with chords) Recorder (g-d′) Autoharp (chording)
Ten to twelve (grades four to six)	Increased facility of eye-hand coordination Finger flexibility Control of breathing apparatus	Xylophone (moving drone, ostinato, melody; two mallets striking) Keyboard (both hands, two moving parts) Recorder (c-g′) Guitar (chording) Orchestral wind and brass

the formal introduction of musical instruments into children's performance experiences. Playing techniques introduced at a given age will require practice for refinement.

The Body as a Percussion Instrument

The body can be viewed as a musical instrument. Clapping, slapping, tapping, snapping, stamping, and patting the shoulders, head, elbows, knees, and stomach produce various sounds that delight children everywhere. In some cultures, the body is considered one of the primary sources of musical sound. For example, African American sacred songs, particularly folk spirituals and gospel, often feature clapping, just as African American folk songs frequently include hand jives of slaps, claps, and snaps. The potential for timbral variety through corpophones, the body's sound producers, has gone unnoticed in some cultures but nonetheless can be successfully brought into the culture of the classroom.

Children at play often create their own original body-percussion pieces. They can also learn through imitation body-percussion sounds that can enhance their rhythm skills, increasing their vocabulary of internalized rhythms. With guidance, children can be led to perform ensemble pieces that feature the rhythms of body percussion, one pattern layered on another. Body percussion makes for an exciting performance piece for audiences of parents, other children, and people in the community.

Body-percussion exercises can also be used to prepare children for their performance on nonpitched rhythm and barred instruments. By patting the rhythm of an ostinato on their laps, children are then better able to

The body as a percussion instrument

Jerry Gay

play the pattern on a drum, a woodblock, or a xylophone. Even guitar and Autoharp strums can be played first in the air, while fingers can play imaginary recorders and piano keyboards on the arm, the floor, or a tabletop. A reward for initially working out the rhythm through a body percussion exercise is the opportunity to play it on the instrument itself. Examples of body-percussion pieces and exercises that can stand on their own, or be transferred to instruments, are found in Lesson 10.1.

Nonpitched Percussion Instruments

Also known as rhythm instruments, nonpitched percussion instruments are found nearly everywhere that children are gathered—from preschools to public schools, from child care centers to churches and temples. Rhythm instruments can be played alone or in groups, with or without pitched instruments such as xylophones or keyboards, to accompany songs, chants, poems, or stories. They can accent and interpret narratives, and they provide leitmotif-like sounds to represent story characters. They provide colorful timbres in improvisations and pieces composed by small groups of children. When played together in polyrhythmic fashion, they provide a fascinating complex of sound. Nonpitched percussion instruments may be classified as membranophones (various sizes and shapes of drums that produce sound through a vibrating skin or membrane) or idiophones (instruments of wood, metal, and gourd that are struck, shaken, scraped, or tapped). They may also be categorized according to the material from which they are made: woods, skins, metals, and gourds.

Children enjoy exploring the possible sounds that rhythm instruments can produce, either informally and independently or as stimulated by words of a poem or story. They should also be led by demonstration to learning the traditional ways of holding and playing the instruments, to obtain the greatest resonance from them.

The musical quality of commercially available instruments varies somewhat, but many of them produce pleasant and resonant sounds that are attractive to children through their elementary years. A set of classroom instruments typically includes sticks, flat and notched woodblocks, cymbals, triangles, tambourines, jingle bells, and sandblocks. Additional rhythm instruments in these sets frequently include gongs, finger cymbals, cowbell, and claves. Of the many varieties of drums, those most typically found in well-stocked classrooms include hand drums, bongo drums, conga and goblet drums, and timpani. Still other nonpitched percussion instruments, including those from various world cultures, are the Latin American *guiro*, claves, and maracas; West African double iron *agogo* bells and djembe drum; East Asian temple blocks; and the slit log drum, commonly found in West and Central Africa. Some of these instruments can be made by a teacher or parent, or by children as an art project, although their musical quality may be questionable. A number of nonpitched percussion instruments are described on the following pages, along with techniques for playing them. A vast array of the world's percussion instruments are documented in *Musical Instruments of the World* (1976).

Gourds

Maracas (also rattle, shekere, hosho, cabasa). Found throughout Latin America, maracas are pairs of dried gourds with seeds inside, and they are shaken like rattles. Those played in Mexico, the Caribbean, and South American countries are related to the rattles of Native American and West African cultures. The shekere, hosho, or cabasa, found throughout much of Sub-Saharan Africa, is covered with a beaded netting that is moved by the hand, providing a scraped, rattling sound.

LESSON 10.1 *Experiences in Body Percussion*

1. Teach the rhythms through measure-by-measure imitation, with the intention of engaging all children to perform all parts in body percussion.

2. Transfer rhythms to instruments, to be performed by four groups of children.

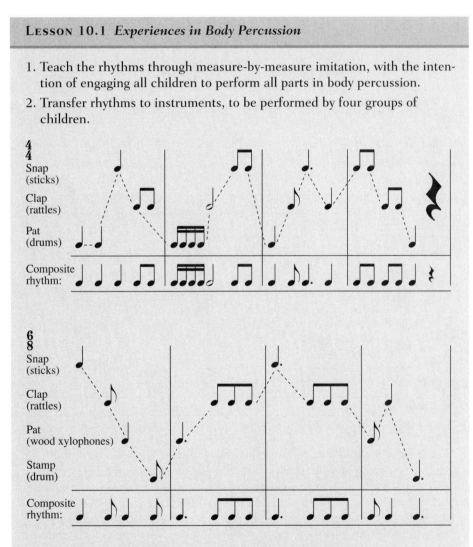

3. Transfer these complete rhythm phrases to xylophones to be played on any keys of the pentaton according to children's personal choices.

4. Teach the following rhythms through imitation. Practice to perform the parts in three groups that gradually combine, overlap, repeat, increase in volume, and conclude on cue.

(Continued)

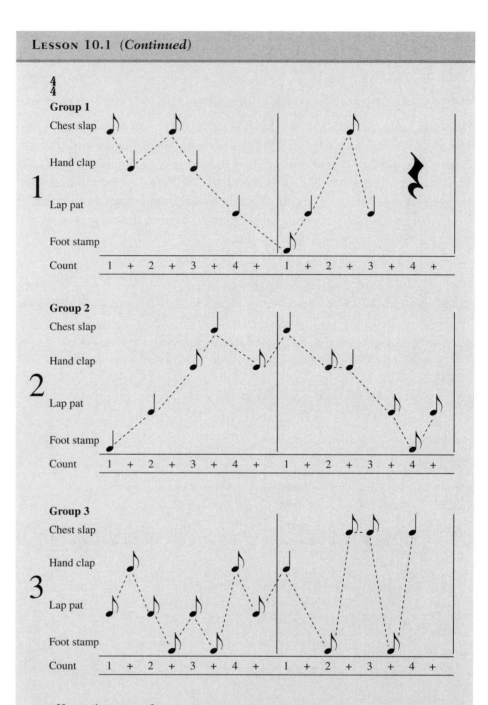

Possible Performance Plan: Arrange children in three groups of equal numbers, to be placed in three circles, one long line, or an open-ended, three-sided square. The director may wish to use claves to keep a constant pulse and to aurally signal changes, additions, or deletions of groups in some pre-planned way. Group one begins performing its rhythm, continuing as group two enters, followed by the entrance of group three. A previous form can be determined, so that groups perform, wait out several cycles, and return again; one such form is given on the next page. The director can cue louder and softer cycles, while the pulse remains the same throughout. Basic movements (such as changes of direction toward which the children face) may be added for visual impact, although the major objective is the performance of polyrhythms through body percussion.

Suggested Form: Numbers stand for group, one complete rhythm cycle per number.

Sequence of Groups in Rhythm Performance, with Dynamics

Group 1	1	1	1	1		1	1	1	1		1	1	1	1		1	1	1	1
Group 2		2	2			2	2		2	2		2	2		2	2		2	2
Group 3				3	3	3		3	3	3		3	3	3		3	3	3	

$p < mf > p$ $f > p$ f mf p f $mf < f$ p f

Alternative Plan: All parts are combined into a six-measure pattern and learned. The six-measure rhythm is then performed in canon, with group two entering one measure after group one, and so forth.

Woods

Sticks. Played in pairs, one stick is struck against the other. Ridged sticks rubbed against each other produce an alternative sound.

Claves. Typically made of rosewood, claves are thick sticks of about one inch in diameter. They are played by holding one clave in the cup of one hand and striking it with the other. Of the many rhythms, one of the best known Latino rhythms is the clave pattern: |♩.♩.♩|𝄽♩♩𝄽|

Woodblock. A partially hollowed block of wood. The most resonant sound is produced by striking a wooden mallet over the slot on the wide surface. The tone block is a variant of the woodblock, with ridges around its hollowed cylindrical shape. It can be struck or rubbed with a mallet.

Temple Blocks. Similar to woodblocks, colorful temple blocks of about four or five sizes are positioned horizontally on a stand at about waist level. When struck by a wooden mallet, they produce sounds that are nearly

Wood, metal, skin, and rattle hand percussion instruments

Jerry Gay

(but not quite) pitched. These East Asian instruments can be used to accent songs from China, Taiwan, Japan, Korea, and Vietnam.

Sandblocks. The friction of rubbing together two blocks of wood that are covered with sandpaper produces the swishing sound of sandblocks. Sandblocks can effectively instill in preschool- and primary-grade children the feel and sound of pulse and meter.

Slit Log Drum. Often just larger than a shoe box, the classroom version of the Sub-Saharan African slit log drums consist of slits cut into the flat top side of a hollowed log or block of wood. The longer and shorter wooden slits are played with mallets, producing lower and higher sounds. Not really a drum at all, the slit log provides a set of colorful timbres in an improvisation or composition.

Guiro. Pronounced "gwee-do," the ridged surface of this wooden instrument is scraped with a stick. Much of Latin America's music features its sound.

Skins (Drums)

Hand Drum. Named because it is held at the rim by the hand, the hand drum is played by striking its head with the other hand or with a mallet. On some, the skin can be tightened or loosened by adjusting the screws at the rim. The hand drum is useful for keeping the pulse and for playing rhythm patterns.

Bongo Drums. Bongo drums are a pair of drums, usually connected by a wooden crosspiece, held on the lap or between the knees. Bongos are played with the fingertips, the palm, and the thumbs. They play an important rhythm role in music from the Caribbean.

The standard hand drum

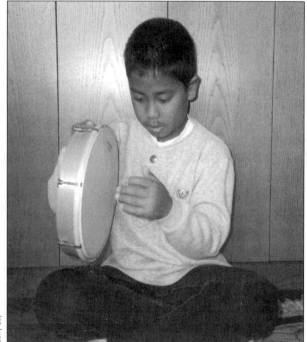

Jerry Gay

Conga Drum. A long upright drum in the shape of a narrow barrel with a skin head stretched across one end, the conga drum produces a variety of resonant timbres when the player strikes its center, edge, or wooden side with the palm and heel of the hand, the flat and cup of the hand, the fingertips, or even with sticks (at the side). Sounds reminiscent of Latin American and Sub-Saharan African cultures emanate from the conga drum. It may be played alone or in pairs.

Djembe Drum. An instrument common to Ghana, the djembe drum is wide at the head and narrow at the base, standing about three feet from the floor. It is played with fingers and palms, often in groups, and personifies for many classrooms the West African sound.

Goblet Drum. An important Middle Eastern instrument, the goblet drum is wide at the head and narrow at the base, about eighteen inches. It is played with fingertips and the palm of the hand at the center and edge of the head.

Timpani. Similar to the symphonic timpani in function, the children's version can be tuned to the tonic, dominant, subdominant, or other prominent pitch of a musical piece by adjusting the screws at the rim. Timpani sit at about waist level on stands with metal legs, and they are played with padded mallets. They come in various sizes, so that several pitches in a piece can be sounded as a percussive bass line.

Metals

Cymbals. Two concave, metal disks (with knobs for holding), cymbals can be struck or rubbed together. They can also be played separately with a mallet or wire brush.

Finger Cymbals. Finger cymbals are smaller versions of the hand-held cymbals. Elastic loops are used to attach the cymbals to the middle finger and thumb of the same hand. Finger cymbals produce ringing and muted sounds, and they are commonly heard in the performance of Middle Eastern music. They can also be played without attachment to the fingers, by touching the rim of one to the rim of the other.

Triangle. This three-sided instrument of metal or steel hangs from a string and is played by striking it with a metal or wooden stick. Its bright timbre is useful for sounding accents.

Tambourine. A tambourine features pairs of metal disks attached to a circular wooden rim that make a jingling sound when shaken. Those tambourines with a drumhead are similar to a hand drum. Most of the countries bordering the Mediterranean, including Spain, Italy, Greece, Turkey, Israel, and Egypt, feature the tambourine in their songs and dances.

Jingle Bells. Small bells on a stick or a plastic ring worn around the wrist or ankles, jingle bells can be added to seasonal music and to the sounds of some Native American Indian groups.

Gong. The flat brass gong found in orchestras is also an important percussion instrument in the music of China, and less so in other parts of East Asia. Played with a padded mallet or wooden stick, various sizes of gongs

1. Gather all of the available instruments together. Experiment with the possibilities for sound on each of them. Seek answers to these questions: Which ones produce pitched or nonpitched sounds? How many different sounds can be produced? What are the traditional ways of sound production? Can you invent new ways? Categorize the instruments according to material (gourd, wood, skin, and metal) or sound production (struck, shaken, rubbed).

2. Read a poem together. Ask children to choose instruments that can aid in the expression and interpretation of the poem.

The Diesel Engine
(P. S. Campbell)

Here,

About half-past eight,

   I like to hear the diesel engine whining.

Once,

It whirred, purred, and clicked,

   ticking track after track in a prearranged pulse.

Now,

It rattles, and coughs,

   spewing smoke in white puffs out its stumpy red stack.

Still,

I like to hear the diesel engine whining,

   about half-past eight.

3. Play a Latin-flavored rhythmic piece with these instruments and their ostinato patterns. First chant the mnemonic syllables and word-phrases of the rhythms, then play by gradually adding one instrument after another. Play the piece with a recording of salsa music.

are capable of playing different pitches, providing bright and long, sustained sounds. These flat gongs are not to be confused with the mellow-sounding knobbed gongs of Southeast Asia, including Indonesia.

Cowbell. A bell found hung around the necks of cows, the cowbell produces open, lower sounds when struck by a mallet near its opening and closed, higher sounds when struck at the top near its handle. It is an important instrument in much Caribbean and South American dance music.

Double Iron Agogo Bells. Found in the West African iron-culture countries of Nigeria, Ghana, Dahomey, and the Ivory Coast, these connected iron bells of two sizes produce a higher- and lower-pitched sound when struck by a mallet. A polyrhythmic layering of patterns played simultaneously adds an authentic timbral color with agogo bells.

Count | 1 + 2 + 3 + 4 + 1 + 2 + 3 + 4 +

Claves
Cla - ves from Cu - ba

Maracas
shake it shake it shake the ma-ra-cas shake it shake it shake the ma-ra-cas

Cowbell
op - en close-close op - en op - en close-close op - en
(open = strike at bell opening; close = strike at top near handle)

Guiro
gwee-do gwee - - do gwee-do

Bongos
bon - go drums are sweet bon-go bon - go drums are sweet bon-go

Conga
heel tips flat heel tips heel cup cup heel tips flat heel tips heel cup cup
L L R L L L R R L L R L L L R R

(Strike conga drum with left hand heel or finger tips; strike with right hand either flat or cupped.)

---

4. Divide children into small groups. Ask them to select a scene (the seashore, a forest, a busy downtown street, the building of a house, the last day of school) and to create the aural image of the scene by making a sound-piece performed by nonpitched instruments. Encourage free rhythms as well as pulsive pieces.

---

5. Encourage children to invent notation for their rhythmic compositions. Allow their own graphic notations to lead (or return) them to the reading of standard rhythmic notation of the Western staff.

These nonpitched percussion instruments provide an array of timbres for children's musical growth. They can develop children's aural awareness and can motivate children to learn to read rhythmic notation. A rhythm band approach (common in the 1930s and 1940s) is to be avoided. Children are capable of far more than merely striking, tapping, rubbing, or shaking instruments without direction or a coherent musical concept in mind. Instead, experiences such as those described in Lesson 10.2 allow children to sample timbral qualities and also to match the durations they hear with how they are symbolized. See the collections of Schmid (1997) and Solomon (1997) for ways of bringing nonpitched percussion instruments, especially the drumming traditions of West Africa and the Caribbean, into a central place in the curriculum.

Pitched Instruments

Children can play melodies and accompaniments on many kinds of instruments. Among them are the barred instruments, such as xylophones, metallophones, glockenspiels, and tone or melody bells; wind instruments, such as recorders and the closely related song flutes; the chording instruments, such as guitar and Autoharp; and keyboards, such as pianos, lap pianos, synthesizers, and organs. A number of these pitched instruments are likely to be found in schools and in the home. They are described here, along with suggestions for their use in developing children's musical understanding and fundamental performance skills. Instructional resources are available for those who wish to teach or to learn these instruments, which also provide children with skills, techniques, and repertoire beyond the beginning levels.

Barred Instruments

The barred instruments developed by German composer Carl Orff are widely known for their exceptional tone quality. These are often referred to as "Orff instruments" and consist of larger and smaller wooden or metal bars laid across a frame, which are struck by mallets made of wood, plastic, rubber, felt, wound yarn, or cloth. Other styles of metal xylophones consist of colored bars or black-and-white chromatic bars similar to a keyboard that predate the increasingly popular Orff-style instruments. Orff instruments were developed to complement the Orff-Schulwerk approach to teaching music to children. Still, they can be employed by all who wish to offer children instrumental experiences. The sounds are pleasing to the ears and are attractive to children who enjoy playing with sound, developing their playing skills, and expressing themselves through improvised and composed

Selected metals and barred instruments

Jerry Gay

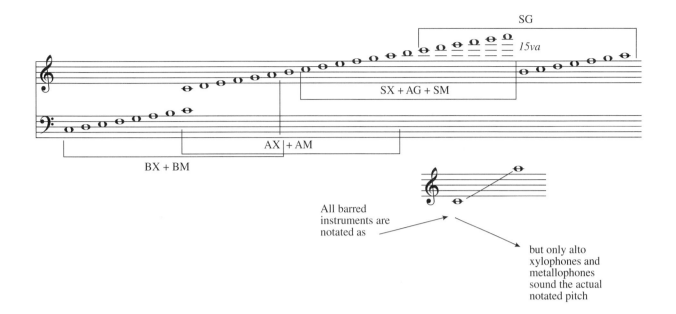

All barred instruments are notated as

but only alto xylophones and metallophones sound the actual notated pitch

FIGURE 10.1

Melodic Ranges of Barred Instruments

Ranges in pitch for the bass, alto, and soprano xylophone and metallophone, and the alto and soprano glockenspiel.

pieces they create. Whether played alone, in ensemble, or as an accompaniment for singing, the Orff instruments greatly enrich children's musical experiences.

The barred instruments of the Orff-Schulwerk consist of xylophones made of wood as well as metallophones and glockenspiels made of metal. The xylophones and metallophones come in three sizes (soprano, alto, and bass); glockenspiels, in two (soprano and alto). All contain a pitch range of a C to A octave (an octave and a sixth), in various registers (see Figure 10.1). The instruments can be played in combinations of different registers or groups of metals and woods.

Barred instruments are usually placed on the floor in front of the musicians, the larger, lower bars to their left, with the players sitting comfortably on the knees or cross-legged. (Glockenspiels can be elevated on a stack of books for easier access, eliminating the need to bend over.) There should be room for movement of the arms and elbows while playing. The mallets are held as in holding a hammer, hairbrush, or toothbrush. Some experimentation and practice may be necessary before the right spot to strike on the bar is found. Eye-hand coordination is critical for mastery in playing. For the best resonance, children should be encouraged to pull out the sound rather than hammer it in; the mallets should bounce away from the bars rather than rest on them.

The bars are removable, so that only those pitches necessary for a particular melody or accompaniment may be played. For example, if a pentatonic melody is to be played, then two bars per octave are removed, making it easier to play the melody. In the case of a repeated accompaniment pattern, or ostinato, all bars not a part of the pattern are removed, clearing the way for the ostinato. Additional bars provide the chromatic pitches for G major (F♯) and F major (B♭); these are provided with the initial purchase. Other accidentals may be purchased, however, as well as fully chromatic instruments.

Barred instruments are most frequently used to supply an accompaniment to a song, using a wide array of musical techniques, from drones to ostinatos. Examples of techniques for accompaniment are ordered from simple to more complex in Box 10.1. While not all-inclusive, these examples convey the flavor of the potential for instrumental accompaniment. These techniques require preparation before playing. Children should pat the patterns on their laps that they will eventually play on the instruments. The success with which these accompaniments are played will depend on children's motor development. Similarly, the extent to which they can be used to accompany folk songs and children's songs will depend on the teacher's musical ear and training. In particular, Orff-Schulwerk training offers lessons in orchestration and mastery of the performance techniques and the pedagogical process. A number of sources on Orff-Schulwerk describe and illustrate the various barred instruments, including Frazee (1987), Steen (1992), and Warner (1991).

Barred instruments also function as melody instruments and as means for improvisation. Children can play songs they know on xylophones, either by ear or by reading notation. A host of familiar songs such as "Little Sally Walker," "Suogan," "Hey, Betty Martin," "Kookaburra," and "Scotland's Burning" are excellent selections to challenge children to play what they already know, while they also master the instrument.

Barred instruments can be their own music-making experience, too, as in the marimba traditions of Guatemala and other coastal regions of Central and South America, and xylophones of the Chopi and Shona peoples of southeastern Africa. Wood and bronze or metal xylophones are found in southeastern Asia, too, as in Java and Bali and in the court music of Cambodia and Thailand. Children can be led to learning styles and structures of these musical experiences through transcriptions (and modified arrangements) of recorded music from these cultures and through collections by Hampton (1996, 1999), Holtfreter (1996), Campbell with Frega (2001), and Sam and Campbell (1992). The prospects of a children's full-blown marimba ensemble for public performances for parents and community members are rich, and the musical results can be nothing short of electric.

From imitative devices to expressive tasks, children can develop creative musical thinking and improvisatory skills through playing these instruments. For example, as children hear a rhythmic pattern of four or eight beats clapped by the teacher, they can then play it back on the instruments, choosing pitches as they play. As they hear a short musical question played for them by a leader, children can then play back an invented short musical answer. In another task, children can be directed to listen to a simple melody, and then to play it back as closely as they can to the way they heard it—without delay. They can experiment with playing the simple melody softer or louder. They can also attempt to play it twice as fast or twice as slow. With partners, children can play musical dialogues, questioning and answering each other every four, six, or eight beats. They can take a known melody and vary it, adding an ostinato pattern. Alternately, they can

Box 10.1 Accompaniment Techniques on Xylophones, Metallophones, and Glockenspiels

Simple drone, in place

Simple drone, in different registers

Simple drone, in a different rhythm

Simple drone, broken

Simple moving drone, treble pitch

Simple moving drone, lower pitch

Double moving drone, drone 5th

Double moving drone, 5ths / 6ths

Double moving drone, broken

Ostinato, one hand

Ostinato, two hands

Ostinato, layered

glock.

sop. xylo.

alto xylo.

bass met.

Several ostinati can be combined to provide for colorful textures.

take a drone and invent a melody for it. The possibilities for building their musicianship through instrumental improvisation are nearly endless, and the rewards are great.

Tone bells, also known as melody bells, belong to the family of barred instruments. They are separate metal bars attached to a resonating box, which are played with a plastic or rubber mallet. Tone bells are kept in a large box and can be played as a xylophone, or they can be distributed to a group of children for playing a collaborative melody similar to the manner in which a handbell choir may function, with each child contributing separate pitches to the melody. The tone quality is soft and bell-like; thus, tone bells function well as harmonic accompaniment to children's voices. In this function, children can contribute the root, third, and fifth (and seventh) of tonic, dominant, and subdominant chords to accompany a vast selection of folk and popular songs.

The Recorder

The recorder was a popular instrument of the European Renaissance period. It is also among the most common melody instruments played by children in the elementary grades today. Various other instruments are related to the recorder, using the same playing techniques and featuring a similar pure, clear tone quality, including song flutes, flutophones, and tonettes.

Recorder playing position

Jerry Gay

CHAPTER 10 / THE PLAYING CHILD

When children have been singing, listening with discrimination and in directed ways, and playing percussion instruments in their early years at home and in school, a logical next step is reading and playing melodies. When they show the physical development that enables them to move their fingers with ease, they are ready for the coordinated tasks of reading, breathing, and finger dexterity that are required to play the recorder. Beginning at about the age of nine, children in the third, fourth, and fifth grades are able and eager for the recorder, a pathway for furthering their musical understanding.

Children often relish the chance to play the recorder. For some, the recorder is an important precursor to the study of band instruments, and it is used to give them the feel of fingering the wind instruments they may later choose to study. The recorder is also an important means of understanding melody—its highs, lows, contours, and intervallic pitch relationships. In typical ensembles of Orff instruments found in elementary classrooms, the recorder is the only nonpercussive instrument (with the exception of the voice). The smooth and sustained melodic flow of the recorder is complementary to the more static and percussive sounds of the barred instruments.

Soprano recorders are best for beginners, and alto recorders can be added after fundamental playing techniques are learned and after fingers have grown long and wide enough. Professional recorder musicians play wooden instruments, but those made of plastic are inexpensive and offer a surprisingly mellow tone when played gently. Most beginners' recorders come with a soft or plastic tubular case. The mouthpieces can be sterilized with hot water or with aerosol spray sanitizers. Instructional books are available for playing recorder, although a chart of fingerings, musical exercises, and familiar songs are all that may be needed to introduce children to the instrument.

Children will follow the model of the teacher in finding the correct playing position. The top of the mouthpiece is placed in front of the teeth between the lips. The left hand is placed above the right hand, and its fingers cover the back hole and the top front three holes. The right hand's fingers will cover the bottom front four holes (including the bottom two double holes). Children must meet the challenges of (1) feeling the holes that they cannot easily see; (2) balancing the recorder with the thumbs at the back, the fingers at the front, and the mouth at the tip; (3) curving the fingers and placing the fleshy finger pads on the appropriate holes; and (4) blowing gently while forming the sound of "doo" with the mouth and tongue. Fingerings are shown for the c-d" in Figure 10.2. When the sounds are incorrect or piercingly painful, the most common problems will be resolved by blowing more lightly and covering the (appropriate) holes.

One way to teach the recorder involves singing a familiar song, then singing it with letters, numbers, or solfège syllables while fingering it on the recorder, and finally playing it. Because children know many songs, they may be more quickly able to play them in that they have already mentally processed the rise and fall of the melody and the repeated patterns. Songs such as "Hot Cross Buns," "Mos' Mos'," "Polly Wolly Doodle," and "Hey,

FIGURE 10.2

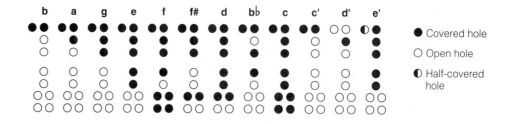

Betty Martin" feature limited ranges and repeated patterns that children may find more easily transferable to their recorders. The second stage of singing while silently playing is a critical one, because it links the sound with the kinesthetic feeling. During this stage, which may be repeated numerous times until the fingers move easily, children may hold their recorders at their chin to ensure that no tones are sounded.

The recorder is neither a toy nor an instrument limited to playing simple folk songs and exercises. An exciting repertoire is available for children who learn the fundamental performance techniques, stemming from fourteenth- through seventeenth-century Europe. Further, the music of other cultures, particularly some East Asian and Native American genres, can be played on recorder. Children can continue to play songs they know on recorder, as well as to invent their own. Those children who continue past the introductory lessons can eventually play the sophisticated music of a Renaissance consort or melodies found in Latin American (including Andean) wind ensembles (King, 1998). Recorders combined with other timbres can be beautiful and aesthetically pleasing. Also, many songs that students hear on the radio, on their cassettes, or on compact discs (CDs) are simple enough to play on the recorder. Children can develop high levels of skill on recorder when challenged to learn high-interest songs as extra-credit projects on their own time. There are several recorder books noteworthy for classroom use, including those by Burakoff and Burakoff (1997) Cox and Richard (1985), and Etkin (1975).

Harmony Instruments

While all melody instruments are capable of producing a melody that functions harmonically in playing an ostinato or descant against a melody (such as xylophones, metallophones, and recorders), several instruments are known for their primary function as accompaniments for singing. The Auto-harp and the guitar are chordal instruments found at school or at home. Both are social instruments arising from American musical heritages steeped in evening sing-alongs on the back porch, around the campfire, and in the parlor. While the guitar has long been an important part of the American pop and rock music scene, it still remains, along with the Autoharp, an important means of producing chords for any folk, popular, or personal music that children may wish to sing and play.

The Autoharp

As recently as the 1950s, one of the most important instruments for the accompaniment of folksingers in the Appalachian hill-country, the Ozark Mountains, and Anglo-American communities elsewhere was the Autoharp. It became useful to teachers who wanted a portable instrument to provide harmony to songs sung by children in the classroom or outdoors, one that could be easily learned by teachers and children alike. Its sound is soft enough to support children's singing voices without overwhelming them. By following chord markings in songbooks and music series texts, the Autoharp functions as a bona fide musical instrument almost immediately.

The Autoharp is a zither, commonly equipped with twelve, fifteen, or twenty-one chord bars that are depressed by pressing on buttons. When a button on the chord bar is pushed, the felts on the bottom of the bar are pressed against the strings that are not part of the chord, which silences those pitches. The chord names are printed on the buttons. The Autoharp player reads the chord names found above the melody line of notated songs and presses the corresponding chord bars with one hand while strumming the strings with the other. Different strumming patterns can be used to enhance rhythmic characteristics of a variety of songs.

While the Autoharp is generally easy to play, there are two challenges to consider. One is in the player's adjustment to the traditional Appalachian playing position, in which the Autoharp is held upright and somewhat diagonally, with the left hand pressing the buttons and the right hand crossing over the left to strum the strings. Alternative positions for children include laying the instrument flat on the lap, on a tabletop, or on the floor.

Autoharp playing position

Jerry Gay

The second challenge is tuning the Autoharp, a time-consuming task even for those with a good ear. The instrument is affected by weather conditions, thus tuning is necessary almost daily—and sometimes more frequently than that. A metal tuning key is provided for tightening the string to raise the pitch and for loosening it to lower the pitch. By pressing one chord button (for example, G major) and then slowly brushing across each G, B, and D string from highest to lowest, flat and sharp pitches can be heard and adjusted with the tuning key. At the very least, all pitches in chords of the song(s) to be played should be tuned. If the Autoharp is not in good tuning, it should not be played or it may lead to out-of-tune singing. Electronic tuners greatly simplify this chore.

The advent of the Omnichord, a type of electronic Autoharp, eliminates the tuning difficulties of the acoustic instrument. The Omnichord has no strings but retains the push-button chord system. In addition, the Omnichord plays rhythmic ostinati, waltz, and rock-style rhythms, and it can be set at various tempi, volumes, and timbres that include piano, guitar, brass, banjo, and chimes.

The Autoharp and its newer cousin facilitate children's awareness of harmony—major and minor chord qualities, the function of chords in their support of melody, and the relationship of tonic, dominant, subdominant, and mediant chords to one another. For children in the primary grades, the teacher may wish to press the chord buttons while a child strums the strings. Just as children in the intermediate grades are beginning to hear harmonic changes, they can also play the instrument by themselves. Familiar songs with one chord ("Are You Sleeping?," "For Health and Strength," "Row Your Boat"), two chords ("Sandy Land," "Down in the Valley," "Polly Wolly Doodle"), and three chords ("Red River Valley," "Knick-Knack Paddy Whack," "Old McDonald") can be played by reading chord charts—or by ear, providing children with exercises in hearing harmonic changes as they sing. Further information on the Autoharp is available in Peterson (1966) and Carlin (1982).

The Guitar

Children are eager to learn the guitar long before they are able to play it, motivated by seeing and hearing it in many popular styles of music, from rock to country to folk, on TV, radio, recordings, and films. When their hands are sufficiently large to stretch around the neck to the strings, they are ready to play; for most children, that occurs around fourth grade.

There are many types of guitars, but the nylon-strung folk or classical guitars are easier on the fingers than the steel strings found on larger acoustic instruments. Nonamplified electric guitars can also be played by children because, despite the steel strings, their necks are narrow and thus easier on the hand and finger expanse.

As a chording instrument, the guitar can accompany songs with as few as one, two (I, V), or three (I, IV, V) chords. The right-hand strums can be as basic as one chord per measure or per pulse, to syncopated rhythms and patterns that combine plucking with strumming. While there are many manuals for playing guitar, children often learn to play through observation and experimentation. Time spent in practice pays off, so that children who play at home or who come to the music room before or after school can become proficient. The use of a capo, a plastic-covered bar that is clipped across the strings, extends the possibilities for playing song accompaniments in practically any key.

Children can be playing guitar accompaniments to songs they know even in their first lesson. Once they find a comfortable way of holding the guitar, imitating the teacher's seated position with the guitar resting on the crossed leg, they are ready to play their first chord: e-minor. Figure 10.3 presents tablature, or fretboard diagrams, of a minor, E major, G major (simplified and more sophisticated versions), C major, and D major (and D7) chords. When they are played correctly, the left-hand fingers are curved, their tips pressing the designated strings to the fingerboard. Children should be checked and reminded to avoid touching other strings that are not a part of the chord configuration.

Once the fingers of the right hand are comfortable in their chord positions and in changing chords, then children can begin to learn strumming patterns. Several common patterns are featured in Figure 10.4. They are best learned by saying "down" and "up" in rhythm before and while playing. Down refers to the downward brushing of the thumb from the lowest string to the highest; up is the thumb's upward brush across the higher to lower strings and toward the player's face. Strumming patterns add distinctive flavors to songs and soon separate beginners from the more proficient players.

Children who have mastered a few chords and their strums can be playing the harmonic accompaniment for a great variety of songs. The e-minor chord alone enables children to play "Shalom Chaverim," "Hey, Ho, Nobody Home," and "Zum Gali Gali." The great majority of children's songs often require no more than three chords and often only the tonic and dominant. Guitar accompaniment is especially appropriate for such Latin American songs as "Tinga Layo" (Dominican), "Ambozado" (Puerto Rican"), and "La Raspa" (Mexican). Collections of folk and popular songs are readily available with guitar accompaniment.

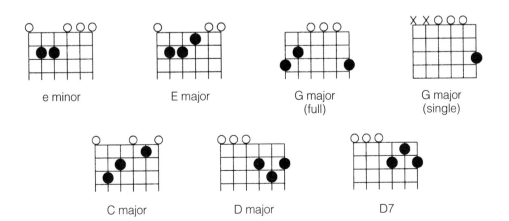

FIGURE 10.3

Guitar Tablature for the Left Hand

FIGURE 10.4

Guitar Strums

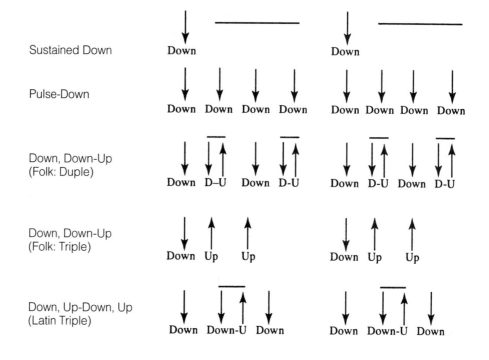

Tuning the guitar can present still another challenge, and the parent or teacher often must match the pitches of the six strings (E, A, D, G, B, e) to each other or to a pitch pipe, piano, or the guitar's special tuning pipes. Most instructional manuals feature tuning along with a great variety of chord tablatures and strumming and picking patterns. For a sequential handbook on playing folk guitars, including chording and picking patterns, see Kuhn and Reid (1984); for classical styles, see Noad (1994). The logistics of, and sequence for, teaching guitar in a classroom setting, with guitars for every child, are outlined in a manual by Bay and Christiansen (2000).

Keyboards

Either at home or in school, children are bound to have opportunities to play a keyboard; that is, pianos, organs, synthesizers, MIDI instruments, and lap pianos. Keyboards are the most popular type of instrument in American homes. Over half of American families today own acoustic and electronic pianos or organs.

Some electronic keyboards are inexpensive to own individually (for example, Casio models) and come with color-coded notation for playing familiar melodies and their chords. Frequently, children play with these or other types of pianos at home and are likely to have explored the black and white keys to figure out familiar songs. Keyboard instruments are often responsible for children's first chance to play music and may be the source of their growing interest in music. Some children have sampled chords and timbres with the press of a button. They may even have access in their homes to more sophisticated keyboard technology, including MIDI and assorted attachments that allow the sounds of rain forests, windstorms, and outer space to be mixed with violin, guitar, koto, and talking drum timbres.

Most schools are likely to have available at least one classic grand or upright acoustic piano. The music room, auditorium, and assembly space are the most likely locations for the piano. When in tune and played well, the piano can bring unity to the group singing of patriotic and traditional songs as well as add to the artistic quality of a choral performance. Yet it is far more than an accompaniment instrument. It can stimulate eurhythmic movement to music through its percussive quality and its broad spectrum of expressive capacities. It can illustrate musical features, from pitch to duration to dynamic intensity. It can add color and interest to stories and poems. The piano can also underscore and reinforce musical learning for children of every age.

Whether the music is initiated by the teacher to stimulate musical responses in children or whether the music is read and performed or invented by children themselves, keyboards provide an effective avenue of music instruction. Children can learn by observing the teacher play or by exploring on their own the concepts of scale, intervals, register, range, ascending and descending pitches, melodic contour, repetition, and sequence. They can experiment with tone matching (playing and then singing pitch patterns) and can come to terms with the function of the staff, treble and bass clefs, and notation when they take it to the piano. Children enjoy experimenting with the piano's potential as both a melody and a harmony instrument. For those who develop basic facility at the piano (or any keyboard), it will become an important channel for personal expression in the original music that they create.

In some schools, pianos are purchased as keyboard laboratories. A music room may thus be equipped with ten, twenty, or more electronic pianos on stands, with student headphones. The student pianos are linked to a teacher's station that includes piano and audio facilities for listening to the performances of individual students, small groups, or the entire class. Beginning in the intermediate grades, children can learn to read notation as well as basic piano technique through instruction manuals that progress from one-hand melodies, to song melodies with simple chordal accompaniments, to full-fledged piano pieces from the classical and popular repertoire. Group piano classes in the schools are generally focused on learning about music—its structures and sonorities—through performance. See Chapter 4 for a discussion of the Yamaha Corporation's Music in Education program, and Chapter 13 for descriptions of MIDI and other technologies for making music and aiding music instruction.

Music teachers may be an important link to children's further training and development as pianists and as musicians. Because they have presented children with musical problems and have observed the nature of each child's capacity to solve them, music teachers are in a position to evaluate and recommend further instruction. They have noted the rhythmic capacity, aural acuity, and eye-hand coordination of individual children in group piano lessons or in other musical activities, and they can thus predict with reasonable accuracy the prognosis of children who wish to study piano (or other instruments) privately. For those children who enjoy playing piano, classroom instruction in keyboard laboratories is ideal. For those few who aspire to become pianists, the music teacher may offer a pathway.

Assessment of Playing Instruments

Children can rattle around on classroom instruments, trapped in an endless and nonprogressive first-level exploratory stage. They can rigidly step through a routine of school-music skills that do not bring them personal satisfaction or an understanding as to how these skills might be transferred to music making beyond school. Or they can succeed in developing the techniques and the musical intelligence for playing instruments as soloists and ensemble members, from notation or by ear, and with both technical facility and interpretative, improvisatory power. Pitch by pitch, and rhythmic duration by rhythmic phrase, children can progress to a repertoire of songs and musical sounds that give pleasure to them and those that listen. They can be so motivated by their own progress as to want to travel with their recorders, playing the tunes they learned in school and making up new ones, or to play their school keyboard compositions on the old family upright piano. They can be inspired by the rhythmic instruments they have begun to learn to want their own at home to play with their favorite CDs, or they can be driven to transfer the sense of harmony learned on xylophones (and the cooperative spirit of playing together) to a more perceptive ability to listen to harmonic changes, to perform harmonies on other instruments, and to create their own music with a refined sense of how melodies and chords move.

Children can sense their own progress in learning to play instruments, and they can be assessed (or can learn to self-assess) this progress in numerous ways. The following questions can frame this assessment.

1. Is the tone quality of your instrument, however simple the music, pleasing to your (and others') ears? Why or why not? (Check your playing position, and breath control and mouth and tongue actions for wind instruments.)

2. Is the performance of your instrument musically accurate? Are you reading the rhythms and pitches correctly? Are you listening carefully to the musical models, particularly in the case of traditional and popular music from oral traditions?

3. Are you playing with ease? (Check your fingerings, work on transitions between phrases, and play the harder parts repeatedly.)

4. Does the music sound like you or as you would like it to sound (within the parameters permitted by the musical work or tradition)? Are you able to express yourself as you would like to?

5. Can you play a piece alone, from start to finish, accurately and expressively? Can you play your instrument in tandem with others, listening to them and blending with them in their playing?

Checklists of exercises and specific phrases, scales, and songs learned can be posted to the classroom wall or stapled to the back of the instrumental manuals, to be filled in by the teacher for each individual student as he or she meets the requirements. The teacher may wish to engage parents, too, in assessing the amount of daily or weekly practice time (particularly on instruments such as the recorder that all children may be required to have, to take home to practice). As in all musical activities that occur within the classroom, children's musical skills can be subject to ongoing and regular assessment, with teachers calling out remarks like "Good tone, Jenny," "Watch your rhythm on the second measure, Sean," "Take a bigger breath to float you through the phrase," and "We've got it, the whole piece by the whole class." Still, it is useful to provide individual feedback to children and to pull them into the realm of self-assessment by questioning them in ways that lead them to their own recognition of what it takes to play an instrument well.

The Benefits of Instrumental Study

For some children, making music is equivalent to playing musical instruments. The appeal of tapping, striking, shaking, blowing, and strumming musical instruments is one of the great joys in their lives. Because musical instruments are extensions of the musical self, when children play they are often demonstrating what they know and can express musically. To play a musical instrument is to deliver to others ideas that are not easily expressed verbally.

Musical instruments enhance the development of musical understanding. Why count rhythms when they can be felt and played? Why learn staff notation unless the symbols can be realized musically? Along with the singing voice, classroom instruments are teaching aids for experiencing musical concepts such as high and low, loud and soft, long and short, fast and slow, and choppy and smooth. The practice of playing a minor third, a perfect fourth, a legato phrase, or a chord progression underscores principles of music theory. Until children can be engaged in the practice of music making, they are not likely to fully understand the musical structures behind the sound. The playing of a musical instrument can precede, and later coincide with, the reading and writing of notation.

Teachers and parents who are aware of children's attraction to musical instruments, and of their capacities for playing them, can facilitate their musical growth. Children can develop performance skills quite rapidly when they are developmentally ready; that is, when they have arrived at the motoric and perceptual stages required for successful performance. There is the danger that when instruments and their performance techniques are introduced before children are capable of playing them, they may experience frustration and failure that may result in negative attitudes and demotivation. Teachers should recognize the importance of preparatory experiences that set in motion the physical skills necessary for playing with rhythmic accuracy, and they should allow children repeated opportunities to practice their parts while avoiding the possibilities for boredom by delivering a variety of rapid-fire rehearsal strategies.

The old adage "practice makes perfect" should be reinforced for children who hope to develop their performance skills on instruments such as the recorder, piano, or guitar. Daily practice at home will undoubtedly result in marked improvement. At school, the teacher may wish to institute an open-door policy for children to spend before—or after—school time practicing. Where there is interest in the study of a musical instrument, the motivation to become a proficient player may be awaiting general encouragement of the teacher and parent.

Scenario

A combined class, Mrs. Barr's second- and third-grade group, has arrived to Miss Hailey's music room for their late-morning class. They settle themselves into places just behind the instruments that have been laid out in sections on the carpeted floor. There are three xylophones and three metallophones (soprano, alto, and bass). Two glockenspiels; two conga drums, a goblet drum, and four hand drums; two woodblocks, two claves, a slit log drum, and a *guiro*; and one each of the metal instruments (gong, cowbell, triangle, finger cymbals, maracas)—they are grouped together in each of the four corners of the room. Children know the routine, but Miss Hailey reminds them, "Do what I do. Listen to me, watch my cue, then you do it." She picks up claves and plays a four-beat pattern, extends her arms and nods her head to the children, and they immediately imitate her. That pattern is followed by another and another and another. She increases the length of the patterns to eight beats, and some of the children are unable to produce a completely accurate imitation. The children on the eight xylophones are playing on the keys of the pentatonic scale (the Fs and Bs have been removed) with less rhythmic precision than, for example, the children on claves, woodblocks, or conga drums, but Miss Hailey continues to maintain a steady pace to keep the class on-task and motivated.

Miss Hailey switches gears as she begins to chant, "A stitch in time saves nine," accenting the second, fourth, and sixth syllables, and clapping twice at the end of the phrase. The children join in the chant as Miss Hailey plays the claps on her claves, and they are soon following her lead and also playing the claps on their instruments. She moves over to the xylophone group, takes the mallet to the bass xylophone, and alternately plays c and g on every chant syllable as the chanting proceeds. While the children continue to chant and play, she moves to the metal instruments, cues them in on the second and fourth syllables, and then invites the drums to play on the words "time saves nine." This leaves only the woods to play the double clap at the end of a phrase, and so instruments sound across the proverb's eight-beat phrase. Miss Hailey is listening now, asking the children to phase out their chanting to hear the textures. Some children are rushing the tempo, and so she waves her arms above her head in an exaggerated fashion to keep them together. Taking it one step further, Miss Hailey reminds the children again to watch her, and with her body stretched high or low, she conducts their dynamic levels. She is pleased with their playing (although the drum players have been playing very hard and very loud, and talking and laughing as they play) and tells them so.

As has been done in the past, Miss Hailey distributes photographs of landscapes (the seashore, mountains, a river, a volcano) and assigns the children on each instrument group the task of creating a soundscape for the scene. "You have five minutes to work together with your group to make up an aural image for your scene." The children set out to work on this open-ended project, and Miss Hailey sets the timer and sits at her desk to thumb through a new instrument catalog. She feels that the din of four groups of children playing at once is vital and a clear indication that the children are productive. At the sound of the timer, each group plays its soundscape, and while it is difficult to distinguish between pieces, Miss Hailey firmly believes that the children have had an opportunity to explore their instruments and to express themselves. There is still time remaining, so directing the children to take their places behind instruments in a different group, she repeats the soundscape exercise. As the class comes to a close, Miss Hailey asks them to describe what they have learned in the class session, and one little girl's answer brings much agreement among the children: "To wear ear-muffs to music!"

Questions

1. Which of Miss Hailey's three musical activities was the most musically valid or pedagogically sound? Explain.

2. If the children were more, or less, skilled, would it influence the success of the lesson? Could Miss Hailey have intervened at any point in developing the children's instrumental skills?

3. Would it have been possible to involve the children in more singing, moving, or listening along with their instrument playing? How? Why?

REVIEW

1. Why are xylophones recommended for use by school-age children instead of by kindergarten and preschool children?

2. What is a corpophone? How many corpophones can you demonstrate?

3. How can classroom instruments be categorized, so that children can understand similarities among instruments regarding their function and the materials from which they are made?

4. What are children's challenges for playing recorder? What direction can the teacher provide to meet these challenges?

5. How is an Autoharp tuned? A guitar?

6. Discuss the contributions of the piano in reinforcing children's musical learning.

PROJECTS

1. Create a body-percussion piece. Begin with a poem or song that can serve as the stimulus for the rhythm and can then be performed together with or as an alternate to the body-percussion piece.

2. Collect a set of children's songs from various cultures that can be performed with one or two non-pitched percussion instruments. Determine which instruments are representative of the cultural tradition.

3. Experiment with various accompaniment techniques for xylophones, metallophones, and glockenspiels. Arrange or orchestrate one folk song to feature each of the following techniques on Orff xylophones: simple drone, moving simple drone, moving double drone, ostinato, layered ostinato.

4. Practice guitar strums shown in Figure 10.4, and invent three new strums for 4, 4, and 8 meter.

5. Write a letter of appeal to the parents of your students, in which you inform them of the importance of home practice in learning a musical instrument. Choose recorder, guitar, or keyboard. Be persuasive in your support of the educational value of playing a musical instrument—individually and in the class ensemble.

REFERENCES

Bay, W., and M. Christiansen (2000). *Mastering the guitar class method.* Pacific, MO: Mel Bay.

Burakoff, G., and S. Burakoff (1997). *Hands on recorder.* Ft. Worth, TX: Sweet Pipes.

Campbell, P. S., with A. L. Frega (2001). *Canciones de America Latina: De su Origen a la Escuela.* Miami, FL: Warner Bros. Publications.

Carlin, R. (1982). *How to play autoharp.* New York: Music Sales.

Cox, H., and G. Richard (1985). *Sing, clap, and play the recorder* (books 1 and 2). St. Louis, MO: Magnamusic-Baton.

Diagram Group. (1976). *Musical instruments of the world.* New York: Paddington Press.

Etkin, R. (1975). *Playing and composing on the recorder.* New York: Sterling.

Frazee, J. (1987). *Discovering Orff: A curriculum for music teachers.* New York: Schott.

Hampton, W. (1996). *Hot Marimbas!* Danbury, CT: World Music Press.

———. (1999). *Mojo Marimbas.* Danbury, CT: World Music Press.

Holtfreter, L. (1996) *Flowing waters: The Javanese gamelan.* Danbury, CT: World Music Press.

King, C. (1998). *World winds: Pan-American pipes.* Memphis, TN: Musicraft Publications.

Kuhn, T. L., and H. D. Reid (1984). *Modern folk guitar.* New York: Alfred A. Knopf.

MENC (1994). *What every young American should know and be able to do in the arts: National standards for arts education.* Reston, VA: Music Educators National Conference.

Noad, F. M. (1994). *Solo guitar playing, Book I* (3rd ed.). New York: Schirmer Books.

Peterson, M. (1966). *The many ways to play autoharp.* Union, NJ: Oscar Schmidt-International.

Sam, S. A., and P. S. Campbell (1992). *Silent temples: songful hearts: Traditional music of Cambodia.* Danbury, CT: World Music Press.

Schmid, W. (1997). *World drumming curriculum.* Milwaukee, WI: Hal Leonard.

Solomon, J. (1997). *Drum.* Miami: Warner Bros. Publications.

Steen, A. (1992). *Exploring music.* New York: Schott.

Warner, B. (1991). *Orff-Schulwerk: Applications for the classroom.* Englewood Cliffs, NJ: Prentice-Hall.

SOURCES OF CLASSROOM INSTRUMENTS

Andy's Front Hall. P.O. Box 307, Wormer Road, Voorheesville, NY 12186.

Bergerault, Inc. (Peripole). 2041 State St., Salem, OR 97301.

Elderly Instruments. 1100 N. Washington, Lansing, MI 48906.

House of Musical Traditions. 7040 Carroll Avenue, Takoma Park, MD 20912.

John's Music Center. 4501 Interlake North #9, Seattle, WA 98103.

Magnamusic-Baton, Inc. 10370 Page Industrial Blvd., St. Louis, MO 63132.

Music Education Group. Oscar Schmidt. 230 Lexington Drive, Buffalo Grove, IL 60089.

Remo, Inc. 28101 Industry Drive, Valencia, CA 91355.

Rhythm Band, Inc. P.O. Box 126, Fort Worth, TX 76101.

Sonor, HSS. Department ED-3, P.O. Box 9167, Richmond, WA 23227.

Suzuki Corporation. P.O. Box 261030, San Diego, CA 92196.

The World of Peripole, Inc. P.O. Box 146, Lewiston Road, Browns Mills, NJ 08015.

West Music. 1212 Fifth St., Coralville, IA 52241.

Yamaha Music Corporation, U.S.A. P.O. Box 6600, Buena Park, CA 90620.

11

The Creating Child

To a great extent, everything the young child does musically comes out of his or her creative imagination and exploration. Anna engages in the typical vocal sound play of the infant with her "bahs," "duhs," and "gurgles" throughout her range. Juan rhythmically strikes a wooden spoon against a pan, and Marianne laughs and claps with joy when she discovers she can make sounds on the piano. All of these responses represent a satisfaction of the inherent desire children have to generate and manipulate sounds and, eventually, to place them into meaningful structures.

This desire continues through the elementary years and beyond as children eagerly invent words and rhythms for a rap, improvise a pentatonic melody on a soprano xylophone, or work in a group to choreograph a favorite musical selection. The creative impulse is alive in children of all ages, and the music classroom is an ideal setting to stimulate the growth of that creativity beyond the initial stages of exploration and discovery.

The arts come into being through the creativity of individuals and groups. To deny children the opportunity to work creatively with the materials and structures of music is to limit their capacity to think artistically and, ultimately, to limit the full exploration of what it means to be musical. Teaching music without having children compose would be like teaching art without having children draw or paint, or teaching writing by having children copy other people's work. Including composition, improvisation, and arranging as important aspects of a general music program provides the third element of a balanced program of listening, performing, and creating.

Developmental Sequence

The development of musical creativity, both conceptual and practical, appears to be the result of the interaction of factors of environment, musical thought or cognition, and individual intellectual and personality traits. Children are exposed to a wide range of music as a result of enculturation and have much to draw from as composers. As children grow in their musical experience and their capacity to physically manipulate or control the sounds of their instruments or voices, they can move to higher levels of creative production. If they are in environments that encourage them to improvise, arrange, and compose music, they will perceive these activities as natural and as part of what one does to express musical ideas. Some children may feel more comfortable with this process than others and express more musically sophisticated ideas. All children, however, can benefit, both musically and cognitively, from active involvement in the creation, not just the recreation, of music.

Several theories have been proposed about the development of creative thinking and creative production in music. Although these theories need to be tested in classroom settings where children are allowed extended time to craft pieces, they are included in Table 11.1 to suggest the growth of creativity during preschool as well as the elementary years. Critics of these studies suggest that children at the ages of five and six do compose pieces

TABLE 11.1 *Development of Creative Production*

AGE	FLOHR (1985); KRATUS (1985, 1991)	TILLMAN AND SWANICK (1989)	TEACHER ACTION
Birth to four-to-five years	Driven by motor energy. Highly individualistic in approaches and patterns. Lacking musical syntax.	Mastery of materials and range of sounds through sensing and manipulating.	Provide age-appropriate instruments to explore. Encourage and reinforce discovery and respect individuality.
Four-to-five to nine (kindergarten to grade four)	Predictable rhythmic and tonal patterns, influenced by familiar music. Changing meters and emerging sense of tonality. Lack strong sense of phrase structure and cadence.	Imitation of both personal and vernacular ideas occurs with greater expressive quality. Meter emerges, greater use of dynamic expression, ostinati.	Encourage growth of ideas and craftsmanship. Build musical concepts and awareness of many conventions. Build skills of self-evaluation.
Ten to twelve (grades four to six)	Music becomes organized according to cultural rules or structures. Use of melodic and rhythmic motives. Increased use of sounds and patterns of familiar music. Often less original.	Imaginative play in which surprise is an element but using more references to popular music idioms. Concern for form and structure, use of harmony emerges.	Keep expanding the repertoire of conventions for structuring music. Help students to avoid becoming too critical of their or others' works. Encourage self-expression.

that reflect structural thinking in music. This is most often done when children use their voices or when they are given more time to develop confidence in using instruments than is typically allowed in a research setting. (See a summary of these ideas by Barrett, 1996, 1998.)

Creative Thinking

Much of the thinking teachers ask children to do is convergent thinking, the type of thinking that results in a single, correct answer. When children are asked to name things such as signs, symbols, composers, or pieces of music, they are directed to think convergently. In performance, children are asked to conform to the correct pitches and rhythms of a song, although often creativity is encouraged in the area of interpretation.

At the heart of creative thought is a different type of thinking, divergent thinking. This is when teachers ask children for many possible answers. For example, children could be challenged to discover how many different sounds a percussion instrument makes or how many techniques might be used in playing it.

Webster (1990) has developed a theory of creative thinking in music. According to that theory, qualities of divergent thinking include:

1. Musical extensiveness—how many ideas are generated

2. Flexibility—the ease of shifting within parameters such as high and low or loud and soft

3. Originality—how unique the musical ideas are

In the area of originality, for example, creative children may generate their own songs and themes instead of using more familiar ones. These

Young children exploring sounds

Jerry Gay

qualities interact with others such as a child's musical understandings and sensitivities, ability to imagine pitches and rhythms, aesthetic sensitivity, and ability to craft a piece to effect the final product of the creative effort. From the standpoint of the teacher, the key is to establish an environment where these various skills and understandings are consciously developed.

Exploration and Discovery

The first stage in the creative process for all students is to explore and discover possibilities that exist for manipulating sounds. Children need to have the freedom to explore the range of sounds an instrument or voice might make in terms of color (ringing, thunking, raspy, rattle); techniques (scraping, shaking, striking, rubbing, blowing, plucking, strumming); and dynamics (loud or soft), pitch (definite or indefinite, high or low), duration (long, short, or sustained impression), and texture (thin to thick).

In the process of free exploration, children are building a repertoire of sound possibilities and techniques from which they can later draw to make musical or artistic decisions. As a stimulus for exploring sounds, the teacher might give every child a piece of paper and say, "Discover as many different sounds as you can make with this piece of paper in the next two minutes. The signal for you to stop and look at me will be when I flash the lights." When the two minutes have passed, students share their discoveries. During this time, the teacher can guide by asking questions that help the children to compare sounds or group them into categories. "Who has rattling sounds?" "Whose sound was almost like that sound?" The teacher can use this time to build musical vocabulary such as high and low or loud and soft: "Play that sound again but change from loud to soft." "Make your buzz swoop from low to high." "Repeat the sound of the 'thunk' five times, letting it fade gradually."

Over time, children should be encouraged to explore the sound possibilities of a wide range of sources and to use those sounds creatively. Some suggestions are found in Box 11.1 with additional suggestions in Biasini, Thomas, and Pogonowski (1971).

Once children have discovered what their instruments or voices can do, they can move into either a mode of improvisation, arranging, or composition. Whatever mode the strategy involves, the teacher's role is to establish the parameters for the piece.

Improvisation

Improvisation at a beginning level allows children to play with sounds and with musical syntax (or putting those sounds together). Improvisation at the highest level—in jazz or certain world traditions such as Indian sitar

Box 11.1 *Sound Sources*

Found Sounds

Paper

Objects (rulers, cups, pens, keys)

Kitchen implements (egg beater, whisk, grater, spatula)

Garage sounds (hammers, saws, nails, drills, tin cans, wood, springs)

Mouth Sounds

Voiced (hum, shout, sing, sigh, shriek, buzz, animal sounds, machine
    sounds)

Nonvoiced (pop, click, whistle, slurp, hiss)

Room Sounds

Pencils, notebooks, rulers, grates, shades, doors, music stands

Body Sounds

Hands, fingers, feet, arms, chest, head

Toy Sounds

Whistles, hummers, drums, xylophones, music boxes, rattles, doll, kazoos,
    Zube-Tube

Environmental Sounds

Birds, animals, machines, vehicles, water, wind, waves

Instrumental Sounds

Classroom (nonpitched percussion, xylophones and metallophones,
    Autoharps, recorders, pianos, guitars)

Electronic (keyboards, synthesizers, tape recorders)

Ethnic (membranophones, chordophones, idiophones, aerophones)

Band or orchestra (brass, strings, woodwind, percussion)

Student-Invented or -Constructed Instruments

Give students simple materials (canisters, string, wood, beans, paper, tape,
    nails, metal, glass) and have them invent an instrument.

---

and tabla duos, Nigerian drum ensembles, or Chopi (Mozambique) xylophone ensembles—involves advanced performance technique combined with deep knowledge of the idiom being used (Campbell, 1991). Regardless of the age or musical sophistication of the improvisers, this process is essential to developing an ease and flexibility in manipulating the language of music. Opportunities to improvise should occur throughout children's development, stimulating them to converse in music in the same way they converse using words, freely and spontaneously with meaning. National Standard 3 is dedicated to improvisation. Ideally, children should be invited to improvise during portions of each class. (See issues of *Music Educators Journal* and *Teaching Music* listed in references for ideas about composing and improvising.)

Generally, an improvised piece or section of a piece is invented spontaneously. It is neither formalized, refined, nor repeated. There are numerous possibilities to use in structuring improvisation with children. A whole-class improvisation with the paper sounds that the children have discovered could include the following activities.

1. Ask each person to select three paper sounds he or she found the most interesting.

2. Perform each sound once over one minute and distribute the sounds across the time.

3. Conduct the work—either student or teacher—and mark the passage of time visibly with an arm acting as the second hand of a clock

4. Record the piece, listen to the results, and discuss them in terms of musical interest and success.

Lesson Activities 11.1 offers many ideas to stimulate individual improvisation. Although individual children would be inventing ideas, many of these could be done simultaneously by the whole group vocally or using body percussion. As children gain skills and confidence, individuals can share their improvisations as solos. Many of these can also be done on instruments.

Each of the European approaches to elementary music teaching includes improvisation as a deep part of developing children's musical vocabulary and imagination. An improvisation characteristic of Orff-Schulwerk might feature children's invention of the B section of an ABA or ternary-form piece, where A is a composed or known section. The children, using soprano xylophones, would be directed to invent a melody on a C pentatonic scale, fitting it into an eight-beat frame. Rondo form (ABACA, ABACADA)

LESSON ACTIVITIES 11.1 *Improvisation Starts*

Rhythm	Improvise over a steady beat using body or mouth sounds. Use an eight-beat cycle and have different children enter on different beats.
	Improvise over a rhythm pattern or ostinato.
	Improvise over a recording, fitting rhythms into the musical ideas.
	Improvise over a metric pattern.
	With older children, have one group in threes and another in fours.
Melody	Improvise on a neutral syllable over a drone or an ostinato.
	Improvise on a familiar melody over the top of a chord sequence.
	Improvise a melody using scat syllables such as do-be-do, do-wop, shu.
	Improvise in a particular style using pitches from a known scale.
	Improvise based on a melodic theme, embellishing it.
	Improvise a short song or instrumental piece or an accompaniment.

would allow multiple sections for solo or group improvisation. Children might also improvise a section of a piece using vocal syllables or creative movements.

In a Kodály setting, children might be asked to generate four-beat rhythm patterns for echo clapping or pitch patterns using sol, mi, and la for echo singing. Once children have built an internal collection of rhythm and pitch patterns, they might be asked to improvise a longer melody, a melody with additional pitches, or, perhaps, the "answer" to a "question."

The Dalcroze tradition also uses improvisation as an important component in its pedagogy. Children may listen to their teacher's improvisation at the piano and then be expected to complete or continue the piece, retaining the same style in the extension. They could perform melodically using the piano or voice, or rhythmically on a hand drum or through movement. Through this process they learn to improvise within an established musical quality.

Children should also be called on to improvise: accompaniments to songs using body rhythms or classroom instruments, movements to music, and music for dramatizations and storytelling. The possibilities for improvisation are endless.

Improvisation can play several valuable roles in the creative process. It can help to develop and expand musical ideas that may be used in compositions; it can help children attain a sense of structure, form, and style; it can be used to introduce and reinforce concepts and technical skills; and, at the highest level, it provides an opportunity for the synthesis of these concepts and skills.

Although not always included as a part of the improvisational process, children can be asked to reflect and comment on the musical effectiveness of the improvisation. Questions could focus on whether it met the requirements of the limits imposed and what was inventive or interesting about the ideas. These reflections should not focus on mistakes as improvisation by its nature requires risk taking. Further ideas for improvising in classroom settings can be found in Aebersold, 1988; Biasini, Thomas, and Pogonowski, 1971; Campbell, 1985; Chatterley, 1978; Choksy, Abramson, Gillespie, and Woods, 1986; Dadson and McGlashan, 1995; Mead, 1994; Steen, 1992.

Composition

A more planned realization of the creative process is the act of composition. It differs from improvisation in that it involves the opportunity for crafting a piece, for reflection and revision. Arranging can also reflect this process. National Standard 4 is composing and arranging within specific guidelines.

Box 11.2 *Motivations for Compositions*

Themes: "Life and Death of a Mosquito," "Clouds," "A Day in a Factory"

Emotions or moods: angry, happy, sad, excited, proud, regal, frustrated, mysterious

Pictures or images: photographs from magazines, paintings, designs, maps, scores

Stories: wordless books, children's own stories, fairy tales

Poetry: sound or a melodic setting of children's own or other's poetry

Sounds: families of sounds, individual sounds, contrasting sounds

Patterns or cycles: "The Seasons," "A Day," "A Storm," "The Butterfly," "The Water Cycle," "The Life Cycle of a Salmon"

Musical elements: melody, rhythm, harmony, tone color, tempo, dynamics

Aesthetic ideas: density, texture, tension and release, repetition and contrast

Musical structures: ostinato, phrase, motive, AB, ABA, rondo, layered, theme and variations, blues, free form

Recorded music: any music has the potential of evoking creative responses; works need to be carefully selected for various age levels based on complexity

The teacher serves as a catalyst by establishing the limits of the composition or giving composition problems to be solved, as in Box 11.2. (For ideas to inspire student compositions, see also Bramhall, 1989; Dennis, 1975; Evans, 1978; Hamann, 1992; Harris and Hawksley, 1989; Haines, 1996; Katz and Thomas, 1992; McNicol, 1992; Paynter, 1972; Paynter and Aston, 1971; Schafer, 1976; Thomas, 1970; Upitis, 1990, 1992; Wiggins, 1990; Winters and Northfield, 1992.)

Even though composing is highly regarded for what it contributes to children's musical and cognitive growth, few teachers choose to spend the time it takes to have children compose. Ideally, each teacher will plan three or four composition units per year lasting two to three weeks.

With very young children, the teacher may participate throughout the compositional process, pulling ideas from the group and helping the students refine their thinking. From late first grade on, children may work in groups of four to five to solve a composition problem with the teacher serving as a resource person (see Lessons 11.1 and 11.2). Once the compositions have been performed and taped, the teacher helps to guide the students in evaluating their work. Building skills of critiquing or reflective evaluation is crucial to the compositional process. Evaluative skills are covered in National Standard 7. Finally, the teacher can help students transfer what they have learned to other pieces of music by bringing in recordings that incorporate ideas or techniques the children have developed. Books by Thomas (1970) and Paynter and Aston (1971) illustrate clearly this process.

Aural Plans

The first stage in the formal compositional process is to help children structure aural plans for their pieces. This simply means that they will work together to refine a piece, trying many different ideas, selecting and rejecting, and finally reaching consensus on the end-product through an aural plan. No graphing or notation will be used to record their work. To a certain extent, aural plans are improvisational because, even though the children may rehearse their piece several times, surprises usually occur.

An example of a whole-group composition for primary children with teacher guidance is given in Lesson 11.1. Extensions of this composition would be to use the tape of the music as a basis for creative movement. Another day, listen to the "Carnival of the Animals" by Saint-Saëns and discuss the ways the composer conveys a sense of the various animals. Identify and discuss similarities, if any, to their compositions. Discuss differences, such as the use of animal sounds. Add creative movements to sections of the Saint-Saëns work.

Because older children can work with less teacher guidance, compositions are often best crafted by groups of children; the ideal group size is four to five. Groups can be created by counting off, formed from existing cooperative groups, or devised by the children themselves. Wiggins (1994) found that working in groups facilitates musical thinking as children

---

LESSON 11.1 *A Group Composition Built on a Trip to the Zoo*

TEACHER ROLE	STUDENT ROLE
Ask children to notice the qualities of movements of various animals during their field trip to the zoo.	Carefully observe movements such as smooth or jerky, fast or slow, even or uneven, continuous or random, upward or downward.
Review with the children what they noticed about the movement qualities of the animals. Help them generate sample rhythms that might illustrate those qualities.	Share what they noticed. Generate various rhythmic responses.
Divide children into groups based on the animal they wish to represent, and provide instruments for them to play.	Develop a short piece that conveys the sense of movement of an animal. Practice and refine it.
Select a child to conduct by walking to a temple block from animal to animal. Tape record the results.	Perform rhythm pattern as long as the conductor is standing in front of the group.
Play tape recording and lead children in a discussion of the results. What animal did each group represent? How could one tell? What could be done differently?	Listen to tape. Respond to questions. Evaluate your performance. Suggest ideas for revision.

Jerry Gay

challenge each other's ideas. They often start with a large picture of what
they want, work on details, and then return to large ideas, completing their
compositions.

The same assignment can be given to each group if the goal is to discover or reinforce a particular concept or theme via composition. It is exciting for children to discover the variety of solutions that can be generated by
a single idea. Different assignments can be given to various groups if the
goal is a multimovement composition with each group contributing a part
(that is, types of clouds), or if the goal has more to do with the process of
composing than with a particular outcome. Lesson 11.2 gives an example of
an aural plan that might be developed by children from the age of eight or
beyond.

This particular strategy could expand into a unit in which children invent and construct their own instruments out of unusual and found materials, then tune them in unique scales in the style of American composer
Harry Partch. Ideas could also be developed on a synthesizer or MIDI (Music Instrument Digital Interface) keyboard where children have a rich opportunity to invent their own sounds.

Notational Systems

Children grow gradually in their ability to utilize aspects of music notation.
Research on children's self-constructed notational systems suggests that
they move from pictorial or iconic means of representing their music to
more discrete or symbolic means of notating rhythm and pitch, means
which may use numbers or letters (Upitis, 1990, 1992). Later they move to
actual or discrete notation. Figures 11.1 and 11.2 show two examples of
children's invented notations.

LESSON 11.2 *Group Composition of Layers of Long and Short Sounds*

TEACHER ROLE	STUDENT ROLE
Assign composition limits: Compose a piece for contrasting patterns of long and short sounds in which the texture never gets thicker than three sounds. Group students and provide instruments. Serve as resource person to groups if necessary.	Select instruments that will play long and short sounds (xylophones, sticks, metallophones, drums, woodblocks, temple blocks, triangles, and so on). Experiment with various patterns. Select the most interesting ones. Structure the piece, deciding when the various patterns will sound and what creates a sense of completeness. Refine it so it is ready to share.
Make either audio or visual recordings of the pieces.	Perform own piece and listen to others.
Guide children in assessment of their own work and the work of others. Expand thinking and vocabulary as the opportunity arises.	Access the work of your own group and individual roles in it. Assess the composition and suggest ideas for refinement. Help assess the compositions of other groups.
Encourage students to expand or refine compositions. Help expand their thinking by bringing in recorded works that use the same principles. (*Daphne of the Dunes* by Harry Partch is a good example.)	Refine own work to make it more satisfying. Listen to other works, including recorded works that illustrate the same principles.

FIGURE 11.1

Invented Notation Using Abstract Symbols

This piece is notated with tear drops to show that it is in a minor key. Other symbols are used as well, but it is not possible to reproduce the piece from the notation itself.

Reproduced with permission from Upitis (1990, p. 66).

FIGURE 11.2

**Invented Notation
Using Letter Names
of Pitches**

*The backwards 2 [upper
left] means "with two
hands and two times."
The knife next to the F
indicates the note F♯
("It is a pirate's knife,
and a pirate's knife is
very sharp").*

Reproduced with permission
from Upitis (1990, p. 63).

Once children have a sense of the compositional process through creating aural plans, the use of notation can be introduced. Children should be free to devise their own systems. Ideally the initial system should be a representation of a piece they have already crafted with an aural plan. For example, second graders are each asked to compose a "one-tone tune," lasting as long as one breath. They experiment with varying the tone color, dynamics, pattern, and vowel and consonant sounds. Once the piece is refined and shared, each child devises a means of notating the ideas in a way another person could understand. They then share their notation with another child and ask that child to interpret it. Dialogues between composer and performer about notation as a means of communication result in interesting insights. A sample notation of a "one-tone tune" is:

Buh ——————— Zzzzzz z *te te te te m___ ah-t*

As children experience standard notation through the use of music texts and training in reading, they will want to incorporate it in notating all or part of their compositions. They might start by notating rhythm patterns using stick notation or pitch patterns on a three-note staff.

G
F
E

Compositions using notation can also tie into skills children are acquiring. For example, once children have learned to play B, A, G on a soprano recorder, they could be asked to compose and notate a four-measure melody in $\frac{4}{4}$ time using B A G, ♩♫♩♩ rhythmic values, and ending on G.

Older children will be stimulated to use notation programs available on computer. (See Chapter 14 for a list of programs suitable for children during the preschool and elementary years.)

Regardless of age, children need to remain free to create aural plans, invent devised systems, or use discrete notation or a combination thereof. Exposure to performing contemporary works that use devised systems will help children to understand that notation is malleable and must convey what the composer intends.

Inventing Songs

Children are natural inventors of song. Any preschool teacher can testify to the fact that young children are constantly singing self-made songs as they play. Campbell's 1998 ethnography, *Songs in Their Heads,* is a profound testament to the richness that song invention and elaboration plays in the lives of both individual children and groups of children. Often, teachers do not leave a place for children to share these songs in their music classes. Wise teachers can continue to encourage the singing of spontaneous, self-made songs by providing both a context and encouragement for children to share their ideas. Children from preschool through grade one could have a song circle where a child in the center sings a spontaneous song about a pet, something he or she has been doing, or perhaps about a story in a picture book. Older children might be encouraged to develop a tape of their invented songs, keeping it as a portfolio. A song recording center could be set up in a corner of the room. Each child could create a tape cover by inserting his or her photograph inside the tape carrier. Children who wish to share their songs with the larger group could also be encouraged to do so.

Sometimes, a teacher will want to establish a more formal structure and procedure for creating songs. Teachers can work with young children to create a song using the following procedures.

1. Select a topic. Create a word bank of descriptive words generated by the children. The children suggest phrases for a poem that the teacher transcribes on the board.

2. When the poem is completed, children chant it together, getting a feel for its rhyme and rhythm. The teacher then could play a tonic chord on an Autoharp or keyboard and have different children sing melodies for the first line of the poem.

3. After trying several ideas, the class votes on their favorite melody, and it is sung by all and tape-recorded.

4. The process continues with the teacher supplying underlying chords, which support the harmonic structure of the melody. (An alternative is to provide a harmonic structure in which children create the melodies.)

5. Children listen to the entire song and suggest changes. The song is sung and tape-recorded in its entirety. The teacher can notate it at a later time and share it with the class in that form.

The song "Freckles" (see Box 11.3) was composed by a group of second graders in collaboration with their teacher, Jackie Wiggins (1990, p. 45). She suggests the following procedures for writing a song with elementary children. This procedure reflects one of the many ways professional songwriters work, beginning with lyrics and moving to an accompaniment and melody. It is also possible to begin with a melody, chord sequence, or rhythm and have the lyrics emerge.

Day 1

1. Invite students to suggest a topic and a title.

2. Ask students for a good first line to introduce the topic. Write it on the board.

3. Develop that into a poem. [Younger children may need more guidance in finding rhyming words and structure.]

4. Guide children into writing a short refrain around the topic, usually four lines with some repetition.

Day 2

1. Write the poem on the board.

2. Play two or three possible accompaniments, contrasting style such as rock and roll, blues, or lullaby and tonality—major or minor.

3. Have students vote on the accompaniment style they think is most appropriate.

Box 11.3 *"Freckles" by Jackie Wiggins's Second-Grade Class*

Wiggins (1990, p. 45).

4. Play the accompaniment and speak the words over the top, making them fit a metric pattern.

5. Have the class improvise a melody over the accompaniment. Experiment with various melodies, shaping them until students come to a consensus about which melodies they want to use. Move back and forth between the chanting and the singing until children are satisfied.

Day 3

1. Distribute a notated copy of the song to the children with their class name at the top.

2. Decide to leave it as is or invite children to arrange the piece, adding introductions, interludes, and codas to be played on various instruments.

3. Rehearse it and either record it or perform it for others.

Older children can use a similar process but can work more independently. They might be given a poem with the rhythm notated and encouraged to experiment with different melodic shapes on a keyboard, staying within a single tonal center. They could experiment using stepwise motion, small leaps, and repeated tones. Later, build in concepts of repetition and contrast and melodic sequence. As children grow in their abilities, use ideas of tone painting and have students compose their own words and melodies. Other devices such as a twelve-bar blues progression could be provided as an underlying framework for melodic composition:

I	I	I	I
IV	IV	I	I
V	IV	I	I/V^7

When children are ready to start notating their own rhythms, the teacher can show them how the lyrics suggest rhythms and how the rhythms suggest a meter, paying special attention to heavy beats and lighter beats. (They might need to practice this first with familiar nursery rhymes, then advance to notating the rhythms of unfamiliar poems or song lyrics.)

Individualized Plan

As children mature, many prefer to work on their own or in small groups. Teachers can structure the classroom with learning stations where children develop skills by working on their own with keyboards, guitars, synthesizers, and recorders, as well as areas dedicated to listening and composition. In each learning center, folders are provided that tell students the requirements for that center.

Folders for a composition center could be color-coded and numbered for type of assignment and level of complexity. Instruments, blank tapes, and tape recorders are made available for the students. File folders have the title on the outside; the left inside pocket contains pictures, scores, maps or other images; and the right pocket contains the chart shown in Lesson 11.3.

Assessment

Any creative individual learns to critique his or her own work using objective as well as intuitive standards. Building skills in self-assessment and evaluating the work of others is crucial to the compositional process. This can be done verbally with the teacher guiding the entire class, individually, or within peer or small group settings. Students can share comments about what they liked about a composition. All students can engage in a guided critique of their own work using the questions below. Assessment sheets could be kept by individual students as a part of a portfolio project along with selected compositions on tape. Teachers or students could also develop rubrics to use in assessing compositions. (See Chapter 13 for suggestions for creating rubrics.)

Regardless of the method used, critiques need to focus on the following questions:

1. How well did the composition meet the requirements of the assignment?

Problem	State the limits of the composition.
	Compose a sixteen-beat piece in duple meter for Autoharp and nonpitched rhythm instruments.
Materials	State the size of the group, the materials and equipment needed.
	1. Four students
	2. One Autoharp and pick
	3. Various rhythm instruments
	4. Tape recorder and blank tape
Procedures	State the steps to be followed in a logical order.
	1. Experiment with various chord progressions until you find one you like.
	2. Write the progression down, indicating each of the sixteen beats and the chord changes. Make sure the final chord is one that gives a sense of resolution.
	3. Select rhythmic percussion instruments that will enhance your piece and add the rhythmic accompaniment.
	4. Use an interesting strum to create a rhythm on the Autoharp.
	5. Practice your piece, refining as necessary.
	6. When you are satisfied, tape record the piece, label the tape with your group name and the folder name, and place the tape in the box on the composition table.
Assessment	List questions the students need to answer as part of the process of reflecting on their composition and the process. Each group member answers the following questions separately and submits them with the tape.
	1. How satisfied are you with your composition and why?
	2. Did you change anything? Is there anything else you would like to change? How might you change it?
	3. What contributions did you make to the process of composing this piece?
Challenge	Ideas for further compositional work, reflection, or transfer into listening.
	Listen to the tape in the composition folder. These ideas represent other people's solutions to this problem. Compare them with your own. Discuss your responses with other members of your group.

2. Did you revise? What did you change? How did you change it?

3. Did you hear music inside your head? When and how did this happen?

4. What worked or was interesting musically about the composition?

5. If you had more time to spend on the composition, is there anything you would change?

6. How successful was the process? Does anything in it need to change?

Should the teacher wish to keep a written record of student progress in composition, Harris and Hawksley (1989) suggest assessing compositions on qualities of musical features, general style and effectiveness, originality, and performance directions. Their assessment form also records student growth in attitudes, commitment, interpretation, confidence, and discretion. Other ideas for student and teacher assessment of compositions and the compositional process can be found in Winner, Davidson, and Scripp (1992), Paynter and Aston (1971), and *Performance Standards for Music* (MENC, 1996).

Any of these ideas could be adapted to fit the teacher's criteria for creativity, commitment, and skill development. Formal evaluation would not need to be used each time a student composed but could be used several times a year to keep track of the quality of a given student's work. Along with tapes of various compositions, the assessments could become a part of documentation included in student portfolios.

The Rewards of Nurturing Creativity in Music

A challenge in teaching music is to implement a curriculum that balances performing, listening, and creating. Teachers are naturally drawn to teach those things with which they are the most familiar. Because so much of their own musical training required the development of sophisticated performance skills, teachers are drawn to emphasize performance with children. Yet, teachers who are willing to develop the processes of listening and creating with children will find the rewards gratifying.

Quality programs in composition and improvisation will foster many important skills. Children will develop a sense of control over the materials of music as they engage in aesthetic decision making. The result is a feeling of pride and of ownership of their ideas. They will develop a musical vocabulary of sounds, patterns, and concepts with which to create musical syntax, assisting them in thinking musically. They will learn to apply critical and creative thinking skills to the process of making musical decisions. These skills will transfer from composing to listening and performing. Children will learn to work cooperatively with others in the composition process. They will learn to assess their own work and the work of others. They will discover that effective composition involves craft, not just inspiration. Children will grow creatively, critically, musically, and aesthetically. As Pablo

Picasso remarked, "Every child is an artist. The problem is how to remain an artist once she grows up."

Scenario

The sixth graders in Mr. Jensen's music class love to compose and have been doing so for two years. They are used to groups and to working through the problem-solving process. Today they are working on the beginning stages of writing a two-part song in their groups. Each group has a synthesizer station at which to work. The details of the assignment are on the board. Mr. Jensen uses his familiar technique of counting students off by fives and having them go to a station with other students who have the same number. The students have twenty minutes to work that day and are expected to come up with lyrics around a theme that they choose in their groups. The next class will be devoted to writing their tunes.

All of the groups go to their station and seem to be working. One boy, Jared, comes up quietly to Mr. Jensen and says that he prefers to work alone and wants to compose a piece all by himself. Mr. Jensen knows that Jared will probably succeed at that task, so he sends him over to work at the piano, once Jared excuses himself from his group. Out of the corner of his eye, Mr. Jensen notices that one group of four girls and one of the more popular boys are not focused on the assignment. The girls seem uncomfortable and shy. He applies his cardinal rule not to interfere with the dynamics of a group and simply stays at the side of the room watching and listening to the exchanges in the various groups. Jared works away happily by himself.

When the twenty minutes are up, Mr. Jensen flicks the lights on and off, which is the signal to the children to stop what they are doing and share their progress with the whole group. Jared quickly volunteers that he was writing a song about the adventures of Harry Potter, one of his favorite storybook characters. Four of the groups share their ideas. When Mr. Jensen turns to the fifth group, the students just stare at him and look embarrassed. They do not have anything to share, and they try to shrug it off by looking cool.

Questions

1. Why do you think students in the fifth group failed to meet the assignment?
2. What could Mr. Jensen have done to avoid such potential problems?
3. Do you think that it was appropriate or inappropriate for Jared to work alone? Why?
4. How appropriate was the compositional assignment for sixth graders?
5. What did you use as the basis for your decision?

REVIEW

1. What is the difference between composing and improvising? What is the difference between convergent and divergent thinking?

2. How is the type of thinking developed during creative activities different from the type of thinking in most of the rest of schooling?

3. What are the benefits to children of improvising? Of composing?

4. What role(s) does the teacher play in the composition process? What role(s) does the student play?

5. List several ways you and your students could keep track of their growth as composers.

6. Which methods include improvisational strategies as a regular part of their instruction? How do strategies vary between those approaches?

7. What motivates young children to invent their own songs? How could you build on that as teachers?

CRITICAL THINKING

1. Is it important to build skills in evaluative or critical thinking as a part of the composition process? Why or why not?

2. Why might teachers be reluctant to include compositional assignments in their classrooms?

3. How could teachers overcome those blocks?

PROJECTS

1. Find some nonconventional sound sources and work with a group of children to help them explore and discover the sound possibilities. Help guide them through a simple improvisation using those sound sources.

2. Find a composition assignment from one of the books listed in the chapter references and implement it with a group of children or with college classmates. Try to include all of the elements of the compositional process listed in this chapter. Discuss your response to this process and the response of the participants.

3. Write three composition assignments for older elementary children using the format explained in the section "Individualized Plan." Share your assignments with a classmate to check for clarity and logic.

4. Develop a two-paragraph rationale to be used with parents for having composition as a significant part of the general music program.

5. Read and review one book on composition or improvisation from the references. Note a minimum of five ideas you would want to use with your students.

6. Find a picture from a magazine that might be a good start for a composition. Write a composition assignment to go with it.

7. Review a text with activities oriented toward Orff Schulwerk, Dalcroze, or Kodály methods. Discover strategies that promote improvisation and those that promote composition.

8. Examine through experimentation any of the computer programs listed in Chapter 14 designed to encourage children to develop song-writing skills. Decide which would be most appropriate for your setting, and develop a plan for its use.

9. Interview three teachers to find out whether or not they have their students improvise and compose. If they do not, find out why. If they do, find out what procedures they use and what benefits they see for their students. Report your findings to your class.

10. Get permission to visit an early childhood center to observe and record instances of spontaneous singing during a forty-minute period. Document who sang, what the nature of the singing was, and what the children were doing as they sang. Summarize your findings and reflect on what this means to you regarding children's inherent musicality as well as what this might mean for your teaching.

REFERENCES

Aebersold, J. (1972–1988). *Play-a-longs*. New Albany, IN: Aebersold.

Barrett, M. (1996). Children's aesthetic decision making: An analysis of children's musical discourse as composers. *International Journal of Music Education, 28*, 37–62.

———. (1998). Researching children's compositional processes and products: Connections to music education? In B. Sundin, G. E. McPherson, and G. Folkestad, ed., *Children composing*, chapter 1. Malmö, Sweden: Lund University, Malmö Academy of Music.

Biasini, A., R. Thomas, and L. Pogonowski (1971). *MMCP interaction*. Bardonia, NY: Media Materials.

Bramhall, D. (1989). *Composing in the classroom*. New York: Boosey & Hawkes.

Campbell, P. S. (1991). *Lessons from the world*. New York: Schirmer Books.

———. (1998). *Songs in their heads*. New York: Oxford University Press.

Campbell, L. (1985). *Sketching at the keyboard*. London, England: Stainer & Bell.

Chatterley, A. (1978). *The music club book of improvisation projects*. London, England: Stainer & Bell.

Choksy, L., R. M. Abramson, A. E. Gillespie, and D. Woods (1986). *Teaching music in the twentieth century.* Englewood Cliffs, N.J.: Prentice-Hall.

Dadson, P., and D. McGlashan (1995). *The from scratch rhythm workbook.* Portsmouth, NH: Heinemann.

Dennis, B. (1975). *Projects in sound.* London, England: Universal Edition.

Evans, D. (1978). *Sharing sounds.* London, England: Longman.

Flohr, J. (1985). Young children's improvisations: Emerging creative thought. *The Creative Child and Adult Quarterly,* 10(2), 79–85.

Hamann, D. L. (ed.) (1992). *Creativity in the music classroom: The best of MEJ.* Reston, VA: Music Educators National Conference.

Harris, R., and E. Hawksley (1989). *Composing in the classroom.* Cambridge, England: Cambridge University.

Haines, N. (1996). *Composing at the electronic keyboard.* Oxford, England: Oxford University Press.

Katz, S. A., and J. A. Thomas (1992). *Teaching creatively by working the word: Language, music, and movement.* Englewood Cliffs, N.J.: Prentice-Hall.

Kratus, J. (1985). The use of melodic and rhythmic motives in the original songs of children aged 5 to 13. *Contributions to Music Education,* 12, 1–8.

———. (1991). Growing with improvisation. *Music Educators Journal,* 78(4), 35–40.

McNicol, R. (1992). *Sound inventions: 32 creative music projects for the junior classroom.* Oxford, England: Oxford University Press.

Mead, V. H. (1994) *Dalcroze eurhythmics in today's classroom.* New York: Schott.

Music Educators Journal. September 1993; January 1995; November 1996; November 1997; November 1999.

MENC (1996). *Performance standards for music.* Reston, VA: Music Educators National Conference.

Paynter, J. (1972). *Hear and now.* London, England: Universal Edition.

Paynter, J., and P. Aston (1971). *Sound and silence.* Cambridge, England: Cambridge University.

Schafer, R. M. (1976). *Creative music education.* New York: Schirmer Books.

Steen, A. (1992). *Exploring Orff: A teacher's guide.* New York: Schott.

Teaching Music, by Music Educators National Conference. December 1994; April, 1995.

Thomas, R. (1970). *Manhattanville Music Curriculum Project (MMCP) synthesis.* Bardonia, NY: Media Materials.

Tillman, J., and K. Swanick (1989). Towards a model of development of children's musical creativity. *Canadian Music Educator,* 30(2), 169–174.

Upitis, R. (1990). *This too is music.* Portsmouth, NH: Heinemann.

———. (1992). *Can I play you my song?* Portsmouth, NH: Heinemann.

Webster, P. (1990). Creativity as creative thinking. *Music Educators Journal,* 76(9), 22–28.

Wiggins, J. (1990). *Composition in the classroom: A tool for teaching.* Reston, VA: Music Educators National Conference.

———. (1994). Children's strategies for solving compositional problems with peers. *Journal of Research in Music Education,* 42 (3), 232–252.

Winner, E., L. Davidson, and L. Scripp (1992). *Arts propel: A handbook for music.* Cambridge, MA: Harvard Project Zero and Educational Testing Service.

Winters, G., and J. Northfield (1992). *Starter composing packet.* Essex, England: Longman Group.

12

Curriculum Design

In early May, Ms. Santiago finished a production of the Broadway musical *Cats* with her elementary children. Her principal and the parents of the children were thrilled to see the children in lights. Ms. Santiago was pleased with their reactions because the entire school year had been spent preparing for this event. Each year she has done a different musical, and her reputation for high-quality productions has spread throughout the region. Some talented children have become stars, although all children are involved in some way, many behind the scenes.

In a neighboring school, Mr. Congdon also just completed his annual spring concert to the acclaim of parents, other teachers, and administrators. During April, the children voted to share with parents two or three things they had done in music class during the year. The choices were wide-ranging. First graders sang and dramatized some songs they had learned during their unit on bears; second graders sang and shared a dance they had invented to go with a folk song; third graders played their soprano recorders accompanied by orchestrations on Orff xylophones and metallophones; fourth graders performed some partner songs that they accompanied on various instruments; fifth graders sang a medley of songs related to American history and small groups performed their own compositions; and sixth graders sang a song in three-part harmony and shared a short film they had made, accompanied by electronic music they had composed. Students from each grade level introduced their selections and explained why they had chosen those pieces and what they had learned from involvement in music.

In a third elementary school in the same district, Ms. Solecki's students presented a theme concert called "Our Musical World." Students from each grade level performed music and dances from cultures they had studied during the year. Children dressed in simple, but representative, costumes from each culture. Some classes created instruments that they incorporated into the performance. Children's artwork, reflecting styles and techniques from the various cultures, decorated the gymnasium. Slides of specific artworks were projected during the performances. During the final number, all of the children joined hands and voices to sing a song about world peace. The entire audience sang with them on the last chorus.

The Nature of Curriculum

These spring concert vignettes illustrate the wide differences among music programs and the freedom individual teachers have in determining the content of their own curriculum. Curriculum can be thought of as the activities that occur in the classroom. It is usually hoped that those activities promote significant musical learning. Although spring concerts rarely represent an entire year's work, they do reflect what teachers value and what they have emphasized out of the myriad of possibilities existing in music education.

These examples clearly indicate that the operational curriculum, or that which is implemented, is dynamic rather than static and is subject to such variables as teacher attitudes and training, parental and administrative expectations, and current trends in education. They also show that the experiential curriculum, or that which the students receive, can differ remarkably, even within the same school district.

The curricular goals for Ms. Santiago appear to revolve around achieving a quality and entertaining performance, with certain students receiving a high level of recognition. Mr. Congdon's curriculum reflects an emphasis on student leadership and clear development of a range of musical performance skills in singing, dancing, and instrument playing, as well as composition. In addition, children are encouraged both to think about what they are learning in music and to make values choices about what they have produced. Ms. Solecki's curriculum appears to be stimulated in part by its connection to the rest of the school program, particularly social studies. It also reflects attention to issues of multiculturalism and societal values. Students learn to express ideas through several art forms and experience an integration of those within and across cultures.

None of the preceding choices is inherently right or wrong. Each curriculum could be justified based on different philosophies and circumstances. However, some reflect more closely than others what the profession of music education has come to value as a comprehensive and balanced approach to the early childhood and elementary curriculums. This is called the ideal curriculum (Abeles, Hoffer, and Klotman, 1993).

Children signing a song in preparation for a concert

Types and Sources of Curriculum

Curriculum plans exist in many forms at many levels and are available from a range of sources (see Table 12.1). Most are highly structured and suggest a logical sequence of concepts, skills, and attitudes to be achieved through the scope of an entire music program. A formal curriculum helps to provide all the teachers in a school or district a frame for their plans and helps to assure that some consistency exists within a program. It helps provide for articulation as students move from one level to another, such as elementary to middle school. Most important, a formal curriculum helps establish clear goals or outcomes and becomes a structure for directing teacher and student activity and for musical learning to be measured.

A quality formal curriculum establishes large goals, competencies, and outcomes, leaving teachers free to develop an instructional curriculum for their own classroom and a personal method for attaining the goals. A quality formal curriculum reflects the nature and content of music; is balanced, comprehensive, and sequential; and reflects what is known through research about musical development in children.

A music curriculum may be established for teachers by a school district or state. Teachers may be held accountable for achieving state standards. Such documents generally are created by committees made up of music teachers and administrators. Usually these curricula are revised every seven to ten years to reflect current trends in education, research in learning, and changing national standards in music education. They may or may not be followed by every teacher in a school district. Successful implementation is usually dependent on training teachers in how to use the curriculum.

TABLE 12.1 *Type and Sources of Curricula*

IDEAL	FORMAL	INSTRUCTIONAL	OPERATIONAL	EXPERIENTIAL
National standards of the Music Educators National Conference; Kodály; Orff; Dalcroze	Individual states, school districts, and schools; consultants and other outside experts	District or school guides; music series texts; technology; individual teachers; outside experts; school curriculum	Individual music; teacher and methodology chosen; students; other teachers; school administrator; music administrator; parents	Students; parents; other teachers; administrators; school boards

Highly formal ⟵————————————————⟶ Less formal

In private schools, teachers often create their own curriculums. These tend to be much more idiosyncratic, reflecting the values and training of the teacher(s) and the values of the school. They are more likely to be followed because they are determined locally. They may or may not be formally assessed.

Many sources are available for individual teachers and committees to consider in determining their own curriculum. These sources range from formal to informal and are highlighted in Table 12.1.

Planning a Curriculum

Teachers need to think through what they want to accomplish each year in their instructional curriculums. If there is an established formal curriculum for music where they are working, they should follow its guidelines in developing their own program. If there is not a curriculum, teachers may wish to use state or national standards in music education as a guide. Virtually every state has adopted state standards that reflect the National Standards (MENC, 1994) in significant ways. Those standards are the ideal. It is up to teachers to make them real. Tables 12.2 and 12.3 show how a general program outcome on the state or national level becomes increasingly specific as it is realized in the classroom.

A curriculum should be balanced, appropriately sequenced, and comprehensive. It should reflect what musicians do with music, should help children discover the nature of music, and should show how music is put together. It should challenge the children to grow artistically, creatively, and aesthetically, and it should give them a wide repertoire of vocal and aural literature that they can enjoy through a lifetime.

One possibility for organizing a year's curriculum would be to establish comprehensive, age-appropriate goals and procedures for attaining:

1. *Skills* of singing, moving, listening, playing, reading, creating, and critical thinking

2. *Concepts,* including elements (melody, harmony, rhythm, tone color, and expression), form (how the elements are put together), style and

TABLE 12.2 *Relationships between Levels of Outcome and Music Elements*

STATE LEVEL	DISTRICT OR SCHOOL LEVEL	SPECIFIC GRADE LEVEL
Students will use the conceptual language of music to organize musical concepts, ideas, and sounds.	Students will develop and apply musical concepts of rhythm, melody, harmony, tone color, expression, form, and style through listening, performing, and creating.	First graders will understand the concept of beat as an organizing device, be able to recognize it in a variety of settings, and use beat as a basis for composition and improvisation.

General ◀——————————————————▶ Specific

TABLE 12.3 *Relationships between Levels of Outcome and Skills Development*

NATIONAL OR STATE LEVEL	DISTRICT LEVEL	SPECIFIC GRADE LEVEL
Students sing expressively, with appropriate dynamics, phrasing, and interpretation.	Students sing a wide range of songs demonstrating vocal control and expressiveness.	Fourth graders will sing the song "Wings of a Dove," using breath support, correct phrasing, and soft dynamics.

General ◀——————————————————▶ Specific

genre (what emerges from structure and culture), and context (the relationship of music to culture, history, and the other arts)

3. *Attitudes* about music and children's preferences for various kinds of music and commitment to involvement in music; increased aesthetic sensitivity

4. *Repertoire* of vocal music including American heritage and folk songs, composed songs, and songs from various parts of the world; a listening repertoire of a wide range of quality works that students can identify, discuss, and evaluate

These four curriculum elements are implemented differently reflecting how they are developed in the learner. Skills must be developed gradually, moving from simple to complex tasks. For example, the skill of singing expressively and confidently across a wide range needs to be developed in small steps (see Chapter 7). Skills must also be practiced regularly to be retained. Reasonable goals can be established for children's vocal growth during a given year, and attainment of each step measured throughout that year. Chapters 7–11 will help in formulating developmentally appropriate skill sequences in each of the major processes of music. The National Standards also establish benchmarks or standards for levels of attainment for fourth grade and eighth grade in skills development and provide a guide for stages of development in reaching those benchmarks from prekindergarten to grade four. [See *Performance Standards for Music: Grades PreK-12* (MENC, 1996).] Table 12.3 shows how skills might move from the general level of national and state standards to the specific behaviors found in a classroom.

Concepts, once learned, do not need to be practiced. A person either does or does not understand a concept. However, once a concept is attained, it does need to be applied to new situations or used in new ways. During a year, a teacher might implement a short unit that introduces the concept of beat, go on to teach several other concepts, then return to beat, applying that concept to new pieces of music at a more sophisticated level. Once the concept of beat is understood, then children have the basis for understanding concepts of rhythmic durations and metric organization. Chapters 5 on rhythm, 6 on pitch, and 8 on listening are sources for specific concepts about elements typically taught at the elementary level.

All music should be placed in a cultural and stylistic context when taught, and children should be helped to perform in the appropriate style as they learn new pieces. (See Chapters 8 and 15 for examples.) Very young children are not ready to understand the history of music, but they can learn about individual composers, and they are very sensitive to style. Older elementary children can begin to gain a conscious understanding of the attributes of music that come together to create specific musical styles, periods, and genres.

Attitudes do not need to be taught but should emerge in response to musical experiences. The kinds of questions the teacher asks the students throughout the year will help them to grow in their valuing of and sensitivity to music. Asking questions such as these will help the children to consciously make musical decisions and will build patterns of aesthetic thinking. "What did you find interesting about that piece of music?" "How shall we shape the song when we sing it this time?" "What do you want to change in your composition now that you've heard it?" "What should we change to make this arrangement more musical?"

Repertoire develops from engaging children in quality music through singing, playing, and listening. Concern here is having children internalize key works to gain a sense of mastery and ownership. Such internalization results from many experiences with a work of music. Excellent literature is available in music series texts with recordings that use authentic instruments from various cultures, played in a style true to that culture. Many separate song collections of contemporary music are available through music stores and online services. Numerous Kodály-inspired books provide collections of American folk music. The Orff-Schulwerk American edition books include many songs, chants, and instrumental works (see Chapter 4 for names of resources). Various published collections of songs and listening experiences from throughout the world are available (see Chapter 15). Other ideas for building a listening repertoire can be found in Chapter 8.

A suggested framework for a year's plan appears in Box 12.1. Teachers need to adapt it to their own settings and to put in specifics for each grade

Box 12.1 _A Planning Map for a Year's Curriculum_

	SEPTEMBER	OCTOBER	NOVEMBER	DECEMBER	JANUARY	FEBRUARY	MARCH	APRIL	MAY	JUNE
Concepts										
Melody										
Harmony or texture										
Rhythm										
Tone color										
Expression										
Form										
Style or genre										
Cultural context										
History										
Relation to other arts and subjects										
Skills										
Singing										
Moving										
Listening										
Playing										
Reading										
Creating										
Thinking										
Attitudes										
Musical judgments and preferences										

Programs   Autumn Parent Teacher
                     Student Association   Holiday   Spring

_____   _____   _____

Repertoire

Vocal works to be mastered
(minimum of fifteen per year)

_____

_____

Recorded works to be internalized
(at least six per year)

_____

_____

level. Units of study can be superimposed on the framework. Many of these things will be accomplished in the same lesson—singing, context, form, playing, moving, attitudes. By nature, these are interwoven. Additional considerations are:

1. The number and type of programs or concerts to be given each year
2. The structure of the school and goals for the integration of the music program with the rest of the curriculum
3. Expectations of administrators and other members of the community
4. Whether there is more than one music teacher involved in implementing the music curriculum in the school

How much can realistically be accomplished will depend on the contact time the teacher has with the children. An ideal would be thirty minutes daily with each class. Much more common is two to three times a week for thirty to forty minutes each. An inadequate program is thirty minutes per week or less.

Other factors that often influence the successful implementation of the curriculum include:

- Teacher attitudes, priorities, and training
- Facilities and equipment
- Socioeconomic status of the community
- Stability or transience of the student population

Of these, the most important factor is the first. It is discouraging for a teacher to spend more time disciplining than teaching, to adjust to a yearly turnover of one-third in student population, or to teach by going from room to room with equipment on a rolling cart. However, if a teacher truly cares about connecting children with music, a great deal can be taught, even under adverse conditions. With dedication and innovation, most challenges can be met.

Implementing a Curriculum

Lesson Planning

Once the yearly curriculum has been established, individual lessons can be planned. Lessons weave together the strands of the yearly plan. Skills, concepts, and attitudes merge as the imaginative teacher decides how to achieve the goals established. Key considerations to effective implementation are (1) each group of children and their unique learning needs, (2) the yearly curriculum, and (3) method (how to reach curriculum goals with a particular group of children). This aspect of the curriculum often provides teachers with the greatest satisfaction, because it requires their creativity and musicianship as well as their insight into what children need.

Effective lessons can be thought of in three parts: (1) objectives, or what this lesson is trying to achieve in terms of student growth in music (these come directly from the curriculum goals and outcomes); (2) strategies, or what procedures and materials will be used to achieve the objectives (this is where personal method and technology enter); and (3) evaluation, or reflecting on whether the objectives were achieved and whether the strategies were effective. (See Pasch, Sparks-Langer, Gardner, Starko, and Moody, 1991, for ideas as to decisions teachers must make.) This should include assessments of the children as well. In addition to these core ideas, teachers need to think of what prerequisite understandings children need to be successful in achieving the goals of a particular lesson and what follow-up activities might be done to extend the ideas from that lesson over time. This model is shown more specifically in Table 12.4. Movement, as shown by the arrows, is from left to right, then back again. Other models of lesson planning that show the flow through a lesson can be found throughout this book.

Regardless of the model selected, it is important that teachers develop clear goals and objectives that are supported by classroom activities. Some teachers get so caught up in selecting appealing materials or in following an approach that they lose sight of the larger reasons for what they are doing. It is as if they have entered the process of planning, as noted in the middle column of Table 12.4. When asked to state their goals, such teachers often reply, "to learn the song" or "to have fun," instead of to build a foundation of musical skills and concepts children can carry through their lives.

Lesson 12.1 takes this planning model and illustrates how it can be used for a music lesson in the first or second grade. Note the relationship

TABLE 12.4 *The Three-Legged Model of Lesson Planning*

National or State Standards _____

OBJECTIVES	STRATEGIES	MONITOR AND EVALUATE
Concepts, skills, and attitudes specific to the curriculum. Most music lessons have multiple objectives, not just one.	All of the materials and activities, in logical order, that will help children to achieve the lesson's objectives. Questions can be listed. Processes from specific approaches to music education as well as technology can be incorporated.	Monitor whether students understand the task to be done and where they are in their understanding or skills at the end of a lesson. Evaluate whether objectives were realistic and whether strategies were effective.

between the columns and the variety and flow of the activities through the lesson. The activities are linked to specific National Standards for children at this age.

Prerequisite understandings for this lesson would be knowledge of the syllables sol, mi, do and their hand signs; familiarity with tracking a melody on a staff; and knowledge of a range of repertoire songs as well as experience in shaping music expressively. Follow-up activities could be to transfer the sol, mi, do awareness to another song; understand the cultural context of "Jubilee" and learn the traditional dance for that song, relating it back to

OBJECTIVES	STRATEGIES	MONITOR AND EVALUATE
1. To develop skills of pitch matching, sight singing, interval awareness, and inner hearing. (National Standard 5)	Warm up with sight singing exercise, drawing patterns of sol, mi, do from the song "Mouse, Mousie." Use hand signs. Work on internal hearing of pattern.	Listen for intonation and accuracy. Correct as necessary. Note whether children are maintaining hand signs while moving from inner singing to singing out loud.
2. To discover sol, mi, do pattern in a song and to add a bourdon accompaniment. (National Standards 4 and 5)	Put fingers on sol, mi, do pattern in "Mouse, Mousie." Sing the song. Sing again while patting an F, C bourdon on laps to the beat. Select children to play the bourdon on xylophones.	Watch to see that everyone is pointing to the pattern in the book, tracing it as they sing. Monitor accuracy of playing. Note on file cards who performed and how well they did.
3. To begin focus on the concept of binary or AB form. (National Standard 6)	Sing the song "Jubilee." Clap hands on the A section, pat laps on the B section. Once children get a sense of where to switch, have them suggest other contrasting movements. Invite children to discuss why the movements changed.	Observe whether children switch movements at the B section. Monitor responses to the question.
4. To review one or two repertoire songs and refine a sense of style in singing them. (National Standards 1 and 7)	Have children vote for the songs they want to refine using a thumbs up or thumbs down procedure. Experiment with various interpretations using suggestions from the class.	Observe where individual children still need help with words or melody. Guide children in reflecting on the success of the various interpretations.

Source: "Mouse, Mousie" and "Jubilee!" reproduced with permission from *World of Music*, Grade 1 (Parsippany, NJ: Silver Burdett & Ginn, 1992).

the AB form; and selecting an interpretation of a repertoire song and internalize it to prepare for an upcoming concert.

Another approach to lesson planning is to establish a problem for students to solve. Lesson components of setting goals or objectives, planning strategies, and assessing will still be present, but the structure will be slightly different. Students will be more involved in constructing their own learning through their problem solving. This approach is particularly useful for composition and listening assignments but can also be used for performance. Lesson 12.2 is an example of a lesson based on problem solving.

LESSON 12.2 *Based on Problem-Solving Model*

National Standards:

4b. Create and arrange short instrumental pieces within specified guidelines

4c. Use a variety of sound sources when composing

Level	Grades two to six
Objective	To allow students to demonstrate their understanding of ternary form through composition.
Materials	An array of classroom instruments and synthesizers
Problem	Work in a small group to compose a piece in ABA form, showing clear contrast of ideas between sections.
Process	Children choose groups and brainstorm initial ideas about how they want to demonstrate their knowledge of a simple structure involving repetition and contrast. They will select the instruments they want to use and experiment with developing the contrasting themes. Through experimentation and dialogue they will refine their themes and rehearse their piece until ready to share.
Assessment	After each piece is performed, invite students to reflect on whether the piece met the requirements of the problem; what in the piece was particularly satisfying; what they might want to change if they had more time; and what decisions they made in the process of refining their pieces. It is also valuable to compare solutions to the problem among the different groups—how were they similar and different?

Other examples of this type of lesson can be found in Chapter 8 on listening and Chapter 11 on creating.

The Quadrant Approach to Lesson Planning

Yet another approach to lesson planning is to apply a model developed by Bernice McCarthy (1987)—called the 4-Mat System®—that incorporates in its structure the principles of research into learning styles. She created a strategy for presenting lessons that teach to all four cognitive styles identified by David Kolb's research: divergers, assimilators, convergers, and accommodators.

McCarthy's elaborate system visualizes a lesson as a circle divided into quadrants—one for each type of learner. She goes on to subdivide each quadrant into right- and left-brain stimulation and other factors. The model becomes complicated. The main point of structuring lessons in quadrants is to remind the teacher constantly that he or she is dealing with many kinds of learners and must teach with different emphases to build on

Jerry Gay

the strengths of each learner and to encourage development in weaker methods of processing.

Quadrant 1. Why? This part of a lesson answers the students' questions (either asked or unasked), "Why are we doing this?" "What is the significance to me, to now, to the future, to other ideas, to meaning?" This quadrant usually takes very little time and can be in the form of words of introduction or relationship, cues for focusing on specific musical events, provocative questions to stimulate thinking, or any other activity that hooks students' interest.

Quadrant 2. What? This part of a lesson answers the students' question (either asked or unasked), "What is it we are supposed to be learning?" The teacher explicitly informs students exactly what the skill or concept to be learned is, checks for understanding, and re-teaches as necessary until all students are clear about what they need to learn.

Quadrant 3. How? This part of a lesson answers the students' questions (either asked or unasked), "How exactly do I do this?" "How do I relate it to other learning?" "How do I do the skill?" This section usually consists of some kind of practice, repetition, or activities to reinforce and internalize the concept or skill.

Quadrant 4. What if? This part of a lesson answers the students' question (either asked or unasked), "If I have learned this concept or skill, what else can I do with it?" This section helps students see the bigger picture, stimulates their creativity, encourages divergent thinking and personal meaning making. Students are often asked to apply their new knowledge or skill to a new situation and to evaluate the success of their learning. Lesson 12.3 illustrates this model in a series of activities designed to explore popular music with older elementary children. (See also Box 12.2.)

Lesson Objective	Develop skills in evaluating popular music using musical criteria.
Grades	Five, six.
National Standards	6a. Identify simple music forms when presented aurally.

6b. Demonstrate perceptual skills by answering questions about, and by describing aural examples of, music of various styles representing diverse cultures.

6c. Use appropriate terminology in explaining music, music notation, music instruments and voices, and music performances.

6d. Identify the sounds of a variety of instruments, including many orchestra and band instruments and instruments from various cultures, as well as children's voices and male and female adult voices.

7a. Devise criteria for evaluating performances and compositions.

7b. Explain, using appropriate music terminology, their personal preferences for specific musical works and styles.

Materials	Recording of "La Bamba" or other popular music, music description forms, T-chart for each class, and recorded popular music brought in by students.
Procedure	**Quadrant 1. Why?**

1. Listen to "La Bamba," then ask group to whisper the meter to the captain; captains stand when they are ready to answer. Award points for correct answer (4).

2. Ask students to discuss with their group as many things as they perceive in the music: what the instruments are (jarana [eight-string chord guitar], requinto [small guitar], harp); how many vocal parts there are (2); who is singing (men); what language (Spanish); how to clap the rhythmic ostinato that runs through the whole song (titi ta titi ta titi ta ta); whether the melody in the vocal part moves mainly by step or leap (step); whether the tempo is fast, medium, or slow; where the music is from.

3. In a round robin answering format, give one point for each new description item the captains can name. Use incorrect answers for teachable moments.

Quadrant 2. What?

4. On a scale of zero to ten, predict whether this music is very popular (ten) or not at all popular

(zero) in the country from which it comes. Groups discuss with captain who gives answer.

5. What makes music popular? Think of some music you know that you and many people like. What are its characteristics? Pass out the form and have groups work on writing responses in each category. Have each group report to the whole class. Award points for thoughtful, meaningful, accurate responses.

6. If you and your friends like a piece of music, do you think everyone in the world likes it the same as you? Why or why not? What do you think causes differences? Should there be just one popular music? Why or why not? What would we gain or what would we lose?

Quadrant 3. How?

7. To practice identifying things we like and why we like them, you are encouraged to bring in one of your favorite songs on compact disc (CD) or tape. By listening to each others' favorites and discussing why music is popular, we will gain a greater understanding of ourselves, our musical preferences, and what makes music interesting. There are some guidelines we will follow, listed on your information form. (Review guidelines.)

8. Listen to several examples brought in by students. When discussing musical preferences in class, comments may be made only about the music. No comments about the person who brought the music or that person's musical taste will be made. Our goal is to understand what makes music popular, not whose or what music is popular.

Quadrant 4. What if?

9. What if we were writing a book on popular music. What would we write about the characteristics of popular music? Make a T-chart to agglomerate ideas. Have each group work together to create a summation that arranges these ideas in a logical, coherent, paragraph form. Award twenty points for each thoughtful, meaningful, and accurate summation that exhibits higher-level thinking skills and includes all the ideas generated by the class.

Method of Evaluation   Teacher continuously observes students' working together, answers to questions, music contributed, and written summations.

Box 12.2 *Guidelines for Exploring Popular Music in the Classroom*

Throughout history, music has always had a lighter side that appealed to many people. Much of it is popular for a short time then discarded when new music catches people's attention. People's taste in music changes over time just as their taste in clothing or hair style changes. Different groups of people have different preferences in their music.

What is popular right now among students at this elementary school? Does everyone like the same kind of music, or are there differences among different people? Why is some music well liked and other music less liked? What characteristics in the music are most appealing?

Students are urged to bring their favorite recorded music to school to share with others in music class. By listening to each others' favorites and discussing why music is popular, students will gain a greater understanding of themselves, their musical preferences, and what makes music interesting. Here are some guidelines to follow:

✦ Write your name and homeroom teacher's name on the compact disc (CD) or cassette tape case so the teacher can return it to you.

✦ Recordings brought to school may not contain (1) profane language, (2) glorification of violence, (3) advocacy of drug use, (4) advocacy of intolerance toward any individual or group of people, or (5) promotion of a specific religious doctrine.

✦ When discussing musical preferences in class, comment only on the music. No comments will be allowed about the person who brought the music or that person's musical taste.

✦ For each music title you want the class to hear, fill out an information form [see form on the reverse side] and tape it to the CD or cassette tape case.

✦ Give the music and attached form(s) to the teacher at least one day before it is shared with the class. Cue your tape to the starting place of the music you want the class to hear.

Name of music _____ by _____

Name of student _____ Homeroom teacher _____

Cooperative group name   _____

Write below at least one specific characteristic in the music that appeals to you and why. General statements, such as "I like it," "It's cool," "It's got a good beat," "The melody goes up and down," do not qualify.

Melody _____

Harmony _____

Rhythm or meter _____

Form _____

Expression _____

Lyrics _____

Other (specify): _____

You will earn five points for every category containing a thoughtful and accurate comment about the music. (Attach another sheet of paper if you need more space.)

Courtesy of Dr. Kirk Kassner.

Unit Planning

Some teachers prefer to divide their year into units around specific ideas rather than using a kind of spiral approach in which concepts of elements are used as a basis for organization and skills are woven in, gradually becoming more and more complex. Early childhood programs frequently use a unit plan because young children do not yet separate life into subject areas to be covered; they learn more holistically. Units can be of different lengths but usually last at least three class periods at a minimum. Some units may extend across several weeks, depending on the reason for the unit. Units can also be interjected into a more traditional spiral curriculum.

Units have the advantage of allowing students to become deeply immersed in a topic over a period of time. They are often rich and stimulating for children because an idea can be approached from so many perspectives. American education has been accused of trying to accomplish so much that only the surface is covered and the understandings that can come from delving into a topic simply do not occur, leaving children mentally impoverished. Sometimes it may be good to give teachers permission "not to do everything" so that they may do a few things very well.

Units can focus on many different topics and they can take many different forms. A range of possible subjects for units—by no means exclusive—follows.

Curriculum Connections (National Standards 8 and 9)

1. A culture or subculture, including music, dance, visual arts, stories, and other aspects of that culture (see Table 15.2)

2. A topic that relates to an area of the classroom curriculum such as the Westward Movement, nature, journeys, the planets, and so on (see Chapter 17)

3. Children's literature (see Table 8.10)

4. A composer or musician (see Table 8.8)

5. Connecting music with an artwork, style, or artist (see Chapter 17)

Topics within Music (National Standards 1 through 7)

1. Instruments of the orchestra

2. Opera

3. Folk dance

4. Patriotic music

5. Holiday music including such holidays as Martin Luther King Day, Chinese New Year, Cinco de Mayo

6. The process of composing (see Chapter 11)

7. A skill such as playing the recorder

8. A particular work of recorded music explored from many perspectives (see Chapter 8)

FIGURE 12.1

*National Standards
Web for Planning
Unit of Study*

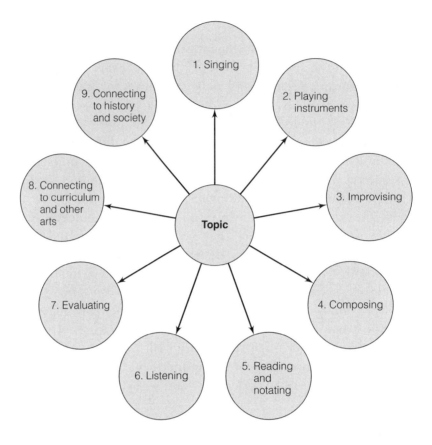

Regardless of the focus, units still need to address key concepts and skills in music to be valid as part of a music education program. See Barrett, McCoy, and Veblen (1997) for excellent suggestions on developing series of lessons that view music from many perspectives. Figure 12.1 suggests another model for planning a unit, using a web based on the National Standards. Teachers will be more likely to achieve important musical learnings if they make sure they approach a topic from as many of the standards as are valid. They should not force an activity if it makes no sense.

Units may be accomplished in collaboration with classroom teachers or other school personnel. Parents can also become involved in sharing expertise. For example, in a unit that focuses on a cultural study, the teacher may have individuals in the school from a particular tradition who can help to teach songs and dances and share in-depth understandings about their culture of origin. Other specialists such as the librarian, art teacher, or physical education teacher may wish to collaborate on a unit so that their combined expertise will benefit the children. Artists-in-residence can also add their expertise. Artists and the funds for residencies are available through local, regional, or state arts commissions, and Parent Teacher Student Associations (PTSAs) are often willing to provide matching grants from the school.

Lesson 12.4 is an example of a unit that could be accomplished with the collaboration of classroom teachers and an art specialist. The process involves "Spinning a Thread through the Arts." Appropriate in grades two

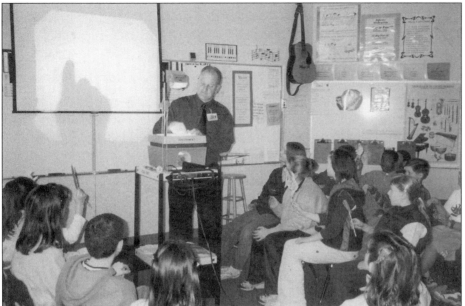

through four, the lesson can stand on its own or connect with a unit on sea
life for greater richness.

Other Sources of Curriculum

Contemporary music series textbooks can be of tremendous help to both
the music specialist and classroom teacher in planning and implementing a
core curriculum in music, as well as in integrating music across the curriculum. The most frequently adopted series are based on diverse musical
materials woven carefully into a scope and sequence of significant musical
skills and understandings and placed within a cultural, historic, and artistic
context. These series also incorporate the National Standards. In addition
to print materials, recordings of high quality accompany the texts. Materials
can be used in a sequential fashion, or teachers can select and implement
lessons or units they find compelling for their children in their unique setting. Textbook companies have gone to great expense to provide a richness
of materials and ideas that would be very difficult and expensive for any
teacher to gather in one place. Much can be learned about teaching and
curriculum from utilizing these resources. Silver Burdett Ginn (2000,
2002) and Macmillan (2000) are the two leading textbook publishers in
general music. They publish new texts approximately every seven to ten
years with revised editions in the interim years. The state or a local district
will take the leadership in the adoption of music series texts and recordings.
Sometimes, individual buildings find ways to purchase these resources.
These companies can be contacted through their Web sites listed in the reference section.

A small collection of lessons based on the National Standards is available from Music Educators National Conference (Stauffer and Davidson,
1996). In addition, pedagogies such as Orff-Schulwerk, Dalcroze, and

Day 1 *Classroom Teacher*	Children's literature ✦ Read the book *The Rainbow Fish* to the children. ✦ Have them discuss the plot and the characters. ✦ Invite children to suggest the moral of the story. ✦ Ask them to think about what kinds of sounds they would use if they were going to compose music to tell this story.
Day 2 *Art Teacher*	Visual art ✦ View photographs of tropical fish. ✦ Discuss the range of sizes, shapes, colors, and designs. ✦ Using colored paper, oil pastels, and glitter glue or foil, have each child create a rainbow fish, applying some of the designs they have seen in real fish. Use the initial shape as a template to create the opposite side. Fasten both sides together leaving some room to stuff the fish. ✦ Add a dowel to turn it into a stick puppet.
Day 3 *Music Teacher*	Music ✦ Review the images in *The Rainbow Fish* with the children. Ask them to recall what sounds they imagined using to tell the story. ✦ Tell them that a French composer named Camille Saint-Saëns wrote a piece called "The Aquarium," in which he tried to suggest the movement of fish. ✦ Listen to the music and describe the sounds. ✦ Listen again and ask the children to follow the shape of the melody and map it in the air with their fish puppets. ✦ Have them draw musical maps of the melody.

Kodály often provide detailed sequences of concepts and skills along with materials and processes for how to achieve those goals. Some even suggest specific lesson plans based on curriculum in addition to process. Books by Choksy, Abramson, Gillespie, and Woods (2000), Choksy (1981, 1988), Mead (1994), Steen (1992), and Frazee (1987) provide useful models for incorporating some of these pedagogies within the framework of a sequential curriculum. Woods and Gordon (1985) have developed a series called *Jump Right In,* which implements the learning principles espoused by Edwin Gordon. Yamaha Corporation's program *Music in Education*™ or MIE (1989) is an extensive curriculum for teaching general music using electronic keyboards and computers that is available in many schools. Key to thoughtful use of these or other pedagogies is to reflect on whether they

Days 4 and 5 *Music Teacher*	Music and nature ◆ View the video of "The Aquarium" by Saint-Saëns on *Tropical Sweets* © by William Patterson (2001). ◆ Discuss how the videographer and editor were able to realize the music through images of tropical fish. ◆ Ask the children to use their music maps to compose their own music on a synthesizer, bells, or metallophones or tell the story of *The Rainbow Fish* musically. ◆ Consider having the children experiment with using a whole tone scale. ◆ Ask the children to refine their pieces, share them with others, and evaluate them.
Days 6 and 7 *Music Teacher*	Creative movement ◆ Discuss the ways that fish move through the water. Discuss what happens when they move individually and in schools. ◆ Ask the children to experiment moving their bodies and using that flow and awareness of space. ◆ Work in groups to choreograph either the music of "The Aquarium" or some of the student compositions. Share those works. Video tape them and evaluate them. (These could become part of children's portfolios.)

constitute a comprehensive and balanced approach that engages students actively in music and musical thinking that stimulates musical growth.

Distilling the Essence of Curriculum

Because the role of the arts in education is constantly being questioned, music educators must be clear about the importance and value of music. One of the best ways to convey that is by having a clearly stated curriculum with a sense of direction in which students are growing through active involvement in listening to music, creating music, and performing music.

Many excellent sources are available to provide that structure. There are numerous ways to achieve those goals. Thoughtful and creative instruction by dedicated teacher-musicians will help to assure that the journey is meaningful and the destination worthwhile.

REVIEW

1. What is a curriculum, and why is it important to have one?

2. Describe the differences between an ideal curriculum, a formal curriculum, an instructional curriculum, an operational curriculum, and an experiential curriculum. Give sources for each type.

3. What constitutes a balanced and effective curriculum in music?

4. What considerations are important when establishing a curriculum? What factors might influence its successful implementation?

5. What are the elements of a three-legged lesson plan, and how do they relate to each other?

6. How do these elements relate to any effective lesson plan format?

7. Where do specific lessons belong in the curriculum and how do they connect back to the curriculum framework?

8. How are unit plans different from a sequential curriculum?

9. What are some models for effective unit planning?

CRITICAL THINKING

1. What role(s) does the individual teacher play in regard to the curriculum? Where does personal method fit in?

2. What are the benefits of using the National Standards as a basis for your curriculum and what might be the limitations?

3. Critique the following idea. "I see the children only once a week, which is totally inadequate, so I choose materials and activities that I think are fun. I want them to have a good time. It's impossible for me to follow a sequential curriculum."

4. What might be the limitations of basing your whole curriculum on a series of units? What might be the benefits?

5. Critique the following statement. "Good lesson planning is a formula and once you learn that formula, you are set for success."

PROJECTS

1. With another person, review and discuss at least two music curriculums, preferably from different levels such as national and local. Notice their similarities and differences. Determine how comprehensive they are in light of the standards set forth in this chapter. Discuss how useful they would be as a frame for your teaching. Would they help in assessing student growth?

2. Review an instructional curriculum, whether it be in a music series text or from a specific pedagogy. Determine what goals and outcomes are being emphasized in skills development, conceptual development, attitudes and values in music, and listening and vocal repertoire. How are these being developed? How are they being assessed in the lessons provided?

3. Observe a model music lesson based on a three-legged model. Follow the lesson and assess how effective it was and how the parts related to each other. Observe another model music lesson without knowing the goals and objectives. See if you can determine what the teacher was trying to accomplish. Discuss that with a partner and with the teacher.

4. Find two different goals or outcomes from a formal music curriculum. Write specific goals for an operational curriculum that would come out of the general goals. Develop a lesson plan using one of the models in this chapter to achieve those goals.

5. Plan and implement lessons based on the three different models provided in this chapter. Compare the level of student engagement and thinking involved in each type of lesson. Discuss the results with others in your class.

6. Select a topic you believe is worthy of a unit focus. Identify the materials you will use to teach that unit and the key ideas that will hold that unit together. Sequence those ideas and the accompanying activities across the days you think it will require to implement the unit.

REFERENCES

Abeles, H. F., C. Hoffer, and R. H. Klotman (1993). *Foundations of music education* (2nd ed.). New York: Schirmer Books.

Barrett, J. R., C. W. Mc Coy, and K. K. Veblen (1997). *Sound ways of knowing: Music in the interdisciplinary curriculum.* New York: Schirmer.

Choksy, L. (1981). *The Kodály context.* Englewood Cliffs, NJ: Prentice-Hall.

———. (1988). *The Kodály method* (2nd ed.). Englewood Cliffs, NJ: Prentice-Hall.

Choksy, L., R. M. Abramson, A. E. Gillespie, and D. Woods (2000). *Teaching music in the twenty-first century.* Upper Saddle River, NJ: Prentice-Hall.

Frazee, J. (1987). *Discovering Orff: A curriculum for music teachers.* New York: Schott.

Mead, V. H. (1994). *Dalcroze eurhythmics in today's classroom.* New York: Schott.

McCarthy, B. (1987). *The 4-Mat System: Teaching to learning styles with right/left mode techniques.* Barrington, IL: EXCEL.

Macmillan (2000). *Share the Music. http://www.mhschool.com/teach/music/sharethemusic/.*

MENC (1994). *National standards for arts education.* Reston, VA: Music Educators National Conference.

———. (1996). *Performance standards for music: Grades preK-12.* Reston, VA: Music Educators National Conference.

Pasch, M., G. Sparks-Langer, T. G. Gardner, A. Starko, and C. D. Moody (1991). *Teaching as decision making: Instructional practices for the successful teacher.* New York: Longman.

Patterson, W. (2001). *Tropical Sweets,* video and teaching materials available online from *http://www.AlphaDVD.com* or *http://www.tropicalsweets.com,* or by calling 1-888-448-4648.

Steen, A. (1992). *Exploring Orff: A teacher's guide.* New York: Schott.

Silver Burdett Ginn (2000) *The music connection. www.sbgmusic.com.*

———. (2002). *Making music.* www.sbgmusic.com.

Stauffer, S. L., and J. Davidson, eds. (1996). *Strategies for teaching K-4 general music.* Reston, VA: Music Educators National Conference.

Woods, D. G., and E. E. Gordon (1985). *Jump right in.* G.I.A. Publications, 7404 S. Mason Ave., Chicago, IL 60638.

Yamaha®, (1989). *Music in Education™: Technology Assisted Music Program.* The Music Suite, Yamaha Corporation of America, P.O. Box 899, Grand Rapids, MI 49512-0899, or 1-800-253-8490, or *http://www.yamaha.com.*

13

Assessment and Evaluation

In Mrs. Bourne's class the children eagerly raise their hands to share their ideas as to specific ways the student conductor might work with them to interpret the music they are learning in elementary chorus. Children in Mr. Yin's class are quietly circling ideas on a rubric they have developed to evaluate their compositions on form. Later, they will share and discuss the results of their thinking with the rest of the class. Mrs. Taylor is writing in her professional journal about what she observed today in working with a child who is having particular problems paying attention. She writes a description of the child's behavior, her responses to that behavior, and then reflects on what she learned and other techniques she might use in the future. The principal, Mr. Abbott, is preparing for his semiannual evaluation of the music specialist, Ms. Shadduck. This evaluation is required by law, and the school district has a standard procedure that he must follow. Before he goes in to watch her teach and to conference with her, he reviews her professional development plan that she submitted before the beginning of the school year so that he can discuss her progress in meeting her goals.

Each of these snapshots is a way of looking at some aspect of assessment or evaluation that occurs daily in the lives of teachers and children. Some of these are informal and happen automatically as a part of thorough lesson planning and implementation. Others are more formal and are a part of teaching in an educational environment that requires assessment and evaluation. All are deliberate, meaning that they have been consciously planned and have not happened by accident.

Evaluation

One of the most important and often challenging tasks educators engage in is evaluation. *Evaluation* is often used as an umbrella term to describe taking stock of a program or the people in it. Other terms such as *assessment*, *measurement*, and *testing* may be used to describe specific tools in the evaluation process. Each of these tools can help to increase the base of objective information to use in making evaluative decisions.

Evaluation involves making a value judgment about something or someone. According to law, principals must formally evaluate teachers each year. Teachers constantly evaluate their students, sometimes formally, sometimes informally. Teachers also evaluate their administrators, often based on how supportive they are, how well they communicate, and how well they lead. Parents evaluate the success of the music program based on the attitudes of their children toward the music classes and on the musical quality of the concerts. Ideally, teachers evaluate their own curriculum on a regular basis and reshape it as necessary. Table 13.1 illustrates a variety of ways, both formal and informal, that evaluation of curriculum and of teachers occurs.

As can be seen from these illustrations, evaluation is often subjective or highly personal, lacking in objective or measurable standards. A complete lack of objective standards could be troublesome. For instance, teachers would find it distressing to have their music curriculum evaluated solely on how well the students performed in a spring concert or to have their abilities evaluated on impressions the principal received about them and their program from faculty room discussions over coffee.

TABLE 13.1 *Evaluation of the Curriculum*

IDEAL	FORMAL	INSTRUCTIONAL	OPERATIONAL	EXPERIENTIAL
National testing of student achievement Accreditation of teachers and programs	Statewide or district-level testing School or program accreditation	District testing Individual teacher testing Tracking of students Ongoing assessment of curriculum	Individual teacher testing Tracking of students Ongoing assessment of goals and procedures Student self-assessment and peer assessment Evaluation of program and teacher by administrators	Student attitudes and growth Teacher reflections and comments Parent observation of student achievement and attitudes

Highly formal ⟵——————————————————⟶ Less formal

Effective evaluation involves collecting a combination of objective and subjective data as well as affective or feeling responses, using many different perspectives or sources of information. Lehman (1992) suggests that evaluation should be a part of every music program and should be built in from the start of the program, not added afterward. It is best done if the goals of the program have been clearly stated from the beginning. Music teachers who anticipate a formal evaluation of their program need to be proactive in communicating their vision and clear goals to their administrator early in the school year. The administrator would then conduct formative evaluation, which is a kind of ongoing series of interactions with the teacher about the program to help it progress. Ultimately, the best evaluation is constructive, helping the learner, administrator, teacher, or program to grow.

Regardless of whether a formal evaluation of a teacher's program is done by an administrator, the teacher needs to engage in regular evaluation of his or her program. That begins by establishing what the teacher hopes to accomplish during the year through the curriculum. It continues by monitoring student progress toward those goals on a regular basis and also by assessing how well the teacher has achieved other goals set for the program such as public performances, acquisition of music and instruments, and projects with other teachers. The teacher will also need to evaluate his or her own progress in achieving goals for professional growth. Ideas in this chapter should be of help.

Testing and Measurement

Testing involves the systematic observation of a person's behavior, and then quantifying that behavior in a numerical scale or by placement in a category. A teacher might test children's knowledge of basic musical terminology through a written test or understanding of a concept through administering a test of aural perception such as a "what do you hear?" test that is often included in music series texts (see Figure 8.3). Attitudes could be formally sampled via a rating scale using a like-to-dislike continuum or an interest inventory. Skills might be tested by rating performance accuracy. To be valid, the test needs to be specific to the behavior it is measuring, and it must be constructed to be consistent across different sets of students. Tests can be constructed by the teacher, or a standardized test such as those available to test musical achievement could be used.

Nationally standardized tests are available in music to measure aural perceptive or aural-visual perceptive abilities such as pitch discrimination, interval discrimination, meter discrimination, and cadence recognition (Colwell, 1969 and 1970; Gordon, 1970). Some teachers utilize these tests to screen children for select groups or to gather an overall profile of where their students are in their music achievement on these tasks. It must be remembered that these tests measure a limited portion of what it means to be musical. They cost both time and money to administer. Teachers using

Students taking standardized test

Jerry Gay

them need to have a clear sense of why it would be important to do so (Boyle and Radocy, 1987).

Measurement also involves assigning a range of numbers to individuals or events but is less specific to a particular behavior than a test. It allows the comparison of individuals or groups, and it often involves statistical treatment of the data collected. Teachers could measure individual student progress across time by using rating scales or rubrics or student self-assessments. Once ratings are collected, teachers could compare the data with each other or compile it for a final grade. Also, teachers might measure all the students in a class and compare the results with those of another class.

Assessment

Assessment is often used synonymously with evaluation. However, it can also mean a more deliberate collection of information for specific purposes. It does not necessarily involve numbers. Through it, students receive and participate in continuous feedback on both process and product. It may be subjective within the framework of standards. For example, children might be asked to assess the quality of their own performance (self-assessment) or that of others (peer assessment). Criteria related to expression, tone, phrasing, and rhythmic and pitch accuracy could be used. Teachers could assess a child's progress in playing the Autoharp or xylophone. Children could assess their own musical growth by writing about their progress in a music journal.

Assessment has become a hot button issue in education. This is partly due to the public demand for accountability and partly due to the standards movement. Parents, business leaders, administrators, and politicians want to know that students are learning what teachers claim they are teaching. Are they meeting the standards? In addition, learning theorists have raised the issue of assessment in their critique of the narrowness of traditional ways of conducting assessment. They have called for alternative assessments to traditional paper-and-pencil tests for measuring student achievement. The cry throughout the education community is for authentic assessments or assessments that reflect tasks that people perform in the real world.

In many ways, music educators have always used authentic assessments, particularly of performance. They measure performance by having children perform, not by having them take paper-and-pencil tests. Performing is a real-world skill in music. At the same time, music educators have often been led to believe that to grade children, they had to administer real tests. They have resorted, therefore, to giving children written tests on such things as the names of the notes and other musical signs and symbols to fit into a system that saw these measures as objective evidence of learning. Happily, many other and more effective alternatives now exist for assessing children as well as having them assess each other and themselves.

Teacher Assessment of Children

Teacher assessment of children should be continuous. Teachers are constantly monitoring many dimensions of the learning process as well as the learners. Much of this is done almost intuitively as they note which children are paying attention and which are not; which children seem to understand the task and which need more instruction as to what they are to do; and how well each child is performing or answering questions. Effective teachers process this information and adjust their teaching to meet the needs of the situation and of individual learners. This is part of the art of teaching.

One of the more provocative questions in assessing music learning is how to get at what is happening inside a student's head. Success in music, a performance art, is most often measured by performance. That is something tangible that can be seen and heard. However, the comprehensive elementary general music program is not based solely on musical performance, but also attempts to help children attain a variety of concepts and skills.

Musical behaviors can be overt (observable to others) or covert (internalized and private). Overt behaviors most commonly developed at the elementary level are singing, moving, playing, reading, identifying, and creating. (Specific ideas for assessing those behaviors have been included in each of those related chapters.) Covert behaviors are such things as listening, conceptualizing, perceiving, discriminating, recognizing, imagining, feeling, and valuing.

Developing techniques for measuring overt behaviors is relatively simple. All teachers have to do is observe what children produce and use musical standards to evaluate their performance. Developing techniques for

Box 13.1 *Measuring Covert Behaviors*

COVERT RESPONSE	OVERT RESPONSES
Listening—a complex aural response to music that depends on attention and perception and is influenced by attitudes and past experience.	Ideas presented in Chapter 9 suggest how to focus perception and how to assess what children perceive. Some options are describing, diagramming, pointing, sequencing, circling, listing, moving, singing, and playing.
Perceiving—the act of noticing something through one or more of the senses. Auditory perception is the most important in music, but reading music and following a conductor demand visual perception and performing music demands muscular and touch perception.	Children could identify, discuss, shape, draw, diagram, notate, point to, circle, order, sing, play, conduct, or move to what they perceive.
Discriminating—the ability to tell the difference between two things, people, or events.	Present children with two musical events and have them tell you verbally or through thumbs up (same) or thumbs down (different) whether those events are the same as or different from each other. It could be two pitches, two rhythm patterns, two phrases, two melodies, or two chord sequences.
Recognizing—the knowledge that something is familiar.	Children could point to or circle or talk about what they recognize. The next level would be to have them identify or name what they recognize, such as a song or a recorded work, a composer, a style, or a country from which a work comes.
Conceptualizing—the formulation of a generalized understanding based on grouping similar but different objects or events into a category based on their commonalities; this depends on skills of discrimination and perception.	Children can group sounds based on commonalities, such as all high sounds or all ringing sounds. They can group patterns such as similar melodic shapes or styles of music such as rock or folk. Once they attained a concept, they could

measuring covert behaviors is more challenging and needs to reflect as much as possible what is happening mentally and emotionally. Box 13.1 suggests ways that teachers can help make internal responses observable.

Questioning is also a powerful way to assess student thinking as well as to challenge them to think in new ways. Pautz (1989) says, "To be an [ef-

Box 13.1 (*Continued*)

COVERT RESPONSE	OVERT RESPONSES
	(1) define it in their own terms, (2) bring in examples that illustrate that concept, (3) perceive it in unfamiliar music, and (4) compose using that concept. *Note:* People can understand a musical concept without being able to demonstrate it through accurate performance. Performing a chromatic scale vocally is a high-level skill, different from understanding what a chromatic scale is.
Imagining—the ability to internally image musical ideas or to image other ideas that are stimulated by music.	Aural imagination can be examined through sight-reading or sight-singing; strategies using internal or external responses within a piece; improvising; and composing. Other images could be shared through describing, writing, drawing, or moving.
Feeling—the emotional or affective response to music. This is influenced not only by the music itself, but also by the experiences the listener may associate with that music. Feelings are not right or wrong, they just are.	Have children discuss or write down their feeling responses to music. They could also dance, move, or draw their responses or write poetry to describe their feelings.
Valuing—the worth people attribute to a piece or style of music or to musical experiences. Values cannot be imposed as in "You will like this music" but must emerge from active involvement with music. Values can be influenced by other factors including families, peers, live concerts, and the media. Values can change.	Observe students' responses to a variety of music, and have them discuss or write down their responses. After they state a value response, such as "I really like that music" or "I hate that music," encourage them to discuss why in terms of the music. Observe what recordings they purchase, what concerts they attend, or what pieces they want to sing or perform over and over. Encourage them to discuss their musical preferences.

fective] teacher is to be a facilitator, a guide, a nurturer of curiosity, a cognitive referee rather than a teller, an expert, a disseminator of knowledge." To be a facilitator and guide, teachers need to know how to ask questions at a variety of levels. Kassner (1998a) lists a series of dos and don'ts that are helpful in developing effective questions. They are shown in Box 13.2.

Box 13.2 *Effective Questioning*

QUESTIONING "DO'S"	QUESTIONING "DON'TS"
Ask stimulating questions	Ask questions that can be answered with a "yes" or "no"
Ask personal and relevant questions	Ask vague questions
Vary the length and difficulty of the questions	Ask multiple questions before students can answer
Keep questions clear	Ask questions that require a long answer
Move around the classroom when asking questions	Call the name of a student unless a particular reason exists for seeking information from that person only
Ask questions that allow students to demonstrate what they know, understand, believe, or value	Ask questions only of students who volunteer to answer
Stretch students' thinking, but ask questions easy enough to answer	Trap, trick, or punish with questions
Use humor whenever appropriate	Use sarcasm
Wait a minimum of three to five seconds before soliciting an answer to give all children time to think	
Use a variety of techniques to engage all students in answering a question—everyone who agrees, show thumbs up; disagree, thumbs down; not sure, thumbs sideways. (Student responses can be varied.)	

Small group decision making

Jerry Gay

Teachers often fall into the trap of only asking questions that measure knowledge-level thinking such as "name this note" or "who wrote that piece?" Asking some questions of this nature is fine, but they do not challenge children to think at higher levels. More sophisticated questioning engages children in such behaviors as summarizing and describing; demonstrating and classifying; analyzing and contrasting; inventing and predicting; and justifying and critiquing. (See Kassner, 1998b.)

Questions and challenges that help children to stretch could be phrased in the following ways:

+ What ideas do you have for interpreting this piece, reflecting the essence of what it is about?

+ What key ideas do you need to think of when composing your next piece?

+ Can you show your learning partner how to finger this pattern on your recorder?

+ Compare these two arrangements of *Beauty and the Beast* and be prepared to explain how they are the same and how they are different.

+ Justify your choice of music to serve as an accompaniment to a video based on the qualities in the music and the qualities in the video.

+ Devise criteria for evaluating your performance in the spring concert.

Effective questioning takes time to develop, and it is helpful for beginning teachers to write the questions they are going to ask into their lesson plans to assure that they are encouraging children to think about music, their own performance, and ideas in challenging ways. (See also Boardman, 1989.)

Rubrics

A popular form of assessment used by many teachers is the rubric. Rubrics provide a set of scoring criteria that can help to determine the value of a student's performance on a task such as singing, playing, reading, improvising, or composing. The rubric can be specific to a limited task or it can be stated in terms of benchmarks that measure student progress toward a standard such as the National Standards. (See *Performance Standards for Music: Grades PreK-12*, published by the Music Educators National Conference in 1996.) They can also be used to evaluate children's thinking such as their ability to analyze or critique their work using musical criteria. A well-designed rubric will not only help to establish performance standards for students, but it can also help provide feedback as to what must be done in the future to improve their performance. Students can even be involved in helping to designate those standards and they can use rubrics in self-assessment. Table 13.2 shows a rubric for assessing the skill of singing based on the National Standards (MENC, 1996).

To be effective, rubrics must clearly state what students should be able to do as a result of instruction. They need to be multilevel and rich in detail, helping to motivate students. They need to relate to real-life situations students are likely to face outside of school. Rubrics can be used to quickly score students, and points could be assigned if necessary for awarding grades. Remember that a single measure of a child on any skill would be unfair or invalid. A single measure only reflects that particular time and can be influenced by many factors. These rubrics could be used throughout a year

TABLE 13.2 *Rubric Scoring the Skill of Singing "America"*

ADVANCED LEVEL	PROFICIENT LEVEL	BASIC LEVEL	NEEDS IMPROVEMENT
Maintains accurate pitch throughout	Pitch is good, with some minor discrepancies	Pitch is generally accurate but there are mistakes	Difficulty in maintaining pitch or showing contour of melody
Rhythm is excellent and beat is steady	Rhythm is generally good and the beat is maintained	Rhythm is generally good but lacking in precision, beat is unsteady	Rhythm is uncertain and beat is unsteady
Tone, resonance, and articulation are excellent	Tone, resonance, and diction are good	Tone and diction are generally good, but there is breathiness and some words are hard to hear	Tone is harsh and there is little evidence of support, words are unclear
Posture and support are excellent, mouth is open	Posture and support are good, mouth is open	Difficulty supporting tone and posture is marginal	Poor posture and breath support, head is often down and mouth closed

Teacher rating singers in small group using vocal rubric

Jerry Gay

CHAPTER 13 / ASSESSMENT AND EVALUATION

to track a student's growth in his or her skills and understandings. Details in the rubric would need to change depending on the nature of the individual tasks or materials to be performed.

Hickey (1999) advocates the use of rubrics in assessing compositions. She has developed a rubric using general criteria for assessing any composition and rubrics using criteria tailored to specific compositional assignments. In a modification of ideas suggested by Hickey, Table 13.3 shows a rubric that could be used to assess a composition in ABA form.

Other more elaborate forms of teacher assessment of students are valuable when teachers need to gather detailed information on an individual student for purposes of getting a better understanding of what is happening with that child. Teachers could write a descriptive narrative of a child's behavior, reflect on that, try other techniques of working with the child, write another narrative, and reflect on the impact those changes made. Often this process helps a teacher to stand back and view other possibilities.

Student Self-Assessment

One of the goals of assessment is to help children develop ownership of their own growth. Instead of always being assessed by the teacher, in a top-down fashion, students are encouraged to make decisions about their own performance. This can happen informally through questioning. It can also happen more formally through student journals, either audio or written, and reflections on their own growth. If teachers use a portfolio system to collect student work from throughout the year, each child needs to reflect

TABLE 13.3 *Assessment Rubric for Composition in ABA Form*

COMPONENTS	Needs work ⟶			Terrific
ABA form	No form is evident	Clear A idea but B section is not developed	In ABA form, sections need a more clear delineation	In clear ABA form with distinct contrasts between sections
Melody	Does not feel complete or coherent	Seems complete but not intriguing	Musically complete and has some interesting qualities	Musically coherent and aesthetically satisfying—it makes sense
Rhythm	Erratic and does not make musical sense	Stable but predictable	Makes musical sense and helps create the form	Clearly helps to delineate the form, coherent and satisfying
Timbral choices	Choice of instruments and combination seems erratic	Tone color choices blend and are used to help create contrast	Tone color choices are interesting and are clearly used to highlight differences	Uses timbral change to create musical interest and define sections in ways that are satisfying and imaginative

on the contents of his or her portfolio. Students can also help to develop rubrics to use in assessing performance or the culmination of a project. Ideas can be stated in simple terms for young children or in more detail for older children. National Standard 7 encourages teachers to help students to develop and apply criteria for evaluating music as well as their own work. Ideas for student self-assessment of their improvisations and compositions can be found in Chapter 11 and for listening in Chapter 8. Teachers will need to assess the quality of thinking students are using in their self-assessments. See ideas in Wells (1998) and in *The Arts Propel Handbook for Music* by Winner, Davidson, and Scripp (1992).

Peer Assessment

Another way to involve students in real-world assessment in music is to have them critique the work of their peers. Teachers are often afraid to open to this possibility because they do not want children to be negative. They can keep this positive by inviting children to answer questions such as, "What did you like about that performance?" Or they can ask the children to make at least one positive comment, then a suggestion for refinement. Children can also use rubrics to assess peer work or they can use other forms such as those suggested in *The Arts Propel Handbook for Music* or in Freed-Garrod (1999). An efficient way to get everyone involved in peer rating is to have them play the role of Olympic judge. Every child holds up from one to ten fingers to rate a performance, with ten being Olympic quality. A discussion of the ratings can follow. Finally, students can conduct peer interviews about involvement in music activities and likes and dislikes in music (Smith, 1995) and reflect on what they have learned from that experience.

Children rating peer performance using the Olympic rating system

Jerry Gay

Teacher Self-Assessment

Many resources are available to teachers to become more self-aware. Teachers could maintain a journal of reflections about their work, highlighting areas they need to grow or ways they have made progress. Teachers who want the input of a colleague in music education to help them grow could invite someone to be their mentor. That person could talk with them on the phone, via email, or over coffee. He or she could come to see a teacher in the classroom or view a videotaping of a class meeting and provide feedback.

Teachers can also challenge themselves to grow in their use of different levels of reflective practice. Griffiths and Tann (1996, pp. 45–47) suggest that teachers frequently stay on the first level of reflection (see Box 13.3) but need to work across all of these levels over time to change. Typically, teachers go through periods of growth and plateau, with the first five years representing rapid growth. The key is to continue growing after that. Reflective practice should help in that process.

Box 13.3 *Levels of Reflection for Teachers*

Rapid reflection	This is immediate and automatic as you teach. It is part of a teacher's thinking as he or she notices how students respond to material. Teachers instinctively answer a question or help a student who asks. It is private. It is called reflection-on-action.
Repair	This is thoughtful reflection-on-action. The teacher may notice a student behavior, think about it briefly, and change his or her actions to fit the student's needs. It may mean ignoring a student's behavior based on previous experience with the student's response to feedback. This is also private.
Review	This takes place after the incident and can happen at any time during a teacher's workday. It may involve a dialogue with a colleague and gathering perspective. It could involve collaborating with others and changing direction. This is reflection-on-action at a particular time.
Research	This may happen over weeks or months as a teacher reflects on an idea or a needed change and gathers information from colleagues, professional journals, or through staff development. This is more systematic reflection-on-action.
Research and retheorizing	This results from advanced academic study and learning current theories. It could occur in the process of obtaining a master's degree or fifth year of study. It happens gradually over a long period of time and much reflection. When teachers receive new information, they change many of the ways they think and, therefore, change the ways they work with children.

Many school districts require teachers who are on continuing contract to construct an annual professional development plan that establishes their goals for their program for the year and professional goals for growth. These are reviewed by the principal and discussed with the teacher at the end of the year, providing a wonderful opportunity for the teacher to assess his or her progress. All states require continuing credit for teachers to maintain their certificates. Some require advanced degrees. These opportunities for further study are meant to enlarge the frameworks of thinking teachers bring to their work and to enhance their practice and feelings of success.

Tracking Student Growth

To both document how each child is growing in music and measure the effectiveness of instruction, it is valuable and important to develop a system for tracking student growth. Often preschool or elementary teachers rely solely on informally gathered impressions of children, and they fail to take the time to establish a system that will provide a more objective basis for evaluation.

Systems for gathering and recording data may vary from simple to elaborate, depending on the teacher's preference, how many students are in each class, student contact time per week, what reporting system(s) are used, and how much technical and physical support the teacher gets for accomplishing this important task. For instance, it would be virtually impossible for a teacher assigned to two schools, seeing 1,200 students one time each week, to do much more than instruct. However, a teacher assigned to one school with 350 students, seeing them two or three times a week, should be able to establish a more formal system.

One method is to identify key behaviors or markers to follow, consistently measure, and record. This might include skills such as singing accurately, expanding vocal range, performing a bourdon on the beat, or playing an ostinato using a crossover pattern. It might also include recording attitudinal responses or age-appropriate understandings. A separate file card for each child in a class could be made with key behaviors listed. File cards could be color-coded for different classes or grade levels. The file cards should be randomly ordered and selected from the top of the pile as those students are asked to demonstrate skills or understandings in the context of a lesson. Notes could be made immediately about level of understanding or skill and the card placed on the bottom of the pile. This system assures that, over time, every child in the class gets to play instruments or lead a game or a song, and in turn be carefully observed by the teacher. Grades on tests could be entered on the card, in a grade book, or on a computer database where all of the data are finally compiled.

Another system might be to keep a file folder for each class. Duplicate charts with student names, listed alphabetically, could be pasted inside on both halves of the folder. On one chart, the teacher could track student behaviors regarding attitude, attendance, and participation. On the other

Box 13.4 *Record Keeping System of Individual Student Progress toward National Standards*

Child	Singing	Playing	Improvising	Composing	Reading and Notating	Listening	Evaluating	Music and Other Arts	History and Society
Beth									
Chet									
Dena									
José									
↓									

Class _____ Grade Level _____

Note: 0 = minimal; + = beginning competence; ++ = proficient; +++ = outstanding.

chart, skill and concept goals for various segments of the year could be listed, and individual student growth toward or attainment of those goals could be marked using a rating or checkoff system. A system based on the National Standards might look like Box 13.4.

Scott (1999) suggests that it may be too much to try to assess the progress of every child on all of the standards each year. She proposes a workable alternative to implement four assessment units during the year that relate to different combinations of the standards. The first and last might focus on assessing singing and performing with a group. The other two could focus composition and evaluation. Each year thereafter, teachers could assess some basic skills and focus on some other standards. Students could be assessed in groups and also engage in self-assessment.

Teachers can record information about children's musical behaviors directly onto a computer database. Advantages of this system include the ability to (1) sort in each category, (2) group information for measurement, and (3) generate detailed personalized reports for parents.

Portfolios

Some models focus less on outcomes and more on the ongoing process of assessment. This process includes what students are able to learn from assessing themselves and their own and others' products. In these models, each child is given a portfolio to record evidence of their work, including drafts. Portfolios must reflect the domain in which the child is working. Because music is a discipline that involves performance, perception and cognition, and creativity, evidence that reflects those dimensions must be included. Table 13.4 indicates the various means of collecting and recording data in music classes.

TABLE 13.4 *Porfolio Contents in Music*

MUSICAL BEHAVIOR	EVIDENCE	CONTEXT
Performance	Videotapes and audio tapes	Individual and group performances
Perception and cognition (including listening)	Tests, journal entries, charts, grids, interviews, discussion, rubrics, poetry, and videos	Individual growth and reflection
Composing and improvising	Drafts of ideas in journals, scores, and recordings of compositions and improvisations	Individual and group efforts

Also key to portfolios is students' reflection on their own artistic growth and the growth of the groups in which they participate. Through reflection they become active in the learning process and learn to apply musical standards to production, be more inventive, and generate ideas for new work. Reflection can be done in journals or on forms developed for those purposes. Projects are long term and portfolio work ongoing. Portfolios can be assessed by teachers, students, and parents. Sources for portfolio assessment ideas in music come from Winner (1991) and Winner, Davidson, and Scripp (1992). Additional ideas for alternative assessment including how to structure a system can be found in Herman, Aschbacher, and Winters (1992).

Reporting to Parents

School systems, whether public or private, usually establish standards or procedures for reporting to parents both about the curriculum and about student progress. A variety of methods are typical to the early childhood and elementary levels for reporting about the curriculum. They include:

1. Autumn open house or curriculum night when teachers describe the program to parents

2. Informal programs at the end of units to which parents, other classes, and administrators are invited

3. Descriptions about the program that go out in brochures or in school or music newsletters

4. Parent Teacher Student Association (PTSA) meetings that feature the music program and can include teachers and children discussing the curriculum and modeling lessons

5. Music in Our Schools Week (MIOSW), an international celebration with children, teachers, and community, with supporting materials available annually from the Music Educators National Conference

6. Parent observation in the classroom during MIOSW or throughout the year

There are also many methods to report to parents about student progress and achievement. With the exception of concerts, these are specific to each child and usually involve a dialogue that helps to educate parents, not only about their child or children but also about the music curriculum. The following ideas reflect practices that exist in many different settings. There may be some places where the only sense parents receive of the music program is through concerts and discussions with their child about how they like music.

Parent/Teacher Conferences. These are usually with the classroom teacher and rarely involve the music teacher. In schools where the arts are central to learning, arts specialists may also hold conferences with parents or the music specialist may be required to be in the building during conferences in case any parents want to come and ask questions.

Concerts for the Community. These are important vehicles for recognizing student achievement in music. They are most useful when they feature all students, although individuals may be recognized. Performances can be turned into "informances" by including program notes or student presentations that help parents understand how these things emerged from the music curriculum and what was learned by the students.

Student Contracts. These are signed by students and parents outlining what the student hopes to achieve in music.

Student Projects. These result in a culminating event and in sharing of student portfolios.

Individual Conferences. These take place any time during the year as requested by the parent or the teacher. This could include an individualized education program (IEP) conference about children with special needs.

Report Cards. These might include any of the following, depending on the school district:

1. Letter grades or marks of satisfactory or unsatisfactory in music, assigned by music teacher or the classroom teacher

2. Comments about each child's performance in music written by the music teacher

3. Checklist in music that shows progress in specific skills areas, attainment of understandings, and attitude toward music assigned by the music teacher

4. No acknowledgment of the music program on report cards

Music teachers need to consider how to make those communications as effective as possible so that parents understand that the purpose of the music program is to educate children, not simply to entertain them. Grades and comments, if required by a system, need to be based on systematically collected and broadly based data about musical growth, not just about attitudes or behavior in the music classroom. Teachers who rely only on a big show to impress parents or who grade strictly on whether a child is cooperative in music limit the purposes of music education.

Distilling the Essence of Assessment and Evaluation

Effective evaluation, whether of individual students, groups of students, teachers, or programs can be accomplished with greater ease if it is based on a clearly articulated curriculum and substantive data. Information that has been gathered regarding student learning and teacher effectiveness should be drawn from a range of sources, both formal and informal, subjective and objective. Parents, administrators, and the broader community will be more likely to support programs that offer both substance and results.

Teachers also need to challenge themselves to reflect not only on the growth of their students and the effectiveness of their program, but also on their own growth as a professional. Teachers can gain tremendous satisfaction from helping children to grow as well as from growing themselves—and turning what could merely be the job of teaching into a profession.

REVIEW

1. What are the differences and similarities between assessment, evaluation, testing, and measurement?

2. What are the reasons for the call for alternatives to traditional forms of assessment?

3. What are four different ways teachers can assess children in music?

4. What does authentic assessment mean, and why is it important?

5. What is the difference between overt and covert behaviors?

6. What are five ways teachers can understand what is going on inside children's heads?

7. What are ways that teachers can grow in their ability to reflect and to self-assess?

CRITICAL THINKING

1. Is it ever valuable to administer a standardized test in a general music classroom? Why or why not?

2. Why might teachers struggle with asking higher-order questions of children?

3. What are the potential challenges to assessing elementary general music students, and how could those challenges be overcome?

4. What kinds of goals might you want to state on a professional development plan and why?

5. Critique the four different types of report cards that you might find in the schools. Which one of the four would be the most ideal and why? What might be the challenges in completing such a report card?

PROJECTS

1. Interview music teachers from three different school systems about how they evaluate their children in music and how they are expected to report to parents. Discuss with them their perceptions of that process.

2. Observe a music teacher in action and note all of the ways children are assessed—from asking ques-

tions to monitoring and adjusting his or her teaching. Interview the teacher afterward about what he or she was thinking while teaching and how he or she changed depending on student behavior. Ask what caused the change. Ask how his or her thinking grows.

3. Keep a journal of your emerging vision of yourself as an elementary music teacher. What are possibilities that you find exciting? What are areas in which you feel you need to grow? What are some goals you might set for your growth?

4. Collaborate with others in your class to collect examples of report cards from elementary schools in your area. Compare them to find what systems are in place for reporting on musical growth.

5. Develop a rubric to assess student performance on performing a song on the soprano recorder. What would you look for at different levels of attainment?

6. Read and report on two articles on assessment in music that can be found in recent issues of the *Music Educators Journal* or *Teaching Music*. Include implications of these ideas for your own teaching in your report.

REFERENCES

Boardman, E., ed. (1989). *Dimensions of musical thinking*. Reston, VA: Music Educators National Conference.

Boyle, J. D., and R. E. Radocy (1987). *Measurement and evaluation of musical experiences*. New York: Schirmer Books.

Colwell, R. (1969). *Music achievement tests 1 and 2*. Chicago: Follett Educational Corporation.

————. (1970). *Music achievement tests 3 and 4*. Chicago: Follett Educational Corporation.

Freed-Garrod, J. (1999). Assessment in the arts: Elementary-aged students as qualitative assessors of their own and peer's musical compositions. *Bulletin of the Council for Research in Music Education*, 139, Winter, 50–63.

Herman, J. L., P. R. Aschbacher, and L. Winters (1992). *A practical guide to alternative assessment*. Alexandria, VA: Association for Supervision and Curriculum Development.

Gordon, E. E. (1970). *Iowa tests of music literacy*. Iowa City: University of Iowa, Bureau of Educational Research and Service.

Griffiths, M., and S. Tann (1996). Cited in K. M. Zeichner and D. P. Liston, eds., *Reflective teaching: An introduction*. Mahwah, NJ: Lawrence Erlbaum Associates Publishers.

Hickey, M. (1999) Assessment rubrics for music composition. *Music Educators Journal*, 85(4), 26–33.

Kassner, K. (1998a). Would better questions enhance music learning? *Music Educators Journal*, 84(4), January, 29–36.

————. (1998b). Improving your IQ—Intelligent questioning. *Music Educators Journal*, 84(5), March, 33–36.

Lehman, P. (1992). Curriculum and program evaluation. In R. Colwell, ed., *Handbook of research on music teaching and learning*, chapter 18. New York: Schirmer.

MENC (1996). *Performance standards for music*. Reston, VA: Music Educators National Conference. Issues of the *Music Educators Journal and Teaching Music* from 1992 on include numerous articles on assessment in music.

Pautz, M. P. (1989). Musical thinking in the general music classroom. In E. Boardman, ed., *Dimensions of musical thinking*. Reston, VA: Music Educators National Conference.

Scott, S. J. (1999). Assessing student learning across the national standards for music education. *General Music Today*, 13(1), 3–7.

Smith, J. (1995). Using portfolio assessment in general music. *General Music Today*, 9 (1), 8–12.

Wells, R. (1998). The student's role in the assessment process. *Teaching Music*, 6 (2), October, 32–33.

Winner, E. (1991). *Arts propel: An introductory handbook*. Boston: Harvard Project Zero and Educational Testing Service.

Winner, E., L. Davidson, and L. Scripp, eds. (1992). *Arts propel: A handbook for music*. Boston: Harvard Project Zero and Educational Testing Service. Find current work of the Arts in Education Program at Harvard online at http://www.gse. harvard. edu/~aie_web or on Harvard Project Zero at http:// www.pz.harvard.edu.

14

Technology for Music Instruction

Some children need extra time to learn music concepts and skills, and others need to be stimulated with more advanced and challenging tasks. Technology can help the teacher customize music learning for differently abled students, as well as provide exciting whole-class lessons. Kevin was a typical student having a hard time remembering the names of music pitches on the treble staff (National Standard 5), until he went through lesson seven of *Music Ace* and played the games at the end. The wacky cartoon character featured in the software humorously engaged Kevin in the learning of pitch names, gave him opportunities to interact with new information each step of the way, and periodically tested his new knowledge with frequent note-naming tasks. When he did some tasks incorrectly, the program patiently offered correction and presented new problems, then rewarded him with praise as if he had completed each task without error. Following the lesson, he chose to play the games over and over, trying to improve his score, and, in the process, became an excellent note reader. And because the computer sounded the correct pitch of each note that was presented on staff, Kevin effortlessly learned to associate note position with its pitch. His newly found self-confidence showed radiantly in his face like a prisoner released from bondage. He could read music now.

Mr. Badillo had seen similar remarkable success in developing listening skills with his second-grade music class using the *Making Music* (Subotnick, 1995) computer program. The children begged him to play *Making Music* every class, and almost all his children could identify musical phrases that were either identical, higher in pitch, lower in pitch, in retrograde, or in inversion (National Standard 6). Throughout the rest of the year, Mr. Badillo noticed the spectacular ripple effect *Making Music* had on the children's ability to remember motives and melodies when listening to and analyzing music. He also noticed that their compositions were using more interesting melodies and compositional devices: The children seemed to have moved beyond the experimental stage of sound exploration to a stage of intentional design (National Standard 4). He was especially pleased to learn from the librarian that the music software he had placed in the library was the most often checked out by students for use in free time and at home. Several children reported receiving music software for their birthdays or downloading software from the Internet. They were continuing to expand their music skills at home.

Although it may seem like magic, the success of technology in music classes is simply the result of good instruction. Technology has improved dramatically. Early technology for music education was similar to early airplanes and early Ford mass-production automobiles—they got you where you wanted to go (usually) but did not do it with much style, grace, or comfort. Early software had a number of problems They were mainly drill-and-skill exercises, had poor sound quality and poor-quality colorless graphics, isolated children, did more testing than give instruction, and gave feedback that was more defeating than stimulating. In sharp contrast, the latest generation of software is intellectually stimulating, involves students in genuine musical tasks, uses intriguing colorful graphics and musical sounds, and guides students to competence through musical rewards, humor, and gentle corrections. Airplanes and automobiles have grown more complicated and expensive, while new software has become easier to use and less expensive as it has improved. Some music teachers may still choose to travel on foot and to teach without technology, but their journeys will be limited and their students will learn less (Kassner, 1999).

Computer music technology is approaching the blissful state of being transparent and fully integrated into general music and performance curriclums in all areas of the National Standards. Buy-and-run software is as easy to use as cassette recordings, compact discs (CDs), or videos. Computer programs are becoming almost as useful as having a human teaching aide in the music classroom. Advances in storage and retrieval of information have made it possible to create complex programs with intriguing visual and aural stimuli. Improvements in programming architecture give responses to student input a more human, less mechanistic, feel. Technology is beginning to achieve a sophistication that Skinner (1968) only dreamed of when he advocated for increased use of teaching machines over three decades ago. Much of the latest music software has been written by savvy music educators, and it wisely leads children from the known to the unknown in small steps. Students are challenged by intriguing questions, led to competence with skillful tutoring, and have their feelings of self-confidence reinforced with encouragement, appropriate praise, and correction. Students have many ways and opportunities to feel successful (Kassner, 2000a).

In addition to tutorial types of programs, open-architecture programs expand students' abilities to think in musical sound and construct musical compositions without the need to know myriad complexities of tonal harmony and standard western notation. Students also do not have to spend years learning instrumental skills. Technology, through sequencing and printing software, eliminates traditional barriers to music composition by giving students tools to transform their ideas into actual sound, listen to their creations, self-critique, and revise as desired (National Standard 4). (For more details for sequencing and music printing programs, see Kassner, 2000b.)

Human teachers are absolutely essential for teaching music, but they are limited in the amount of time and attention they can give to each child. Luckily, the technological revolution brings music teachers the assistance they have long desired. "The latest wave of technology not only gives teachers and students a huge supply of new resources, but it breaks down the traditional boundaries of time and space: *students can learn music 24-hours a day, seven days a week, in their own homes, without a costly investment in software, and without direct involvement of an adult.* As in all other aspects of today's living, music education can take place through the Internet. And as with all new technology, it will take us some time to learn how to use the Internet to best advantage. Typing into a search engine the terms, 'music' or 'music education,' yields more web sites than a person could visit in a lifetime. It can be overwhelming." (See Kassner, 2001, for more details).

Technology has many advantages, but it does add another layer of complexity (and sometimes anxiety) to the teacher's many tasks. Three important issues will be considered here about technology for teaching music to children:

- ✦ What is available?
- ✦ How can technology best be used?
- ✦ What is likely to happen in the future?

Technology Available for Teaching Music

In the broadest sense, technology includes all kinds of communication devices and products, such as clarinets (and other acoustic instruments), radios, televisions, audio recordings (records, tapes, and CDs), audiovideo recordings (slides, filmstrips, motion pictures, videocassette recordings, videodiscs, and CD-ROMs), synthesizers, computers, computer software programs, MIDI (Music Instrument Digital Interface) devices, and interactive programs that link two or more technological devices. Each application of technology has its important uses in music education, but, because other devices are discussed in other books, this discussion will concentrate on the use of synthesizers, computers, software programs, and interactive programs and hardware.

The term *computer* has come to represent an entire system of electronic parts, known as hardware, including a central processing unit (CPU), random-access memory (RAM), read-only memory (ROM), input devices (keyboards, disk drives, MIDI devices, sampling devices, modems, mouses, light pens, touch pads, joysticks, trackballs, scanners, and so on), and output devices (monitors, printers, sound systems, modems, fax machines, MIDI devices, and so on). MIDI is an especially important component of technology for music. It is a set of specifications regarding the connection of and communication among various types of digital equipment capable of generating, sampling, controlling, recording, altering, or reproducing sound. MIDI-compatible instruments are equipped with specific hardware for information receiving, transmitting, or both, and they are connected to each other by five-pin cables. A precise code has been established that specifies information about musical data such as pitch, note on, note off, channel, key velocity, aftertouch, and program change. Through this code, MIDI allows a wide variety of equipment to communicate with and control each other, including computers, synthesizers, sequencers, pitch-to MIDI converters, drum units, and signal processors.

Computers and MIDI devices do what they do because programmers have written lists of instructions, called programs or software, telling the equipment what to do and in what sequence. As with any other teaching resource, teachers need to choose TAIM (Technology-Assisted Instruction in Music) programs based on their overall curriculum goals. The Music Educators National Conference has developed nine National Standards for music learning. Most school districts and states, as well as textbook publishers, have established written curriculum guidelines to define and describe the goals and objectives of music education for children in preschools and in the elementary grades. Music teachers should review these guides and choose only those programs that can teach these skills and concepts more efficiently than human teachers. Once teachers know what they want to teach, they need to become familiar with the particular software programs available for teaching each skill or concept.

Usually, the software chosen will determine the kinds of equipment needed. Sometimes, however, the kind of computer has already been selected by previous teachers or the school district, and teachers will need to confine, at least temporarily, their software choices to the platform(s) available. There are good reasons for using more than one kind of computer, but financial considerations often restrict teachers to one kind. Box 14.1 presents a short sample list of software, not so much for the purpose of recommending specific programs, but to give the reader an idea of the scope of software available. The list by no means represents all the software available, and the particular programs cited are not necessarily the best for all applications. Only one thing is for sure: The list will become out of date quickly. As with anything else connected with technology, software for teaching music has been developed and will continue to develop rapidly.

To keep up with the latest developments teachers should:

1. Attend college classes or workshops specifically designed to acquaint teachers with many programs and equipment

Box 14.1 *Sample Computer Software for Teaching Music Skills and Concepts*

SKILL OR CONCEPT	SOFTWARE
Rhythm reading and performing	*ECS Tap-It, Rhythm Ace, Rhythmaticity*
Identifying written pitches	*Music Ace* I and II, *MiBAC Music Lessons* I and II
Scales and key signatures	*Music Ace* I and II, *Practica Musica*
Ear training	*Thinkin' Things* I and II, *Practica Musica, Play It by Ear*
Composing	*Making Music, Music Ace* I and II (*Doodle Pad*)
Sequencing and printing	*Sibelius, Finale, Cakewalk, MasterTraxPro Nightingale, Songworks, Encore*
Technology-integrated instruction	Yamaha Corporation's Music in Education
Piano pedagogy	*ECS Kids, Musicware Piano, Piano Suite*
Music appreciation and history	*ECS TimeSketch* Series; *Zane Home Library: Great Composers* Series, *History of Music* Series, *Music Appreciation* Series
Harmonization	*Band-in-a-Box, Music Ace* III
Singing and voice training	*Sing!, Bach Chorales* I and II, *Barbershop Quartet*
Prerecorded Music Instrument Digital Interface song accompaniments	Hundreds of songs in many collections— "Songs Made Famous by . . .," "Classical Arias," "Hits from the Movies," and so on
Instrumental performance	*Guitar Magic* II, *Guitar Coach*
Instrumental accompaniments	*Music Minus One series, Band-in-a-Box*

Note: Most of the software are dual-platform; that is, they run on either MacIntosh or Windows-based machines. These software programs were available in early 2001 and could be purchased from many different sources. Prices vary considerably from one source to the next, so teachers need to shop the market for best deals. If change continues as rapidly as in the past, this list will be out of date in a few years. Teachers can find currently available software through local music retail stores, catalogue companies, and Internet companies.

2. Attend software and equipment demonstration sessions at professional in-services and other conferences

3. Attend demonstrations by technology producers and dealers at conferences or in their plants or stores

4. Obtain demonstration disks through the mail or download previews of software through the Internet (most companies offer this free service)

5. Read descriptions of technology in the catalogue of the Association for Technology in Music Instruction

6. Read descriptions in trade catalogues, such as Lentine's Catalogue, Musical Software.com, LMI Music Products, or Cascio Interstate Music Company

7. Read software reviews in the *Music Educators Journal, General Music Today,* and other music education periodicals

8. Discuss technology with colleagues who currently use TAIM

9. Surf the Internet for research and discussion of the latest developments in TAIM

Evaluating Music Software

When evaluating music instruction software, teachers should run the programs to determine if their content and scope fit their needs.

1. What skills or concepts are being taught, and what ages would they be suitable for?

2. What procedures and techniques are being used to convey information? Is there simply text on the screen, or are there interesting graphics and musical illustrations?

3. What is the quality of graphics? Are they interesting, colorful, animated, accurate, easy to read?

4. What is the quality of the sound? And will special equipment (and extra funds) be needed?

5. How easily do children interact with the program?

6. What kinds of feedback are given to children—especially when they make errors?

7. Does the program review appropriate information if children respond incorrectly?

8. Can teachers and children easily control the scope and sequence of the lessons?

9. What kinds of positive reinforcement are used?

10. Can the software be used in a variety of instructional settings? Individual? Small group? Whole class?

11. How expensive is the software relative to the amount of learning material supplied?

12. Are musical examples of high quality, and do they accurately reinforce the concepts being taught?

Teachers should also evaluate the printed documentation that comes with most software in terms of its helpfulness in planning and executing lessons. Because many important things must be taken into consideration before purchasing software, teachers are strongly encouraged to write formal evaluations of programs as they go through the review process. A consistent form or database should be used for these evaluations, so that complete information can be collected and compared easily. It is difficult to

Box 14.2 *Sample Product Evaluation Form for Technology-Assisted Instruction in Music (TAIM)*

Product name: _____

Current version: _____ Copyright date: _____ ISBN/ISSN: _____

Product author: _____ Publisher name: _____

Contact person: _____ Telephone: _____

Publisher address: _____

_____

Cost:
 single copy: $ _____ multiple copies: $ _____ site license: $ _____

Demo disk available / cost: _____

Description of contents: _____

Hardware required (type of computer): _____

Hardware suggested: _____

Additional requirements (memory): _____

Suggested grade or ability level(s): _____

Note: This form was adapted by permission from TAIM.

---

remember all the details about each piece of software without written evaluations. Box 14.2 presents a sample evaluation form.

Using Technology to Teach Music

Even in teaching situations in which all the curriculum and software and hardware decisions have been made, questions still arise about how technology is used in music classrooms. To use technology, most teachers need to make a paradigm shift—a new way of thinking about music learning and music instruction. Traditional music instruction for children usually includes:

1. Whole class grouped together for instruction, with some instruction given in small groups and very little, if any, individual instruction

2. Instruction paced at the whole-group level, with virtually no individual pacing

3. When the teacher needs to give special instruction to a section or individual, other children are not actively engaged in learning, which reduces time on task and creates opportunities for behavior problems

4. Individual children are not often tested and given specific feedback about their progress

5. TAIM is very rarely used, if at all

In contrast, instruction with technology has the following characteristics:

1. Instruction is by individual or small group, with only a small amount of time spent in whole-class instruction

2. Instruction is paced mostly at the individual and small-group level

3. When the teacher gives instruction to some, others are usually productively engaged in learning activities

4. Individual child responses are tested often and given much corrective feedback

The use of technology allows for individual differences in background, motivation, aptitude, and learning rate.

Many strategies have been developed for organizing and integrating technology instruction into typical elementary general music settings, and each is useful for meeting specific needs. Some teachers send individuals or small groups of children to the media center or computer lab to graze randomly in whatever programs interest them at the moment; other teachers have developed more directed and integrated sequences using individualized or Cooperative Learning settings. Tyler (1949) suggests that "continuity, sequence, and integration" (p. 86) are very important considerations when structuring learning experiences. When several different computer programs are available, children may use them haphazardly, not in a logical sequence that builds from one skill or concept to the next (Adams-Nepote, 1991). Some important pedagogical principles must be considered when designing strategies for using technology:

+ Decide who will use the technology

+ Sequence learning in small steps

+ Do not isolate children

+ Consider using a Mastery Learning approach

Decide Who Will Use the Technology

Research shows that high-ability students are least likely to enjoy and learn from drill programs, while low-ability students are the most likely to enjoy and learn from them. Software drill programs can be especially effective when used by learners who have not yet acquired good study habits. Computer-assisted instruction seems to be especially effective at the elementary school level and less so as children grow older. Students with special interests and students who need remedial tutoring seem to get the most out of technology uses.

Technology can also be used for entire classrooms to introduce or reinforce musical skills and concepts. Network systems can be used to serve several computers, and effective instruction can also be provided by having an entire class take turns running a program on a single computer (see Kassner, 2000a). Tutorial programs, videodiscs, and CD-ROMs work well in whole-group situations, much like a film or videotape resource, except

Jerry Gay

children have more control and interact more with computers. For example, the program *Peter and the Wolf* can be projected on a large screen instead of having children crowd around a small computer monitor. Children can control the pace and progression through the program by clicking the mouse when the cursor is over preprogrammed screen areas, called buttons. Children are able to command the software to play the music, play the story, show visual representations of the characters in the story, display information about the instruments, display the music score of the different themes, and experiment with substituting different instrument sounds for the themes.

Teachers can also invent game formats for adapting drill or game programs to whole-class reinforcing activities. The *Music Ace* program (Casey, 1996), for example, instructs children about music note-reading and music theory. This software was designed to be used by one or two students working at a computer, but it can be adapted for use as a game for the entire class.

1. Divide the class into teams of three or four children.

2. Have each team send one member to the computer for a turn to operate the mouse.

3. Award three points to the team whose member follows the teacher's directions through the program.

4. In the game section, give the points earned on the scoreboard.

In this way, all children learn from the technology at the same time as they would from a video or recorded lesson. Once children are familiar with using particular software from the whole-class setting, they can use the software independently in the computer lab, in their classrooms, and at home to expand music learning beyond the music classroom.

Sequence Learning in Small Steps

Learners prefer well-organized, logically sequenced instruction. Bloom (1971) advocates dividing the total curriculum into small, easily learned units that children must master before going on to the next step. Most tutorial and drill programs incorporate these principles within their design, and the music educator also needs to keep these principles in mind when incorporating TAIM into the overall curriculum goals for musical skills and concepts. This can be easily accomplished by matching Student Learning Objectives (SLOs) itemized in curriculum guides with SLOs described in the printed documentation included with most software programs.

Do Not Isolate Children

Try to invent strategies that encourage child-to-child interaction. In the process of working together, children are required to discuss, explain, interpret, demonstrate, relate, generalize, compare, and justify their understandings. Hooper and Hannafin (1988) believe that it is probably unnecessary and unwise to assign a computer to each child individually, because children who explain to others will develop descriptions that also help them in the learning process. In an interview with Brandt (1988), Slavin reports that students working alone on individualized materials often failed, because they no longer received explanations and motivations from qualified teachers. Bloom (1971) strongly advocates Cooperative Learning strategies. Johnson, Johnson, Holubec, and Roy (1984) believe that increased motivation and greater understanding result from group discussion. This is especially important in music performance groups, which are not simply collections of individuals making music together, but highly integrated groups (Kassner, 1992).

Consider Incorporating Mastery Learning

Mastery Learning is an instructional delivery approach, developed by Bloom (1981), in which the curriculum is divided into small parts and children are allowed to take as long as they need to learn each part to a mastery level as measured by frequent tests. Children who do not achieve mastery in the first exposure to new material are retaught with ancillary materials and approaches, and then retested until they achieve mastery. Research on Mastery Learning has demonstrated significantly improved learning of music skills and attitudes toward music learning, increased speed of learning (particularly in low achievers), and quick learning of psychomotor skills (especially with low-aptitude children). From their meta-analysis of research in Mastery Learning, Guskey and Gates (1986) found several prominent effects of Mastery Learning:

1. Better student achievement
2. Higher grades
3. Higher standardized test scores
4. Better ability to learn complex and abstract ideas

5. Better ability to apply ideas to new problems

6. Longer retention of ideas

7. More positive attitudes and greater interest in the subject matter

8. Better motivation for further learning

TAIM combined with Mastery Learning holds children ultimately responsible for the learning and provides opportunities for exchanging machine success with human approval and recognition (children report scores to the teacher, who marks criterion mastery on wall charts).

Funding Technology-Assisted Instruction in Music

Several strategies have been used to obtain the money necessary to buy equipment and programs. In some enlightened school districts with adequate funding, teachers are encouraged to buy and use technology with district funds. These districts seem to be in the minority, however, and, more often than not, teachers need to be proactive to get their technology needs funded. Many districts have grant money available to teachers who write grant proposals. Teachers should investigate the grant programs their district promotes. Parent-Teacher Associations, local businesses, and service organizations often will also entertain grant requests. To get money through the grant process, teachers need to include clear information about (1) what they want to buy, (2) how much the technology will cost, (3) why they want to buy the technology (what can it do), (4) how the technology will fit into the existing curriculum, (5) which children will use the technology, and (6) the technology-use background of the teacher. Some districts or organizations employ people to help write effective grant requests or provide forms for this purpose. For more detailed suggestions on grant writing, see Kassner (1998).

Another means of obtaining money for technology is fund-raising projects. This often is the choice of last resort but may be the only way to get technology in the classroom. Many companies exist to provide goods or services for fund-raising projects, and they advertise widely in educational journals. Teachers need to choose a company with a good reputation, good product that sells itself, and a high return for effort with a minimum of bookkeeping and product management. Be sure to check with the school district to get permission and follow the proper process adopted by the district for fund-raisers (Rohner, 1994).

The Likely Future of Technology for Music Teaching

Technology for teaching music continues to expand and improve rapidly. There has been a revolution in the use of technology in the last two decades, and this will undoubtedly see much more expansion and development in the future. Computers have become faster, able to store and manipulate more information, and more able to interact with humans in a variety of ways. Future programs will most likely continue these trends and also become more interactive; that is, they will become more sophisticated in not only stimulating users with high-quality audiovisuals, but also responding to attempts to acquire the skills of music making. Artificial intelligence, digital sampling, and high definition television, for example, will probably be incorporated in more software as the technology improves and the cost becomes more affordable. Networking throughout the world will become commonplace, as will interactive learning through the Internet. Scanning software

LESSON 14.1 *A Sample Lesson Using Technology in the Music Classroom, Grades Four to Six*

Divide a music class into cooperative learning groups. Distribute the lesson organizers to each group, and have them follow the directions. The teacher's role becomes one of demonstrator, facilitator, and helper.

Cooperative Project: Creating Music Using Technology

Group name _____

Group members _____

_____

All members of the group should be meaningfully involved in all phases of music decision making and performance. Work together productively with respect for each other's feelings and opinions. Using pencil or erasable pen, write all your music decisions on the composition form at the end of this packet. Be careful with the equipment. Do not touch any of the synthesizer buttons except those needed for each step. For example, on steps one and two, you only need to use the on/off switch and the white and black keys.

Step 1: Invent a Melody

Part A. Turn to the A Phrase composition form and have everyone clap the rhythm to a steady beat. Do this several times until everyone can repeat it easily. (Note that both lines begin with the same rhythm, but they end differently.)

Part B. Everyone find the pitch C somewhere on the synthesizer and play the printed rhythm together. (C keys are white keys located to the left of a group of two black keys.)

Part C. Move beyond playing all Cs and explore several melodies by playing different pitch sequences on the printed rhythm. Begin and end your melodies with C. Because many interesting melodies contain at least one repeated note, one step, and one skip, try to invent melodies that have at least one of each.

Part D. After exploring several different pitch sequences, select one melody that is interesting, yet easy enough to be played by someone in your group.

will improve enough in accuracy that teachers can easily turn printed music into MIDI files. Teachers will never reach the end of their learning about new technology, and they need to keep themselves informed. Technology cannot replace the music teacher, because technology is only the method of communication, not the creative, thinking, musical force that can be provided only by humans. Technology can, however, provide new, more powerful means of support for music educators and children. (Lesson 14.1 offers a complete sample lesson using technology in music.)

(Do not choose a familiar melody that someone else has invented.) Write your melody's pitches below the rhythm symbols. Notice that the first and last pitches have already been assigned. Play your written melody several times and, if necessary, rewrite until it sounds good to you. When all members of the group agree on the pitch decisions and you have writing on the form, one group member will play the melody for the teacher, who will verify that you followed directions correctly and can play what you have written.

Step 2: Add Harmony

After you have completed the phrase melody, add at least one type of harmony. Here are three of many types of harmony:

Ostinato: a short, stubborn, repeating musical idea.

Countermelody: a different melody that sounds good with the original melody.

Triad: three pitches (played simultaneously) of the keyboard pattern play-a-key/skip-a-key/play-a-key/skip-a-key/play-a-key. A melodic pitch will harmonize with one of three triads. For example, you could harmonize the pitch C with the triad C-E-G, or A-C-E, or F-A-C.

For convenience, triads are named the same as the lowest (root) note, for example, a C triad contains the pitches C-E-G.

Experiment with different harmonic ideas, and write down and develop your ideas under the melody of step one on the form. You may choose to add more than one type of harmony. When all members of the group agree with the harmony decisions, ask the teacher to listen to your group play. One person plays the melody and another (or others) plays the harmony. Be sure to keep a steady beat so the parts will stay together.

Step 3: Change or Add Rhythm

After you have completed step two, choose to either change the rhythm of the melody or add a new rhythmic accompaniment and write this rhythm under

(Continued)

the melody and harmony. You may choose a rhythmic sequence built into the synthesizer. When all members of the group agree with the rhythm, ask the teacher to listen to you play the composition.

Step 4: Make Expressive Decisions

Explore different expressive possibilities of your phrase: mood, fast or slow, loud or soft, different sounds (timbres) on different parts, expressive words (text), and so forth. When all members of the group agree with the finished phrase, write down your decisions, practice it, then ask the teacher to listen as everyone performs.

Step 5: Turn to the B Phrase

Create another melodic phrase that is different in pitch and rhythm from the first phrase and add harmony, rhythm, and expression to it. Write this second phrase on the composition form with the heading B Phrase.

Put this together with the first melody in the form ABA or AAB or ABB (whichever pleases you most). If you have time, create yet another different melody (called "C") and decide on a new form: ABACA or ABCAB or ABCBC or some other grouping that pleases your group. When all members of the group agree with the form, ask the teacher to listen to everyone perform.

Step 6: Perform for Others

Perform your composition for the class or visitors and try to earn an Olympic rating of a perfect ten points. The class will judge your composition based on how well you followed the directions and the emotional effect your music has on them.

Step 7 (Optional): Sequence or Transcribe Your Composition

Play your composition on a Music Instrument Digital Interface keyboard connected to a computer running a suitable computer program. See the teacher for step-by-step instructions on how to run the particular program in your classroom.

Group name _____

Group members _____

_____

Title of composition _____

A PHRASE

Line 1

Pitches: C   — — —   —   — — — — —   Rest

Harmony 1: _____

Harmony 2: _____

Rhythm: _____

Expression:_____

Words: _____

Line 2

| | | ⊓ | | | | | | | | | Rest

Pitches: — — — — — — — C

Harmony 1: _____

Harmony 2: _____

Rhythm:_____

Expression:_____

Words: _____

B PHRASE

Line 1
Melodic Rhythm

Pitches: _____

Harmony 1: _____

Harmony 2: _____

Accompanying Rhythm: _____

Expression: _____

Words: _____

Line 2
Melodic Rhythm

Pitches: _____

Harmony 1: _____

Harmony 2: _____

Accompanying Rhythm: _____

Expression: _____

Words: _____

Scenario

Ami Sowinski has been a general music teacher at Lake Rosemont Elementary School for several years. Her district just passed a special levy for technology that provides $5 in matching funds for every $1 raised at each school. Ami's principal wants to get as many of these matching funds as possible and is requiring all teachers to develop a grant proposal for purchasing equipment and software. Ami remembers a little about music technology from college in the early 1990s, but she has not used technology in her classes and has never written a grant proposal or organized a fundraiser.

This project is definitely out of Ami's comfort zone. She has not kept current on software developments, does not have the foggiest idea of how technology will fit with her Kodály/Orff-based curriculum, and has no idea what to include in a grant proposal or how to raise the money for matching funds. She has strongly considered quitting the profession and comes to you for help.

Questions

1. What suggestions would you have for fitting specific software into her curriculum?

2. Where would you direct Ami to find information and models for writing a grant proposal?

3. If the technology Ami needed totaled $4,800, she would need to raise $800 at her building level to match the district's $4,000. What suggestions would you give her for raising this money?

REVIEW

1. Write the terms from which the following acronyms are coined: TAIM, CAIM, CPU, RAM, ROM, CD-ROM.

2. What does the acronym MIDI stand for? What is special about a MIDI instrument?

3. List as many sources as you can (at least five) from which to learn more about technology for music teaching.

4. Circle the letters of the statements that are *not* true regarding TAIM: (a) children work at their own pace; (b) computer programs patiently repeat drills as many times as needed; (c) computers will probably replace human teachers within twenty years; (d) open-ended technology (such as CD-ROMs and videodiscs) allow children to explore randomly a vast amount of musical information; (e) a single computer should never be used to instruct an entire class; and (f) because technology is so complicated, teachers should begin using it in their classrooms only after they understand it completely.

CRITICAL THINKING

1. Discuss the rationale for combining Cooperative Learning techniques with TAIM.

2. Discuss the rationale for combining Mastery Learning techniques with TAIM.

3. Discuss the important considerations that a teacher must think about when evaluating software.

PROJECTS

1. Visit a music classroom where technology is being used. Ask the teacher and children what they like about using technology, what they do not like, and how effective they think it is for music instruction.

2. Visit a music store that sells the latest electronic music equipment. List in categories that most interest you the equipment available for music instruction. Establish an organized notebook of descriptive (promotional) materials and price lists.

REFERENCES

Adams-Nepote, S. (1991). Enhancing mastery learning with instructional technologies. *Outcomes*, 10(3), 17–20.

Bloom, B. S. (1971). Mastery learning and its implications for curriculum development. In E. W. Eisner, ed., *Confronting curriculum reform*. New York: Little, Brown, and Company.

Bloom, B. (1981). *All our children learning: A primer for parents, teachers, and other educators*. New York: McGraw-Hill.

Brandt, R. (1988). On research and school organization: A conversation with Bob Slavin. *Educational Leadership*, 46(2), 22–29.

Casey, D. (1996). *Music ace*. Evanston, IL: Harmonic Vision.

Guskey, T. R., and S. L. Gates (1986). Synthesis of research on the effects of mastery learning in elementary and secondary classrooms. *Educational Leadership*, 43(8), 73–80.

Hooper, S., and M. J. Hannafin (1988). *Cooperative learning at the computer: Ability based strategies for implementation*. ERIC Document Reproduction Service No. ED 295-647. New Orleans: Association for Educational Communications and Technology.

Johnson, D. W., R. T. Johnson, E. J. Holubec, and P. Roy (1984). *Circles of learning*. Washington, DC: Association for Supervision and Curriculum Development.

Kassner, K. (1992). Effects of computer-assisted instruction in a mastery learning/cooperative learning setting on the playing abilities and attitudes of beginning band students. Doctoral dissertation, University of Oregon, 1992.

————. (1998). Funding music technology. *Music Educators Journal*, 84(6), 30–35.

————. (1999). Technology for teaching: Making music. *General Music Today*, 13(1), 27–28.

————. (2000a). Technology for teaching: *Music Ace I and II*. *General Music Today*, 13(3), 28–31.

————. (2000b). Technology for teaching: Music sequencing and printing software. *General Music Today*, 13(3).

————. (2001). Technology for teaching: Using the Internet for music instruction. *General Music Today*, 14(2), Winter.

Rohner, J. M. (1994). Fundraising for fun and very large profits. *The Instrumentalist*, 49(5), December, 12–17.

Skinner, B. F. (1968). *The technology of teaching*. New York: Appleton-Century-Crofts.

Subotnick, M. (1995). *Making Music*. Irvington, NY: Voyager. (CD-ROM dual platform [Macintosh and Windows], http://www. voyagerco.com, ISBN 1-55940-662-3, ca. $50).

Tyler, R. W. (1949). *Basic principles of curriculum and instruction*. Chicago: University of Chicago Press.

15

Music, Multiculturalism, and Children

Children come in many sizes, shapes, hues, and views. The music they know well and can perform derives from the rich cultural traditions of their homes and ethnic communities. Mikael hums the songs of his grandmother's Russian childhood. Maisa sings the way she does with her Norwegian relatives, adding harmonies in parallel fourths and fifths to the melodies she hears. Ramon comes to school with the tunes of his uncle's Mexican mariachi band in his ears, with the Spanish words at the tip of his tongue. Luis claps and pats the sophisticated syncopations of Puerto Rican claves and congas easily, never missing a moment in time. Shirelle sways as she sings, because "that's the way it's done" in the gospel choir in which she performs on Sundays. Bisi sings a duple-metered melody while clapping in three, performing with ease the typical cross-rhythm of a Nigerian game song. With encouragement, Charoen performs the graceful ramvong dance of Laos, Li-Chen demonstrates the ribbon dance of China, Joseph steps the circle dance of the Sioux, and Saroda communicates through the gestural language of the Bharata Natyam, a South Indian classical dance. A gathering of children such as Mikael, Maisa, Ramon, Luis, Shirelle, Bisi, Charoen, Li-Chen, Joseph, and Saroda is an occasion for a microcosmic classroom experience, a reflection of the world's multiethnic variety.

The circle of uniform and evenly measured three-by-three-foot carpet squares often found in a music classroom belies the rich cultural diversity of American schools and society. Diversity is apparent in the faces of children in schools, on playgrounds, and in neighborhoods. It is apparent in the various perceptions of the world they share, in their languages, dialects, and variations of English, in the holidays they celebrate, and in the customs they choose to share with their friends and schoolmates. The cultural traditions of so many varieties of children do not melt into some all-American "people-pot." Instead, the classroom is like the image of a quickly changing multiethnic society: a mosaic of many colored tiles that comprise the new America.

Recent trends in immigration and birth rates in the United States have resulted in a population spread of 14 percent African Americans, 12 percent Hispanic or Latin Americans, 5 percent Asian Americans, 1 percent Native Americans, with the remaining two-thirds of European heritage. These are broad demographic categories, such that there is diversity within diversity. A Latin American may be of an elite class of Argentinians who trace their roots to Spain, Italy, or Israel, or a Chicano whose family has known border crossings, migrant work, and barrio neighborhoods of any of dozens of American cities. Nonetheless, by the mid-twenty-first century, the average American will trace his or her roots to multiple regions and cultures in Africa, Asia, the Hispanic world, the Pacific Islands, and the Middle East—almost anywhere but Caucasian Europe. Americans are living in a fast-changing society, with the statistical charts on race and ethnicity turning upside down and inside out.

Definitions

If schools are the vehicles through which children are presented with the knowledge and values of a given nation, then the music program should offer to children (1) opportunities to experience a broad sampling of the world's musical traditions, (2) more thorough-going journeys into selected musical cultures, and (3) multiple approaches to musical skills and understanding that appeal to their varied modes of learning. While this stance seems logical enough, sometimes the prospects of teaching music from a multicultural perspective may seem overwhelming. One reason for this is the all-encompassing definition of multicultural education, which includes the study not only of groups distinguished by race or ethnic origin, but technically also by the music of people of different ages, social classes, genders, religions, lifestyles, and exceptionalities (Banks and Banks, 1995). Within this framework, the tasks of multicultural music education are enormously broad, and perhaps too comprehensive to be applied to the curricular changes that are occurring.

"Multiethnic" is a label applied to curricular developments that focus exclusively on the study of groups distinguished by ethnic origin. Music programs that focus in-depth on musical styles of a group of people united by national or ethnic origin, such as the music of the Chinese, Filipinos, the Yoruba of Nigeria, and Brazilians, are referred to by the rubric "multiethnic music education." While *multicultural* is the term featured prominently in

Jerry Gay

curriculum and instruction materials in North America, *multiethnic* refers more directly to ethnicity rather than age, social class, gender, or other issues. (See Chapter 16 for a discussion of music for children of special needs, of which each handicapping condition may constitute a culture all its own.)

The term *multiethnic* suggests an intensive study of music from more than one ethnic group. Fourth-grade children who are learning to sing Japanese and Chinese songs, to listen analytically to the music of the Japanese koto and the Chinese zheng (zithers), and to play Japanese shakuhachi and Chinese di (flutes) melodies on recorders are reaping the benefits of a multiethnic curriculum. First-grade children who are learning the melodies, movements, and functions of singing games from Zimbabwe and Venezuela are also being served a multiethnic-flavored music curriculum. Even an intensive study of one new and less familiar musical culture begins to approach the mission of multiethnic music education, because children are already making subconscious comparisons of their mother-tongue music acquired in their homes with the music of the teacher's choice. The intent of multiethnic music education is, in addition to the provision of a variety of musical experiences (singing, listening, moving, playing instruments, and creating), to offer children an understanding of how the music reflects people's lifestyles and ways of thinking across cultural boundaries.

Yet it must also be said that in reference to teaching music—or any other subject—to children, multiethnic refers to the varied instructional approaches that need to be provided to children from different cultural perspectives such that they can develop skills and understanding that are as complete as those developed by children from the mainstream majority. In the past, children who have fared best from instruction have tended to be those whose cultural understanding and learning styles have matched the teacher's own experience and training. Teacher education programs, curricular materials, and even instructional delivery systems have been oriented toward the white middle-class teacher and her children. In a multiethnic approach to music education, children's own ethnic-cultural heritage(s) must be kept in mind not so much in the selection of repertoire (although that can be a way to develop meaningful learning) but in the design of processes by which children's individual interests, learning modes, and special linguistic, social, and religious needs can be considered with the utmost sensitivity. All music, from Mozart canons to folk tunes from Mozambique, must be taught with the knowledge of who the children are and how their cultural heritage may season their learning.

Another curricular concept in music education programs for children is "world music education." As distinguished from multiethnic music education, world music education features the study of musical components as they are treated in various musical styles across the world. For example, preschool children may learn to clap or step the steady pulse to the music of an African American blues song, a Chinese luogu (percussion ensemble), an Indonesian gamelan piece, and a Puerto Rican salsa number. Third-grade children may learn about timbre by listening to fiddles and musical bows from Ireland, Pakistan, Malawi, Cambodia, and Mexico. Sixth-grade children may come to understand syncopation as a prominent characteristic in the music of Ghana, Cuba, China, and African American gospel music. Like the term *multiethnic*, world music education suggests another type of comparative approach to music. Unlike multiethnic music education, world music education is concerned with cross-cultural comparisons that span a great many musical styles, instead of concentrating more narrowly and more deeply on a smaller selection of ethnic groups. World music education may also allow less contextualization of musical experiences, as the emphasis is placed on more extensive (instead of intensive) musical (instead of cultural) experiences.

Which is better: to teach a small selection of musical traditions thoroughly, as in the case of multiethnic music education, or to teach music conceptually through cross-cultural examples, as in the case of world music education? There may be room for both within the design of musical experiences for children. In the scope of a year's plan, children can learn aspects of melody, rhythm, timbre, texture, and form by engaging in active listening to many samples of the world's musical styles and genres. Just as the examples of a musical concept can be historically broad—from the music of Monteverdi through Messiaen—they can also be culturally broad, chosen from Bulgaria, Bali, and Brazil, for example. Within the same year, a series of lessons on one musical tradition or genre (for example, dance music of the Pueblo Indians of New Mexico or the Macedonians of southeastern Europe) can lead children into a knowledge of people and their musical ways of thinking. Side by side in a single school year, children can experience the best of both musical and multiethnic understanding. There is no limit for ways in which many musical styles can be brought to children to develop their understanding of music.

One thing is certain, as products of a multiethnic and multiracial society, children must be led to listen and to respond to the aesthetic components and cultural meanings of more than a single musical tradition. They are living in a less-homogenized world than any earlier generation, one that demands their understanding of many people. Ideally, through their musical experiences sensing its ebbs and flows, learning its logical structures, and feeling its power, children may come to understand not only the music, but also the music makers. They may learn to take note of not only the differences among people and their musical expressions, but also the similarities that transcend all people.

Uncertainties in Teaching New Musical Styles

There are misgivings, uncertainties, and well-founded questions to consider in offering a broader palette of musical colors and styles. Consider the often-quoted statements both for and against offering children the music of many cultures.

"My kids are not ethnic; they are white." In fact, everyone is ethnic, including European Americans. All music is ethnic, too, including the masterworks of Mozart and Mahler, of Charles Ives and Paul Simon. Each song and instrumental piece manifests the characteristic musical components of the culture from which it derives. Even those rare teachers who still teach homogeneous groups of children whose ancestors arrived from Europe generations ago know that those children will venture beyond their neighborhoods. They will have the opportunity to associate with people in diverse ethnic communities in an increasingly pluralistic American society. It may be that by knowing about other ethnic groups' values, their traditions, and their artistic and musical expressions, children will also come to know the world's people better.

"My schedule is too packed to include multiethnic music." According to the manner in which multiethnic and world music education are defined, it is unnecessary to offer additional classes to explore a variety of music traditions. Teachers can inject the new or less-familiar music into their lessons to illustrate the cross-cultural similarities and yet vast diversity of musical thought and expression.

Musical experiences intended to bring about multiethnic understanding may also require new ways of teaching across the curriculum. Teachers of music, art, and classroom subjects can team together to develop monthly and quarterly units on a given country, cultural region, or ethnic group. Colloquial expressions can be spoken, customs can be practiced, stories can be told, read, and reenacted, visual arts and crafts can be viewed and copied, songs can be sung, and traditional instrumental pieces and dances can be performed. In a collaborative and thorough way, music teachers can join together with others to enlighten children about the worlds of people and their cultural expressions.

"I don't know the languages of the foreign songs." Although foreign language songs challenge teachers and children, the cultural experience can be very powerful. There is an added dimension when the original language of a song intermingles with the song's rhythm and melody, rather than singing an English translation. Music teachers whose ears are fine-tuned to discriminate fractional sound variations can often easily learn the phonemes of new languages as well. A foreign-language song is best learned by listening—at home, in the car, and at school—with the ears perceiving the music and language as one. Once it is aurally channeled and internalized, there is a growing confidence in transmitting the song to children. The song becomes a part of the listener's and singer's repertoire.

Children can also be initiated to a musical culture through music listening experiences, movement, and opportunities to play instruments of the culture and by music educators with a commitment to multiethnic or world music education. Listening can be active, engaging children to gesture the rise and fall of a Japanese shakuhachi (flute) melody or to snap, clap, pat, and stamp the ostinato of a Cuban bomba drum. Basic circle and line dances of the Middle East, Eastern Europe, and Native American cultures can be performed by young children as early as first or second grade. Children can play West African polyrhythms on various nonpitched percussion instruments and selected melodies from many cultures on recorders. They can play the melodies and polyphonic textures of selected Southeast Asian and sub-Saharan African music on xylophones, if in a somewhat modified manner. Occasionally, listening, movement, and instrumental performance can be combined with songs, a four-dimensional experience for children.

The Musically Competent Teacher

Increasingly, courses within collegiate music and teacher education programs expose students to musical styles beyond Western European art music. Prospective teachers can gain initial acquaintance with musical cultures through one or more broad-based world music survey courses, and they can follow that with specialized seminars for the in-depth study of the music of African, Asian, European, Latin American, Native American, Australian, and Pacific Island cultures. Although these may be offered only as elective or optional courses in collegiate music programs, they are nonetheless invaluable for teaching music to children from multiethnic and global perspectives.

In addition to full-fledged courses, workshops are also occasions for learning the music of other cultures. These workshops are commonly offered through summer school programs by musicians from various traditions, by ethnomusicologists with considerable study of one or more musical cultures, and by music educators with a commitment to multiethnic education. For those who cannot squeeze additional courses into their undergraduate program, these workshops can be taken during the summer interim period soon after teaching certification is completed. In addition to courses and workshops, musicians in the community may offer lessons on traditional instruments and singing styles for a moderate fee.

Many teachers have chosen to learn to play or sing music other than Western European art music. Those who are competent in a musical tradition or style are the ones who are best able to teach it accurately and easily. The musical competence they achieve through specialized training includes aural competence, or the ability to listen to and understand the structural components of a musical style. Ideally, musically competent teachers also attain a measure of performance proficiency, vocally or on an instrument. Children are fascinated with the music that is performed live for them and are eager for opportunities to play instruments or sing in the style of a confident performer. When fundamental instrumental techniques and pieces can be demonstrated by the performing teacher, and when songs can be sung using their original language and appropriate vocal timbre and inflections, the music becomes more appealing to children. The performing teacher also gains credibility in the children's eyes.

Gaining proficiency within a musical tradition requires time and effort. Just as aural and performance competence in Western European art music requires many years of listening, reading, and practice, it is also the case in knowing well the music of the Zulu of South Africa, the Han Chinese, the Sephardic Jews of Spain, or African Americans. Those who take the time to sing or study an instrument of a favorite other culture, and then build a school or personal library of recordings, writings, and videotapes on the music and culture, are well on their way to gaining proficiency within

Andrew playing West African shekere

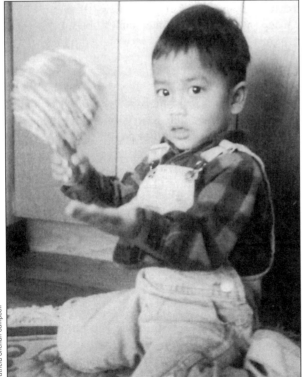

that tradition. By becoming musically competent in a style, they have the skills, knowledge, enthusiasm, and confidence for presenting it to children.

Teachers of music usually become competent in Western European art music through their training, but they can also progress to the study of another musical culture. Those with aural and performance competence in more than one music are said to be bimusical; it is this quality that approaches the goals of bicultural and eventually multiethnic (multicultural) education. A modified bimusicality is a goal to be achieved in children as well, so that they can listen to and perform the music of more than one culture. Becoming musically competent in more than one tradition may develop an appreciation for the complexities of other music, as well as the recognition of their validity and logic. Performance proficiency is not necessary for selecting examples of a pentatonic piece, a triple-metered song, or a polyrhythmic texture from a variety of musical traditions (a curricular tactic featured in world music education). Still, any attempt to know musical traditions more than superficially will excite both teachers and their children.

New Repertoire for Familiar Pedagogies

Teaching music from the perspectives of multiethnic or world music education does not mean negating or discarding the old or the well-established pedagogical approaches. Techniques such as speech rhythms, rhythmic syllables, movable do, stem notation, melodic mapping, instrumental performance, listening grids and call charts, part-singing, eurhythmic movement, and improvisation may be readily used in teaching nearly all music traditions. In fact, three of the classic methods associated with teaching music to children may find new freedom in the repertoire that is introduced.

Orff-Schulwerk provides children with experiences that are as social as they are musical. Many of the world's music traditions beautifully suit its components. Many music traditions are inseparable from poetry, stories, and movement, because their musical events are comprehensive and integrated. The music of West African cultures such as the Akan, the Ewe, the Ibo, and the Yoruba offer call-and-response songs, layered polyrhythmic compositions on nonpitched percussion instruments, stories replete with music in choral response, and movement created to follow the repeating and contrasting phrases. The xylophone cultures of Bali, Guatemala, Java, and Zimbabwe are natural repositories of music that can be performed on Orff's familiar xylophones and metallophones. The possibilities for exploring the world's musical styles through one or several of Orff's components are rich, readily available, and ripe for experimentation. Hampton's volumes (1996, 1999) are exemplary of how an ensemble of Orff-styled instruments can launch children's exploration of a musical culture (the Shona of Zimbabwe) in an active, engaging manner that is not unlike the Orff process itself.

Proponents of the Hungarian approach that Kodály inspired consider folk and traditional music to be at the heart of music instruction. Unadulterated folk music is alive and well in every culture and applicable to children's learning of both music and their national heritage. The child-centered Kodály sequence for teaching melodic and rhythmic concepts can extend to many of the world's musics. Transfer of the tools of the method—movable do, rhythmic syllables, hand signs, and the shorthand notation of stems and solfège initials—from Hungarian to Anglo-American and African American songs occurred as early as the 1960s. Given the goal of the Kodály approach to foster musical and cultural understanding, such tools could transfer to the traditional and art music of Asian, African, Latin, and Native American cultures as well. The musical vocabulary used by a culture in its children's songs, folk and folk dance music, and instrumental and choral works may be better understood through the application of Kodály techniques.

If rhythm is the primary element of almost all music, and the source for musical rhythms is contained within the natural movements of the body, then the techniques of the Dalcroze approach should be suited to the development of a thorough understanding of music from many cultures. The eurhythmics techniques of follow, quick reaction, and canon can apply aptly to styles as diverse as the rhythmically dynamic Jamaican soca (soul calypso) style and the rhythmically subtle Japanese koto concert repertoire.

Walking the pulse, conducting the meter, and changing directions as each new phrase appears are Dalcrozian responses for music of any style, period, or form. When an unfamiliar selection from a little-known tradition becomes the stimulus for movement, the challenge to respond correctly to a different but equally logical musical structure is considerable. The reward, however, is greater intimacy through natural body movements that express musical understanding. The Dalcroze approach may provide the difference between simple exposure to, and integral, intensive experience of, the world's music.

The application of classic pedagogical techniques to a new repertoire of music is an appropriate balance for achieving the aims of a multicultural music education. Like Orff, Kodály, and Dalcroze, other approaches also can serve as frameworks for the development of musical and multicultural understanding: the eight-step learning sequence of Edwin E. Gordon; the perception, performance, and creativity processes of the Manhattanville Music Curriculum Project; and the integration of performance with the study of theory and literature as espoused in Comprehensive Musicianship. Whatever the approach, possibilities exist for infusing a greater variety of music into classes for children.

The Aural–Oral Transmission Process

One of the marks of Western thinking is the tendency to emphasize the end, or product, not the ways and means, or process, by which the product is achieved. Children can be guided to bring music they study to concert-level perfection in their performance, but product-oriented instruction without attention to process is only half the musical and cultural experience. The emphasis on how music and music learning evolves is central to valid experiences for children in the various musical styles the world can offer them.

An emphasis on process also distinguishes many of the world's great music traditions: the classical music of India; the African American gospel song; the gamelan music of Java; the Chopi (Mozambican) xylophone and drum ensemble; the Bulgarian polyphonic song; the rock, reggae, and rap music of North America; and the siku (panpipe) music of the Bolivian Andes. While musicians strive for a finished musical work in any tradition, their interaction with each other and with the musical components in the process of learning and rehearsing together is critical in defining both the music and the musical culture.

If authenticity is to be taken seriously, the transmission of much of the world's popular, traditional, and even art music can only be delivered orally—as it can only be received aurally. Notation, a marvelous technological invention, is not pervasive, and it cannot replace direct contact with the musical sound. Teachers and children can best become familiar with unfamiliar music through listening, the most direct route.

How then should the teaching of the world's music proceed? The transmission process by which the teacher can facilitate both musical and multiethnic understanding involves familiar teaching and learning practices. The use of teacher modeling, student imitation, and exploration and improvisation are important components of the transmission of music in many cultures, just as they are often integral to any well-planned lesson. When a traditional song or instrumental piece is transferred from a listening mode into the realm of performance, an aural or oral delivery system can be easily applied. The teacher as transmitter of a musical piece owes it

Children performing in an African drumming ensemble

Jerry Gay

to the tradition to maintain the authenticity of the transmission process as well as of the finished musical product. Notational literacy is an important goal of music instruction, but for achieving the goals of cultural literacy and understanding, the oral or aural process by which music is taught and learned may temporarily override the more traditional curricular objectives. See Campbell (1991) for further discussion of classroom teaching in light of world music transmission systems.

Curricular Design

Many established curricular programs are undergoing revitalization to meet the needs of children growing up in a changing American society. Education in social studies, language arts, math, sciences, and the arts is becoming more inclusive of African American, Asian American, Latin American, and Native American cultures. Music is no exception. A study of textbooks over the past few decades underscores the tremendous leap the profession has taken to teach a broader variety of musical styles that are more fairly represented as they are also more authentically presented. Curricular change comes slowly, however, and both the revision of pedagogical materials and the infusion of a more comprehensive perspective on music and music making into classes for children take the time, effort, and creativity of the teacher.

In the pioneering efforts to achieve the curricular goals of multiethnic music education and world music education, several important determinants should be considered. (1) Many of the instructional materials, and the longer-range curricular plans, are not written down, so that they must be invented through the teacher's own cultural immersion, musicality, and knowledge of how children learn. (2) An understanding of children's learning styles and attitudes can guide the teacher in designing a curriculum that provides active participation in music-making experiences along with initial exposure to selections of a culture's music. (3) Arrangements with members of particular ethnic-cultural communities to sing their traditional songs, play folk instruments, and tell traditional tales can provide children with the human interaction so vital in understanding music and culture. These considerations can be supported, although not replaced, by the recorded, filmed, and printed materials that are becoming available, so that children become more broadly experienced in the music of many cultures.

Box 15.1 offers questions as a guide to choosing recorded and printed music that brings the world of music to children. Both listening and performance experiences in a variety of music traditions can be selected in accordance with these principles. Affirmative responses to these questions indicate that the teacher's selection is a probably a wise one.

The design of an all-inclusive music curriculum can take several directions. Multiethnic music education is likely to be packaged within a curricular unit of several weeks, a month, two months, or longer, and it will

Box 15.1 *Confirming Authenticity in a Selection of Music*

1. Is the recorded music performed by a musician from within the culture? Is the printed music notated, transcribed, or attributed to a musician from within the culture? Is a scholar with training and experience within the culture involved in the recording or notating of the score?

2. Are notated instrumental pieces characteristic of the musical style, not arrangements for instruments outside the tradition?

3. If a song contains lyrics, are they in the original language? Is it accompanied by a guide to its pronunciation? Is an English translation provided? Is it literal or amended to fit the melodic rhythm?

4. If a song involves a game, dance, or movement, are the instructions clear for how to perform it? Is there a photograph, a diagram, an illustration, or a clear outline of how to perform the game, dance, or movement?

5. Is there a recorded version of the song or instrumental piece to be performed, so that the real music can be heard, used as a model, and later compared with the children's version?

6. Is a cultural context provided for the music? Are there accompanying notes or a book to offer a description of the culture—values, customs, historical, geographic, and economic issues that may add to an understanding of the music? What is known of the function and meaning of the music to the people who make it?

Adapted from Judith Cook Tucker.

---

feature a variety of experiences in the music of a selected culture or country. In the larger realm of year-long curriculum design, the intensive study of one musical culture can lead to the study of further cultures (including the music of the teacher's training, or the mother-tongue music of the teacher or of the majority of the children within the classroom or school). The phrase *multiethnic music education* suggests that more than a single musical culture will be explored and that comparisons will be made among several musical cultures.

In a study of China's music, for example, a unit may begin with samples of instrumental sounds, followed by exposure to the appearance and sound production capacities of the huqin (fiddle), pipa (lute), zheng (zither), di (flute), and luogu (drum and gong ensemble) through live demonstration or videotapes. The unit may unfold to include vocal music, with opportunities to perform several traditional children's songs and chants, and to view videotapes of the premiere Chinese performing art, Peking Opera. Maps, slides, transparencies, posters, and photographs of China, and its people, places, and paintings can provide a cultural context for the music, along with occasions for reading Chinese traditional poetry and folktales. With ample experiences in listening analytically to Chinese music, children can be guided to create music in the Chinese style, using recorders, cymbals, gongs, and drums to render pentatonic melodies with syncopated rhythms in duple meter. Lesson 15.1 presents a calendar of events in a study unit on Chinese music for children in the intermediate

Lak Gei Moli
(Jasmine Flowers of the Sixth Moon)

Lak gei__ mo li__ jin jian__ shui. Long gun__ si(n) zui__
Lahk gay__ moh lee__ jin john__ shwee. Long gun__ see(n) zwee__

jin__ go zhui. Ho hui lan_____ die__ xien xiang__
jin__ goh zhwee. Hoh hwee lan_____ dee__ zhehn zhahng__

dui__ Xin bin(n) mou_____ gun xiung_____ ka_____ kui.
dwee__ zhin bihn moo_____ gun zhung_____ kah_____ kwee.

Weekly Class Meetings	Two at thirty minutes each (Note that suggestions are oriented toward student rather than teacher behaviors)
Lesson One	Enter class while listening to Chinese music*
	Listen to tape of Chinese instrumental music selections
	1. How do you play these instruments?
	2. What do these instruments look like?
	See illustrations (photos, slides) of instruments
	Find China on a map; discuss geography
	Depart class while listening to Chinese music*
Lesson Two	Match listening samples to illustrations of instruments (huqin, pipa, zheng, di)
	Play "Jasmine Flowers of the Sixth Moon" (Lak Gei Moli) on recorder
	Read and discuss text of "Jasmine Flowers"
	Sing "Jasmine Flowers"
	See photos of China's people and places
	Discuss lifestyles of people in China; host Chinese "culture-bearer"
Lesson Three	Review by identifying instruments by sight and sound
	Review "Jasmine Flowers" on recorder
	Add woodblock and bells on "Jasmine Flowers"

*All classes can begin and end with sounds of Chinese traditional music.

(Continued)

Match listening samples of illustrations of instruments (luogu ensemble of gongs, cymbals, drums)

Play luogu parts for "The Flower Drum Song" (Huagu Ge)

See videotape clip of Chinese instruments

Lesson Four Review luogu parts for "The Flower Drum Song"

Sing (or play on recorders) "The Flower Drum Song"

Sing and add luogu parts for "The Flower Drum Song"

See photos of Chinese festivals; describe festivals; host Chinese "culture-bearer"

Review "Jasmine Flowers" for recorder, woodblock, bells

grades, to provide one of several pathways to realizing the goals of multi-ethnic music education.

In designing lessons that incorporate the goals of world music education, the teacher may choose from among several pathways. The musical components avenue was highlighted in the earlier definition of world music as a curricular concept, where cross-cultural comparisons are made regarding specific aspects of melody, rhythm, timbre, texture, and form. The mu-

Lesson Five	Listen to tape of Chinese instrumental musical selections (presented in first lesson)
	1. Can you tap the steady pulse?
	2. What is the meter? [duple]
	3. Can you hum the melody?
	4. How many pitches are there? [five]
	Sing "Jasmine Flowers" and "The Flower Drum Song"
	Repeat questions 1–4; summarize meter/melody concepts
	Tell the Chinese folktale "Money Makes Cares"
Lesson Six	Watch videotape clip of Peking Opera
	Review "The Flower Drum Song" with luogu
	Review "Jasmine Flowers" for recorder, woodblock, bells
	1. Do you hear uneven syncopated rhythms?
	2. Can you clap them as you sing the songs?
	Discuss syncopated rhythms, pentatonic melodies, and duple meter as characteristic of Chinese music
	Review/retell the Chinese folktale "Money Makes Cares"
Lesson Seven	Review characteristics of Chinese music
	Review tale of "Money Makes Cares"
	Children are assigned to groups to prepare
	1. narration of tale
	2. dramatization of tale
	3. creation of incidental instrumental music for tale (on recorders, gongs, drums, woodblock, bells)
	4. performance of "Jasmine Flowers" and "The Flower Drum Song" for inclusion in tale
Lesson Eight	Rehearse performance project in individual groups
Lesson Nine	Continue rehearsal
	Integrate groups into performance/production of tale
Lesson Ten	Perform tale
	Teacher-directed evaluation to determine children's understanding of Chinese music/culture

Sources: Anderson & Campbell (1989) "Jasmine Flowers of the Sixth Moon"; Cole (1982) "Money Makes Cares"; Han & Campbell (1992) "The Flower Drum Song" and "Jasmine Flowers"; and JVC: China (1989).

sic material approach features a study of similar musical instruments across cultures, for example, the incidence of lutes in Europe, Asia, and the Middle East, or the spread of bamboo and bronze instruments in Southeast Asia. Still another approach is parallel genres, the study of theater, dance, orchestral, wedding, or opera music (to give a few examples) in a variety of cultures. Lesson 15.2 presents examples of these directions in world music education for children of various ages and grade levels. Note that Western

Grade	Any
Musical Concepts	Triple Meter
Suggested Listening or Song Experience	Korea: "Ahrirang." JVC World Sounds. JVC 1009. Austria: Mozart, Symphony 40, K440, Movement 3. Sweden: "Vals from Orso." *Folk* Fiddling from Sweden. Nonesuch 72033.

Mos', Mos'!
(Hopi, Native American)

Tritonic Melody
(d, m, s)

Mos', mos', nai-ti-la Mos', mos', nai-ti-la
[neh-tee-lah]

Ka-nel per-kye nai-ti-la Ka-nel per-kye nai-ti-la
[Ka-nel pehr-kyay]

Mo - sa Mo - sa nya-nya-ya-ya etc.

Sorida
(Zimbabwe)

(d, m, s)

So-ri-da So-ri da ri-da ri-da So-ri-da
[Soh-ree-dah]

So-ri-da ri-da ri-da da da da da da da ri

da ri-da da da da da da da ri-da ri-da

Yuyake
(Japan)

(s, l, t)

Yu - ya - ke   ko - ya - ke   A - shi - ta ten - ki - ni   na___ re!
[Yoo - yah - keh   koh - yah - keh   Ah-shee-tah ten - ke - ne   nah___ reh]

Leak Kanseng
(Cambodia)

(s, l, t)

Leak   kan - seng   chma kaim   keng   oh   long   oh   long
[Lee ahk kahn - sahng   chmah kahm   kehng   oh   long   oh   long]

Syncopation

Ghana: "Chalala Eh" and "Wateh Eh." *Mustapha Tetty Addy: Master Drummer from Ghana.* Lyrichord 7250.

China: "The Hero's Defeat." China's Classical Master-pieces. Lyrichord 7182.

Cuba: "A Los Rumberos de Belen." *Sabroso! Havana Hits.* Virgin/Earthworks 91312.

Lutes

'Ud (Egypt, the Middle East). *Music in the World of Islam.* Tangent 131-136.

Sitar (India). *The Sounds of India: Ravi Shankar.* Columbia 9296.

Shamisen (Japan). *Japan: Kabuki and Other Traditional Music.* Nonesuch 72084.

Pipa (China). *Floating Petals, Wild Geese, The Moon on High: Music of the Chinese Pipa.* Nonesuch 72085.

Bronzes in Southeast Asia

Balinese metallophones/gongs. Music from the Morning of the World. Nonesuch 72015.

Javanese metallophones/gongs. *Javanese Court Gamelan, Vols. 1–3.* Nonesuch 72044, 72074, 72083.

Cambodian metallophones. *Silent Temples, Songful Hearts.* World Music Press.

Vietnamese coin clappers. *Music of Vietnam.* Lyrichord 7337.

Filipino gongs (kulintang). *Philippine Gong Music.* Lyrichord 7322.

(Continued)

Theater Music	Italy: Puccini, *Gianni Schicchi.*
	China: Peking Opera, "Hu Hung-yen: Aspects of Peking Opera" (videocassette). The Asia Society.
	Japan: Kabuki. "Martial Arts of Kabuki from the National Theater Institute of Japan" (videocassette). The Asia Society.
Suite	Peru: Suite of dances. *Music of the Incas: "Ayllu Sulca."* Lyrichord 7348.
	Iran: Suite in Dastgah Mahour. *A Persian Heritage.* Nonesuch 72060.
	Bach: *French Suite.*

European art music is not abandoned in these approaches, because it is one of the important world music traditions.

Many resources are available for use in teaching the world's musical traditions. Community resources, including traditional performing artists, are rich and waiting to be tapped for assembly programs, long-term residencies, and contractual teaching. Readers may wish to collect a set of ethnomusicology references, including books by Malm (1996) on Asian music, Nettl (1991) on European, African, and Latin American musics, and Nettl, Capwell, Bohlman, Wong, and Turino (1998), Titon (2000), and Fowler (1994) on these and other selected world musical traditions. Lessons for children are found in books by Anderson and Campbell (1996) and Dunbar-Hall and Hodge (1991). Books accompanied by recordings of children's songs from various world cultures include collections by Campbell, McCullough-Brabson, and Tucker (1994), East (1989), and Vanaver (1990). Recordings are plentiful, and those on the Smithsonian/Folkways, Nonesuch, Lyrichord, Monitor, and Rounder labels are among the most accessible. Ethnic-flavored instruments, a host of videocassettes, and CD-ROMs such as Microsoft's *Musical Instruments of the World* complete the basic package of instructional materials that deliver a quality program of world music to children.

Many Musical Worlds

Multiculturalism is a big word and a broad concept, but certainly, the objectives of multicultural education can be at least partially met through children's exposure, experience, and education in music. The world of music offers a comprehensive view of the sounds, functions, and meanings of music globally and within the many ethnic groups of a single nation. The musical expressions of groups of people are the focus of multiethnic music education, where children are offered intensive study of one and then another musical culture. Likewise, world music education provides children with knowledge of how groups of people organize the elements of music in unique modes of musical expression.

Formal as well as informal experience in listening and (ideally) performing the music of another culture increases children's understanding and thus appreciation of unfamiliar musical styles and music makers. Carefully planned experiences in the music of many cultures can bring about improved musicianship, increased preference for new (to the children) musical styles, and a deeper understanding of people and their music. Through the intermediate grades, children are open to changing their values and attitudes, so that the palette of music offered to children in their early years can be a powerfully awakening and broadening experience.

Scenario

Ms. Johnson is teaching at Baker Elementary, a school that she describes as "mildly diverse," with 20 percent African American children; 10 percent Hispanic (mostly Puerto Rican, Dominican, and Cuban); another 10 percent children whose parents or grandparents arrived from Vietnam or the Philippines; 5 percent Jewish children; a few children from Somalia, Eritrea, and Ethiopia; and all the rest of the children from one or another European heritage. She is becoming aware of diversity in the array of languages spoken by the children, the many religious and seasonal holidays they celebrate, the variety of foods brought in brown bags for lunch, the varied manner of dress and hairstyles sported, and most relevant to her, the songs and records that children bring to share with her at music time. Times have changed since her own elementary school experience out in a suburban school, and she is adamant in her goal to allow her music program to reflect the diversity of the school community.

It is just a few weeks before the winter program, and Ms. Johnson has been rehearsing the fifth graders (a microcosmic composite of the larger school population) on music that will comprise a "Festival of Lights" concert. There is a carol for Christmas, a xylophone arrangement of a song for Divali (India), a Hanukkah song with countermelody for recorders, a dance with recorded music to commemorate St. Lucia's Day (Swedish), music for Kwanzaa to sing and drum, an a cappella song for Loy Kratong with partner-game (Thailand), and a circle dance with recorder-and-drum accompaniment for Solstice. As she is distributing the recorders and drums for the Solstice song, Jamal murmurs something about "honky music." Several other boys join in while chanting, "We won't play that h-o-n-k-y music," rhythmically waving their arms while their fingers take on contortionist positions. They are rhythmic but they are loud, and Ms. Johnson worries about whether the message they are sending to the other children is offensive—both by way of word and gestures. She orders them to stop. Jamal (an African American boy) protests, "That song is lame. It's so white." And Ms. Johnson nervously replies in a sweet tone, "But we've already done your music, so you can do ours." The hip-hop boys hold their recorders to their mouths, but they do not play.

The class is invited next to review the song for Divali. The children take their places by the wood and metal xylophones, and Ms. Johnson conducts the singers and players through several repetitions of the unison song. Shanta, who arrived two years ago from India, raises her hand to inform the class that, "We really don't have xylophones in India." Ms. Johnson grimaces, several children look at each other and roll their eyes (why? she wonders), and while she carries on with the song's arrangement as planned, she is feeling uneasy inside.

"Okay, let's see what we remember of the Loy Kratong. Partner up so we can sing and perform the actions." Ms. Johnson walks up to Isaias and Kaleta and pairs them up. They are not pleased with the arrangement and will not join hands in the opening position. While others sing and play the partner game, the two boys stand stiffly facing each other, silently glowering. (Later, Ms. Johnson learns that Isaias is from Ethiopia and Kaleta is from Eritrea, two warring nations with deep-seated feelings of animosity toward one another that spreads from adults to children.)

"Why aren't we doing 'Feliz Navidad'?" asks Marisol. Ms. Johnson realizes that she has committed another faux pas in her selection of repertoire, having assumed that the Hispanic children knew "The First Noel" in English (because it is a Catholic hymn, and they are Catholic). There is not enough time to learn another song for the program, so she invites Marisol, Maria, and Ramona to sing it in the winter program. The girls look shy yet pleased at the prospects of being featured until Katerina and Anna complain, "What about us? Can we play one of our Ukrainian songs on our accordions?" As their classroom teacher arrives at the door to pick up her class, Ms. Johnson realizes that the class has disintegrated into cultural enclaves and animosities that she never would have predicted. She is beginning to think that an "all-American" program might be safer next time around.

Questions

1. How did Ms. Johnson's best intentions to celebrate cultural diversity go sour? Could any of these circumstances have been averted through more careful planning?

2. Is Ms. Johnson approaching the design of the winter concert in a manner akin to multiethnic music education or world music education or both? Explain.

3. Would the outcome have been any different had Ms. Johnson been teaching children in a less diverse setting than this one at Baker Elementary? In what ways?

REVIEW

1. Define multiethnic music education and world music education. How are their goals distinguished from one another? In what ways are they similar?

2. What uncertainties may have slowed the curricular advances in the teaching of world music?

3. Describe ways in which classic methods of music for children can be used in teaching world music traditions.

CRITICAL THINKING

1. What are some of the important issues to consider regarding authenticity and representativeness in the selection of music for children?

2. How might a teacher go about teaching a unit of study on African American gospel music (a) to a group of African American children, (b) to non-African American children, (c) if she were African American, and (d) if she were not African American? Or would it make a difference?

PROJECTS

1. Launch a demographic study of the city or district in which you may teach. Study the recent changes in the ethnic composite of the school population, as well as projections for the future.

2. Choose a favorite culture. Develop an annotated list of books, recordings, and videocassettes useful in teaching the music of this culture.

3. Develop a month-long curricular plan in teaching children the music of a favorite culture.

4. Choose one avenue of world music education (musical components, music material, parallel genres), and collect songs and listening experiences from various musical traditions to illustrate selected features within that category.

5. By listening to a recording, prepare to teach a song or instrumental performance from an oral tradition, with careful attention to rendering an authentic sound.

REFERENCES

Anderson, W. M., and P. S. Campbell, eds. (1996). *Multicultural perspectives in music education*. Reston, VA: Music Educators National Conference.

Banks, J., and C. M. Banks (1995). *Handbook of research in multicultural education*. New York: Macmillan.

Campbell, P. S. (1991). *Lessons from the world*. New York: Schirmer Books.

Campbell, P. S., E. McCullough-Brabson, and J. C. Tucker (1994). *Roots and branches*. Danbury, CT: World Music Press.

Cole, J. (1982). *Best-loved folk tales*. Garden City, NY: Anchor Press/Doubleday.

Dunbar-Hall, P., and G. Hodge (1991). *A guide to music around the world*. Marrickville, NSW, Australia: Science Press.

East, H. (1989). *The singing sack: 28 song-stories from around the world*. London: A & C Black.

Fowler, C. (1994). *Music!: Its role and importance in our lives*. New York: Glencoe.

Hampton, W. (1996). *Hot Marimbas!* Danbury, CT: World Music Press.

———. (1999). *Mojo Marimbas*. Danbury, CT: World Music Press.

Han, K.-H., and P. S. Campbell (1992). *The lion's roar: Chinese luogu percussion ensembles*. Danbury, CT: World Music Press.

The JVC video anthology of world music and dance. (1989). Washington, DC: Smithsonian/Folkways.

Malm, W. P. (1996). *Music cultures of the Pacific, the Near East, and Asia* (3rd ed.). Upper Saddle River, NJ: Prentice-Hall.

Nettl, B. (1991). *Folk and traditional music of the Western continents* (2nd ed.). Englewood Cliffs, NJ: Prentice-Hall.

Nettl, B., C. Capwell, P. V. Bohlman, I. K. F. Wong, and T. Turing (1998). *Excursions in world music*. Englewood Cliffs, NJ: Prentice-Hall.

Titon, J. T., ed. (2000). *Worlds of music*, shorter version. Belmont, CA: Schirmer/Wadsworth.

Vanaver, B. (1990). *Sheaves of grain: Songs of the seasons from around the world*. Danbury, CT: World Music Press.

16

Music for Exceptional Children

Malinka, age eight, loves to sing; she does so with great enthusiasm but has a difficult time controlling her voice and her impulse to sing constantly. Trebon, age ten, is an active composer; he can replicate, by ear, challenging piano pieces he has heard two or three times. Jessica, age eleven, is withdrawn; she comes to music class but sits there, looking downward. James, age six, seems to need constant attention; he moves all the time, hits the children next to him, talks out of turn, and rarely sings without shouting, but he loves to play the African drums.

Each one of these children has unique needs and abilities, some of which are being met through special education and some through regular education. All attend music classes with children of their own age in a regular education setting as a part of their school's goal to place them in an environment where they can achieve their maximum growth. This is called the least restrictive environment (LRE). Although these children have been labeled exceptional, they are more like other children than they are different. Musically, they are frequently similar in their interests and abilities (Jellison and Flowers, 1991).

The music teacher who works with these children is part of a child study team that helps to determine how to accommodate each special-needs child. As a team member, the music teacher is able to communicate with the others the goals of the music program to make sure each child can be successful. He or she also learns from the other team members how to help meet the unique needs of each of these children and what support can be expected in the process. He or she helps decide how mainstreaming or inclusion in music can help achieve goals set forth in each child's annual individualized education program (IEP).

The following descriptions outline the factors that the child study team considered in placing Malinka, Trebon, Jessica, and James in a music setting.

Malinka is a Down syndrome child, moderately retarded, with a gift for relating with joy to the people around her. Although she has some problems inhibiting her responses, she is developing increased control. Her performance in school suggests she should be able to live in a group setting as an adult and hold a job provided there are some supports for her. The committee decided that she would benefit from the structure of the music setting, the challenge of learning to match her voice to those of the children around her, and the intellectual and physical stimulation of being with children who learn more quickly than she does. Although she will largely learn music by rote, her participation is immediate and feeling of success immense.

Trebon is a highly gifted child, particularly in music, although he is also a part of his school's pull-out gifted program where he receives additional instruction. When the music specialist recognized Trebon's exceptional gifts in music, she encouraged his parents to get him private lessons. Although they wanted that for him, they could not afford the cost. The music specialist contacted the district music supervisor who had begun a program, funded through a combination of school funds, Parent Teacher Student Association (PTSA) grants, and community corporate grants, to give private music lessons to economically disadvantaged children. Members of a local private music teachers association agreed to come to the schools to offer lessons at reduced rates as part of their dedication to public service. In her music class, the specialist offers Trebon opportunities for leadership as an accompanist and a teaching assistant, helping her when she divides the class into smaller groups for guitar instruction and for composition assignments.

Jessica is a child who has been emotionally and physically abused by her parents. She is now living in a foster home and is receiving counseling. She has coped with her abuse by withdrawing, and her self-esteem is at a very low level. She has normal intelligence but poor social skills. Her teachers are eager to help her learn to express herself and to trust and interact with others in group settings. Because the music classroom is based on group expression of musical ideas, the team decided to place Jessica with a class of fifth graders. Although Jessica withdraws during group singing, she is willing to play accompaniments on Orff xylophones. She is also starting to express some ideas, both verbally and musically, in the small group composition sessions. (The music specialist has elected to form cooperative groups that retain a stable membership for three months.) As a result, Jessica is beginning to trust the other students in her group and is making some friends. Her teachers report she is increasingly eager to go to music class.

James has been diagnosed as having attention deficit-hyperactivity disorder (ADHD) and some learning disabilities. His parents have decided not to control his behavior with Ritalin because they are concerned about the negative effects of continued medication. James comes to music from a resource room where teachers are working with him on specific academic and social skills. The resource-room teachers have worked with the music specialist to implement a behavior-management procedure that is consistent with the one they are using with James. Some of the musical goals for the year include reducing the amount of energy James uses in singing, building accuracy in reproduction of patterns through techniques of echoing, and having James notate and then read and perform his own patterns.

Who Are Exceptional Children?

Although it could be said that on some level every child is exceptional, with unique abilities and needs, current practice defines exceptional children as "those whose physical attributes and/or learning abilities differ from the norm, either above or below, to such an extent that an individualized program of special education is indicated" (Heward and Orlansky, 1992, p. 27). This includes children who are identified as gifted. In 1990, PL 94-142 was amended to redefine handicapped children as children with disabilities. The new law, PL 101-476 (Individuals with Disabilities Education Act or IDEA), addressed a number of issues to help students receive needed services and assistance, including children with attention deficit disorders. It lists disabilities as:

+ Mental retardation

+ Specific learning disabilities that require special education

+ Behavior disorders (emotional disturbance)

+ Communication (speech and language) impairments

+ Hearing impairments including deafness

+ Visual impairments including blindness

+ Orthopedic impairments

+ Autism

+ Traumatic brain injury

+ Other health impairments

The language used to describe a child's disability is frequently open to misinterpretation and confusion. It is useful to think of these children as "differently abled" instead of "disabled." For example, exceptional children may or may not have a disability, or "the reduced function or loss of a particular body part or organ" (Heward and Orlansky, 1992, p. 27). Children who cannot perform tasks involving seeing, hearing, or moving the way others can may be said to be disabled. Persons with disabilities may or may not be handicapped, referring to the "problems a person with a disability or impairment encounters when interacting with the environment" (Heward and Orlansky, 1992, p. 28). A person using a wheelchair may be handicapped when trying to go to the second floor of a building without elevators, but not handicapped intellectually in the school classroom. PL 101-336, Americans with Disabilities Act (ADA), passed Congress in 1990. This sweeping law created a national mandate for the elimination of any discrimination against people with disabilities and named the federal government as the enforcer of these laws. Title III of this law applies to schools, ensuring equal access and services.

A category of at-risk children is often described in the literature. Although these children are not currently identified as disabled, they run a greater-than-usual chance of developing a problem. They are often preschoolers whose conditions of birth (such as premature birth or fetal drug or alcohol syndrome) or home environment (such as abuse or economic deprivation) suggest that they may be at risk for developmental problems and may need special help. At-risk children are those in the primary or intermediate grades who demonstrate learning problems in the regular classroom and are at risk for placement in special programs or, if older, for school dropout. These children are not currently classified as exceptional but their needs are real, and early intervention by schools and social agencies is becoming common.

Educating Exceptional Children

In 1975, Congress passed Public Law (PL) 94-142, the Education of the Handicapped Act, which was later renamed the Individuals with Disabilities Education Act. This legislation was instrumental in changing the ways schools had historically dealt with children who have special needs. It requires that schools offer free public education to all students regardless of the severity of their need; that individuals and families of individuals with handicaps have a say in their education; that an annual IEP is developed for each individual that helps to place him or her in the LRE for growth. Gifted children are the only group of exceptional children not covered in this act but may be included in corresponding state laws for the education of children with special needs.

Since 1975 schools have responded in various ways to this legislation. Schools have moved away from isolating or even warehousing handicapped children to mainstreaming them into different parts of the school program with support from resource rooms and teachers trained in special education. Historically, mainstreaming has usually occurred in areas typically taught by specialists: music, physical education, and art.

Since the late 1980s, many schools have integrated disabled children into the regular classroom throughout the entire day using a model called inclusion. In such schools, other children and faculty are taught to assist these children as needed, and support is usually provided to meet their additional physical and educational needs. Paraprofessionals or teacher aides are frequently assigned to assist individual children to help assure success.

The federal government encourages but does not require states to create and fund special programs for gifted and talented students. Forty-eight states have such programs, but the relative amount spent on them is minimal compared with that spent on children with disabilities. Many models exist for serving gifted and talented children; one of the most common is to pull them out of their regular classroom for enrichment classes. Entrance into these classes is usually a measured IQ (intelligence quotient) of 130 to 135. Some schools teach the most intellectually gifted children (the top 1 percent) in completely separate programs. Other schools, particularly at the secondary level, screen students based on specific gifts in math and science, humanities, or the arts. Selected students are placed in magnet schools that stimulate them to achieve advanced levels of performance in the area(s) of their gifts.

Of the children in special education (about 9.4 percent of the total population), 48 percent are diagnosed as having learning disabilities, 23 percent with speech and language impairments, 14 percent with mental retardation, and 9 percent with emotional disturbance. Two-thirds of these children receive at least part of their education in a regular classroom with the support of a resource room, and the remainder are in self-contained classrooms. The most severe are usually educated in special schools. Ninety percent of children receiving special education are mildly handicapped (Heward and Orlansky, 1992).

Mainstreaming and the Music Classroom

The decision to mainstream or to include a child in music is justified for a variety of positive reasons that relate directly to the nature of music and of music learning.

1. Music taps into nonverbal ways of knowing and allows children to express ideas regardless of verbal abilities. At the same time singing can help children to develop vocabulary and understanding of language.

2. Music is multimodal in nature, stimulating the eyes, ears, and muscles along with the mind. Children who have a disability in one sensory area may still participate in music via other senses. The joy of producing sounds and movements draws children actively into the process of music making instead of requiring them to be passive receptors of new ideas.

3. Music can be performed at very sophisticated levels by rote. It is not necessary to be able to read music to perform it well. Although an important outcome of a quality music program is the skill of music reading, children who have difficulties with abstract symbols, such as reading words or translating numbers, can enjoy success in music.

4. Music making is generally a collaborative endeavor. Music is usually made and learned in groups, not alone. This is particularly true of

preschool and elementary general music programs. Therefore, children can gain a sense of belonging and commitment to a group that is important to social development.

5. Music, as a performing art, allows for the expression of a wide range of emotions, and it can communicate on very deep levels without the use of words. It stimulates and challenges people to grow aesthetically.

6. A single activity in a music classroom can be adapted to a wide range of ability levels.

7. Music, as a temporal art, challenges the mind to recognize patterns across time, a skill that often needs to be developed in children with patterning and memory deficits.

Yet, in spite of the many potential benefits of mainstreaming children in music, such decisions need to be weighed carefully for each child in terms of (1) his or her unique needs and abilities and (2) the demands of the music classroom. The purpose of the LRE is to place children in a situation in which they can succeed and grow, not where they will be ignored or fail.

The goals of a quality music program for children are many but largely focus on the development of musical skills and musical thought. Children who have been through such a program should be able to perform, create, read, and discuss music. There are many demands on complex motor-coordination skills and on thinking at the critical and creative levels. A quality music program is far more than a series of activities designed to help children have fun musical experiences together.

Also, although it is tempting to focus on the possible therapeutic values of musical involvement for exceptional children, general music teachers are rarely trained as music therapists. Therefore, they do not have the background or credentials to plan for placement of children in music classes for therapeutic reasons or to systematically implement therapeutic uses of music.

The most effective decision to mainstream a child in music will result from clear communication and cooperation among the members of the team involved. One of those members should, by law, be the music specialist if he or she is being asked to receive a child. The music specialist needs to consider whether a child with a particular set of needs can succeed in the context of a particular classroom, and he or she needs to gain insight from the team members about how best to work with each mainstreamed child.

Regrettably, many schools ignore this requirement and simply send the children to music classes without any warning, a practice known as dumping. Results of such decisions have led to anger and confusion on the part of music teachers, lack of acceptance of the mainstreamed child by the other children, and, ultimately, a more, rather than less, restrictive environment.

The Music Educators National Conference (MENC) has clearly stated standards for mainstreaming in *The School Music Program: Description and*

Standards (MENC, 1986). This booklet can be used to communicate with administrators the National Standards for a quality music education program. It reads:

> When handicapped students are mainstreamed into regular music classes:
>
>   a. Music educators are involved in placement decisions.
>   b. Placement is determined primarily on the basis of musical achievement.
>   c. Placement does not result in classes exceeding standard class size.
>   d. Placement does not result in a disproportionate number of handicapped students in any class.
>   e. Music instruction is provided in special education classes for those handicapped students not mainstreamed for music.
>   f. Special education music classes are no larger than other special education classes, and teacher aides are provided for special education music classes if aides are provided for other special education classes (pp. 25–26).

As part of a successful placement in music, the music teacher will need to join other members of the child study team to make sure that the IEP for that child reflects realistic goals for musical attainment. By law a child study team must include at least (1) the child's teacher(s), (2) a representative of the local school district other than the child's teacher, (3) the child's parents or guardian, and, (4) whenever appropriate, the child herself or himself. Other specialists, including music specialists, can be added as necessary.

Each IEP is required to contain basic information about and goals for the child, and it must be established at the beginning of the school year and reviewed once during the year. Local school districts have usually developed their own forms. Ideally these plans should help identify the student's level at the beginning of the term, goals for the class, how these goals will be achieved, and how the student's progress will be evaluated. Box 16.1 shows an example of an IEP in music.

Although involvement in this process clearly takes time, music specialists need to understand that their right to participate is protected under the law and that doing so can help create a more positive environment for the mainstreamed child. Specialists also need to know that schools should be committed to educating all students in music whether they are mainstreamed or not.

Inclusion in Music

Because of the shift in schools from mainstreaming to inclusion, the music teacher may not have been formally involved on a child study team, deciding whether music would be the best placement for a particular child. Regardless of whether a child with disabilities enters the music classroom

Box 16.1 *Individualized Education Program (IEP)*

1. Student

Name: James King
School: Paxton Elementary
Grade: III
Current placement: Resource Room
Date of birth: 8/7/69
Age: 9

2. Committee

NAME	POSITION	INITIAL DATE
Ms. J. Strong	Music teacher	
Dr. T. Forman	Assistant principal	
Ms. J. Kane	Resource teacher	

3. Present Level of Functioning	4. Annual Goal	5. Instructional Objective	6. Assessment Procedure
Strengths: Plays rhythm instruments well, maintains rhythm most of the time. Can imitate simple sounds.	Will imitate short phrases in songs.	Will imitate a short random phrase.	Will imitate the phrase accurately in pitch and rhythm in two of three consecutive sessions.
Needs: To improve use of his singing voice. To improve his ability to respond to music rhythmically in a less inhibited manner.	Will respond by running, synchronizing his steps to the drumbeat.	Will respond to a fast drumbeat by running, though not necessarily synchronizing steps with beat.	Will run to the drumbeat (sixteen measures of 2/4) with 80 percent accuracy.

7. Educational Service to Be Provided

a. Services Required	b. Date Initiated	c. Duration	d. Individual Response
• A full-frequency-range hearing aid. • Music in a regular classroom having a hard surface floor. Sixteen twenty-minute sessions with the music therapists to develop the singing voice and synchronize running movement with the drumbeat.	10/1/78	8 weeks	Joan Reed

e. Extent of Time in Regular Educational Program

Placed in the regular third-grade music class, one thirty-minute period per week.

f. Justification for Placement

Placement based on music-assessment instrument.

8. I have had the opportunity to participate in the development of this individualized education program.

Parent's signature _____

Reproduced with permission from Graham and Beer (1980, p. 87).

through mainstreaming or inclusion, an IEP will have been written. Knowledge of that information will be helpful in integrating the child successfully. The more awareness the teacher has of each child's unique needs and abilities, the more effectively that teacher can tailor learning strategies to meet that child's needs.

Successful integration means providing an environment where each child participates to the highest level possible, has experiences that all children are having, learns to interact with other children, and receives respect for his or her unique needs (Adamek, 2001). To accomplish this, the music teacher may wish to request a Summary Sheet of Information on the Special Needs Children in Class (Adamek, 2001, p. 24). Such a sheet should include the following information:

Name

Grade

Teacher

Date

Strengths, Skills, and Talent

Weaknesses and Limitations

IEP Objectives

Strategies for Success

The Music Classroom and Exceptional Children

Whether teachers work with exceptional children in a mainstreamed classroom, through inclusion, or in a self-contained setting, the key to success is the willingness of the teachers to adapt instruction to meet the needs of those children. Each category of exceptionality has unique characteristics as does each child within a category.

For some students, teachers need to adapt the pace and clarity of instructions, slowing down what they do, repeating directions, and modeling tasks. For some children, teachers will need to adapt the complexity either of the task, of the music, or of the level of thought required, sometimes simplifying it and other times making it more challenging. For other students, teachers will need to adapt the materials and instruments, making print larger, using sequencing cards, or adding Velcro fasteners to gloves so children can hold bell mallets. And for others, teachers will need to adapt the processes and support they provide, using student buddies and cooperative groups, allowing students to experience instruction (seeing, hearing, moving) and demonstrate knowing (telling, singing, playing, writing, moving) through multiple instead of single modalities.

Ultimately, deciding how to adapt instruction can be an exciting and challenging process that will increase a teacher's repertoire of strategies designed to meet the needs of all children. The following ideas should provide an initial base. Other resources include the special education teachers and specialists (hearing, speech, and psychologists) assigned to work with exceptional children, the parents, the children themselves, print resources, and classes in working with disabilities. (See Alvin and Warwick, 1991;

Atterbury, 1990; Birkenshaw, 1977; Bitcon, 1976; Edwards, 1974; *Journal of Music Therapy*; Michel, 1976; dedicated issues of the *Music Educators Journal.*)

Mentally Retarded

Children who are classified as mentally retarded (MR) are significantly below average in general intellectual functioning, which either results in or is associated with deficits in adaptive behavior (average IQ is 100). Some children with low IQs are able to function well in school and society. Those children would not be classified as mentally retarded. However, if a child has a low IQ and does not meet age level standards of personal independence and social responsibility, then he or she will be labeled mentally retarded.

There are typically four levels of mental retardation that are defined in terms of levels of IQ.

Mild Retardation (IQ of 50–55 to approximately 70)

This group is the most likely to be mainstreamed into music classes with the assistance of a resource-room teacher to meet individual needs. Often these children are not identified until they begin schooling. Many do well in school and function independently as adults.

Moderate Retardation (IQ of 35–40 to 50–55)

These children have usually been identified at an early age and often have other handicapping conditions and physical abnormalities. They are usually taught in a self-contained classroom where focus on daily living and functional skills usually outweighs academics. Many of these children have Down syndrome or are brain damaged. They continue to need support as adults.

Severe Retardation (IQ of 20–25 to 35–40)
Profound Retardation (IQ below 20–25)

Most children in these categories are identified at birth and have significant central nervous system damage. They usually have not been taught in schools, although that is beginning to change. New technologies are helping to reach children who are profoundly retarded. Most of these people will need care, some twenty-four hours a day, throughout life. However, some may be able to function semi-independently as adults.

Music teachers are most likely to be asked to work with mildly and moderately retarded students either in mainstreamed or self-contained settings. Box 16.2 provides a breakdown of characteristics of mildly retarded children and specific teaching strategies to meet their special needs.

Box 16.2 *A Breakdown of MR Characteristics and Specific Teaching Strategies*

1. Mentally retarded (MR) children may have problems with focusing attention or distinguishing the important from the unimportant. They may also be unable to generalize learnings to new settings.
   - Use color highlighting of notated melodic and rhythmic patterns.
   - Notate their part (such as an ostinato) separately; use color highlighting.
   - Teach songs without recordings or other accompaniment.
   - State lesson goals clearly, and repeat during the lesson.
   - Speak in short simple sentences without talking down.
   - Ask children to perform only one musical task—for example, chant or sing, or maintain a steady beat or ostinato—not multiple tasks.

2. MR children may have problems with memory from one lesson to another and also short-term memory of patterns within a lesson.
   - Repeat materials, skills, and concepts across several lessons.
   - Keep musical patterns for echo clapping or singing short, simple, and slow; repeat them if necessary.
   - Break tasks down into small units and teach with simple directions; use hand movements to practice dance patterns ahead of time or patschen (patting the lap) to practice instrument patterns.
   - Use visual cues such as pictures or movements to help them remember the order of events in a song; for example, "I Know an Old Lady Who Swallowed a Fly."
   - In learning a new song, have them join in on the part that repeats; for example, "Sandy Land."

3. MR children may have trouble with cognitive organization of ideas and abstractions.
   - Use iconic notation to represent patterns.
   - Teach ideas by rote instead of note.
   - Let them develop their own way of writing down music.
   - Help them chunk or group information using visual, verbal, or movement cues; for example, music charts that come with music series or bulletin boards that highlight or review concepts.

4. MR children may have trouble singing in tune across a wide range or may sing with too much energy.
   - Work to expand their tessitura upward (often it is low, from B to g).
   - Have them sit next to an effective singer and encourage them to match that singer's voice.

5. MR children's mental age (MA) is behind their chronological age (CA) yet they often identify with same-age peers.
   - If mainstreamed based on CA, adapt instruction per suggestions above; have them work with a partner who can monitor and assist but not solve or take over for them.
   - Respect their CA when selecting song and listening materials; do not treat older students like little children.
   - Discover something they do well in music, and let them offer leadership or have them lead a cooperative group with a sensitive buddy as their assistant.

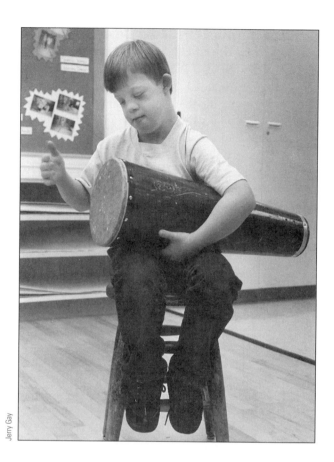

Jerry Gay

Learning Disabled

The area of learning disabilities is perhaps the most difficult to define of all of the areas of exceptionality. Generally children identified as learning disabled (LD) are of normal intelligence but have "significant difficulties in the acquisition and use of language, listening, speaking, reading, writing, reasoning, or mathematical abilities" (Heward and Orlansky, 1992, p. 137). It is assumed that these limits are intrinsic and stem from some problem in the central nervous system, and not a result of other handicapping conditions or extrinsic influences such as environment or lack of education.

By far, the largest number of exceptional children served in schools today are identified as learning disabled, although the form(s) that the disability takes varies greatly. The majority are males (a three-to-one ratio), identified in the elementary grades, are more deficient in spelling and reading than in mathematics, and have increased difficulty in learning with increased age.

Because *learning disabled* is an umbrella term covering a wide range of behaviors, it is difficult to state principles that will apply in every case. A careful dialogue with the resource-room teacher and a review of each mainstreamed child's folder should help the music teacher to better meet individual needs. Box 16.3 provides some general characteristics and specific teaching strategies to address the students' needs.

Box 16.3 *General Characteristics of Learning Disabled*
Children and Specific Teaching Strategies

1. In general, develop strategies that allow learning disabled (LD) children to hear, see, move, or touch either simultaneously or sequentially. LD children have difficulty receiving and translating input from one or more of the senses used for learning.

   Visual (verbal and nonverbal)

   ✦ Highlight visuals using large print, color, frames that isolate patterns on overheads or in their books.

   Auditory (verbal and nonverbal)

   ✦ Slow down verbal input and recordings; teach difficult parts separately.

   ✦ Separate the reading of rhythms from pitch.

   ✦ Learn songs by rote, then add the tracking of words; print one line of words under a song, not multiple verses.

   Tactile (touch) or kinesthetic (muscle movement)
   (verbal and nonverbal)

   ✦ Use concrete manipulables to reinforce musical ideas such as notation: magnet boards or hand staffs for pitch work; Popsicle sticks for rhythm work; and also felt or sandpaper notes.

   ✦ Practice instrument parts kinesthetically away from the instrument first.

2. LD children may have problems cognitively integrating all of the different information they receive during a music lesson. Depending on the complexity of the task, they have to move from paying attention to what it is the teacher is emphasizing, to perceiving the place in the music, to forming an image of what that is, to interpreting a symbol of how it is represented, to conceptualizing it in terms of other similar musical events or in terms of the task. This is particularly challenging in music because even a simple folk song printed in a music book is full of information. Most of the musical tasks children are asked to perform involve complex coordination of the mind and the body.

   ✦ Perform a task analysis of the skills or concepts children are expected to do or understand.

   ✦ Teach LD children to perform something in a series of smaller steps:

   • How to hold a mallet and how to strike it

   • Later, how to coordinate with complex patterns

   • Later, how to read

   • Later, to understand an ostinato

   ✦ Know that motor coordination may be a problem and simplify motor tasks.

3. LD children may have difficulty showing what they know through writing or reading.

   ✦ Provide alternative means of showing what they know: pointing, circling icons such as arrows or lines, matching, manipulating, singing, moving, and telling.

Behavior Disordered

The term *behavior disordered* (BD) is increasingly used to apply to children who might have previously been labeled emotionally disturbed, socially maladjusted, or psychotic. Health impaired or autistic children are also placed in this category. The behaviors may have either a biological or a psychological cause.

Children identified as BD are usually either very aggressive and act out (externalizers) or shy and withdrawn (internalizers). The level of their behavior puts it consistently outside of the social norms. As a result of that behavior, they are often socially isolated and in trouble academically. Happily, most of these children have normal intelligence and can be helped to gain needed social skills in the regular classroom and at home.

Because the range and variety of behaviors in BD children is so broad and potentially disruptive, it is essential that the music specialist communicate with the resource teachers and school psychologists to know how best to adapt their teaching for successful mainstreaming of these children. This planning needs to be done ahead of time because BD children need (1) consistency in expectations, (2) clarity in the communication of those expectations, (3) options or choices, not mandates, and (4) extrinsic guidelines and support for behavior modification.

Music teachers need to anticipate places in their lessons that might be difficult for behavior disordered children and implement procedures that will result in appropriate behaviors. The classroom procedures and adaptations highlighted in Table 16.1 are relevant to the teaching of all children. Many of the techniques in Chapter 3 will also be useful with BD children.

Counting out to choose a leader

Jerry Gay

TABLE 16.1 *Classroom Management Procedures*

CLASSROOM PROCEDURE	POSSIBLE ADAPTATION
Entering and leaving classroom and finding place to sit	Lines with leaders, single file, no talking, assigned seats or carpet squares—make it more musical by moving children to a drum, piano, or recorded signal
Distributing, holding, and collecting books	Include behavior disordered (BD) children as leaders for the day or week to distribute and collect books—one book per child so there are no difficulties with sharing. Establish clarity on respect for the books.
Distributing and playing instruments	Model correct way to hold mallets or other instruments and correct playing technique. Have children imitate teacher's model. Move around, not over, Orff-barred percussion instruments, mallets left in holders or on top of instruments. Distribute instruments one at a time to add color to a piece instead of taking a rhythm band approach. Place hand percussion instruments under chair when finished, or collect immediately by instrument type, for example, placing all tambourines on the front table. Develop silent freeze signal if noise gets out of hand, for example, hand on chin or lights out. Immediately remove instrument from possession of student who is not respecting it.
Selecting a partner for a dance or giving an instrument to another person	Avoid saying, "choose a partner." Use colored tags, shapes, numbering off, or letters signifying individuals. "Everyone with a red tag stand with someone with a blue tag. Move to the drumbeat for eight beats."
Forming a circle or other formation for a dance	Place Xs on floor with tape or white (washable) shoe polish in the proper formation. Stand on the X with no touching until given the signal.
Working in small groups for composition or other projects	Establish cooperative groups of four to five with a balance of different types of children in them. Keep the groups consistent for at least three months. Let them select a group name. Always have them work in the same area of the room.
Establishing and reinforcing behavior standards	Have students generate a list of class rules (or teacher does so if necessary). Keep the list short and clear. Post it in front of room. Discuss the rules to make sure children understand what their responsibilities are. Refer to them regularly. Have children understand consequences of not following the rules such as warnings, time-outs, or discussion with the teacher or parents. Try to use praise and positive reinforcement as much as possible. Be patient and calm. If a BD child is on a behavior modification plan, follow its guidelines in teaching music.

Sensory Handicaps

Hearing-Impaired

Hearing-impaired students are often assumed to be incapable of perceiving sounds or of learning to make music, but nothing could be further from the truth. The term *hearing impairment* refers to a wide range of hearing losses. Most students who are hearing impaired are capable of hearing some musical sounds and responding to and performing music. Even deaf children can perceive vibration and pitch changes through their sense of touch, and they can learn to play various percussion and wind instruments as well as dance in time to music.

A person who is deaf may perceive some sounds, but not clearly enough to understand speech either with or without a hearing aid. It is very hard for deaf children to communicate aurally; they rely on vision. A person who is hard of hearing can perceive enough sounds to be able to understand speech and communicate similarly to the normal hearing child. Most hearing-impaired children do not require special services. Most deaf children are now being served in regular schools, not in special schools for the deaf.

In effectively working with hearing-impaired children in music, the music specialist would benefit from knowing answers to the following questions:

1. What is the degree of the hearing loss?
   a. Mild (20–55 decibels): can understand conversation from three to five feet, gets confused in groups, may speech read (read the movements of the mouth of a speaker)

Teacher signing with a hearing-impaired child

b. Moderate (55–70 decibels): can understand loud conversation only, may have impaired speech and language comprehension

c. Severe (70–90 decibels): may hear loud sounds about one foot from ear, may identify some environmental sounds, probably has difficulties with speech (consonants) and language, uses vision to understand

d. Profound (90–110 decibels): may hear some loud sounds but mostly senses vibrations, difficulty with speech and language, relies on vision rather than sound for communication

2. How are they receiving information?

a. Through auditory learning (learning to listen to actual sounds)

b. Through amplification instruments: hearing aid, microphone and hearing aid, or cochlear implant (find out what frequencies they can hear)

c. Through speech reading (trying to understand through careful attention to a speaker's face)

3. What methods are being used to teach them? (See Box 16.4.)

a. Oral approaches: emphasis is placed on auditory, visual, and tactile means of reaching children; speech reading; amplification; and talking (will need to sit where they can read speech)

b. Total communication: use of speech reading, signing, and finger spelling (may need an interpreter or a note taker and must sit where they can read speech)

Box 16.4 *Strategies for Working with Hearing-Impaired Children*

Adapting for the hearing-impaired student may involve some or all of the following suggestions.

✦ Seat the child at the front of the room and make sure light falls on your face.

✦ Face the child and speak directly to him or her.

✦ Speak clearly but not too fast.

✦ Do not shout or raise the level of your voice.

✦ Cue children if you are going to ask them a question.

✦ Assign a note taker for older children.

✦ Use visual communication such as pictures, icons, charts, overheads, chalkboards, written notes. For example, for songs and words representing key concepts, place their page numbers in order on the chalkboard.

✦ If you are wearing a microphone, be sensitive to the potential of distortion from ambient noise and instruments. Have students adjust hearing aids accordingly.

✦ Model fingerings and mallet techniques for playing instruments.

✦ Have children touch instruments to feel vibrations: piano sounding board, body of the guitar, frame of a drum, the body of Orff bass bars (good for pitch discrimination).

(Continued)

Box 16.4 (*Continued*)

◆ Give children instruments that have low frequencies or can be felt through the hand such as rhythm sticks. Avoid instruments that have bright, piercing sounds.

◆ Do not expect that children in the moderate to profound loss categories can hear recorded music clearly.

◆ Use instruments such as alto recorders or Melodicas (with or without extensions) to work on pitch motion, articulation, breathing, and rhythm.

◆ Tap patterns on desks or other sound conducting surfaces to help children feel meter and rhythm.

◆ When possible, teach music in rooms with wooden floors so that vibrations can be felt; a wooden platform increases the resonance potential of sounds from instruments such as pianos and xylophones.

◆ Place stereo speakers on the floor of a gymnasium, select music with a strong beat such as popular dance music, and encourage hearing-impaired children to dance with their shoes off, feeling the music through vibrations in the floor.

◆ Help all children learn to sing some songs by signing; all children need to understand that there are many ways to communicate.

Visually Impaired

Visually impaired children constitute a very small percentage (0.1 percent) of the school-age population. The causes of visual impairment and the degrees of loss of sight vary greatly. Some children have blurred vision, or poor peripheral vision, are very near sighted, can only see light and shadows, or see nothing. Many (about 30 percent) have other handicaps. Most attend regular classes with peers.

Again, the key for the music teacher is to understand the type of visual impairment a child has and to learn how to maximize use of any residual sight that might exist. Children who are legally blind (20/200 vision in best eye with correction) will probably be learning through a Braille system. Other visually impaired students may use technological devices such as the Optacon that enlarge and raise regular print for easier reading.

Music, an aural art, is readily accessible to the blind child through listening and imitation (see Box 16.5). Even if reading notation is involved, children can learn through a variety of concrete manipulables (such as tongue depressors for rhythm patterns or magnet boards with raised staff for melody work) or through Braille notation. The ideas in Box 16.5 may help in adapting for the visually impaired child.

Physical Handicaps

Children who are physically handicapped may have an orthopedic impairment (involving the skeletal system and muscles) or a neurologic impairment (involving the nervous system) or both. Cerebral palsy (CP) is a major

Box 16.5 *Strategies for Working with Visually Impaired Children*

1. Develop manipulables to use for sensing through touch: sandpaper or felt notes, notes outlined in string, individual staffs to use at seats with staff raised up with layers of Elmer's glue or tape, tongue depressors for rhythm work, listening maps with raised patterns using glue or string, Braille notation or labels if necessary.

2. Enlarge notation through: patterns notated with black pen on tagboard, blowing a song up to a larger size through magnification on a copy machine, large notation on chalkboards or overheads, chart books available with music series, using an Optacon.

3. Use auditory sense by: recording on tape lessons or song materials, explaining unusual noises, training auditory perception of sounds in foreground and background, verbally cuing when they are to play instruments or change chords, using playground balls with bells for activities using balls in music, identifying persons who are speaking by name.

4. Increase confidence in movement by: consistently placing chairs and instruments in room; using sighted partners for dancing or hula hoops, ropes tied in circles, parachutes for circle dances; talking students through patterned movements for dances or instrument playing; guiding individual movement in personal space in time, flowing with music; helping children move by walking next to them while supporting with a hand under their elbow (do not push or pull).

cause of physical handicaps. In addition to CP, a whole range of accidents and diseases can result in physical handicaps. Some of them result in limited physical functioning because they affect breathing (asthma) or energy (diabetes or AIDS—acquired immune deficiency syndrome). Usually, focus in treatment and schooling is on what parts of the body are involved (one or more limbs) and whether the motor and perceptual motor handicaps are mild, moderate, or severe.

Children with mild handicaps are usually able to improve motor and perceptual functioning with intervention, and they are able to keep up with peers in academic work. Children with moderate and severe handicaps may have some academic delays as well as motor-coordination problems that keep them from achieving age-level expectations. Physical and occupational therapists can help the music specialist understand how to best serve these children. For example, output for children who cannot verbally express their ideas can be through a communication board attached to their wheelchair.

Because there are so many different types of physical handicaps, it is important that the music teacher know the specific needs of each child to adapt instruction for them. The goal for all of these children is physical independence, participation, and control.

Adapting for Movement

✦ Create space for wheelchairs that is accessible for activities and sight lines (do not isolate nonambulatory children in back of music room or concert hall)

- If doing creative movement, have children move a part of their body they can still move: "Open and close your mouth to the beat"; "click the rhythm pattern with your tongue"; "stand and rock to show the beat"; "lift your legs up and down"
- Use a standing table or walker for support for movement activities
- Do patterned dances in a space large and open enough that nonambulatory students can dance in their chairs; use music with a tempo they can manage
- Assign a sensitive ambulatory partner to dance with a nonambulatory student

Adapting Instruments and Materials

- Insert mallets, strikers, or small handles through a foam ball or small rubber ball for easier gripping
- Attach mallets or small instruments to hands or gloves by Velcro
- Use baby teething rings or rubber doorstops to strum Autoharps if child lacks pincer grasp
- Restring guitars or ukeleles if necessary for child to strum with left hand and chord with right
- Tape holes on soprano recorders closed to allow children with missing fingers to play
- Tape or clamp small instruments to desks or music stands for children to strike
- Use magnetic tape to attach lightweight bells or other small instruments to metal surfaces
- Have one child hold an instrument while a partner with limited mobility strikes it
- Clip and tape paper to a clipboard for easier writing or drawing

Gifted and Talented

Children who are gifted (who show advanced, natural abilities, usually in the preschool years) or talented (who have a disposition toward something that they work hard to develop) are most likely to come to a music classroom without being previously identified for the music teacher as exceptional. Although some schools have separate self-contained classes for gifted and talented students, the music teacher will probably work with such children in the context of a heterogeneous group and will have to discover the gifts a child brings. It is rare that a program for gifted students will have screened for or recognized musical giftedness.

Generally, schools have used high IQ scores or achievement test scores as the single measure of giftedness. However, the federal definition of giftedness moves beyond intellectual giftedness to recognize advanced abilities in creativity, leadership, academics, and visual or performing arts. A focus on a broader view of intelligence has been supported by the theories of Guilford (1967) and Gardner (1983). Teachers who are aware of these more encompassing theories of intelligence are better prepared to recognize and build on the gifts each child may bring.

Because there is a range of ways of being gifted, it is difficult to create a single list that would apply to all children. However, gifted children usually are quick to relate ideas to each other (they are good conceptualizers); can acquire and manipulate symbol systems easily, including those used in the arts; and make good judgments and can see broader implications of ideas than most of the general population. Furthermore, creatively gifted children often suggest unusual solutions to questions, use their intuitive sense, and have a sense of humor.

Sometimes, these gifts make it difficult for children to work in class as they may become frustrated when the pace is slow, may dominate discussions, fight rules and regulations, use humor to manipulate, and be glib rather than thoughtful in their answers (Heward and Orlansky, 1992).

Although not all gifted students are musically gifted or talented, and not all elect to perform musically, much can be done to recognize the capacity of gifted children for accelerated learning.

If children show early musical gifts or talents:

✦ Encourage private lessons with competent teachers

✦ Introduce notation to them so they can use it as a tool for musical independence

✦ Give them opportunities for musical leadership in class: teaching other children, conducting

✦ Have computer programs available so they can advance on their own in music theory and composition

✦ Have synthesizer or Music Instrument Digital Interface (MIDI) hookups available so they can compose independently and print out their own music

✦ Make sure that school instrumental teachers are aware of their gifts, and help develop plans for careful articulation between the general music program and the instrumental program

If children are gifted in other ways:

✦ Provide activities that will allow them to expand their study of various musical ideas such as the study of a composer or a kind of music that interests them; encourage independent research activities resulting in reports

- Challenge them with small group and individual composition assignments such as those suggested in Chapter 11; have a range of instruments available for their use
- Create a classroom with learning centers where gifted children can work independently on a range of projects such as music listening and research, learning to play the electronic keyboard or the guitar, composing, playing musical games, using music software on the computer, and exploring the World Wide Web
- Bring in artists in residence or guests from the community to challenge children musically

The Joys of Reaching All Children

Working with exceptional children can be a rewarding experience for the music teacher. The keys to success are a willingness to learn, curiosity about how to be effective, clarity of communication with people who understand the needs and abilities of the children involved, and flexibility to change when something is not working.

Many resources are available to help teachers or parents who need more information on music therapy and music for children with special needs. Other resources include classes in mainstreaming and the resources of a range of people who are committed to helping children learn. Through collaboration and cooperation, both teachers and children will be enriched and challenged to grow.

Scenario

Ms. Smeltzer is an enthusiastic teacher who enjoys having a lot of activity in her music class. It is time for the third-grade class of Mr. Mayes to come to music. Ms. Smeltzer stands next to the door and greets each child as they move to their assigned seats in the rows she has created. She happily greets the five children in wheelchairs who are mainstreamed into this class from their resource room. Those children take their place in their own row at the back of the class.

The class begins by singing a familiar song and discussing the patterns in the melody. Children sing those patterns in isolation and shape them in the air with their hands and then with their heads. They go on to learn to play two different melodic ostinatos and a bourdon on the barred percussion instruments. She uses adaptive techniques to allow the children with limited mobility to play the bourdon. Those children are assisted by the teacher aides who accompanied them to the class.

At the end of the class, the children from Mr. Mayes class beg to play their favorite note name game in which groups identify names of patterns of notes that Ms. Smeltzer reveals and team captains race to the front to be the first to write the word those notes spell on the board. The children in wheelchairs observe from their row.

Questions

1. What did Ms. Smeltzer do that showed sensitivity to the needs of the mainstreamed children?

2. What teaching strategies did not take the needs of those children into consideration?

3. Based on what you have learned in this chapter, how would you change any or all of the following to make this classroom more inclusive?
   a. Seating
   b. Relation to other students
   c. Adaptation of materials
   d. Adaptation of procedures
   e. Adaptation of support
   f. Classroom atmosphere

REVIEW

1. Define the following terms: child study team, LRE, IEP, mainstreaming, at-risk, and inclusion.

2. Describe the role the music specialist should play in mainstreaming decisions for music.

3. What is the difference between a disability and a handicap?

4. The key to effective integration of exceptional children in music is adapting. List several dimensions of the learning situation the music teacher needs to think about adapting.

5. What levels of mental retardation is the music specialist likely to work with? What are some key ideas in adapting for the MR child?

CRITICAL THINKING

1. What would you say to the parents of a hearing-impaired child who ask to have their child excused from music because of their hearing loss?

2. How would you respond to the request of a special education teacher that your select elementary chorus include her developmentally delayed children?

3. Work with a partner to create an example of a handicapping condition in an elementary general music class. Describe a way to change that situation so it would not be handicapping.

4. What could you do to establish an environment where all students were responsive to the needs of exceptional students?

PROJECTS

1. Interview two elementary music specialists to determine how they work to integrate children with exceptional needs. Find how they learn about the unique talents and needs of those children.

2. Visit a music classroom where exceptional children participate either through mainstreaming or inclusion. Note ways in which the teacher is adapting for the children. Note how the children respond.

3. Visit a music classroom in which the teacher is working with self-contained children. Describe the children and their responses to music. Describe ways the teacher is working to meet the needs of the children.

4. Review one or more references in music therapy, mainstreaming, or inclusion in music. List additional suggestions for adapting for children in a category of exceptionality of particular interest to you.

5. Create music materials to use with children who are visually impaired.

6. Do some one-on-one teaching with a child in one of the categories of exceptionality discussed in this chapter. Experiment with different musical tasks to discover how to best reach this child. Describe in a written report what the child was and was not able to do. Describe how you adapted instruction to meet the needs of the child.

REFERENCES

Adamek, Mary S. (2001) Meeting special needs in music class. *Music Educators Journal,* 87(4), January, 23–26.

Alvin, J., and A. Warwick (1991). *Music therapy for the autistic child* (2nd ed.). Oxford, England: Oxford University.

Atterbury, B. W. (1990). *Mainstreaming exceptional learners in music.* Englewood Cliffs, NJ: Prentice-Hall.

Birkenshaw, L. (1977). *Music for fun, music for learning.* Toronto, Canada: Holt, Rinehart and Winston.

Bitcon, C. H. (1976). *Alike and different: The clinical and educational use of Orff-Schulwerk.* Santa Ana, CA: Rosha Press.

Edwards, E. (1974). *Music education for the deaf.* South Waterford, ME: Merriam-Eddy.

Gardner, H. (1983). *Frames of mind: The theory of multiple intelligence.* New York: Basic Books.

Graham, R. M., and A. Beer (1980). *Teaching music to the exceptional child.* Englewood Cliffs, NJ: Prentice-Hall.

Guilford, J. P. (1967). *The nature of human intelligence.* New York: McGraw-Hill.

Heward, W., and M. Orlansky (1992). *Exceptional children.* New York: Macmillan.

Jellison, J. A., and P. J. Flowers (1991). Talking about music: Interviews with disabled and nondisabled children. *Journal of Research in Music Education,* 39(4), 322–333.

Journal of Music Therapy. Official publication of the National Association for Music Therapy.

MENC (1986). *The school music program: Description and standards.* Reston, VA: Music Educators National Conference.

Michel, D. E. (1976). *Music therapy in special education.* New York: C. C. Thomas.

Music Educators Journal. Issues dedicated to special learners: April 1972; April 1982; February 1985; April 1990; January 2001.

17

Music in an Integrated Curriculum

M s. Luebke's general music class is alive, not only with sounds but with colors and designs, movement and dance, poetry and stories, and creative drama. Children often work in small groups to solve problems involving several art forms. Ms. Luebke is committed to integrating other arts into her music classroom. She believes that her role is to help children understand the nature of the arts, interpret and express ideas through them, and develop their aesthetic sensitivity.

Mr. Parker's music classes are busy practicing Sub-Saharan African songs and dances. With each new song or dance, the children learn something about the culture from which it came and the meaning it has for its people. The older children have just finished constructing African-style drums, two-toned bells, and rattles with the help of parents and a visiting artist from Nigeria. The artist will teach them some traditional drumming patterns. Mr. Parker works in a school where everyone is immersed in the study of Africa for nine weeks. At the end of that time, the children, teachers, and parents come together for an evening of Sub-Saharan African food, culture, and festivities, where children share what they have learned and African guest artists perform with them.

Ms. Steinhurst met with the primary teachers to determine what the children are learning in science during their study of insects. The children created chants, movement patterns, and instrumental accompaniments in music class to describe their insects. Each class selected one insect to represent at a program for their parents. Ms. Steinhurst is helping them create

Children playing African stick-passing game

Jerry Gay

original songs with accompanying movements for that program. Insect sounds, habits, and motions have been carefully observed and are reflected in the music. Children are creating a story line that places these insects in a larger environment.

Ms. Steinhurst has a double degree in art and music. In her role as art teacher, she uses simple materials such as paper sacks, construction paper, cardboard tubes, and tinfoil to help the children design and create their costumes. They are looking through books of insects for design details, which are reflected in their costumes.

Each of these teachers was hired to teach music, and each has gone beyond the boundaries of what has traditionally been taught in the elementary general music curriculum. Yet, in each instance, children are developing important musical understandings and skills. Ms. Luebke and Mr. Parker are committed to helping to integrate music across various areas of the curriculum. They know that they cannot do this with every aspect of the school curriculum throughout the school year. At the same time, they realize that it is very important to incorporate music into a broader whole. It helps to weave music into the fabric of all school life, rather than isolating it from other subjects to periods of once or twice a week.

Ms. Steinhurst teaches in a school where the entire curriculum is integrated and the arts are at the core. The classroom teachers, who lack deep training in the arts, tend to begin with activities, then introduce content. The fact that Ms. Steinhurst has training in both music and art helps to ensure that significant artistic growth will occur in the students.

Challenges of Integrating the Curriculum

Trends that call for the integration of the arts across the entire curriculum have sometimes caught music teachers by surprise and left them defensive. Music teachers become understandably distressed when a classroom teacher suddenly wants them to suspend the music curriculum to teach frog songs, because her class has begun a frog unit in science. It is important that music specialists and classroom teachers communicate early in the school year about issues of curriculum coordination and integration, so that mutually beneficial goals can be established.

Models for integrating the curriculum vary, but key to all of them is that true integration respects the integrity and uniqueness of each of the disciplines to be combined. The integrated curriculum seeks to relate fragmented learning experiences, by planning that combines the significant curricular goals in music and the arts with the other curricular areas. This might be conceived of as co-curricular education. (See resources for planning listed under general references.)

Singing a song about frogs is not music education, even though it may be a delightful way to enhance learning about frogs. If the classroom teacher wants frog songs, the music specialist can provide those resources for the teacher, who can incorporate them as he or she wishes. However, without prior planning, the music specialist should not be expected to interrupt his or her planned curriculum.

Given the opportunity for prior planning, the music specialist may find that the first-grade frog unit coincides with work she is doing on pitch motion, including melodic leaps. She also sees ways that working with poetry about frogs would help her further develop planned rhythm work, as well as reinforcing the concepts of ostinato and motive. As the classroom teacher communicates some of the vocabulary and concepts the children will be learning about frogs, including the life cycle of the frog, the music specialist sees that she could use the stages of the life cycle as a basis for creative movement and composition, further expanding children's awareness of form. Careful planning and communication among teachers can enhance and integrate the curriculum and bring greater meaning to all that the children do. Books by Drake (1993) and Jacobs (1989a, 1989b) help to give insight into principles and structures for planning the integrated curriculum.

Goldberg (2001) notes that, in spite of the challenges, efforts to provide artistically rich environments for children have many benefits. In a multicultural society where many children do not speak English, the arts provide other forms of literacy that are accessible to all. Such classrooms focus on the development of multiliteracies. Children learn with music by studying and performing existing works and connecting them to other curricular areas, and through music by using creative processes in music to demonstrate learning across the curriculum.

Integrating Other Arts into the Music Curriculum

Music specialists are frequently the only arts specialists hired at the elementary level. In that role, they are often called on to be an advocate for all the arts and to bring a broader awareness of the arts to the children with whom they work. Many teachers have responded with excitement to the opportunity to help create aesthetic literacy through their program. However, this can be a challenge to specialists who may have had strong training as musicians but minimal training in the other arts. Numerous workshops are available for all teachers in creative movement, visual arts, literary arts, and creative dramatics that can help to expand skills and understandings about those forms. Orff-Schulwerk training can be helpful in developing skills for using language and movement in the music curriculum. University courses in aesthetics and interrelated arts are rich sources, as are programs for teachers through museums and other community arts organizations.

Each art form is unique. Visual arts, dance, theater, music, literature, and media arts each have their own language, expressive medium, set of symbols, and technical demands. Yet the arts are deeply connected because they all (1) challenge people to grow aesthetically; (2) are languages of the emotions, mind, and spirit; and (3) embody meaning far beyond what humans can express with words or numbers. In working with multiple arts, teachers need to be sensitive to the commonalities between the arts and to the things that make each unique or different. (See resources for various art forms listed under specific art forms references.)

Interdisciplinary Curriculum in the Arts

Common links among the arts can be found in such aesthetic principles as tension and release, repetition and contrast, pattern, motive, theme and variation, balance, foreground and background, and density. Teachers can enhance children's awareness of how these principles work in various arts by bringing in illustrative examples from different art forms and comparing them. Although the generative impulse may be music, this could be thought of as an interdisciplinary curriculum that focuses on the understanding of broad aesthetic principles. Many disciplines are viewed in terms of a broader set of ideas.

To teach the principle of repetition, the teacher could help children notice it as a forming device in nature, a song or instrumental work, a poem, a painting, and a dance. Discuss the impact of the use of repetition. (It creates a sense of rhythm, fulfills expectations, creates unity, and, taken to an extreme, it could be boring.) Have the children create their own short composition that uses repetition as the main structural device. These activities not only teach music, but also expand children's awareness of a concept that permeates all the arts as well as life.

National Standard 8 asks that music teachers help children to understand relationships among music, the other arts, and disciplines outside the arts. The publication *What Every Young American Should Know and Be Able to Do in the Arts* (MENC, 1994) provides a helpful guide for standards in all of the arts. This can be particularly helpful in finding significant ways to integrate significant content from the various art forms.

Shared Curriculum in the Arts

Another means by which teachers can stimulate the development of children's broader understanding and skills in the arts is to find ways in which aspects of other arts intersect with music. The intersected or shared curriculum attempts to find areas in which two content areas overlap (see Figure 17.1). There are many ways in which an individual teacher can plan lessons and activities that readily accomplish multiple objectives in the arts. The following ideas may help to stimulate thinking about some of those possibilities.

Creative Movement and Dance

The art form that is probably the most analogous to music is dance. They are both arts that unfold through time and occupy space, either acoustic or physical. Music teachers frequently use creative movement and dance to get children physically involved with the music. At the same time, they often miss opportunities to help children to grow in their consciousness and skills as dancers in the process. Box 17.1 outlines the elements of dance. Dance is a language, similar to that of music but different because the expressive medium is the body, not sound. Through capturing the language of dance and incorporating it in the music curriculum, teachers can do a great deal to build and reinforce dance concepts, helping children to express themselves more creatively through movement.

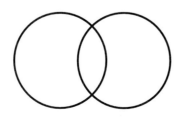

FIGURE 17.1

The Shared Curriculum Design

Two subjects come together and common understandings are developed.

Box 17.1 *Elements of Dance*

Time
    Tempo: fast, medium, slow, stillness
    Duration: long, short
    Beat: steady, even
    Accent: stressing a beat
    Rhythm: patterns of different durations

Flow
    Sustained: smooth, flowing, connected
    Percussive: jerky, segmented
    Vibratory: shaking, swinging

Space
    Personal
      Size: large, small, wide, narrow
      Nonlocomotor movements: stretch, shake, twist, curl, bend
      Force field: protective bubble that surrounds you so you do not bump other things or people
    General space
      Directions: up or down, front or back, right or left, diagonal
      Pathways: curved, straight, angular
      Locomotor: walk, run, leap, skip, hop, jump, slide, crawl, scoot

Force
    Strong or gentle

Shape
    Individual: curved, straight, twisted, balanced, symmetrical, asymmetrical
    Group: lines, clumps, touching, not touching, balanced
    Thematic: animal, sports, emotions

This can often be done by asking open-ended questions using music as the stimulus:

1. "How many ways can you show me a high motion? A low motion? Switch from one to another as you hear the pitches on the bells change from high to low."

2. "When you hear the drum, move across the room in a curved pathway to the rhythm I play. Change levels as you move."

3. "Work in personal space to shape the phrases of this music. Start with one body part and gradually add others until your whole body is involved."

4. "Listen to the suspended cymbal as I strike it once. Be ready to describe the sound." (Model and discuss.) "Show with your body the energy at the beginning of that sound, and keep your body moving

until you can no longer hear the sound. Think of how you will move as the sound dies out." (Repeat the same process with various instruments of contrasting timbre. Play them in a series and have children shift movements in response to the sounds.)

5. "Work with a partner to interpret the contrasting sections of an AB form piece. Decide which of you is A and which is B. Face each other and act as a mirror of your partner. During the A section, partner A gets to lead while B imitates. Try to stay within the style of the music. When the B section occurs, switch leaders."

6. "Work in a group of three to show meter in threes. Plan your movements so that the accented beat is a strong, sharp motion."

7. "Move around the room to the beat, showing the accent in different parts of your body." (Play strong beat music where the accent is on four. Have them show that accent in their head, shoulders, elbows, hips, knees, and so on.)

```
1   2   3   4   1   2   3   4
        >               >
```

Each of these movement strategies helps children to extend a musical concept, gain coordination skills with music, and apply various movement concepts.

The possibilities are endless. If these ways of thinking and moving are instilled in young children, they will be eager to choreograph music in the intermediate grades, showing great ability to connect what is happening in the music with what their bodies can do. Many superb resources connect dance and creative movement with music, and they are referred to at the end of this chapter under specific art forms.

Visual Arts

The visual arts are more removed from music in terms of analogous concepts. Although some of the terms are the same, their meaning is very different, because the visual arts function in space, not time. Box 17.2 highlights the basic elements.

The visual arts can be combined authentically with music in a variety of ways. The following suggestions may serve as a stimulus for further possibilities.

1. Give each child a long, narrow strip of paper. Discuss various types of lines (straight, broken, curved, angular, thick, thin, and so on). Have children draw a line composition moving from left to right across the strip. Each person must use at least three different types of line. Have them interpret the lines vocally, using pitched sounds, or instrumentally on pitched percussion instruments. Extend that by having the children work in groups, combining patterns vertically or horizontally and interpreting them through movement as well as through sound.

Jerry Gay

2. Use lines, shapes, colors, and patterns to illustrate different musical events as they occur in absolute or nonreferential music. For example, listen to a Bach two-part invention. Use different colored lines to show the shape of melodies in the two lines in the invention. Use the same patterns to show where imitation occurs. View art prints based on interwoven patterns. Discuss similarities and differences between those and what the students have drawn.

3. Use art prints from various periods and cultures (often available through school art docent programs or art specialists) to introduce children to stylistic characteristics that are reflected in both art and music. Discuss the commonalities. For example, compare Monet's *Water Lilies* to Debussy's *La Mer.* Discuss the blurring of lines, muted colors, and reflected light of the Monet and the shimmering, dreamy, blurred quality of the Debussy. Experiment with making an

Box 17.2 *Elements of the Visual Arts*

Shape

Square, rectangle, triangle, circle. Created by line and color. Can form pattern creating a rhythm and design.

Color

Red, green, yellow, and so on. It creates intensity and contrast. It gives light.

Texture

Smooth, rough, soft, hard. It is the feel of the work when touched. It can be created by building up layers, carving into, or weaving.

Line

Straight, curvy, zigzag, thin, thick, broken, connected, soft, loud, echoing, parallel. Lines make patterns, designs, shapes, objects.

Space

Negative, positive. Created by placement of shapes.

---

impressionist-style painting using various water color techniques. Tie that in with listening to other impressionist music such as *Nuages* by Debussy. Challenge the children to think of what the clouds might look like. What in the music suggests that?

4. From a range of art prints, have children select the style that most closely matches the style of a piece of music they are listening to. Have them justify their choices.

5. Play works of music that have been stimulated by artworks such as the various movements of *Pictures at an Exhibition* by Mussorgsky or *The Twittering Machine* by Gunther Schuller. Bring in prints of the works that inspired the compositions such as *The Hut of Baba Yaga* from *Pictures* or *The Twittering Machine* by Paul Klee. Discuss the connections among the works. Have children create their own musical compositions using an artwork as a stimulus. (See Kuzniar, 1999.)

6. Use art prints as a stimulus for learning pieces of music, helping to put the music more firmly in a time or place, such as the painting *George Washington* by Gilbert Stuart in combination with the song "Yankee Doodle." This could be expanded to works featuring Jefferson in combination with Mozart.

7. Use program music as a stimulus for painting, drawing, or puppetry. Have children develop their own puppets to dramatize works that tell stories such as *William Tell* or *The Nutcracker*. Help children demonstrate a sense of style in their work. Build art concepts of balance, design, color, and line into the creation of the works. Art skills and techniques can also be incorporated and reinforced. (For example, use the tip or the side of an oil pastel crayon for different

Students connecting styles of art to recorded music

Jerry Gay

effects; place two colors next to each other and blend with a tissue; cut out a shape from another piece of paper and use it as a stencil, flaring the color outward from the edges of the paper.)

Try to avoid nebulous assignments connecting visual arts and music such as "draw the music." The results of such experiences are rarely artistic in any sense, although they may be useful in helping children to represent musical events as suggested in Chapter 8 on listening. Such activities are not arts integration.

Literature and Poetry

As with movement and music, a close relation exists between the literary arts and music. When performed, both are arts of time and sound. Words have many musical elements such as rhythm, pitch, and accent. Ono-matopoeic words (splash, rickety-rackety, and so on) suggest sounds that can be interpreted musically. Both music and language can be used to create imagery. Music can be used to tell stories in an abstract sense, such as *The Little Train of the Capiera* by Villa Lobos or, combined with words, tell an actual story, such as *Peter and the Wolf* by Prokofiev. The combination of poetry with music often results in song. Sensitivity to the elements of the literary arts—phanopoeia or imagery; melopoeia or music; and logopoeia or content, story, and meaning—can be developed within the music classroom, often more readily than in other settings. Children should be encouraged to notice how words and music connect, and be stimulated to combine them through their own creative explorations.

1. Use fine, already existing, children's literature to connect students with music. Many beautiful books exist that (1) illustrate folk, patriotic, and children's songs; (2) tell the stories behind works of program music, ballets, or operas; (3) tell the stories of various composers and musicians; and (4) set the cultural context for various songs or listening experiences. School librarians are eager to assist in

finding children's literature that can enhance their musical experience. Such books can become the stimulus for children's own creative writing or for further research and understanding (Lamme, 1990).

2. Books, stories, and poetry can be used as a stimulus for musical composition. Wordless books and familiar fairy tales can be told through sounds instead of words or through a combination of sounds and words. For example, *Goldilocks and the Three Bears* can easily be transformed to themes in various registers of the keyboard for the characters. Maurice Sendak's *Where the Wild Things Are* lends itself to orchestration, movement, and drama. Literature from various cultures can be set to music using the instrumental sounds, rhythms, and scales of those cultures.

3. Children can generate banks of descriptive words in response to recorded music, then use them to write stories or poetry in various forms to describe the music. The poems might include the title of the music and the name of the composer.

4. Children can write poetry, then set it to music, with or without melodies. Poetic forms that emerge from a specific culture should be written to respect the tradition. For example, haiku from Japan is always about nature; is set in a particular season; describes where, what, and when; is mysterious; and has a syllabic structure of 5–7–5. A musical setting for a haiku can also reflect Japanese music: pentatonic; flowing; bent pitches; no beat; rhythms that punctuate; no harmony; and use of flute, drums, sticks, plucked strings.

5. Children can listen to music designed to tell a story and write their own imagined story based on the music.

6. Children can set existing poetry or literature that uses onomatopoeic sounds or particularly strong imagery to music. (Encourage them to move beyond sound effects by creating a musical setting for the words.) Work with expressive use of the voice in speaking the poem; try single and combined voices for different effects.

Katz and Thomas (1992) suggest a range of ideas for combining literature and poetry with music and movement.

Creative Drama and Theater

Elements of creative drama and theater can readily be developed and incorporated into the music classroom. Skills such as the development of focus, concentration, facial and body movements, and respect for space can be incorporated into any music lesson involving characterization. Many of those skills are common to those developed in creative movement.

Teachers can also help children become sensitive to other elements of a drama or story line.

1. Setting: where the drama takes place and the mood of the place
2. Characters: who is involved and how do they relate to each other

3. Action: what is happening including plot and tension and why are the events happening, the motivation of the characters

4. Theme: what is the main idea being communicated

5. Dialogue: what are the verbal and gestural communications

6. Spectacle: what is needed in terms of costumes, props, lights, music, sounds, or scenery

Many of these ideas can be incorporated into any dramatization. The elements of dialogue and spectacle will not be needed as frequently, and they only have to be used if a formal production is developed.

1. Sing songs that describe characters or tell stories including story songs from various cultures. Discuss the characters, their motivations, and actions. Experiment with various ways of creating character and conveying the dramatic action of the song. Work with concentration and focus. Try to avoid stereotypical responses. Encourage all children to experiment with each character. (Avoid assigning roles and creating a star system.)

2. Learn the stories of various programmatic works or operas. (*The Metropolitan Opera Boxes,* available through New York's Metropolitan Opera Education Program, are useful for introducing children to opera as a form.) Listen to the music and discuss how it helps to heighten the experience of the drama or tell the story. What musical devices are used? Experiment with ways to tell the story with action using mime or dialogue, characterization, and, perhaps, simple props. Puppetry could be used instead of people.

3. Using a familiar children's story, create an opera, singing the dialogue, and adding other music to be created as necessary, as well as dramatic action, to tell the story. Music teachers may want to collaborate with classroom teachers to have a class write their own opera, creating the script in class and working with the music teacher on the musical aspects. (Regional training for doing this type of work is available for teams of classroom teachers and music teachers through the Metropolitan Opera in the summers.)

4. Create a musical around a theme such as U.S. history. Incorporate traditional folk songs and dances learned throughout the year. Ask children to write a story line to tie together the different aspects. Incorporate all the elements of drama in realizing the musical. Share it with others.

Integrating Music and the Arts throughout the Curriculum

In most cultures, music and the other arts are not separate from daily living. People sing to accompany their work, participate in rituals in which the arts

*Children's opera
production of
Hansel and Gretel*

are central, and surround themselves with decorative images on clothing and in their homes. In Western cultures, the arts are often removed from daily living, relegated to the role of entertainment, and turned over to the talented few who are the designated artists. Many people are even afraid to decorate their own homes, leaving that task to a hired interior decorator.

In the early childhood years, children do not separate the arts from life. They sing and dance spontaneously, eagerly experiment with crayons and paper without fear of judgment, and often create highly imaginative metaphors to verbally describe their world. Trends to integrate the arts across the curriculum throughout the elementary years hold much promise for returning children to a sense of a holistic culture, informed by expressive possibilities and alive with the arts at the center.

The role of the music specialist in such a setting is expanded beyond that of direct instruction with children. The specialist needs to assume the role of collaborator with other teachers to help create an artistically rich environment. This role demands time for careful planning and sensitivity to the uniqueness of the individual arts and to the roles they can play. An effective project takes about twenty hours for a team to plan.

The specialist may also become a resource person, directing teachers and students to key musical, library, and community resources, including visiting artists. Classroom teachers and administrators need to recognize that the music specialist also has a music curriculum with its own scope and sequence to teach. Support needs to be given for planning time and thoughtful communication to occur.

Models of Integration

The Thematic Web Design

Many models exist for integrating the curriculum. The most commonly used at the elementary level is the thematic web design (see Figure 17.2). It strives to build important understandings and skills in all areas of the curriculum. The arts activities help to reinforce learning in other areas of the curriculum but also help children to develop or reinforce important skills and understandings in each of the arts disciplines. The arts are approached with depth or integrity, not superficially. This multidisciplinary approach could be taught by one teacher or by several teachers (see Lesson 17.1).

FIGURE 17.2

Webbed Curriculum Design

An examination of the web shows that children are involved in significant content in each area of the curriculum. The individual subjects keep their boundaries, but the webbed relationships feed a metaunderstanding.

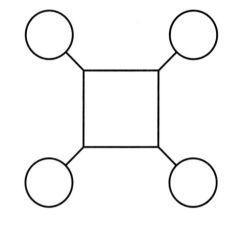

The Threaded Curriculum

A model similar to the webbed curriculum is the threaded curriculum (see Figure 17.3). In this curriculum, children may start with a particular theme or idea and then explore it in a sequential or linear fashion through several disciplines or through multiple intelligences as proposed by Gardner (1983).

In the latter approach, the teacher might introduce a topic such as geologic eras. The children receive input from a variety of sources, then proceed through stations in which they do further research as well as synthesis activities using the various intelligences. The thread is the large theme or

FIGURE 17.3

Threaded Curriculum Design

The thread is the large theme or concept. Each station allows the child to experience the concept through a different intelligence.

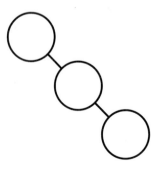

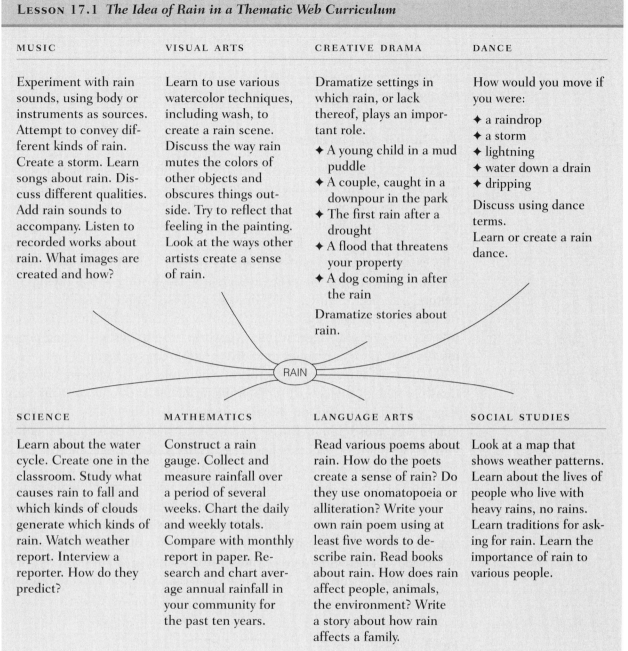

MUSIC

Experiment with rain sounds, using body or instruments as sources. Attempt to convey different kinds of rain. Create a storm. Learn songs about rain. Discuss different qualities. Add rain sounds to accompany. Listen to recorded works about rain. What images are created and how?

VISUAL ARTS

Learn to use various watercolor techniques, including wash, to create a rain scene. Discuss the way rain mutes the colors of other objects and obscures things outside. Try to reflect that feeling in the painting. Look at the ways other artists create a sense of rain.

CREATIVE DRAMA

Dramatize settings in which rain, or lack thereof, plays an important role.

◆ A young child in a mud puddle
◆ A couple, caught in a downpour in the park
◆ The first rain after a drought
◆ A flood that threatens your property
◆ A dog coming in after the rain

Dramatize stories about rain.

DANCE

How would you move if you were:

◆ a raindrop
◆ a storm
◆ lightning
◆ water down a drain
◆ dripping

Discuss using dance terms.
Learn or create a rain dance.

RAIN

SCIENCE

Learn about the water cycle. Create one in the classroom. Study what causes rain to fall and which kinds of clouds generate which kinds of rain. Watch weather report. Interview a reporter. How do they predict?

MATHEMATICS

Construct a rain gauge. Collect and measure rainfall over a period of several weeks. Chart the daily and weekly totals. Compare with monthly report in paper. Research and chart average annual rainfall in your community for the past ten years.

LANGUAGE ARTS

Read various poems about rain. How do the poets create a sense of rain? Do they use onomatopoeia or alliteration? Write your own rain poem using at least five words to describe rain. Read books about rain. How does rain affect people, animals, the environment? Write a story about how rain affects a family.

SOCIAL STUDIES

Look at a map that shows weather patterns. Learn about the lives of people who live with heavy rains, no rains. Learn traditions for asking for rain. Learn the importance of rain to various people.

concept; each station allows children to experience through a different intelligence (Campbell, Campbell, and Dickinson, 1992; and Lazear, 1991).

Sometimes the arts experiences in this model are merely that—experiences. A strategy calling only for the creation of a geologic rap in the music station may result in a demonstration of some of the understandings of geology but may not help the children to grow musically. Teachers wishing to stimulate musical growth need to help children understand that a rap is more than a rhythmic chant. It commonly uses (1) forced rhyme and punctuated words, chanted in rhythm by a single voice; (2) a synthesized pulse and layered rhythmic framework as an accompaniment; (3) two-part form with other voices entering on the chorus; and (4) scratched segments from other music that are layered in to reinforce the theme, usually focused on social protest. Some raps are more effective than others; for example, they have better lyrics and rhymes and are more congruence between chant and accompaniment. Students need to develop a sense of what those qualities are and learn to assess their own raps in aesthetic terms.

The Immersed Curriculum

Perhaps the most difficult curriculum to create is the truly integrated one, because it is largely motivated by a child's interests. This is a curriculum in which children immerse themselves completely in a topic of study or area of interest that they examine from all points of view. Ideas and resources are networked, and the boundaries between subjects are blurred or eliminated. This experience is analogous to living in another culture and having an opportunity to learn the language, understand the history and contemporary culture, interpret the arts, communicate with indigenous people, and experience the geography and ecology. There is no separation among subjects; they all are part of a larger whole. Networks are established among people interested in the same things and ideas are shared (see Figure 17.4).

The truly integrated curriculum helps children to perceive new relationships among subjects through problem solving and to identify life problems, social issues, and individual concerns they wish to address through a kind of metacurriculum. In this curriculum, both affective and cognitive growth is enhanced, and this synthesis occurs in individuals and the group as they derive personal and shared meaning from their experiences.

An example of this curriculum would be when young children explore a curiosity about insects by observing their behavior, counting them, drawing them in ways to reflect their patterns and designs, studying insect biology and habitat, and sharing discoveries with others. Gallas (1991) describes a classroom where children are watching a butterfly trying to emerge from its chrysalis. While one child sketches the process, another

FIGURE 17.4

Immersed and Networked Curriculum

Children immerse themselves completely in a topic of study or area of interest and examine it from all points of view. The boundaries between subjects blur or disappear through a networking of ideas, and resources are networked.

says, "I'll sing him out." Teachers in this setting become facilitators and sources of ideas and information. Depending on the topic, the arts may or may not be directly linked. Teachers in such settings are dedicated, however, to finding ways to help children pursue their ideas through one or more art forms. Such settings respect children's innate capacity for representing their worlds through images, poetry, dance, drama, and music (see Gallas, 1994).

Creating Valid Connections

Perhaps the biggest challenge to using the arts with integrity throughout the curriculum is teachers' surface understanding of the nature of the arts. Yet, thoughtful integration by people who are relatively inexperienced in the arts can happen, provided they are willing to ask the question, "How are children growing artistically by doing this activity?" Music and arts specialists, other teachers, and artists in residence can often be a source of answers for the teacher new to arts integration. Regretfully, many, if not most, of the commercially available materials on the integrated curriculum fail to reflect understanding of the arts as disciplines.

A remarkable exception to these types of materials can be found in the book by Barrett, McCoy, and Veblen (1997) called *Sound Ways of Knowing*. In this book, the authors develop a model of viewing the arts in the interdisciplinary curriculum as if looking through facets in a jewel. In the center of the model is the name of the artwork. In each facet of viewing the artwork teachers ask one of the following questions.

1. Who created it?

2. When and where was it created?

3. Why and for whom was it created?

4. What does it sound or look like?

5. What kind of structure or form does it have?

6. What is its subject?

7. What is being expressed?

8. What techniques did its creator use to help people understand what is being expressed? (p. 77)

The answers to these questions lead naturally to integrating history, culture, other arts and other disciplines.

The following ideas may serve as models for setting goals to achieve artistic growth in combination with goals in other curricular areas. Most of the ideas are examples of integration with subjects coequal, but some represent infusion where an arts activity is used to get at a learning in another area of the curriculum. (See resources for additional ideas listed under arts across the curriculum references.)

Integrating the Arts Process

Regardless of the context in which the arts are integrated, it is helpful to use the arts process as a reminder of ways they can be incorporated without violating their integrity as unique disciplines (Fowler, 1974). Any one mode or a combination of modes from the arts process can be consciously integrated with other aspects of the curriculum. The following modes are central to every art form.

Perceiving (noticing and thinking)—to listen perceptively to music or poetry, to notice patterns of repetition and contrast, to visually discover the use of line in a painting

Responding (discussing, feeling, and producing)—to identify, describe, and discuss what one notices in an artwork; to express how an artwork affects personal mood and thought and connect that with aspects of the work itself; to perform an already existing work in an expressive and stylistically authentic manner

Skills Development (learning to manipulate the materials and processes of the various arts disciplines)—to learn to sing in tune, then with expression, then in harmony; to learn various techniques of working with clay such as coil technique, building, throwing; to develop a range of skills in creative movement involving control of the body in time and space with force and flow

Evaluating (assessing and critiquing)—to grow in the ability to assess one's own and others' works based on their technical, formal, aesthetic, and expressive qualities

Understanding (forming concepts of elements, structures, history, and culture)—to understand pitch, rhythm, melody, harmony, tone color in music; to understand how patterns in music are used to create form; to understand the relationship between a piece of music and the culture and time in which it was created

Creating (generating original ideas and products)—to improvise an eight-beat rhythm pattern; draw a picture that incorporates three different kinds of line

The Arts in Social Studies

Combining the arts with social studies creates natural connections, because so much of what is known and understood about culture comes through the arts. Studying the arts of a culture can help people to understand:

1. What that culture values
2. What makes that culture unique
3. What resources were (are) available to that culture
4. How that culture has changed
5. How that culture is like other cultures

6. What expressive forms and symbols typify that time, culture, and region

In addition, the arts can help people understand individuals within cultures. As a person's stories, poems, diaries, songs, performances, and arts or crafts are examined, others come to know that person in a way that would not be possible if they relied only on others' memories. As the curriculum moves toward an emphasis on helping children to understand and document their own stories and the stories of others, the arts can serve as rich resources for study and expression. National Standard 9 addresses the importance of understanding music in relation to history and culture.

Box 17.3 lists some of the art forms that might be (1) enjoyed and examined for their artistic qualities; (2) performed or replicated with sensitivity to style and technique; (3) studied in terms of their cultural purpose, practice, and value; or (4) studied within their historical context.

Lesson 17.2 presents a series of ideas for integrating the arts into the study of Northwest Coastal Indian Cultures. The left-hand column shows the use of the arts as activities. Ideas in the right-hand column represent a more holistic approach, placing the arts within the cultural context and having children create arts with sensitivity to artistic style and processes from that culture.

Box 17.3 *Forms and Resources of the Arts*

Visual Arts
- Painting
- Sculpture
- Drawing
- Weaving and textiles
- Carving
- Printing
- Calligraphy
- Jewelry
- Costumes and clothing
- Puppets
- Masks
- Pottery
- Decorative arts
- Architecture
- Landscape design
- Interior design

Music
- Folk music
- Art music
- Popular music
- Sacred and ritual music
- Instruments

Drama
- Theater
- Puppetry
- Mime

Literature
- Stories and folk tales
- Poetry
- Plays
- Graffiti

Dance
- Folk dance
- Ceremonial dance and drama
- Dance as pure art form

Media
- Photography
- Video and film
- Laser art
- Computer art
- Mixed media

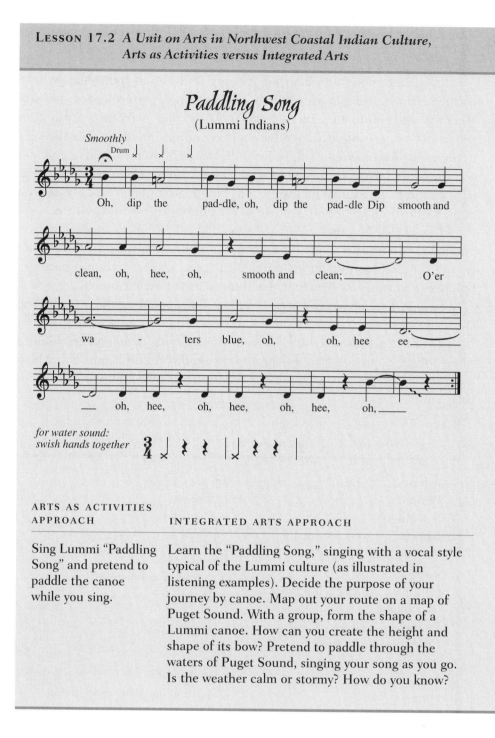

Paddling Song
(Lummi Indians)

Smoothly

Oh, dip the pad-dle, oh, dip the pad-dle Dip smooth and

clean, oh, hee, oh, smooth and clean; _____ O'er

wa - ters blue, oh, oh, hee ee _____

_____ oh, hee, oh, hee, oh, hee, oh, _____

for water sound:
swish hands together

ARTS AS ACTIVITIES APPROACH	INTEGRATED ARTS APPROACH
Sing Lummi "Paddling Song" and pretend to paddle the canoe while you sing.	Learn the "Paddling Song," singing with a vocal style typical of the Lummi culture (as illustrated in listening examples). Decide the purpose of your journey by canoe. Map out your route on a map of Puget Sound. With a group, form the shape of a Lummi canoe. How can you create the height and shape of its bow? Pretend to paddle through the waters of Puget Sound, singing your song as you go. Is the weather calm or stormy? How do you know?

The Arts in Science and Math

Science and math are more remote than social studies for integration of the arts, but some topics provide common ground.

1. Music is made up of scales that are tuned according to frequencies, which are expressed in cents and measurable by electronic tuners.

ARTS AS ACTIVITIES APPROACH	INTEGRATED ARTS APPROACH
	(It is calm because the song glides along smoothly.) Keep your paddles synchronized to the beat. When you get to your destination, show through movement or drama where you were going and what your purpose was.
Read and discuss the legend of how Mt. Rainier came to be.	Discuss the purpose of legends. How does this legend differ from scientific knowledge of how Mt. Rainier came to be? Research the meaning Mt. Rainier holds for the native peoples. Learn to tell the legend in a dramatic style that conveys some of that sacred meaning. Accompany the telling with motions and the sounds of drums and rattles. Later, write your own legend about how a landmark in your community came to be.
Color in the images on a predrawn totem. Cut out the totem and paste it onto a milk carton.	Study various totems and the images on them. Learn what each figure means. Learn why each totem is unique. Notice common aspects of each image: bold, symmetrical, curved lines; shapes are outlined; uses dyes of red, black, and white. Why was cedar used to make the totems? Design a totem for your family or school, selecting images that have symbolic meaning for them. Use images in the style of traditional totems. Carve your totem out of foam, adding colors when you finish. Or, for a school totem, hire a native carver to instruct the children and all design and carve a totem for your school.
Learn a salmon dance and accompany it with drums and shakers.	Research different kinds of dances used and occasions on which they were used. View videos of the dances and ceremonies attached. Note the style of the dancing and the instruments used to accompany them. What makes a salmon dance different from other dances? Construct some of the instruments, decorate them, and play them to accompany dancing.

Children can experiment with using a synthesizer to tune intervals to scales found in different cultures.

2. Children of all ages can discover various principles of the science of sounds such as vibration, amplification, and the relationship of the length of the vibrating surface to the pitch of the sound. Children can experiment with creating their own instruments or use standard instruments to illustrate some of these principles.

3. Equations in math represent symmetrical balance, a principle found in the visual arts.

4. Persian rugs are created with symmetrical patterns based on numerical principles. Students can create their own visual artworks using numbers represented by colors and shapes to create designs.

5. Basic geometric shapes underlie math as well as the visual arts. Children can work to combine shapes to create art. Those shapes can also be represented by individuals or groups in dance movements. Shapes can be used to represent musical forms (AB, ABA, ABACA).

6. Students can number each tone of the scale (twelve-tone or diatonic) and then play with random orders of those numbers in lines, playing them forward, backward (retrograde), upside down (inversion), and any combination thereof. They can also stretch the length of the sounds by doubling them (augmentation) or cut them in half (diminution).

7. Nature consists of patterns. Mathematics describes those in one way, science in another. Use various patterns in nature as a stimulus for composition (see Chapter 11 for suggestions).

8. As with any thematic approach to the integrated curriculum, the arts and arts processes can be integrated in authentic ways with topics that arise from science or math. An example would be a focus on the topic of whales. Children could create their own whales with cloth or paper, showing sensitivity to size, shape, and design. They could listen to any number of recorded works inspired by whales and note how the composers responded musically to whale sounds. They could learn how whales use sounds or songs to communicate, and they could create their own whale-inspired composition. They could move like whales as they migrate or feed. They could sing whaling songs and research their origin, the routes the whaling ships took, and the lives of the sailors. They could learn the hornpipe and other dances and learn to carve scrimshaw out of soap after learning how these activities reflected the life, interests, and culture of the sailors.

The Arts and Language Arts

Although the word *arts* is included in the term *language arts*, much of language arts teaching has focused on the learning of the low-level skills of reading, grammar, punctuation, printing and writing, and spelling.

Approaches to language arts instruction, such as whole language, focus on a generative approach to language learning, where the desire to learn grows out of an experiential base. The arts can provide rich experiences to stimulate language usage and to motivate children to want to read, spell, write, and speak. Many ideas have already been suggested earlier in this chapter under the topics of literary and dramatic arts. The following ideas offer other possibilities.

1. Have kindergarten and first grade children learn to read books that contain the words and illustrations of songs they already know.

2. Have primary school-aged children create books, including shape books of their favorite songs with their own illustrations. (A shape book for "Twinkle, Twinkle, Little Star" would be in the shape of a star.) Have older elementary children create illustrated books featuring familiar songs to share with a young child.

3. Have children practice spelling in rhythm, adding body percussion for accompaniment. Make chants or ostinati out of spelling words. Layer them or group them according to themes. Chant words in relation to the beat and determine how many sounds occur for each word. Notate rhythm patterns to fit the syllables of various words. Chant them and play them on instruments.

4. Punctuate sentences using different vocal sounds for each type of punctuation mark. (Victor Borge was a master at this.)

5. Learn to spell words that are introduced in music or other arts classes. Use them in writing.

6. Listen to recorded music and develop a word bank with young children, or a personal web of words with older children, which are stimulated by the music. Use those words to write a poem or story about the music. Play the music as many times as necessary to stimulate the writing. Play the music as you read the poem or story to others.

7. Read books about the lives of famous composers or musicians. Listen to some of their music. Develop a story or illustrated book about some of that music. Or, write a play about the composer's life, incorporating some of the music performed by classmates or played on recordings.

8. Write the lyrics for a song or work with the class to write the lyrics for a class song. Invite a music teacher or composer in residence to help with the melody.

Again, the possibilities are endless. All that is required is a teacher who is willing to think and act creatively.

Reflections on the Integrated Curriculum

An array of models exists for achieving curriculum integration. In selecting the most useful for a particular situation, teachers need to consider (1) time, (2) focus, (3) expertise, (4) support materials, (5) cooperation, and

(6) assessment. If the model chosen relies on several people, including arts specialists, can all of them be counted on to help? If team teaching is required, will those people work well together? Will schedules be flexible enough to accommodate the sharing of classes and the needed planning time? If an artist in residence is to be part of the team, are funds available to hire that person?

In planning the curriculum, are the goals clear, and are they articulated in written form? Is the curriculum balanced and truly integrated? Is the content, including that in the arts, meaningful and valuable instead of a waste of time for the children? Are ideas and activities sequenced in a way to provide a logical order, if necessary? Or, if the model is one of immersion and networking, are the materials and resources available for a rich experience? Will the ideas chosen be generative? Is flexibility built in so children can explore many different directions? How much time will be spent with a theme or topic (one year, several weeks, a month, a week)? Finally, what plans are there for assessment that is authentic to the goals and processes of the curriculum? What sort of documentation of growth will be used (videos, journals, performance portfolios, creative writing, or other possibilities)?

Integrating the arts throughout the curriculum has the potential for enriching the lives of children and of teachers. To be surrounded by and immersed in the arts is to live more fully and more beautifully. If more classrooms and schools did this well, they might become like the country of Bali where they say, "We have no art. We do everything as well as we can."

REVIEW

1. What are some of the challenges to integrating the arts across the curriculum?

2. What is necessary for true integration to occur?

3. List, define, and give examples of four different models for integrating the curriculum.

CRITICAL THINKING

1. Determine which aspects of the arts process as well as which arts have been integrated into the short series of ideas on Northwest Coastal Indian Culture.

2. What role(s) might an arts specialist play in integration of the curriculum? A classroom teacher? Parents? Administrators? Artists in residence?

3. What factors should be considered in selecting and implementing an integrated curriculum?

4. How could National Standards 8 and 9 be accomplished through ideas suggested in this chapter? Find a specific standard and highlight two or three ways that standard might be accomplished in a way authentic to the various disciplines.

PROJECTS

1. Plan a social studies unit, focusing on a particular culture or subculture, in which the arts of that culture play a major role. Do research on the authentic forms, styles, uses, and meanings of the arts in that culture. Incorporate a series of arts integrated lessons into your unit. Use the arts processes to make sure you have approached this with integrity.

2. Work with a librarian to discover children's books that relate directly to music. (Some ideas are suggested in the references to follow.) Develop at least three different ways to creatively extend the book using music and one other art form.

3. Identify two works of program music that might appeal to children. Develop a series of arts activities that help develop children's knowledge of the music as well as engage them creatively and significantly in another art form.

4. In a team of four people, select a theme that would be appealing to children; develop and collect ideas for integrating the arts into that focus. Use a multidisciplinary approach with a thematic web design similar to the model in Lesson 17.1.

5. Find and visit a school or classroom in which curriculum integration is taking place. What is the atmosphere in the room? The level of involvement of the children? The role of the teacher(s)? The subjects being integrated? The use of the arts, if any?

6. Plan a series of music lessons in which other arts are integrated in artistically significant ways. State at least two objectives for each lesson: one in music and one in the other art form. Make sure your lesson strategies achieve those goals. Use the National Standards in the arts as a basis for forming your objectives.

REFERENCES

General

Drake, S. M. (1993). *Planning the integrated curriculum: The call to adventure.* Alexandria, VA: Association for Supervision and Curriculum Development.

Fogarty, R. (1991). Ten ways to integrate curriculum. *Educational Leadership,* 49(2), 61–65.

Fowler, C. (1974). *The arts process.* Harrisburg, PA: Pennsylvania Department of Education.

Gardner, H. (1983). *Frames of mind: The theory of multiple intelligences.* New York: Basic Books.

———. (1991). *The unschooled mind: How children think and how schools should teach.* New York: Basic Books.

Jacobs, H. H. (1989a). *Interdisciplinary curriculum: Design and implementation.* Alexandria, VA: Association for Supervision and Curriculum Development.

———. (1989b). Interdisciplinary options: A case for multiple configurations. *Educational Horizons,* 68(1), 25–27.

Specific Art Forms

Brookes, M. (1986). *Drawing with children.* Los Angeles: Jeremy P. Tarcher.

Cohen, E., and R. S. Gainer (1976). *Art: Another language for learning.* New York: Citation.

Dimondstein, G. (1971). *Children dance in the classroom.* New York: Macmillan.

Haselbach, B. (1971). *Dance education.* London, England: Schott.

———. (1976). *Improvisation, dance, movement.* St. Louis: MagnamusicBaton.

Jenkins, P. (1980). *Art for the fun of it.* Englewood Cliffs, NJ: Prentice-Hall.

Katz, S. A., and J. A. Thomas (1992). *Teaching creatively by working the word: Language, music, and movement.* Englewood Cliffs, NJ: Prentice-Hall.

Koch, K. (1971). *Wishes, lies, and dreams.* New York: Vintage Books.

———. (1973). *Rose, where did you get that red?* New York: Vintage Books.

Kuzniar, M. (1999). Finding music in art. *Teaching music,* 7(3) 44–47.

Shreeves, R. (1990). *Children dancing.* Sussex: Ward Lock Educational.

Silver Burdett. (1985). *Silver Burdett Music.* Morristown, NJ: Silver Burdett and Ginn.

Spolin, V. (1967). *Improvisation for the theater.* Evanston, IL: Northwestern University.

Arts Across the Curriculum

Anderson, W., and P. Campbell (1996). *Multicultural perspectives in music education.* Reston, VA.: Music Educators National Conference.

Anderson, W., and L. Lawrence (1992). *Integrating music into the classroom.* Belmont, CA.: Wadsworth.

Barrett, J., C. McCoy, and K. Veblen (1997). *Sound ways of knowing.* New York: Schirmer.

Benzwie, T. (1988). *A moving experience.* Tucson, AZ: Zephyr.

Campbell, B., L. Campbell, and D. Dickinson (1992). *Teaching and learning through multiple intelligences.* Stanwood, WA: New Horizons for Learning.

Dunleavy, D. (1992). *The language beat.* Portsmouth, NH: Heinemann.

Edwards, L. C. (1997) *The creative arts: A process approach for teachers and children* (2nd ed.). Upper Saddle River, NJ: Prentice-Hall.

Gallas, K. (1991). The arts as epistemology: Enabling children to know what they know. *Harvard Educational Review,* (1) February.

———. (1994). *The languages of learning: How children talk, write, dance, draw, and sing their understanding of the world.* New York: Teacher's College Press.

Gilbert, A. G. (1977). *Teaching the three R's through movement experiences.* Minneapolis: Burgess.

Goldberg, M. (2001). *Arts and learning: An integrated approach to teaching and learning in multicultural and multilingual settings* (2nd ed.). New York: Longman/Addison Wesley.

Goldberg, M., and A. Phillips, eds. (1992). *Arts as education.* Harvard Educational Review, Reprint Series No. 24. Cambridge, MA: Harvard University.

Jalongo, M. R., and L. N. Stamp (1997). *The arts in children's lives: Aesthetic education in early childhood.* Boston: Allyn and Bacon.

Lamme, L. L. (1990). Exploring the world of music through picture books. *The Reading Teacher,* 44(4), 294–300.

Lazear, D. (1991). *Seven ways of knowing.* Tucson, AZ: Zephyr.

———. (1992). *Seven ways of teaching.* Tucson, AZ: Zephyr.

MENC (1994) *What every young American should know and be able to do in the arts: National standards for arts education.* Reston, VA: Music Educators National Conference.

Upitis, R. (1992). *Can I play you my song?: The compositions and invented notations of children.* Portsmouth, NH: Heinemann.

Wagner, B. J. (1976). *Dorothy Heathcote: Drama as a learning medium.* Washington, DC: NEA Publications.

Walker, P. P. (1993). *Bring in the arts: Lessons in dramatics, arts, and story writing for elementary and middle school classrooms.* Portsmouth, NH: Heinemann.

Werner, P. H., and E. C. Burton (1979). *Learning through movement.* St. Louis: C. V. Mosby.

Index

Teaching methods (*continued*)
rhythm, 98
for rhythm, 110–116
songs in parts, 168–174, 177–178
special needs, adapting, 385–386
Suzuki, 243–244
technology and, 343–344
tonality, phrase, scale, and sequence, 140
for visually impaired, 395
voice training, 152–155
Weikert method, 88, 90–91
Technology
computers, 35, 87, 339–340
computer software, 337–343
future of, 347–349
overview of, 337–339
singing and, 147–148
teaching music with, 343–344
Technology-Assisted Instruction in Music (TAIM), 340, 343, 347
"Teddy Bear" (United States), 216, 218
Temple blocks, 249
Tempo, 161
Tessitura, 149, 151, 162
Testing, 318, 319–320
Texture
active listening to, 188–189
development of, 142–143
movement and, 214
Theater, 411–412
Thinking, creative, 273–274
"This Old Man, He Played One" (United States), 110, 112
Thomas, J. A., 278, 411
Thomas, Ronald B., 86, 90, 144, 274, 277, 278
Thomson, W., 83
Thorndike, Robert, 16
Threaded curriculum design, 414–416
Three-legged model, of lesson planning, 301
Threnody for the Victims of Hiroshima (Penderecki), 192
Tillman, J., 272

Timbre, 214, 327
Time signatures, meter and, 105–106
Timpani, 251
"Tinga Layo" (Dominican Republic), 110, 113, 242
"Tinikling" (Philippines), 233–234
Titon, J. T., 372
Tonal memory, 160–161
Tone, 186–187
Tone bells, 258
Tonic Sol-Fa approach, 77
Transactional analysis, 62–63
Transmission, of musical culture, 12–13, 363–365
Triangle (instrument), 251
TST feedback system, 41
Tucker, J. C., 164, 372
Turing, T., 372
Tyler, R. W., 344

U

Understanding, in integrated curriculum, 418
United States, music education history, 9–10
Unit planning, 309–311
Upitis, R., 278, 280

V

Valuing, assessment of, 323
Vanaver, B., 372
Veblen, K. K., 310, 417
Vertical pitch structures, 139–144
Viennese Classical music, 9
Visual arts, 407–408, 409, 415, 419
Visual impairments, 394434, 395
Visual learning, 29, 193
"Viva la musica" (Germany), 170
Voice
breathing exercises for, 154–155
development of, 148–152
extending range of, 162
Music in Use program (Espeland), 193

training, 152–155
training, software for, 341
vocal model, 162–164
Vygotsky, Lev S., 15, 16, 21–22

W

Warner, B., 81, 103, 256
Warwick, A., 385
Webbed curriculum design, 414
Webster, P. R., 201, 273
Weikert, Phyllis, 88, 90, 229, 230
Wells, R., 328
Werner, Robert, 90
Wheelchair, 394–396
Wiggins, J., 278, 279, 284, 285
"The Wild Horseman" (Schumann), 224
Williamson, S., 164
Winner, E., 288, 328, 332
Winters, G., 278
Witkin, Harold, 17, 29, 32
Wong, I. K. F., 372
Woodblocks, 249
Woods, D., 83, 84, 88, 277, 312
World music education, 358

X

Xylophone, 255

Y

Yale Seminar, 10
Yamaha Corporation, 86, 90, 312, 341
Yarbrough, C., 26
"Yo Mamana, Yo!" (Mozambique), 169, 171
"Yuyake" (Japan), 371

Z

Zemach, M., 200
Zither, 261–262
"Zum Gali Gali" (Israel), 111, 114